ALSO BY JUDITH THURMAN

Isak Dinesen: The Life of a Storyteller

Secrets of the Flesh: A Life of Colette

Cleopatra's Nose: 39 Varieties of Desire

A LEFT-HANDED WOMAN

A Left-Handed Woman

ESSAYS

Judith Thurman

 FARRAR, STRAUS AND GIROUX NEW YORK

Farrar, Straus and Giroux
120 Broadway, New York 10271

"Free Associations" previously appeared in *A Balthus Notebook* (David Zwirner Books, 2020). "Book of Revelation" previously appeared in *The Second Sex* (Knopf, 2010). All other essays previously appeared, in slightly different form, in *The New Yorker*.

Title-page and part-title-page art and hand-lettering by Cecilia Zhang.

Library of Congress Cataloging-in-Publication Data
Names: Thurman, Judith, 1946– author.
Title: A left-handed woman : essays / Judith Thurman.
Description: First edition. | New York : Farrar, Straus and Giroux, 2022.
Identifiers: LCCN 2022023786 | ISBN 9780374607166 (hardcover)
Subjects: LCGFT: Essays.
Classification: LCC PS3620.H88 L44 2022 | DDC 814/.6—dc23/eng/20220727
LC record available at https://lccn.loc.gov/2022023786

Designed by Abby Kagan

Our books may be purchased in bulk for promotional, educational, or business use. Please contact your local bookseller or the Macmillan Corporate and Premium Sales Department at 1-800-221-7945, extension 5442, or by email at MacmillanSpecialMarkets@macmillan.com.

www.fsgbooks.com
www.twitter.com/fsgbooks • www.facebook.com/fsgbooks

10 9 8 7 6 5 4 3 2 1

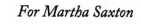

For Martha Saxton

CONTENTS

A LEFT-HANDED WOMAN

INTRODUCTION: COLLECTING ONESELF

———— ✤ ————

I write with my left hand. Left-handedness used to be considered a
malign aberration ("sinister" is Latin for "left"), and in the generations before mine, left-handed schoolchildren were routinely
"switched." Enforced conformity, especially, perhaps, when it selects
an inborn trait to repress or persecute, breeds intolerance for difference of all kinds. Singled out for bullying or conversion, a child inter-
nalizes the message that she isn't "right."

I have a bittersweet memory in this regard. My father had been
switched by an implacable Hebrew schoolteacher who'd made him sit
on his left hand for six years. Even in old age, he still flexed it compul-
sively, though I reckoned that other childhood humiliations had also
numbed him. Our relations were mostly silent, and I pined for his
attention. But when I was learning to write, he sat patiently by my
side, holding my wrist so it wouldn't hunch over "like a cripple's back."
He wanted to endow me with a "beautiful hand"—the signature of a
lady. I don't think he realized how illegible his love was.

In the contemporary world, belonging to the left-handed minority
(about ten percent of the population) is a minor inconvenience. But
when I started kindergarten, at the height of the McCarthy hearings,
my mother, Alice, warned me not to describe myself as a "leftie."
Why, I asked her? "It could get us into trouble," she said darkly. I had
no idea what she meant, and her anxiety was cockeyed, since my

parents' only cell was our four-room apartment. Yet the tone of that caution sobered me to the core. It hinted at a guilty secret that a careless word could betray.

⌾⌾⌾

My mother's demons—her abiding terror of some imminent catastrophe—still haunt me. By the time I could see her with detachment, she was a sedated recluse who had designated the task of living to her only child. In that sense, our roles were reversed; I attuned my behavior to her fragility. I don't know what her own aspirations might have been, except that she revered language, and her gift to me was insisting that I should. During the Depression, she'd taught Latin and English in a Boston high school, but on her wedding day, she forfeited the job. It went to a man, she was told by the principal, "who had a family to support."

Alice accepted her dismissal timidly, without questioning its injustice. Perhaps her ambitions for me were a deflected protest. I was lucky, however, to have two maiden aunts. The feisty old maid in an uptight family is often an ally to her wayward niece. Eva, my father's sister, managed a used bookstore near Harvard Square. She was wraithlike and tweedy, with a smoker's deep voice and wrinkles. "Eva's a character," the family liked to say. Whatever small luxury they sent her—a toaster, a winter coat, a banknote tucked into a birthday card—she gave it away. It went to a poet on scholarship, or to the "unwed mother" who lived upstairs. I first heard the expression "free love" from Eva, uttered with reverence. She meant something heretical, I think; she meant to let me know that virginity is a false idol. Even as a child, I marveled at her ardor.

Unlike Eva, my maternal aunt Charlotte wasn't a romantic, though unlike her sister, she inhabited a body that gave her pleasure. "Arkie," as I called her, was built like an otter and could swim two miles in the ocean. She taught me to ride a bike and to build a campfire. She had spent her youth as an activist in the settlement house movement.

Later, she ran a state unemployment bureau staffed mostly by closeted socialists like herself. Arkie took a dim view of patriarchal institutions—religion, capitalism, marriage. She liked to quote one of her professors at a woman's college: "He has to be a very good husband to be better than no husband at all."

Both my aunts got stuck caring for their elderly parents well into middle age. But then they moved into their own bachelor digs not far apart in Cambridge. They often traveled together, adventurously. Had they been born in a later era, they might have been lesbians, and perhaps they were, covertly—I hoped so—though we never spoke of intimate things. "Of course she was a lesbian!" Alison Bechdel said to me of Arkie. (I was visiting her in Vermont, reporting the profile in this volume.) "Straight women didn't dress up as Gene Autry" (a singing cowboy of the 1950s). When I stayed with my grandparents, as I did every summer, Arkie sang me to sleep in a Stetson, chaps, and a six-shooter.

At the age of eighty, Arkie came to live with me, and helped me to raise my son. (I, too, was an unwed mother.) I once asked her if she was happy. We were living in Paris for a year, while I did research on Colette. She kept house for us without a word of French, and her only company, for most of the day, was a rambunctious two-year-old. "You're too sentimental about happiness," she said. No critique has served my craft better.

The writers I most admire never use a careless word. Their sentences are unimprovable. "Style is character," Joan Didion asserted, in an essay on Georgia O'Keeffe whose surface is as taut as a drum skin. Didion's character was elusive, above all to herself, unlike O'Keeffe's—an artist, she wrote, with palpable envy, who "seems to have been equipped with an immutable sense of who she was." A style like Didion's is often the result of arrogance, painfully unlearned.

"All men are deceived by the appearances of things," Heraclitus wrote, 2,500 years ago, "even Homer himself, the wisest man in Greece." The poet was alerted to his self-deception by boys catching lice: "'What we catch and kill we leave behind,'" they told him, "'but what escapes us we bring with us.'" What we bring with us—embedded in our flesh and bugging it; embedded in art and animating it—is the mystery of how we become who we are.

That mystery has been my subject from the beginning; with every new piece of work, I grope my way into it. "First Impressions," a reportage on Paleolithic art, suggests my point of departure. It recounts the accident by which three spelunkers found an entrance to the Chauvet Cave, which had been sealed for millennia. They were attracted by "an updraft of cool air coming from a recess near the cliff's ledge—the potential sign of a cavity." There's a hidden cavity in every story, a recess of meaning, and it's often blocked by the rubble of your own false starts, or by an accretion of received ideas left behind by others. That updraft of freshness is typically an emotion you've buried.

I write about the lives and work of other people in part to understand my own, while avoiding what I feel obliged to do here: talk about myself. In most of my essays, a passage or even just a sentence surprises me with a private truth I couldn't otherwise have expressed freely. In my study of Emily Dickinson, it's a reflection on depressive mothers. Their daughters, I write, "often feel a propitiary impulse to make some sacrifice of their aggression and desire, perhaps because . . . they feel guilty about their own vitality." In my reading of Elena Ferrante, it's a riff on primal attachments, for which "hostile love" is an antidote. "Ambivalence," I suggest, is Alison Bechdel's "default mode": the voice that narrates her graphic memoirs "both yearns for and mistrusts closeness." In taking the measure of Rachel Cusk, I begin with a description of her narrator—a Cusk-like British writer named Faye. Friends and strangers tell her their stories, "and she listens intently. As these soliloquies unspool, a common thread emerges. The speakers suffer from feeling unseen, and in the absence of a reflection they are not real to themselves." While sharing their dilemma covertly, Faye "lends herself as a filter to her confidants, and from the murk of their griefs and sorrows . . . she extracts something clear—a sense of both her own outline and theirs."

After fifty years of dissembled groping, I thought of calling this collection "Wear and Tear." "You'll frighten off young readers," a friend warned me. "Indefinite Article" was another wry title that appealed to me. But it alluded too obliquely to *The Left-Handed Woman*, a novella by Peter Handke. The connection merits an aside.

Handke found the title I have reborrowed from him one evening in Paris, where we'd met in the early seventies. I'd moved abroad after college, and those years in Europe were my graduate school. Every aspect of its culture—class, speech, dress, food, décor, politics, and sex (especially sex)—was coded in a manner both fascinating and arcane to the provincial American I was. Decrypting the codes was good training for my future vocation. I had one mentor in particular, an elegant Frenchwoman with whom I used to stay. She balanced a prestigious career with her duties as the wife of an important man, and her life seemed glamorous, though I aspired to a different one. Madame G. worried it wouldn't be secure, or not, as she liked to say, "when you're alone at my age."

Perhaps I'd related our conversations to Peter—I don't remember—but when he read the note my hostess had left on the kitchen table, it made him laugh: *"Ce soir, à 9 heures, réunion des féministes gauchères américaines."* (She'd invited another friend to dinner, also a left-handed expatriate, who shared my outspoken allegiance to women's liberation.) I suspect her teasing tone appealed to him as much as its suggestion of a naïvely militant New World sisterhood. He took out a notebook and wrote something down.

Men are a minority in this volume (if not in this Introduction) and four of the seven were couturiers who spent their careers styling—and

eroticizing—the feminine figure, at times perversely. "The true function of fashion," Charles James believed, "is to arouse the mating
instinct." Yet unlikely affinities are sometimes the most revealing
ones. Alexander McQueen, for example, was often accused of misogyny; he was pugnaciously gay and working-class; he brutalized his
clothes, and sometimes his models, and he killed himself at forty. But
on his right arm, he'd tattooed a line of poetry spoken by Helena, in
A Midsummer Night's Dream: "Love looks not with the eyes but with
the mind." That anguished outcry, by a lost woman, whose desire is
mocked and rejected, alludes to a wound that McQueen's work and
mine both seek to dress.

The transcendence of shame is a prominent theme in the narrative
of women's lives. The shame of violation; the shame of appetite; the
shame of anger; the shame of being unloved; the shame of otherness;
the shame, perhaps above all, of drive. Seventy-five years ago, in the
lower-middle-class milieu where I grew up, the career prospects for a
girl who couldn't tap dance were depressingly limited. I scoured literature for exceptions, and there were some. But nearly all of them had
achieved distinction at a price their male counterparts didn't have to
pay. In that respect, one might say they were all left-handed: they
defied the message that they weren't right.

The price of self-possession used to be spinsterhood, if not the convent. ("I'm always happiest when dressed almost like a nun," Miuccia
Prada once remarked. "It makes you feel so relaxed.") A few brazen
rebels braved ostracism. (The two Georges, Sand and Eliot, welcomed
their exemption from polite society; it gave them more time for their
spinning.) A few women writers found exemplary spouses—wives, in
essence—of whom Leonard Woolf and Alice B. Toklas are the epito-
mes. But many of those unions were childless, and it's still a daunting
feat to juggle art and maternity. Even Colette, that great poet of female carnality, felt unsexed by the exercise of her powers. She'd understood before almost anyone that gender is a bell curve, yet she
despaired of being what she enviously called a "real woman." (The
"real" women were her husbands' mistresses.) It wasn't obvious to my
generation how or if one could become oneself, an individual, without

performing what the psychoanalyst Louise Kaplan memorably called a "female-female impersonation."

In resisting a generic definition, many of my subjects have fetishized uniqueness. The witch, the sibyl, the priestess, the martyr, the diva, the vestal, the femme fatale—these are some of their guises. A stylist aims for unsparing specificity, but a stylized persona risks becoming a caricature. Margaret Fuller, born in 1810, is a poignant example. She was the first American foreign correspondent of her sex and the author of a foundational work of feminist history. "I shall always reign through the intellect," she boasted. But her dazzling mind was housed in an unlovely carapace, and she resigned herself to being "bright and ugly."

I recognized my own grandiosity in Fuller's. Until puberty, I, too, was outsized and ungainly. I compensated, as she did, by showing off as a know-it-all. One of my teachers mocked me with the epithet "Miss Importance," and she cast me in our school play, *The Mikado*, as Katisha—a deluded old woman who is spurned by a prince. Since I couldn't carry a tune, I had to deliver her solos in singsong: *"My soul is still my body's prisoner!"* I later destroyed all my class pictures.

In rereading these essays and profiles, all but two of which were published in *The New Yorker* between 2006 and 2021, I was proud to realize how much I managed to write; it was a bleak era in my own history and America's; we were both coming apart. But I also felt a pang of obsolescence—an awareness "of the extent," as Didion puts it, "to which the narrative on which many of us grew up no longer applies." She believed that loss was peculiar to her generation, though I suspect each aging one is similarly humbled. "Whatever I have made for myself is personal," she concluded, ruefully. "If I could believe that going to a barricade would affect man's fate in the slightest, I would go to that barricade . . . but it would be less than honest to say that I expect to happen upon such a happy ending."

There are, however, some endings which give you a taste of happiness. Most of the time, a piece of prose lies on the page bristling with cleverness, yet inert, until I hit upon the precise sequence of words— the spell, if you like—that brings it to life. At that moment, language recovers its archaic power to free a trapped spirit.

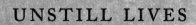

UNSTILL LIVES

ROVING EYE

The American model and photographer Lee Miller was born in Poughkeepsie, New York, a century ago, but spent most of her life seeking adventure in Europe and the Middle East. Last September, a retrospective of her work in front of and behind a camera, *The Art of Lee Miller*, curated by Mark Haworth-Booth, opened at the Victoria and Albert Museum in London. In his introduction to the show's companion volume, Haworth-Booth describes Miller as an artist of "the first electric century," and he invokes the metaphor of electricity—its power to attract, repel, shock, and illuminate—in making a case for her significance.

Miller's power, however, generated an uneven legacy notably indebted to her lover Man Ray, to her mentor Edward Steichen, and to Eugène Atget, Edward Weston, Brassaï, and Paul Strand. Her audacious sexual history has colored perceptions of her art, as has her enshrinement by the fashion world. She traded on her exceptional beauty while it lasted, but she also struggled for respect, and for something more elusive: self-respect. The formal tension in her work is a play between veiling and exposure, glamour and brutality. It carries an erotic charge even when the subject isn't erotic.

On my way to the London preview, I stopped to ponder a startling image of Miller in a show of military and couture camouflage at the Imperial War Museum. The French were the first, in 1915, to experiment with "disruptive patterns" of light, shade, and color hand-painted on uniforms and artillery—a technique indebted to Cubism. In 1940, the rich and eccentric British Surrealist Roland Penrose decided that he could best contribute to his country's defense by recruiting artists for a camouflage unit and lecturing on their research to the Home Guard. The unit had been testing an ointment developed to hide skin from a rifle scope, or at least to disguise it, and on a summer day, in a friend's garden, Penrose asked Miller, his mistress (they married a few years later, to legitimatize their only child, Antony), to play the guinea pig.

Miller was in her mid-thirties. She had been covering the blitz for British *Vogue*, and, after the Normandy invasion, she would help to document the liberation of Europe as one of an elite company of women (Margaret Bourke-White, Marguerite Higgins, Mary Welsh, Helen Kirkpatrick, and Martha Gelhorn, among others) accredited as war correspondents. That afternoon, she gamely stripped for the assembled house party, smeared the dull, greenish paste over her body, and stretched out on the lawn under a caul of camouflage netting. In the course of the demonstration, her groin was covered by a clump of sod bristling with matted weeds—a trompe-l'oeil pubis—and one of her nipples snagged in the net. As a finishing touch, the severed heads of two blood-red lilies were placed between her breasts like a funerary offering. The couple's friend (and partner in a ménage à trois) the American photojournalist Dave Scherman captured the scene, and Penrose used the image in slide shows—no doubt to great effect with the guardsmen.

The earliest known nude study of Lee Miller, who was christened Elizabeth, was made by her father, Theodore, an engineer whose hobby was photography. He titled the picture *December Morn*, even though it was taken in April 1915, two weeks before Elizabeth's eighth birthday. Poughkeepsie had been blanketed by a spring snowfall, and the shivering little girl is posed outside the family house wearing nothing but bedroom slippers. A year before, as Carolyn Burke observes in a fine biography, *Lee Miller: A Life*, the likeness of a fleshier maiden— *September Morn*, by the French painter Paul Chabas—had provoked a storm of outrage and titillation when it was displayed in the window of a Manhattan gallery. The public rallied to one side or the other, and

Theodore, a health faddist, evidently took the liberal view. He had persuaded Lee's mother, Florence MacDonald, a Canadian nurse from a
respectable family, to pose nude for him before they were married, and
if he later philandered with impunity, she considered divorcing him to
marry a lover. They kept up appearances, but something in the household was seriously peculiar. Lee became a promiscuous hellion; her
older brother, John, was a cross-dresser; Florence attempted suicide;
Theodore continued taking nude pictures of his daughter, often with a
stereoscopic camera, well into her twenties. He also talked her girl-
friends out of their clothes and into posing for group portraits, though
when other people's naked children were involved, Florence chaperoned the sittings.

None of those "art studies," or none that survive, cross the line into
obscenity, and the family seems to have been unperturbed by them.
They did, however, bury a painful secret that Antony Penrose revealed
in *The Lives of Lee Miller*, an illustrated biography of his mother. At the
age of seven, Elizabeth had been raped, ostensibly by a family friend
(all attempts to verify his identity, Penrose told me, "have drawn a
blank"), and infected with gonorrhea. Venereal diseases were still incurable, so she was treated at a hospital and by her mother with disin-
fectant "irrigations." The Millers also consulted a psychiatrist, Penrose
said, who counseled them to tell Elizabeth that sex was merely a mechanical act, and not the same thing as love, so the damage wasn't
permanent. But the damage to a violated child, even one as resilient as
Miller, is permanent in incalculable ways.

Given the timing, the kindest interpretation of *December Morn* is
that it represents a form of shock therapy—physical immodesty as a
cure for shame. Whatever it was, Miller's story suggests that beauty
can also be a form of camouflage, one that successfully deceives the
beholder without offering much protection to the wearer. Her art was
always improvised on the run, escaping from or to a man or a place,
and she described her life as "a water-soaked jig-saw puzzle, drunken
bits that don't match in shape or design." The memory of a trauma is
often fractured in the same fashion by that most devious of camou-
flagers, the unconscious. Few artists achieve lasting renown without a

body of work that is cumulative in its power, and Miller wasn't capable of sustained ambition. But her finest pictures—the semi-abstract desert landscapes; the poetic rubble of wartime London; the graphs of desolation from the battlefront; the sculptural female torsos, which were considered shockingly "phallic"—tantalize you, as they tantalized those who championed her career, with the promise of what she might have achieved.

Although Miller was expelled from nearly every school she attended, she was capable of focus when a subject or a teacher, more often the latter, excited her. She and her best friend collaborated on screenplays, inspired by Anita Loos. At eighteen, having badgered her parents for a trip to Paris, she dumped her chaperone and enrolled in a course on stage design taught by the Hungarian artist Ladislas Medgyès, who introduced her to experimental theater, and to her destiny as a bohemian. Back in Poughkeepsie eight months later and pining for the Left Bank, she continued her training in stagecraft at Vassar, did some acting with a local company, and studied dance, which led to a part in the chorus line of a risqué Broadway revue. Success in the performing arts came easily to a quicksilver girl who was usually the most striking hopeful at a casting call. (A few years later, Jean Cocteau, looking for an actress with the features and aplomb of a Greek statue, chose Miller, who had no experience onscreen, for the lead role in his didactically outré first film, *The Blood of a Poet*.)

None of these promising forays, however, held Miller's fugitive attention. By the autumn of 1926, she had moved to Manhattan to take classes at the Art Students League and was earning her pocket money as a lingerie model. If one is to believe the story, Condé Nast noticed her crossing the street just in time to pull her from the path of an oncoming vehicle, and this fortuitous collision led to an interview with Edna Chase, *Vogue*'s editor-in-chief. With a boyish haircut and a new moniker, Lee (a contraction of Li-Li, her family nickname, but also, perhaps, a little bow to that most enterprising flapper, Lorelei Lee), Miller made her debut in *Vogue*—on the March 1927 cover, in a drawing by the French fashion illustrator Georges Lepape—and at the famous parties that Condé Nast hosted in his penthouse. She was soon posing for Steichen, Arnold Genthe, and Nickolas Muray, the leading photographers of the day. But the fact that she modeled for them is more interesting in retrospect than the decorous pictures they took of her. None capture her subversive modernity the way Lepape did: confronting the beholder from under a purple cloche with swollen lips and a sullen gaze that manages to project both wantonness and reserve.

In 1929, with several lovers fighting for the honor of seeing her off, and café society sad to lose its star playgirl, Miller sailed for Europe with the ambition "to enter photography by the back end." It was Steichen, she said, who "put the idea into my head." She planned to do some modeling for George Hoyningen-Huene at Paris *Vogue* while she apprenticed with Man Ray, a leader of the avant-garde and a master of many genres—painting, photography, sculpture, and graphic art. After co-founding the Dada movement in New York with Marcel Duchamp, Man Ray had immigrated to France, where society portraiture and fashion photography helped to support his experiments. To be "done" by this edgy dynamo was as chic in the Jazz Age as to be done by Warhol was forty years later. Despite a bantam physique and a receding chin, Man Ray attracted singular women. Miller succeeded an adorably lewd and fleshy cabaret singer who was a legend of the Latin Quarter: Kiki de Montparnasse.

Man Ray was thirty-nine and Miller was twenty-two when they met. He marginalized their relationship in his autobiography, *Self Portrait*, perhaps in revenge for her infidelities, but she described their chance (or contrived) encounter at an artists' hangout, Le Bateau Ivre, as the "turning point" of her youth. With few preliminaries—she introduced herself as his new student, he told her that he didn't accept students, they left the next morning on a road trip—the affair began. After a summer in the South of France, Miller rented lodgings near Man Ray's studio on the Rue Campagne-Première, and paid tuition for a priceless education in art and worldliness by working as his dogsbody. One of her early tests was to help him photograph the Count and Countess Pecci-Blunt's White Ball of 1930, and, typically, she abandoned her post to dance with other men.

Under Man Ray's tutelage, Miller mastered the use of a Graflex camera, with glass plates, and then a Rolleiflex; studio lighting setups; cropping and retouching; improvisation with a viewfinder; and his techniques for developing. A darkroom accident (Miller turned the lights on before she realized that a batch of negatives was in the open tank) led, by her account, to the discovery of "solarization," a process in which the background of a portrait is overexposed to outline the head with a black penumbra.* Many years later, claiming partial credit for one of Man Ray's most famous solarized images, Miller pretended that it didn't really matter which of them had made it, because "we were almost the same person when we were working."

Man Ray was a generous mentor, but his generosity didn't extend to sharing his protégée with rivals in the arts. He was furious with Miller for lending herself to Cocteau, and resentful of the time that she spent working in London as the still photographer on a feature. "You are so young and beautiful and free," he wrote to her, "and I hate myself for trying to cramp that in you which I admire most." The definitive image of his obsession is a 1930 nude study of Miller, her gaze enigmatic, her head caged by a wire fencing guard. He titled it *La Révolution Surréaliste*, and it expresses an attitude rife in the movement, but also in Miller's life: a contradictory impulse to worship and defile the female body. But Miller's submissiveness in games of bondage was, if not illusory, paradoxical. She claimed the privilege of a man's sexual freedom (while depending, like most women of her class, on subsidies from her men), and Man Ray's jealousy—indeed, any man's jealousy—made her claustrophobic. Man Ray may not initially have known that Julian Levy, his New York art dealer, who included Miller in an important, early group show of European photography, was among her paramours, but in 1931 the couple's fragile illusion of oneness was tested by the arrival in Paris of Theodore Miller, toting

* Miller did not "invent" solarization. The reversal of an image from negative to positive by means of extreme overexposure was known to the earliest pioneers of photography, Louis Daguerre and Sir John Herschel, by 1840. But she and Man Ray were among the first artists to experiment with the technique for aesthetic purposes. She may not have known its history.

his cameras. He photographed his daughter and her roommate, Tanja Ramm, an American model, cavorting in bed, and Lee obliged him, Burke writes, by striking "contorted poses . . . pubic region exposed." She insists that Lee's composure in the pictures is evidence of her implicit trust in the photographer, though "one wonders," she adds, "what went through Man's head as he watched" them.

Perhaps it was trust, or perhaps, as Miller's own work suggests, it was dissociation. She had the gift of finding beauty in a wasteland, and her eye tends to petrify what it looks at. Organic forms and living creatures become abstract in her pictures, but movingly so—the way a nymph fleeing an aggressor is transformed into a star. Where human figures appear in a frame, they are often faceless or disembodied. Her best photographs from the war are of corpses, landscapes, statuary, or distant violence. Once she was proficient with a camera, Man Ray promoted her for commissions that he couldn't fulfill or didn't want, one of which was to document operations at the Sorbonne medical school. Having watched a mastectomy, she asked the surgeon if she could keep the amputated breast. She arrived for a fashion shoot at the studio of French *Vogue* in a buoyant mood, carrying this grisly trophy on a dinner plate, then photographed it at a place setting, next to a knife and fork. She tends to isolate the mechanical act of taking a picture from the visceral connection with a subject, as she was taught to compartmentalize sex and love. Most of her portraits, including her self-portraits, seem wary or disdainful of any true engagement with a sitter except, perhaps, where she was engaged by the drama of seduction. That was the case with two great satyrs who yielded both to her and to her camera: Chaplin, whom she knew from her modeling days in New York, and Picasso.

Miller and Man Ray spent three stormy years together, then, almost as suddenly as she had decamped for Paris, she returned to New York. On the strength of her growing reputation, but also of her errant glamour, she found rich backers for a studio in Manhattan. Theodore had the nerve to sue *Time* for describing his daughter "as the possessor of the most beautiful navel in Paris," and she spent part of the libel settlement to hire a staff, including a young maid who cooked homey lunches for the artist and her clients. The press was fascinated by Miller's new incarnation—paparazzi had been waiting on the pier when her ship docked—and *Vogue, Harper's Bazaar,* and *Vanity Fair* welcomed her to their pages. When she chose to model for one of the pictures *Vogue* had commissioned—a story on headbands—her younger brother, Erik, operated the camera, and their feature is, in its way, a perfect artifact of high fashion in the Depression. Miller sits at an angle in a plush wing chair, against a black backdrop. The light in this hermetic frame glosses the fine planes of her face and neck, the frill of her hair, and the ruching of a velvet gown. Her beauty and expression are as inanimate as those of the figures that were, at the same moment, being carved into the granite of Mount Rushmore. The bell jar that she had sometimes used as a prop in her Surrealist art photographs is here invisible, yet implied. She embodies elegance as refusal—the refusal to inhabit a flawed world of human inferiors.

While the Lee Miller Studio was ultimately an abortive venture (Man Ray was outraged to learn that his ex-apprentice was touting his name and his signature techniques to promote it), for two years, from 1932 to 1934, it made her one of the most sought-after commercial photographers in New York. In addition to her advertising and fashion work, she specialized in celebrity portraits. Julian Levy gave *The Blood of a Poet* its debut at the New York Film Society, enhancing Miller's prestige as a muse to genius. He also gave her art photography a well-received solo exhibition at his gallery. ("We don't think her photos are very good," Levy's wife, Joella, admitted in private, "but they make a surprisingly good show.") Erik Miller, who ran the darkroom, admired Lee's perfectionism as a printer, but noted that his sister could also be "intolerably lazy." She never scheduled more than one sitting a day, and, after work, Penrose writes, "she would resume her social life: the demonic games of poker . . . or wild parties" with friends from the theater world.

In 1933, the director John Houseman engaged Miller to photograph the "all-Negro" cast of Virgil Thomson's opera *Four Saints in Three Acts,* with a libretto by Gertrude Stein. Those portraits, taken in Harlem, have a dignity and a depth of tenderness otherwise missing from her airless portfolio of movie stars, perfume bottles, socialites, and couture. That May, Miller was named by *Vanity Fair* as one of the seven "most distinguished living photographers." Rather than capitalize on her growing renown, she abruptly closed her studio and holed up at a "fat farm" in the Poconos, to lose fifteen pounds. The motive for her apparent self-sabotage was revealed two months later, when she stunned her family and friends by announcing her marriage to a man they had scarcely met, Aziz Eloui Bey, an Egyptian railroad magnate in his forties. Their romance, a well-kept secret, had begun in St. Moritz, in 1931, when Miller was vacationing with Chaplin. Among the pictures she took for *Vogue* that year is one of Eloui's wife, Nimet—"La Belle Circassienne"—in a turban and pearls, and perhaps there was a thrill to stealing the husband of such a formidable rival.

Leaving her brother, a newlywed, unemployed, and her angels incensed, "Lee embarked on marriage as if it were a holiday," Burke writes. Eloui owned a beach house in Alexandria and a mansion in Cairo. He added a European ladies' maid to their staff of fifteen and endowed his bride with a stock portfolio. She had nothing more strenuous to do than enjoy the high life. Eloui believed that this "serene" existence would, as he assured the Millers, cure their daughter's ennui, and a series of exotic pastimes—snake charming, camel racing, desert safaris—did briefly distract her. She also recovered from an ephemeral "loathing" for photography, or for the discipline a career required, to do some of her purest work as a modernist. (Her 1937 *Portrait of Space*, a barren landscape seen through the gash in a patched window screen, was included in the definitive retrospective of Dada and Surrealism at the Arts Council of Great Britain, forty years later.) But life in Egypt was also much like her childhood: charmed on the surface, roiling beneath it, with a doting male footing the bills for her mischief, and a provincial society that was fun to shock. "If I need to pee, I pee in the road; if I have a letch for someone, I hop into bed with him," she boasted to a friend.

One loses sight of how young Miller still was. In June 1937, just thirty, escaping her husband and the heat, she returned to Paris. There she met Roland Penrose, who was married to a lesbian poet and was, or had been, homosexual himself but in any event wasn't the next morning. Later that summer, they vacationed in Mougins with a party of friends who, like Penrose, worshipped Picasso. The acolytes paid tribute to their idol by offering their women to him (although they also shared them fraternally with one another). Miller posed for Picasso, who posed for her, and they recognized in each other a vulnerable quality—the expectation of being looked at without being seen—that others had missed. Those arty revels, staged, in part, for posterity, also produced her homage to Manet's *Le Déjeuner sur l'herbe*. In a dappled grove, three eminent Surrealists (Penrose, Paul Éluard, and Man Ray) and their bare-breasted muses share an amorous picnic. The size of the picture—a one-and-a-half-by-two-inch Rolleiflex contact print that Miller never bothered to enlarge—enhances its peepshow coyness.

When Miller went back to Eloui, she and Penrose exchanged fervid letters, hers astute about her own character. Her betrayal of a man whom she had married for love in the sincere belief that their union was forever "makes me cynically suspicious of any attachment I might make," she told Penrose—"my 'always' don't seem to mean much, do they." But on September 1, 1939, the day that Hitler invaded Poland, the two adulterers, reunited in France after fugues and dramas, caught the last boat for England from Saint-Malo. The stoical Eloui forgave her, and facilitated a last-minute divorce, in 1947, shortly before her child was born, so that she and Penrose could marry. When she returned to Egypt, in the sixties—by which time Eloui had lost his fortune and married the ladies' maid—he was grateful for the visit.

Idleness only ever aggravated Miller's demons: she needed purpose to still them. With Britain girding for the siege, she volunteered at an unlikely venue for patriotic service, but the only one likely to accept her: British *Vogue*. Her cavalier defection from the fashion business had devalued her credit as a professional, and Condé Nast was skeptical of his prodigal's return, so she was hired, on a trial basis, at eight pounds a week, to celebrate handbags and famous faces. But when the *Vogue* pattern house was destroyed by a bomb, Miller was eager to photograph the ruins. The magazine, impressed with the laconic eloquence of her reportage (perhaps one could also describe it as stagecraft—she created, literally, a theater of war, a puppet theater, for the most part, in which objects dramatize human suffering), began to feature it prominently. With an eye for the macabre visual ironies scattered by the bombs like promotional flyers for Surrealism, she photographed a ruined chapel, bricks cascading from its portico like worshippers after the service; a smashed typewriter ("Remington Silent") lying in the gutter; an egg-shaped barrage balloon nesting in a London park behind a pair of geese that are strutting as if they had just laid it; and two air-raid wardens—nubile vestals—masked totemically by their eye shields.

Early in 1942, when American troops and journalists arrived in London, including Dave Scherman, who worked for *Life*, Miller was accredited as a war correspondent with the U.S. forces, a promotion that gave her access to restricted zones. In 1944, six weeks after D-Day, she sailed for Normandy to cover the work of nurses in a field hospital. She also began filing text to accompany her pictures, and, for the next eighteen months, her writing and photojournalism changed the perception of *Vogue*, even among its staff, as an atoll of frivolity in a vast ocean of heroic conflict. "Something had unfettered Lee's talent," her son writes. The model in the ruched gown lived in fatigues and channeled her "insatiable desire for excitement" into a noble endeavor. On her next trip to France, in a tank-landing ship, her convoy ran aground on Omaha Beach, where she was carried ashore by a sailor. Hitching a ride into Saint-Malo, she discovered that, contrary to reports, the siege of the town was still under way, and the Allies were using napalm for the first time in Europe, to dislodge a German unit holding out in the fortress. "Tall chimneys standing alone gave off smoke from the burning remnants of their buildings at their feet," she wrote. "Stricken lonely cats prowled. A swollen horse had not provided adequate shelter for the dead American behind it . . . I sheltered in a kraut dugout, squatting under the ramparts. My heel ground into a dead detached hand." She picked up the hand, and, in a spasm of fury at the enemy, "hurled it across the street, and ran back the way I'd come bruising my feet and crashing in the unsteady piles of stone and slipping in blood." Like one of those feline survivors, Miller was probably too unnerved to have been conscious of how much of herself—of her previous life and imagery—that passage, an inventory of disintegration, contains.

Miller was rewarded for her virtuosity under fire with a working vacation in Paris, and the chance to celebrate its liberation among old friends. She photographed Colette, another feline survivor, at the Palais Royal, and covered the first postwar couture collections. They were enlivened, she wrote, apparently without irony, by "folderols, a splurge of red and a desire for oversized muffs." Scherman turned up at her hotel, the Scribe, and together with him or singly, traveling with infantry divisions, she covered the Allied push to the Rhine on icy roads clogged with refugees, and the reconquest of Alsace, Luxembourg, and Cologne. "It is worth remembering," Penrose writes, "that Lee's Rolleiflex did not have a telephoto lens," and that the only way she could get her pictures "was to go and find the action."

Miller's instinct for detachment was probably the most useful tool in her survival kit, but nothing could steel anyone for the camps. She arrived at Buchenwald, in the wake of General Patton, at the end of April, and dared her editors to publish the photographs that she took there. "Believe it," she cabled them, and that was the headline that *Vogue* ran, in June 1945, opposite an image that was enlarged to fill a full page of the magazine. It was of a human rubbish heap, although the dead—young people with limbs like broken tinder—aren't quite yet corpses. Their eyes still have light in them.

Dachau was liberated on April 29, 1945. The next morning, Miller and Scherman were among the first journalists to document a scene of depravity that sickened combat veterans. Numbly, she did her work. Later that afternoon, they reached Munich, and "wangled a billet," Penrose writes, in Hitler's private apartment on the Prinzregentenplatz—the command post for the 45th Infantry Division. Scherman took a picture of his lover and comrade nude in the Führer's bathtub. For Scherman, it was a great journalistic coup, and it brought him fame. It brought the model fame, too, though not of the kind that her war journalism deserved. That sensational moment of callous clowning after an ordeal is the image of Lee Miller that is, perhaps, best remembered.

Last April, Miller would have celebrated her hundredth birthday. Her father had died only a month short of his, but she was done in, at seventy, by lung cancer. Hard smoking and alcoholism had, by then, ravaged her beauty. "The post-war period was an anti-climax," Haworth-Booth writes, with considerable understatement. Miller had once asked her parents if, should she conceive a child, she could park it with them in Poughkeepsie—for five years or so. Antony, her accidental child, conceived at thirty-nine, was parked with a nanny who displaced her in his affections. Mother and son came to hate each other, Penrose admits, and he left home bitterly estranged. But, after he married, Miller took a liking to her daughter-in-law, Suzanna, who was sunny and maternal, and helped to finesse a détente.

Miller became Lady Penrose (mocking the honor, a dubious one for an orthodox bohemian, she called herself Lady Penrose of Poughkeepsie) when her husband was knighted, in 1966. He had founded the Institute for Contemporary Arts in London, with the writer Herbert Read, and written an authoritative biography of Picasso. The couple had been living for decades on a farm in Sussex with a large and unstable entourage that was held in thrall by her drinking binges and self-pity, which often gave way to frenzies of spite. She put on weight and, despite the odd flare of vanity, gave up on her appearance. Sex lost its savor as she lost her charisma, and when she complained to a doctor friend about her panic and depression, he replied, "There is nothing wrong with you, and we cannot keep the world permanently at war just to provide you with excitement."

In the early sixties, however, Miller found a creative outlet in gastronomy. She earned a Cordon Bleu and amassed a library of cookbooks that she mined for her fantastical recipes: Persian Carpet, a dessert of oranges and candied violets; a plum pudding with a blue sauce; marshmallow-cola ice cream; and the Penrose, an open-faced sandwich of mushrooms and foie gras that won first prize in a Norwegian competition for *smørbrød*. As she approached sixty, she had a face-lift, which, oddly, heightened the mannishness that her sexual pliancy had dissembled. She bossed around the friends and lovers (hers past, Roland's current, including a trapeze artist whom he wanted desperately to marry) when they came, in droves, for the weekend, though she nourished them with memorable food. But her son had no idea, until his wife found Miller's archives in the attic of the farmhouse, of the lives she had lived or of the work that she had accomplished. When pressed about her career by a journalist or a curator, Miller was wont to tell an implausible lie with a grain of truth at its core: that the war had destroyed everything.

Among the Picassos in the Penroses' collection of modern art, one of the greatest in private hands, was *Portrait of Lee Miller as L'Arlési-enne* (1937). Haworth-Booth chose to end the London show with it. It vibrated on the wall of the last gallery, leaving a potent impression of Picasso's genius for the irreducible. What the artist saw was a golden face with green hair and a pert profile; an inverted eyeball leaking a tear and caged by red lids; a blue earlobe with a corkscrew earring; a clenched fist; teeth bared in a smile or a grimace; bulging shoulders—white globes with a brown crust, each bigger than the head—which might be the breasts, displaced, or a bursting heart. But the black cavity of her body has the jagged shape of the torn screen from her *Portrait of Space*, with a void beyond it.

JANUARY 2008

AN UNFINISHED WOMAN

———⊗⊗⊗———

I n May 1850, after four years abroad, Margaret Fuller set sail from
Livorno to New York, bound for her native Massachusetts. She
was just about to turn forty, and her stature in America was
unique. In the space of a decade, she had invented a new vocation: the
female public intellectual. Fuller's intelligence had dazzled Ralph
Waldo Emerson, who invited her to join the Transcendental Club and
to edit its literary review, *The Dial*. She was considered a "sibyl" by the
women who subscribed to her "Conversations," a series of talks on
learned subjects (Greek mythology, German Romanticism) whose
real theme was female empowerment. In 1844, Horace Greeley, the
publisher of the *New-York Tribune*, had recruited Fuller to write a
front-page column on culture and politics (the former, mandarin; the
latter, radical). A year later, she published *Woman in the Nineteenth
Century*, a foundational work of feminist history. When Fuller left for
Europe in 1846, to write for Greeley from abroad, she became the first
American foreign correspondent of her sex and, three years later, the
first combat reporter. She embedded herself in the Italian independence movement, led by her friend Giuseppe Mazzini, and she filed
her dispatches from the siege of Rome while running a hospital for
wounded partisans.

Despite her fame, however, Fuller had always just eked out a living.
So, after the fall of the short-lived Roman Republic, she had to borrow the money for a cheap ticket home on the *Elizabeth*, an American

merchantman. The route was perilous—vessels were lost every year—but Fuller's passage was a gamble for other reasons, too. After a lifetime of tenacious celibacy, this "strange, lilting, lean old maid," as Thomas Carlyle described her, had taken a lover.

One of Rome's eternal stories is that of the bookish spinster from a cold clime, whose life has its late spring in Italy, and who loses her inhibitions, amid the ruins, with a man like Giovanni Ossoli. Fuller's paramour was a Roman patrician, ten years her junior. Her friends described him as dark, slender, and boyish-looking, with a melancholy air and fine manners, but he also struck them as a nonentity. He and Fuller had met by chance, in St. Peter's Square, and embarked on a romance that even she considered "so every way unfit." Ossoli had a "great native refinement," as Fuller advertised it to her mother, but he was virtually penniless and barely literate. He spoke no English and had no profession. It seems unlikely that their love would have endured; Fuller doubted it herself. But early in their affair she found herself pregnant, and they were now sailing home as a couple—"the Marchese and Marchesa Ossoli" (no marriage certificate has ever been found)—with their twenty-month-old son, Nino.

After two months at sea, on July 19, with land in sight, the *Elizabeth* was caught in a violent hurricane that devastated the Atlantic seaboard. It ran aground on a sandbar off Fire Island, only a few hundred yards from the beach. Several crew members made it to shore, and, as the hull foundered, the captain saved himself, abandoning his passengers. Fuller was last seen on the deck, her hair lashed by the gale. Then she was felled by the mast, and disappeared in a swell, shrouded by her white nightdress. Her husband had refused to leave her; neither body was ever recovered. Nino drowned in the arms of a steward.

Margaret Fuller was once the best-read woman in America, and millions knew her name. Her writing and her correspondence have been readily available for almost forty years, and she is a rock star of women's studies programs. Yet a wider public hungry for transgressive heroines (especially those who die tragically) has failed to embrace her.

Few writers, however, have been luckier in their biographers, beginning, in 1884, with Thomas Higginson, best known as the friend in need of Emily Dickinson, who helped to revive interest in Fuller after decades of neglect. She was resurrected for a second time by Bell Gale Chevigny, who published *The Woman and the Myth: Margaret Fuller's Life & Writings* in 1976, just as the second wave of feminism was cresting. This monument of research and commentary, revised in 1994, is the bedrock of modern Fuller scholarship. In 2007, Charles Capper completed the two-volume *Margaret Fuller: An American Romantic Life*, which has never been surpassed as a social history of the period. The Fuller canon was enriched last year with another superb biography, by John Matteson, *The Lives of Margaret Fuller*. (Matteson won a Pulitzer Prize in 2008 for his biography of Louisa May Alcott and her father, Bronson.) And this month Megan Marshall joins the cohort of distinguished Fullerites with *Margaret Fuller: A New American Life*.

Marshall is a gifted storyteller steeped in the parochial society of nineteenth-century Boston and Concord—a world of souls at "a white heat." (The expression was Fuller's before it was Dickinson's; the poet is said to have loved Fuller's work.) Her previous book was an enthralling group portrait, *The Peabody Sisters: Three Women Who Ignited American Romanticism*. "Ignited" is perhaps going too far, but the Peabodys helped to fan the inflammatory changes in attitudes and thought that produced transcendentalism, Brook Farm, Thoreau's *Walden*, Fuller's "Conversations" (most of which were hosted by the eldest sister, Elizabeth), and the novels of Sophia Peabody's husband, Nathaniel Hawthorne.

There is not much that is materially "new" in Marshall's life, beyond a letter from Emerson and some engravings that belonged to Fuller, which survived the shipwreck, and which the author discovered in the course of her research. But there are many ways of doing justice to Fuller, and Marshall makes an eloquent case for her as a new paradigm: the single career woman, at home in a world of men, who admire her intelligence, though it turns them off; and the seeker of experience, who doesn't want to miss out on motherhood yet is terrified that it will compromise her work life. In Marshall's biography, the focus is on the drama of identity that Fuller improvised on the world stage, and on the modern anatomy of her desires—a mind and body ever at odds. Capper's book bests Marshall's in thoroughness, Matteson's in elegance and dispassion, and Chevigny's in tough-mindedness, but Marshall excels at creating a sense of intimacy—with both her subject and her reader.

As is often the case, the most popular life of Fuller, *The Memoirs of Margaret Fuller Ossoli*, is also the most sentimental. In 1852, it was the favorite book in America, until *Uncle Tom's Cabin* usurped its place as the number one bestseller, and it continued to outsell all other biographies for the next four years. *The Memoirs* is a posthumous Festschrift—an anthology of texts and reminiscences—cobbled together by three grief-stricken friends of Fuller's: Emerson, William Henry Channing, and James Freeman Clarke (the latter two were liberal clergymen). Their provisional title, "Margaret and Her Friends," tells you something about an impulse that Fuller often aroused, particularly in her male contemporaries: to normalize her. Men, Emerson observed, felt that Margaret "carried too many guns." Edgar Allan Poe succinctly defined that anxiety when he divided humankind into three categories: men, women, and Margaret Fuller. Her friends intended to praise her, though, in effect, they buried her—morally prettified and embalmed, hands folded piously over her bosom. They took it upon themselves to censor or sanitize the searing emotions of her journals and letters, and to rewrite quotes that might, they feared, tarnish her respectability—especially in the light of her dubious marriage. Emerson had, in fact, urged Fuller to stay abroad with Ossoli and the baby, while a disheartening number of her familiars were of the opinion that a tragedy was preferable to an embarrassment. "Providence," according to Nathaniel Hawthorne, "was, after all, kind in putting her, and her clownish husband, and their child, on board that fated ship."

"Mary Wollstonecraft," Fuller wrote, "like Madame Dudevant (commonly known as George Sand) in our day, was a woman whose existence better proved the need of some new interpretation of woman's rights than anything she wrote." The same could be said of Fuller. She was born in Cambridgeport, Massachusetts, in 1810, the eldest of her parents' eight children. Her mother, Margarett, was a docile, sweet-natured beauty who embodied the feminine ideal. She was a decade younger than her husband, Timothy, a lawyer, educated at Harvard, who later had a career in politics. Higginson describes him and his four brothers as "men of great energy, pushing, successful," and without "a particle of tact" among them. Margaret was her father's daughter.

Mrs. Fuller lost her next child, Julia, when Margaret was three. Both parents were disconsolate and, at around this time, Timothy began to homeschool the precocious little girl who seemed to share his drive. "He hoped," Fuller wrote, "to make me the heir of all he knew." She was reading at four, and writing charmingly at six, when Timothy started her on Latin. "To excel in all things should be your constant aim," Timothy exhorted her. This regime continued, with escalating demands and standards and an increasingly advanced curriculum, until Margaret was nine, when she was sent to school.

Fuller later attributed her "nervous affections"—she was subject to nightmares and sleepwalking in her youth, migraines and depressions in her maturity—to the despotism of her father's tutelage, and some of her more zealous partisans have accused him of child abuse. Timothy was a patriarch of his time, miserly with his approval, which Margaret desperately sought. Yet his ambitions for her—ambitions he never had for his sons—incubated her singularity. So did the romance of an intense shared pursuit that excluded her mother. In her own mythology, Fuller figures as Minerva, the goddess of wisdom who sprang from her father's head. And in *Woman in the Nineteenth Century* she calls her idealized alter ego Miranda:

> Her father was a man who cherished no sentimental reverence for woman, but a firm belief in the equality of the sexes . . . He addressed her not as a plaything but as a living mind.

Shakespeare's Miranda beguiles a prince at first sight. Fuller's Miranda, she writes, "was fortunate in a total absence of those charms which might have drawn to her bewildering flatteries, and in a strong electric nature, which repelled those who did not belong to her, and attracted those who did." A great deal of heartache is thus subsumed.

Margaret was a strapping girl who preferred boys' strenuous activities to girls' decorous ones. But she stopped growing at puberty—her height was average—and her appetite caught up with her. She was described as "very corpulent," and some kind of skin condition, probably acne, spoiled her complexion. Severe myopia gave her a squint that was aggravated by her voracious reading. She compensated for a curved spine by walking with her head thrust forward, "like a bird of prey." Her nasal voice was easy to mock, and, from her school days on, Fuller was the kind of obnoxious know-it-all—brusque, sarcastic, and self-important—who invites mockery. A good deal of her showing off was the bravado of a misfit. She was humiliated when only nine guests came to a party for which she had sent out ninety invitations. She made up her mind, she wrote, to be "bright and ugly." Her journals are full of insecurity and, at times, anguish. George Eliot found one passage in particular "inexpressibly touching": "I shall always reign through the intellect, but the life! the life! O my God! shall that never be sweet?"

Timothy's prodigious daughter would have excelled at Harvard, but no college in America accepted women. In Margaret's case, however, the obstacles that she faced seem only to have whetted her appetite for overturning them. "I have felt a gladiatorial disposition lately," she wrote as a young woman to a schoolmistress. In 1830, she embarked on a course of independent study with a childhood friend, James Freeman Clarke, her future biographer. She set out to learn German, the language of Goethe, and was able to translate him within three months. Once Goethe became her master, Emerson wrote, "the place was filled, nor was there room for any other."

Clarke was not the only platonic friend, man or woman, toward whom Fuller had romantic feelings. These infatuations followed a pattern. A desirable person would be drawn to Fuller's "ebullient sense of power," as Emerson described her charisma. She would fantasize about a mystical union that was, in principle, chaste. In the case of a man, a utopian marriage of equals was usually part of the scenario. In the case of a woman, the two of them might, as was the custom of the time, share a bed. These amorous friendships informed Fuller's prescient notion of gender as a bell curve—the idea that there are manly women, womanly men, and same-sex attractions, all of which would be considered perfectly natural in an enlightened society. But sooner or later her needy ardor would cause the relationship to cool, and the fickle "soul mate" would jilt her for a more suitable partner. It was an "accursed lot," Fuller concluded, to be burdened with "a man's ambition" and "a woman's heart," though the ambition, she wrote elsewhere, was "absolutely needed to keep the heart from breaking."

It was Clarke who suggested, in 1832, that Fuller consider authorship as an outlet for her "secret riches within." But she resented him for thinking her "fit for nothing but to write books." In another century, she later wrote, she would have asked for an ambassadorship. Fuller did begin writing for publication in her mid-twenties, though she was, in a way, right about her inaptitude for a writer's life. Patience and humility were alien to her. She loved flaunting her erudition in gratuitous digressions. Reading her was like spelunking, Clarke said. Lydia Maria Child likened Fuller's style to having "too much furniture in your rooms." Elizabeth Barrett Browning was one of many contemporaries who found Fuller's prose "curiously inferior to the impressions her conversation gave you." But the fairest critique of Fuller's literary efforts may be her own of George Sand's:

> Her best works are unequal; in many parts hastily written, or carelessly. . . . They all promise far more than they perform; the work is not done masterly. . . . Sometimes she plies the oar, sometimes she drifts. But what greatness she has is genuine.

The year 1835 was a turning point in Fuller's life: she made Emerson's acquaintance, and her father died, leaving the family in financial straits. It fell to Margaret to help support her widowed mother and her siblings, so she abandoned plans to write a Goethe biography and to travel abroad, and accepted a teaching job at Bronson Alcott's experimental school, in Boston. The otherworldly Alcott neglected to pay

her, however, so in 1837 Fuller became a schoolmistress in Providence. Her wages, thanks to rich patrons, were the annual salary of a
Harvard professor, a thousand dollars. But striving to elevate the children of philistines was intolerable, and whenever she could she stayed
with Waldo, as Emerson was called, and his put-upon wife, Lidian, at
their manor in Concord. Her first visit lasted two weeks, and Waldo
initially found his house guest conceited and intrusive. Two more dis-
cordant personalities—Waldo's cool, cerebral, and ironic; Margaret's
noisy, histrionic, and sincere—would be hard to imagine. But, as the
days wore on, her caustic wit made him laugh, and her conversation,
he decided, was "the most entertaining" in America. By the time they
parted, Matteson writes, Emerson was "rhapsodic." Fuller's presence,
he gushed, atypically, "is like being set in a large place. You stretch
your limbs & dilate to your utmost size."

Fuller was a passionate pedagogue—just not in the classroom. Alcott, who had also failed at teaching, reinvented himself profitably as
a "conversationalist." A "conversation" was an informal paid talk, in an
intimate venue—a parlor rather than a hall—whose raison d'être,
Matteson writes, was to unite the participants in "sympathetic communion around a shared idea." Inspired by Alcott's model, Fuller
decided that she would offer a series of such talks, by subscription, to
an all-woman audience, with the goals of challenging her "conversers"
intellectually and also of giving them "a place where they could state
their doubts and difficulties with hope of gaining aid from the experience or aspirations of others." Many women, Marshall notes, "signed
on just to hear Margaret Fuller talk," and were too intimidated to join
the discussion, but the "Conversations" that Fuller hosted in Boston
between 1839 and 1844 have been called, collectively, the first
consciousness-raising group.

By this time, Emerson had formed the intellectual society that
came to be known as the Transcendental Club. The transcendence he
espoused was a rejection of established religion in favor of a Romantic
creed in which faith was "one thing with Science, with Beauty, and
with Joy." A soul liberated from blind obedience to Christian dogma
would be free to follow its own dictates, and to seek a direct experi-

ence of divinity in art and nature. The transcendental "gospel" suffused Fuller's "Conversations," but in a more heretical form. She was encouraging women to become free agents not only in relation to a deity but in their relations with men.

The Dial was conceived at club meetings in 1839, and, when Margaret volunteered for the job of editor, Emerson gave it to her gladly. The editorship made, and still does, an impressive entry on Fuller's résumé, especially if you have never read the actual publication. Emerson was dismayed by the cloying piety of the first issue. (Apart from Thoreau, Alcott, and Emerson, the contributors are obscure today.) "I hope our *Dial* will get to be a little bad," he told her.

After five years in the Concord hothouse—"this playground of boys, happy and proud in their balls and marbles," as Fuller put it—she was ready for a worldlier adventure. In 1844, she moved to New York, to work for Greeley, and to live with him and his wife, Mary (an alumna of the "Conversations"), in Castle Doleful, their ramshackle mansion in Turtle Bay, near the East River. The Greeleys were teetotallers and health nuts, but liberal-minded about their house guest's unchaperoned life. Fuller became a regular at the literary salon of Anne Charlotte Lynch, on Waverly Place, where she met Poe, and she patronized a mesmeric healer who supposedly cured her scoliosis. In the chapel at Sing Sing, on Christmas Day, she told an audience of convicted prostitutes that their "better selves" would guide them when they were released. The mistreatment of mental patients mobilized her vehemence, and she compared the humanity shown to the inmates of the Bloomingdale Insane Asylum (a dance was held on the evening she visited) with the wretched conditions of the lunatics on Blackwell's (now Roosevelt) Island. Chevigny writes, "Her job as a reporter gave her access to worlds hitherto closed to a woman of her class." But, she remarks, "liberal as her reportage was for the time, it was still eminently genteel muckraking: the Jew is subjected to age-old stereotyping, the poor to kindly pity."

Fuller's distaste for the Chosen People made an exception for James Nathan, a German-Jewish banker with taurine looks and literary ambitions whom she had met at Anne Lynch's New Year's party. Nathan, who was Fuller's contemporary, was, in his way, as unlikely a match for her as Ossoli, and, Matteson writes, there was no logic to their relations. Love does not obey logic, however—particularly, perhaps, the love of a cerebral woman for a sensual man. Nathan had arrived in New York from Hamburg as a teenager, and had worked his way up from the rag trade to Wall Street. They shared a love for German; Nathan sang lieder to her; they went to galleries, concerts, and lectures.

This artful courtship, which patrician Boston might have considered miscegenation, made Fuller feel "at home on the earth," and she couldn't believe it would suffer from an "untimely blight." But the fact that she imagined the blight suggests that she was braced for its inevitability. Depending on whose story you believe (Matteson's is the fairest to Nathan), the banker was simply caddish. He was using Fuller to befriend Greeley, and it came out that he was living with a working-class mistress. Yet, had Margaret's relations with men not been so naïve, you would have to conclude that she led him on. Her letters dropped hints about an impure past. Their language was overheated. She frankly admitted her "strong attraction" to Nathan, and was coy about joining him on "the path of intrigue." That path led to the banks of the East River, where, one evening, Nathan apparently made an advance from which Fuller recoiled in horror.

Her inchoate feelings for Nathan were not merely virginal. As she herself acknowledged, in forgiving him, they were "childish." But perhaps they suggest why her writing was never as great as her ambitions for it. She could love and desire intensely, but rarely at the same moment, and she could think and feel deeply, but not often in the same sentence.

In August 1846, Fuller sailed for England. She had dreamed of a trip abroad since adolescence, and a philanthropic Quaker couple, Marcus and Rebecca Spring, agreed to pay her expenses in exchange for her tutoring of their son. They tarried in the north for two months, visiting Wordsworth in the Lake District, and also one of his neighbors, a young poet just setting out on his career: Matthew Arnold. They continued to Scotland, where Fuller got lost while hiking on Ben Lomond, in the Highlands, and spent a night marooned, with nothing but the mist for a blanket. She transformed this ordeal, for her *Tribune* readers, into an experience of sublimity.

That October, the companions arrived in London, where Fuller's reputation had preceded her. The British edition of *Woman in the Nineteenth Century* had just been published. In New York, Poe had written that Fuller "judges woman by the heart and intellect of Miss Fuller, but there are not more than one or two dozen Miss Fullers on the whole face of the earth." George Eliot, after noting "a vague spiritualism and grandiloquence which belong to all but the very best American writers," continued:

> Some of the best things [Miss Fuller] says are on the folly of absolute definitions of woman's nature and absolute demarcations of woman's mission. "Nature," she says, "seems to delight in varying the arrangements, as if to show that she will be fettered by no rule; and we must admit the same varieties that she admits."

Even before Fuller left New York, her columns had become more concerned with political engagement than with transcendence, and Europe pushed her further toward militance. Thomas Carlyle and his wife, Jane, had introduced her to Mazzini. She began to describe herself as a socialist. In Paris (where her principles did not forbid the acquisition of some elegant clothes, or a presentation at court), she met some of the radicals—Lamennais, Béranger, Considérant among them—who, as Chevigny puts it, were "preparing the explosion that in the next year would blast Louis Philippe off the throne." She had a thrilling encounter with George Sand after knocking on her door, unannounced. Unlike the "vulgar caricatures" of the libertine crossdresser which even Fuller, to some degree, had accepted, Sand emerged from her library wearing a gown of somber elegance, instead of her infamous trousers. She greeted Fuller with "lady-like dignity," and they spent the day in rapt discussion. A year earlier, Fuller had praised Sand for having "dared to probe" the "festering wounds" of her society, but she deplored the "surgeon's dirty hands." A woman of Sand's genius, she wrote, untainted by debauchery, "might have filled an apostolic station among her people." Now, she declared, Sand needed no defense, "for she has bravely acted out her nature."

The same could not yet be said of Margaret Fuller. A woman could be a sea captain, she had asserted; she could happily do the manual labor of a carpenter; there was no differential of capacity between the female brain and the male. But, ironically, Fuller herself needed a man's blessing to follow the example of Sand's sexual bravery.

That man, whom she met toward the end of her stay in Paris, was the great Polish poet and nationalist Adam Mickiewicz, a forty-eight-year-old exile with heroic features. Expelled from Poland for his political activities, he had lived for a while in Weimar, where he had met Goethe. His marriage was disastrous, and he had taken up with his children's governess. In Paris, Mickiewicz was gathering the forces for a revolution that would free Poland from Prussia, and he was a partisan of freedom in all its guises, including women's liberation. Keen to meet him on every count, Fuller had sent him a volume of Emerson's poems, "guessing correctly," Marshall writes, "that the gift would draw him swiftly" to her hotel. Mickiewicz had been dismissed from the Collège de France, in 1844, for lectures, influenced by transcendentalism, which preached a volatile mixture of mysticism and insurrection.

Fuller inevitably fell in love with Mickiewicz, and it seems, for once, to have been mutual. "He affected me like music," she told Rebecca Spring. But it also appears, from their letters, that he had recognized what vital element—not only sex but honesty about desire—was missing from Margaret's life. "The first step in your deliverance," he told her, "is to know if it is permitted to you to remain virgin."

Several days later, Fuller and the Springs left Paris for Rome. She felt bereft, not only of Mickiewicz but of all the time that she had "wasted" on unworthy others. He had told her, however, that he wasn't yet free to give her what she deserved, which was "all of me." On Holy Thursday, she and her friends went to hear vespers in St. Peter's Square, and became separated. She was approached by a gallant young Italian who asked her if she was lost.

"One is not born, but rather becomes, a woman," Simone de Beauvoir wrote in *The Second Sex*, a hundred years after *Woman in the Nine-*

teenth Century was published. Although her assertion may not be true scientifically, Beauvoir was right in the sense that women are not born inferior but, rather, become inferior, by the process of objectification that she so exhaustively describes. Yet Beauvoir also knew that a woman "needs to expend a greater moral effort than the male" to resist the temptations of dependence.

Few women have fought more valiantly than Margaret Fuller to achieve autonomy. But her struggle required her to create and to endure a profound state of singleness. She had to become, she wrote, "my own priest, pupil, parent, child, husband, and wife." That austere self-isolation, perhaps, is why each new biography excites interest in her, which then subsides. Her example gives you much to admire but not enough to envy.

APRIL 2013

E va Zeisel, the ceramicist and industrial designer, doesn't like to call herself an artist, even though it has been sixty years since the Museum of Modern Art gave her a solo exhibition—a first for a creator of mass-produced housewares. "I am a maker of useful things," she said the other day in her apartment, near Columbia. "Art has more ego to it than what I do." But if it's modesty that makes her wary of enshrinement it's also a pioneer's intolerance for being confined.

Born into a Jewish Hungarian family of freethinking patricians, the teenage Eva was happiest in the wild garden of her parents' villa. She left its sanctuary eighty years ago and apprenticed herself to a potter and oven-maker in Budapest. For the next decade, she camped cheerfully in a series of makeshift lodgings near the various factories in Germany and Russia where she learned her trade. The months in Jazz Age Paris that Zeisel spent with her childhood friend and some-time lover Arthur Koestler, and an interlude in Weimar Berlin, living near the Romanisches Café, were the idylls in a youth of hard travel, ephemeral romance, and the gritty labor of creating beauty.

By her mid-twenties, Zeisel had mastered every phase of manufacture, from drafting to product promotion. She moved to the Soviet Union in 1932, and by 1935 she had become the artistic director of Russia's china and glass industry. Her mother was visiting her in Moscow a year later, when the secret police knocked at their door. Zeisel was imprisoned for the next sixteen months, mostly in solitary confinement, on the charge of plotting Stalin's assassination. She resisted her interrogators until the day that, as she put it in her memoirs, she betrayed her dignity with a false confession. (Koestler drew heavily upon her accounts of this ordeal for *Darkness at Noon*.) But the authorities, rather than shoot her, as they had done to most of her alleged co-conspirators, deported her to Vienna, where she somehow caught the last train out before the Nazi invasion.

Last month, Zeisel celebrated her hundredth birthday. "Still alive, still working—I don't like the word 'still,'" she said. She has lived on the Upper West Side since 1938, when she and her second husband, the sociologist Hans Zeisel, arrived in New York. A few weeks later, she found work in a Manhattan factory designing ceramic miniatures. Her two children were born in the early 1940s, by which time she was also teaching at the Pratt Institute and lecturing at MoMA. The playful organic shapes of Zeisel's Town and Country line for Red Wing and her curvaceous white dinner service for Hall China charmed postwar America.

The mid-century was a second heyday for Zeisel. Her third is right now. To coincide with her birthday, Pratt mounted a retrospective of nine decades in clay, glass, metal, wood, and plastic. The West Fourteenth Street gallery was crowded with design students stunned by her modernity. "What is a hundred?" she asked. "One more than ninety-nine."

The young Eva was a slight, though formidable, girl with an infectious appetite for pleasure. The centenarian has limpid eyes and a crown of white hair. She was nestled in a wing chair under a lap robe, surrounded by her heirlooms. A table of her own design had been drawn up to an Empire divan, and was set with ceramics from her bestselling 2005 collection for Crate & Barrel. Zeisel has always been a maverick modernist, and her formal templates are abstracted from nature: the penguin's belly; the duck's bill; the splash of a milk drop; the oval of an elm leaf; the whorled rim of an ear.

In the kitchen, a young Russian model-maker, Georgii Bogdevich, was shaving Plasticine from the prototype of a chalice-like footed mug that is part of Zeisel's new line of Royal Stafford earthenware. When Bogdevich offered the mug for her inspection, Zeisel chafed it in her cupped palms. Though she wasn't happy with the proportions ("not enough emotion yet"), this "play" with a model, she said, is the defining moment of gestation. "I think with my hands. I design things to be touched—not for a museum. A piece is ready when it has the shape of something to cherish."

DECEMBER 2006

For my tenth birthday, I got the present of my dreams: a piece of Amelia Earhart luggage. It was a small overnight case made of aluminum, with rounded corners, and covered in blue vinyl. Between the latches was a little plaque with an ersatz, feminine signature. (Earhart's actual signature was loopy and uneven, with a runic-looking "A.") I had nowhere to go, so I kept the case under my bed and filled it with dolls' clothes—a use, I suspect, of which Earhart would have disapproved. Play that prepared a young girl for domesticity was anathema to her ideals. When she lectured at colleges—as she did frequently, to promote careers for women, especially in aviation—she urged the coeds to focus on majors dominated by men, like engineering, and to postpone marriage until they had got a degree. On Earhart's own wedding day, in 1931, the thirty-three-year-old bride handed her forty-three-year-old groom, George Palmer Putnam, a remarkable letter, which read:

> You must know again my reluctance to marry, my feeling that I shatter thereby chances in work which means so much to me . . . In our life together I shall not hold you to any medieval code of faithfulness to me, nor shall I consider myself bound to you similarly . . . I may have to keep some place where I can go to be myself now and then, for I cannot guarantee to endure at all the confinements of even an attractive cage.

The place where Earhart went to be herself was the cockpit of a plane, and that may have been the place where she died. On July 2, 1937, she became the world's most famous missing person when her twin-engine Lockheed Electra disappeared in the vicinity of Howland Island, a speck in the Pacific about midway between Australia and Hawaii, where the Department of the Interior had built her a landing strip. She and her navigator, Fred Noonan, were attempting to circumnavigate the equator, a feat for the record books, although pilots before them (all male) had rounded the globe at least six times by shorter routes, and commercial transpacific air service had recently been inaugurated. Critics accused Earhart posthumously of embarking on a capricious joyride that ultimately cost taxpayers millions of dollars, the estimated tab for a huge rescue mission authorized by President Roosevelt, Earhart's fan and friend. Even some of her staunchest admirers disapproved of the last flight. Earhart's biographer Susan Butler quotes one of them, Captain Hilton Railey, who had helped to launch her career. She was, he wrote, "caught up in the hero racket."

Earhart, however, was a heroic figure to millions of her contemporaries, and she still counts as one. She achieved fame dramatically, in 1928, as the first woman to cross the Atlantic in a plane, the *Friendship*, albeit only as a passenger. Railey had recruited her on behalf of Mrs. Frederick E. Guest, née Amy Phipps, a steel heiress and sportswoman who was underwriting the expedition. She had planned to play the starring role herself, until her husband, a former British cabinet minister, expressed his alarm (three women fliers, including a princess, had recently perished in crashes). Railey was commissioned to find a substitute, and Guest stipulated that, ideally, she should be an aviator but, more important, "the right sort of girl." (The wrong sort of girl was her rival in the race to Europe, Mabel Boll, a flamboyant former actress who was known as the Queen of Diamonds. As Guest later put it to her daughter, "It just wouldn't do.")

Wilmer (Bill) Stultz, the pilot of the *Friendship*, who had defected from the Boll party, and Louis (Slim) Gordon, the mechanic, had done the actual flying, and Earhart tried to remind a besotted press and ecstatic crowds hailing her as "Lady Lindy" that she had really been just "a sack of potatoes." In 1932, however, she legitimatized the title by flying the Atlantic on her own, becoming the first woman and the second person, five years after Charles Lindbergh, to do so. (Congress awarded her honorary Major Wings, which she wore with her pearls.) In 1935, she was the first pilot to solo across the Pacific— from Honolulu to Oakland—and to solo nonstop from Los Angeles to Mexico.

Earhart also made or broke a slew of other records, and few Americans would not have recognized her in the street. Her image was managed aggressively by Putnam, a scion of the publishing house G. P. Putnam's Sons, and one of the first über-agents. He specialized in celebrity true-life adventure stories, and he had signed up Lindbergh to chronicle his flight to Paris for the *Times* (which paid him sixty thousand dollars), then turned the articles into a book that sold some 600,000 copies. Even before Putnam met Earhart, he had caught wind of the Guest project—and his next bestseller. By the time the *Friendship* took off, he had a ten-thousand-dollar deal for Earhart's firsthand story, and a file of publicity shots that played up her resemblance to Lindbergh. (They were both lean, fair Midwesterners with winning smiles.) Her legend, to a large degree, was Putnam's creation. He brokered her lecture tours, book contracts, columns, product endorsements, and media exposure, and he was so proprietary that a rival of Earhart's described him as her Svengali. She, however, was the real mesmerist. *Amelia Earhart: Image and Icon*, a handsomely designed album of their teamwork as self-promoters—portraits, press clippings, ads, and illustrations—was published in 2007, with notes and commentary by the editors, Kristen Lubben and Erin Barnett, and essays by Butler and Susan Ware.

Ware regards Earhart's pose of Lindberghian diffidence with critical amusement. She quotes the great aviator Elinor Smith, who was still flying in 2001, at eighty-nine: "Amelia was about as shy as Muhammad Ali." The abuse of the term "icon" incites iconoclasm, or ought to. Earhart was saintlike only as a martyr to her own ambition, who became an object of veneration and is periodically resurrected— her unvarnished glamour, like a holy man's body, still miraculously fresh. Embraced by feminists, she was featured on a 1976 cover of *Ms.*, which promised a story "better than the myth." Read closely, however, Earhart's life is, in part, the story of a charismatic dilettante who lectured college girls about ambition yet never bothered to earn a degree. In the 1990s, Apple and the Gap both featured her in ad campaigns—the Gap to sell khaki trousers, Apple to promote its corporate image of nonconformity. The slogan that appeared with a gauzy, doe-eyed photograph of Earhart in a white helmet was "Think Different." (She thought of herself not only as different but as a special case to whom most ground rules didn't apply.) Three Hollywood movies, starring Rosalind Russell, Diane Keaton, and Amy Adams, have told a version of her story, and a new one, *Amelia*, directed by Mira Nair, with Hilary Swank in the title role and Richard Gere as Putnam, will open in October. The script is based on two biographies, *The Sound of Wings*, by Mary Lovell, and Butler's definitive *East to the Dawn*; and on *Amelia Earhart: The Mystery Solved* (1999), by Elgen M. Long, a veteran pilot, and his wife, Marie K. Long.

There were, in fact, other famous female aces in the early decades of aviation. All of them were daring—some were said to be better pilots than Earhart—and many of them were killed and forgotten. If Earhart became an "icon," it was, in part, because women who aspired to excel in any sphere, at a high altitude, looked upon her as their champion. But it was also because the unburied come back to haunt us.

Earhart had already tried to circle the globe once in 1937, flying westward from Oakland, but she had crashed taking off in Honolulu. Determined to try again, she coaxed additional funds from her sponsors, and "more or less mortgaged the future," she wrote. The plane, hyped as a "flying laboratory" (it wasn't clear what she planned to test, beyond her own mettle and earning power), was shipped back to California for repairs, and, once Putnam had renegotiated the necessary landing clearances and technical support, she and Noonan set off again, on June 1, this time flying eastward—weather patterns had changed. A month and more than 22,000 miles later, they had reached Lae, New Guinea, the jumping-off place for the longest and most dangerous lap of the journey. The Electra's fuel tanks could keep them aloft for, at most, twenty-four hours, so they had almost no margin of error in pinpointing Howland, about 2,500 miles away. Noonan was using a combination of celestial navigation and dead reckoning. They had a radio, but its range was limited.

Early on July 2, on a slightly overcast morning, about eighteen hours into the flight, Earhart told radiomen on the *Itasca*, a Coast Guard cutter stationed off Howland to help guide her down, that she was flying at a thousand feet and should soon be "on" them, but that her fuel was low. Although the *Itasca* had been broadcasting its position, so that Noonan could take his bearings and, if necessary, correct the course, they apparently couldn't receive the transmissions, nor apparently could they see the billows of black smoke that the cutter was pumping out. Earhart's last message was logged at 8:43 a.m. No authenticated trace of the Electra, or of its crew, has ever been found.

After twenty-five years of research, the Longs concluded that "a tragic sequence of events"—human error, faulty equipment, miscommunication—"doomed her flight from the beginning," and that Earhart and Noonan were forced to ditch in shark-infested waters close to Howland, where the plane sank or broke up. There is, however, an alternative scenario—a chapter from Robinson Crusoe. It is supported with methodical, if controversial, research by Ric Gillespie, the author of *Finding Amelia*.

Gillespie is a former airline crash investigator who is notably unimpressed with his subject. (He describes Earhart as an "average" pilot and has little interest in her life or achievements.) He has distanced himself from the kooks and the conspiracy theorists who have suggested, at different times, that Earhart was on a hushed-up mission to spy on the Japanese, who interned her; that she became Tokyo Rose; or that she returned secretly to America and lived out her days as a housewife in New Jersey. In 1988, he launched the Earhart Project, which is devoted to solving what he calls the "Holy Grail of aviation mysteries." Gillespie recently announced that next May he will lead his ninth expedition to the Pacific island where he believes that Earhart landed, and, for a while, survived as a castaway.

Nikumaroro, formerly Gardner Island, is an atoll about four hundred miles southeast of Howland. At low tide, it is surrounded by a broad, flat apron of coral where a plane could safely touch down. The interior is covered with dense tropical vegetation bordering a lagoon. In 1929, a steamer went aground on the reef, and when its crew was rescued, they left behind a cache of provisions. The atoll was deserted until 1938, when it became one of the last outposts of the British Empire to be colonized, and was settled by natives of the Gilbert Islands. (A prolonged drought forced the inhabitants to abandon Nikumaroro in the 1960s.)

In 1940, a colonial administrator and his work party found a liqueur bottle and some corks, a human skull and some bones, the partial sole of a woman's shoe, parts of a man's shoe, and a sextant box. (Noonan had a mariner's sextant on board.) A year later, the skull and the bones were examined by a British doctor on Fiji. The relics subsequently vanished, but when the doctor's notes came to light, in the 1990s, they were reviewed by forensic anthropologists. Their verdict, according to Gillespie, is that they probably belonged to a female, about five feet seven (Earhart was an inch taller), of Northern European origin.

Gillespie's case is circumstantial; Butler and the Longs are among the informed skeptics who take issue with it. But it rests on more than a secondhand analysis of missing body parts: unexplained distress calls from the mid-Pacific on Earhart's frequency which have long been discounted as "freak receptions," or as the work of a hoaxer; "signs of recent habitation" seen from the air on July 9, 1937, by a Navy pilot who was searching the area but saw no one alive; artifacts made by the islanders from scavenged material consistent with an Electra; the last line of position that Earhart radioed to the *Itasca*, which leads straight from Howland to Nikumaroro. But only a DNA sample can lay Earhart's ghost to rest. That, Gillespie hopes, is what the under-brush and the sands will yield.*

Had Earhart returned, she would have celebrated her fortieth birthday on July 24. Only a few intimates, however, knew her true age. She began shaving a year off at twenty-two, when she enrolled in an extension program at Columbia University, to take premed classes, and she later shaved off another. Her birthday was evidently on her mind in Miami, where the Electra was getting a final tune-up from mechanics at Pan Am, and she spoke with an old friend, Carl Allen, the aviation correspondent for the *Herald Tribune*. He told her frankly, Butler writes, that he judged her chances of success at "fifty-fifty," and she didn't argue, noting that she was worried for Noonan's sake but not for her own: "As far as I know I've only got one obsession—a small and probably typically feminine horror of growing old—so I won't feel completely cheated if I fail to come back." Allen, who had covered her career from its outset, might have reminded her of another obsession: to keep proving her singularity.

That "typically feminine" bit of vanity about her age was atypical of a woman who, from childhood, had refused to let her sex either limit or define her. Even in her late thirties, Earhart looked like an adolescent boy who had chopped off his own hair. She was lanky and nonchalant, with no hips or breasts—no visible womanliness—to speak of. One learns from Butler that she flew wearing men's under-pants (they were apparently superior to a woman's for the purposes of a quick pee). For public appearances—at White House dinners, in a ticker-tape parade, on the lecture circuit—her wardrobe was unfrilly but elegant, and for a while she designed and modeled her own fashion label, an undistinguished line of tailored dresses and soft

* Research into Earhart's disappearance continues. As of 2021, the nuclear scien-tist Daniel Beck has been using neutron radiography to study the composition of a metal panel, possibly from the wreckage of her plane, that Gillespie found on Ni-kumaroro in 1991. In 2018, the forensic anthropologist Richard Lanz analyzed the skeletal remains discovered on the island in 1940. His analyses, using modern fo-rensic osteology, strongly suggest the remains are those of a woman whose bone lengths match Earhart's, with a ninety-nine percent margin of certainty.

two-piece ensembles. But in her flight gear—a jumpsuit or jodhpurs ("breeks"); flat lace-up knee boots; a white shirt and a man's tie; a bomber jacket or a leather coat—she seems, at least by the codes of this century, flagrantly androgynous. Butler doesn't raise the question of Earhart's possible bisexuality, and one has to wonder if she put it to any of her sources. She does, however, make a point of noting that two conspicuously virile men donated their boxers, in one case, and their briefs, in the other, to Earhart's wardrobe: her husband and her lover. The lover was "undoubtedly" Eugene Vidal—an Olympic athlete, West Point football captain, flier, airline executive, frequent house guest of the Putnams, and, largely thanks to Earhart's friendship with Franklin and Eleanor Roosevelt, the director of a new agency, the Bureau of Air Commerce. (Butler bases her certainty of the affair on suggestions of it in the diary of Amelia's secretary, and on speculations voiced by Vidal's widow, Katharine, and by Gore Vidal, the son of his first marriage.) When the bureau was reorganized, in 1936, and Vidal was fired, Earhart wrote a breathtakingly cheeky letter to Eleanor, withdrawing a promise to campaign for FDR's reelection unless her protégé was reinstated. The president was said to have guffawed at Earhart's nerve, but a day later Vidal's job was saved.

As far as one knows, Earhart's secret erotic life was heterosexual. On the bell curve of gender, however, she is an epicene, at least in the grammatical sense of the word: that of a noun that has one form to denote either sex ("doctor" or "friend," as opposed to "heroine" or "avi-atrix"). Unlike the cross-dressing sexual rebels of the Belle Époque, whose intention was to be outrageous, Earhart—whose intention was to stay aloft both as a pilot and as a celebrity—projected a confusing mixture of traits with such an aura of virtue and assurance that she disarmed received ideas about femininity, even those of conservatives. Kristen Lubben quotes one of their paeans, published in 1928, which deplores the "decadence" of a generation slipping by stages "from sly gin-guzzling to a calculated harlotry." Earhart, the writer declares, is the antidote to those shameless flappers: "Hers is the healthy curiosity of the clean mind and the strong body . . . She will become a symbol of new womanhood." Yet Putnam, the press, and, no doubt, Earhart

herself were aware that there was something troubling about her appearance that had to be neutralized. Her photo spreads, Lubben
writes, were often laid out like a book of paper dolls, in which pictures
of the cavalier in trousers and leather were juxtaposed with pictures of
the well-bred lady in a long skirt, a fur wrap, a girlish middy, or an
evening gown, her arms full of flowers.

Putnam's Barnumesque title for Earhart's first book, published in
1928, was *20 Hrs. 40 Min., Our Flight in the Friendship: The American
Girl, First Across the Atlantic by Air, Tells Her Story*. Earhart was a "girl"
of thirty-one passing for twenty-nine, but no one can argue with her
purity as a product of America. On her mother's side, she descended
from the Puritans and from Quaker shipowners who arrived with
William Penn. One of her paternal ancestors, Johann Earhardt, survived the winter at Valley Forge. Both branches of the family tree
produced pioneers. Their boldness in facing the unknown was part of
Amelia's heritage, but so was a patrician confidence of her place in the
world.

Amelia was born in 1897, in a Gothic mansion on a bluff overlooking the Missouri River, in Atchison, Kansas. Her mother, Amy, was
the daughter of Alfred Otis, a wealthy lawyer, and of Millie Harres,
who had grown up in Philadelphia society and never quite overcame
her nostalgia for it. Amy defied her father to marry Edwin Earhart,
the son of a destitute Lutheran minister, who had worked his way
through law school but settled for a lazy practice as what one in-law
called a "claims chaser." Otis bought the couple a house in Kansas
City and helped with their expenses, yet the Earharts—he a dreamer
who tinkered with inventions and became a drunk, she a child of privilege, both incurable spendthrifts—still ran out of money. (In later
life, Amelia, like her grandfather, and with some of the same contempt, supported her mother. Accompanying the remittance checks,
Susan Ware observes, were "peremptory" letters full of scolding and
condescension that betrayed an imperious streak that was well hidden
from the world.)

Amelia's sister, Muriel, was born in 1900, and that year, Amy sent
her older daughter, a precociously self-sufficient toddler, to live with

the Otises, in Atchison. There, apparently, she learned to finesse the conflicting demands of her own nature for risk and freedom and those of convention and propriety embodied in an anxious grandmother. In 1908, Edwin took a job in Des Moines as a claims agent for the Rock Island railroad. For the next eight years, the Earharts moved from city to city in the Midwest, as Edwin's drinking inexorably destroyed his prospects. ("There are two kinds of stones," Earhart wrote of life with her father, "one of which rolls.") They sometimes lived in unheated rooms, kept a boardinghouse, or camped with relatives.

After years of litigation with her brother, Amy finally extracted her share of the Otis patrimony, and sent Amelia, at nineteen, to a ritzy boarding school in Philadelphia. Many of her classmates were content to be "finished," but Amelia kept a scrapbook of clippings about self-starting women: a fire lookout, a police commissioner, an engineer. Her plans, after graduation, were to attend Bryn Mawr, but they changed abruptly on a Christmas holiday in Toronto, where she and Amy were visiting Muriel. The city was filled with wounded soldiers. Amelia dropped out of school, enrolled in a nursing course, and volunteered at a military hospital. When Canada was hit by the Spanish-flu pandemic in June 1918, Amelia caught pneumonia from her patients, and her lungs were never quite cured.

In her time off, Amelia visited a military airfield. "They were terribly young, those air men, young and eager," she wrote in *20 Hrs. 40 Min.* "Aviation . . . inevitably attracted the romanticists." Whether or not she saw herself as one of them, she would come to do so. She called herself "a hobo of the air," and described her early flights as "vagabonding." In the meantime, she gave up on the idea of a career in medicine after a year at Columbia, and joined her parents in Los Angeles, in a spacious house on West Fourth Street which, as usual, they couldn't afford. Out of filial duty, or perhaps, as she put it, as a "sunkist victim of inertia," Amelia lived with them for the next three years.

The holy terrors in the annals of fiction and biography—spunky tomboys who, when forced into a dress, hike it up and climb a tree—have often been their fathers' daughters. Edwin encouraged Amelia's exploits, and a sense of their complicity as two profligate rolling stones stirs beneath the clichés of her prose. He had often given her the kinds of present that a man buys his son: a baseball bat, a football, a .22-caliber rifle, which she wanted for shooting rats. A letter that Amelia left for Edwin, in the event of her death, before the *Friendship* flight, reads like the stoic farewell of a manly boy soldier to his sire: "Hooray for the last grand adventure! I wish I had won, but it was worthwhile anyway. You know that. I have no faith we'll meet anywhere again, but I wish we might."

The dry valleys of Southern California were a cradle of aviation, and it was Edwin who took his daughter to her first air meet, south of Los Angeles, and arranged for her first "trial hop" in a plane. Thoroughly smitten, Amelia was "ready at any price" to take lessons, and after only a few hours in the air she decided to buy her first plane, an experimental Kinner Airster. Amy gave her the two thousand dollars for it, and Amelia made some gestures to defray her expenses. But she quit one job after another—as a clerk at the phone company, as an amateur photographer, and, with a partner in the construction business, hauling gravel. Her spare time was devoted to flying, and, in 1923, having learned to "stunt," she was a featured performer in an air rodeo.

Among the admirers of her bravado was the Earharts' new boarder. (They had lost a chunk of Amy's inheritance in a disastrous mining venture promoted by Amelia.) Sam Chapman, an engineer from Marblehead, Massachusetts, was five years Amelia's senior. They played tennis and discussed philosophy, Butler writes, and he shared her progressive ideals, including, apparently, her notions of equality between a husband and a wife. Before he left California, in 1924, he asked her to marry him, and she accepted.

That year was a watershed for the family. The Earharts' marriage finally foundered, Amelia's lung trouble recurred, and she sold her plane. Rather than use the proceeds to pay her hospital bill, she blithely bought a roadster nicknamed the Yellow Peril. Back in New York, she reenrolled at Columbia, but early in 1925 she dropped out yet again and moved in with Amy and Muriel, who were living outside Boston. She took a math course at Harvard Summer School, then applied, unsuccessfully, for a scholarship to MIT. Next, she found a job teaching English as a second language, and worked at a psychiatric hospital, where, according to Butler, "she lasted only a few months before deciding to leave." At that juncture, typically aimless though atypically depressed, she heard of a vocational-guidance service, the first of its kind, that was run by and for women. In filling out the application, she "lied—extensively" about her experience and credentials.

In 1928, when Putnam and Railey were prospecting for "the right sort of girl" to replace Mrs. Guest, Railey called an acquaintance in the Boston chapter of the National Aeronautic Association, Rear Admiral Reginald Belknap. He told Railey about "a young social worker who flies." She was, he added, "a thoroughly fine person. Call Denison House and ask for Amelia Earhart." Denison was a settlement house in the South End of Boston where Earhart ran night-school classes in English and supervised the nursery and the activities for girls. Two years before Railey's call changed her life, an employment counselor had sent Earhart for an interview. Denison's director, Marion Perkins, was intrigued, she wrote, by the applicant's "quiet sense of humor, the frank direct look in her grey eyes," and took a chance on her. So, it would seem, did everyone.

It is hard to know whether, or how long, Earhart would have stayed in social work if Railey hadn't offered her a shot at glory. She could, for a while, throw herself into a high-minded endeavor, but she lacked the discipline to see it through. She dallied with Chapman for six years, breaking their engagement when she became famous. (He never married.) She warned Putnam that she was incapable of fidelity, and she apparently made good on her threat. Her flights were feats of courage and endurance, but compared with the achievements of the women in her scrapbook their significance was ephemeral. Her unique experience might have yielded a memoir that would still be read, yet she published only three slight books, one of them posthumous, which were rushed out, for commercial reasons, in weeks. When people asked Earhart why she flew, she liked to say, "For the fun of it," and *The Fun of It* was the title of her second book. Gravity was uncongenial to her, and she made light even of grave things. There was ether in the very sound of her name. Physically, too, she seemed like an airy spirit—Ariel, impatient to be set free.

The Earhart property that, to a layman, seems to have the greatest cinematic potential was not one that Mira Nair did, or perhaps could, acquire. *I Was Amelia Earhart*, a bestselling novel by Jane Mendelsohn, was published in 1996. It is a desert-island romance based, in part, on an article by Gillespie, and Mendelsohn imagines that Earhart and Noonan have landed on an atoll like Nikumaroro. Amelia builds a lean-to by the lagoon, and Noonan constructs a shack with a veranda that looks out to sea. In the early days of their ordeal, they bicker and mourn, but solitude and need draw them together. They fish, forage, and survive by their wits. He plays his harmonica and talks to the birds, stoned on a narcotic root. She decorates her hut with parts from the Electra. The past recedes. Then, one night, Noonan seduces her. Their wild, "unencumbered" sex leads to a state of oneness "more precious than love." And, when he spots a search plane, they hide on the jungle floor, because "they know now that there is no difference between being rescued and being captured."

The torrid prose and the fantasy of surrender are almost a parody of the genre, and Amelia, of all people, knew that there were no idylls, especially between men and women. Yet the ending rings true. It is one that she herself tried to write. She abandons everything, and flies away.

SEPTEMBER 2009

———⊗⊗⊗———

I spent the summer researching a profile of the German artist Isa Genzken, whose first American retrospective opened last week, at the Museum of Modern Art. Genzken, who lives in Berlin and turns sixty-five today, spent the summer hospitalized with a head injury, so our plans to meet kept being postponed, and we eventually had to cancel the story. I couldn't quite let Genzken go, however. She is, in some respects, one of those lost women who have been my specialty as a writer.

"Lost" is a relative notion. Genzken, an art star in her native country, represented Germany at the 2007 Venice Biennale. She is an important figure in Europe, and her exhibition history fills pages of small print in the show's catalogue. American museums have not overlooked her, and younger artists, especially women, have been inspired by her heretical vitality. But few New Yorkers, I discovered, seem to have heard of her. When her name did ring a bell, it was usually in connection with Gerhard Richter. In the early 1970s, Richter was Genzken's professor at the Dusseldorf Art Academy. They married in 1982 and divorced about twenty years ago. It is time to disentangle them.

The retrospective occupies most of the gallery space on the museum's sixth floor, and part of its lobby. It is fitting that Genzken's belated consecration comes from MoMA: New York, the Ur-metropolis, has been her wolf mother, and the connection is primal on several grounds. Urban architecture—its beauty and desolation—is a central theme of Genzken's work, which mirrors the city's seething heterogeneity and embodies its extremes of rawness and refinement. An incurable wild child, she haunted the downtown club scene of the seventies and eighties, and that experience helped to define her. (She made her first visit as a teenager, and she returned often, sometimes annually.) Genzken's art and life are narratives of defiance. She is too restless to be faithful to a medium or a genre. She has always courted danger, with predictable results—the life force and the death wish are at odds in her. The desire to please is not part of her character. She suffers from alcoholism and from bipolar disease. And perhaps because self-promotion is an aspect of self-preservation, she has resisted that, too. But sexism, it seems, has also contributed to Genzken's relative obscurity, at least until lately. She is a major female artist who doesn't do women's work.

The details of Genzken's biography are as hard to pin down as she is. Her father was a doctor who loved music. Her mother (still alive at close to a hundred years old) renounced her dreams of a stage career to work for a pharmaceutical company. The family moved from the small northern town where Isa was born to West Berlin. She grew up comfortably enough, but during a period of national soul-searching, Cold War tension, and epic reconstruction that transformed a country in ruins. That cleansing—of Germany's rubble and of its guilt—was the unstable scaffolding of her childhood.

Genzken is, par excellence, a child of the sixties who embraced the sometimes violent leftist idealism of her generation. She may or may not have once lent her passport to the terrorist Andreas Baader. A boyfriend of her student years, Benjamin Buchloh, became the eminent art historian who now teaches at Harvard. Buchloh introduced her to a circle of artists with radical ideals and practices, including Sigmar Polke, Bruce Nauman, Dan Graham, Lawrence Weiner, and Richter. In 1974, while studying with Richter, Genzken made her debut as a conceptual artist, with a pugnacious film in which two women, one short and plump, one tall and skinny, strip for the camera and exchange clothing. (Genzken was the skinny one; at the time, she was earning money for her art by modeling. The scrapbook pictures of her, at nineteen, in an ad for a tailored suit—a pretty, dark girl with hair as glossy as her smile—are poignant in their remoteness from the androgynous figure, weathered and scrappy, that she cuts today.)

The film is called *Two Women in Combat*, and Sabine Breitwieser, one of the curators of the MoMA show, interprets its significance in her astute catalogue essay. Genzken, she writes, was publicly shedding the prescribed feminine roles that she had inherited and was trying on the outsize ambition that she would grow into.

The alpha males of the German art world forty years ago, with the notable exception of Joseph Beuys, were not much engaged with performance art, a newborn genre with little prestige or money and without a hierarchy—a perfect niche for women, in other words. But Genzken's fling with performance was ephemeral. By the time she left Dusseldorf, in 1977, to travel to America on a study grant, she had begun making large-scale sculptures ("ellipsoids" and "hyperbolos") in lacquered wood. They were engineered with the help of a computer; she was one of the first artists to experiment with digital technology. These ravishing constructions are cerebral and sensuous. They range in size from ten feet to about thirty feet, and Richter nicknamed them "the knitting needles." ("Weapons," Genzken retorted.)

Her next foray involved sound, which she represented in material form: as prints, photographs, and small sculptures on pedestals. The sculptures—of radios, speakers, receivers, and such—have the eerie charm of clay burial artifacts, the sort of thing a boy pharaoh obsessed with his stereo system might commission for his tomb. Their precision and severity are classical, but, like much of Genzken's work, they have a nerd's macabre sense of humor.

Studies of light and space evolved from her interest in acoustics. A series of monumental freestanding windows pose questions about perceptual triage: the way art gives salience to a fragment of reality and excludes alternative versions of it. (The windows are beautifully installed under a skylight that frames a sliver of sky and the façades of surrounding buildings.)

Throughout this period, Genzken was, typically, working with toxic materials, like epoxy resin, and macho materials, like concrete and steel. She also exposed herself, who knows for how long, to an X-ray machine that photographed her skull as she smoked and drank, two favorite activities.

After her divorce from Richter, and entering middle age, Genzken changed course once again. In the 1990s, she gravitated toward a co-terie of younger gay men who introduced her to Berlin's techno-music culture and to a new brand of militance: for gay rights, for the environment, and against the Gulf War. Her art also shifted radically: from the creation of elegantly austere objects to deceptively makeshift assemblages of crap and garbage that Genzken collected on her urban prowls. (She has always refused to delegate her professional grunt work to an assistant.)

One of her assemblages is a cluster of buildings, like the kind of model that an architect submits to a competition, but fashioned from plywood, pizza boxes, spray paint, construction netting, police tape, and other detritus. It is a picturesque slum whose squalor is both de-pressing and festive. Laura Hoptman, the retrospective's chief curator, interprets this composition, which Genzken called *Fuck the Bauhaus*, as a critique of modernist hubris—a Teutonic ideal of control, order, and rationality that collapsed under Hitler like a house of cards. But she also discerns a redemptive impulse to it. Genzken, she writes, would like to replace dehumanizing, corporate urban development with a livelier, more soulful "accidental modernity." The retrospective con-cludes with a trilogy of room-sized assemblages from the new millen-nium, *The American Room, Empire/Vampire, Who Kills Death*, and *Ground Zero*. (Genzken was in Manhattan on the morning that the towers fell.) These are considerably more sinister and disorienting than anything else she has done. Try to imagine the fallout from an apoca-lypse as the contents of a gigantic piñata full of cheap toys that have been tortured, then arranged in vignettes like graveyard offerings for a murdered child, on the Day of the Dead. But its power is proof against pathos.

No one knew if Genzken would make it to New York to celebrate her opening, but she did. She looked a bit unsteady as she drifted through the galleries, lost in reverie and largely unrecognized, but with an odd stateliness that reminded me of Don Quixote. In a sea of designer black, her motley chic set her apart: a jean-style leather jacket in shiny cobalt blue and a red newsboy cap, from which untidy wisps of colorless hair poked out. You might have guessed, by a process of elimination, that this lanky outsider was the artist. I was about to introduce myself when one of Genzken's minders motioned me away. "She needs her space," he said. It's about time she got it.

NOVEMBER 2013

In 1948, the avant-garde photographer Grete Stern, a German Jew living in Buenos Aires, was hired by *Idilio*, a popular women's magazine, to illustrate a weekly column called "Psychoanalysis Will Help You." The column solicited readers' dreams, and thousands responded—a majority with nightmares. Anxiety, domination, and entrapment were common themes.

The dreams were interpreted by two male intellectuals who—embarrassed to be "agony aunts," as one of them put it—signed their work with a joint pseudonym, Professor Richard Rest. Stern may also have considered the assignment mildly demeaning, at least initially. She had a job with the Buenos Aires urban-planning agency, documenting the city's architecture, and she believed that photography had to have "a social function." A Marxist critic for the prestigious journal *Sur* had praised her style for its "verism."

One of *Sur*'s regular contributors was Stern's friend Jorge Luis Borges, who once admonished, "Let us admit . . . the hallucinatory character of the world." Stern rose to his challenge in the 140 photomontages that she created for the column. Starting with a sketched composition, she juxtaposed photographs of women (enlisting her daughter and friends as models) with stock images of objects and scenery, surreally shrunken or enlarged. Her sense of the grotesque suggests a debt to Goya's *Caprichos*. "Distorted perspective will always give the effect of insecurity," she explained in a note on her technique.

Stern had been analyzed by the Kleinian theorist Paula Heimann, and she understood the punning syntax of the unconscious. She also had a radical intuition about femininity: it becomes nightmarish when its artifice feels inescapable. In her *Sueños* (Dreams), as the montages were known, women daydream inside a corked bottle, or drown help-lessly in a living room as fish snap at them. A monstrous baby threat-ens a cowering mother. Professor Rest decorously avoided the word "sex," but Stern's imagery seethes with allusions to bondage and pre-dation. One of her most famous montages superimposes the figure of a demure housewife on the base of a table lamp, next to a giant male hand that is turning the switch on and off.

An arrestingly creepy feature of many images is the discord be-tween a dreamer's impassive expression and her predicament: she is literally not awake to its horror. Nor was the society she lived in. The intent of the column was to soothe a riled female id; if the woman couldn't resolve her conflict—by ending an unhappy marriage, for example—the professor counseled wifely demurral. But Stern's aim was to satirize misogyny, not normalize it, and she must have been conscious of subverting her assignment. The writers' presumption was that a benign male authority could dictate the solution to women's existential dilemmas. Her montages suggested that the source of most dilemmas was male authority.

When the column launched, Stern was a divorcée of forty-four, with two young children by her former husband, the Argentine pho-tographer Horacio Coppola. The couple had met as students at the Bauhaus, where they joined the Weimar avant-garde and, after Hit-ler's ascension, its diaspora. Before leaving Germany, Stern and a friend, Ellen Auerbach, founded a graphic-design firm, ringl+pit, that pioneered the use of Surrealist photomontage in advertising. Their commercial work had a macabre wit that anticipated the *Sueños*.

After the column's run ended, in 1954, Stern turned back to ver-ism. She worked prolifically as a portraitist, in an austere style that one of her subjects called "facial nudity," and as an ethnographer, spending months in remote provinces to document their ruins, landscapes, and people. This was art with a "social function," but it was also, perhaps, an escape into concreteness from her own nightmares. Stern's father had died in 1910, when she was six. Her mother committed suicide in 1933, in despair at the rise of anti-Semitism. Her son killed himself at twenty-five. Her daughter went into exile during the period of state terrorism in Argentina known as "the dirty war."

Stern's notes on the *Sueños* are impersonal, and she didn't keep the original prints. When she tried to retrieve some of them for an exhibition, in 1967, she discovered that the magazine had thrown them out. Last fall, though, Stern, who died in 1999, shared a retrospective with Coppola at the Museum of Modern Art, and the *Sueños*, in their first major U.S. exhibition, roundly upstaged Coppola's abstract cityscapes. It was as if an urgent message had washed up on a foreign shore, sent by women, long adrift, whose dreams had come back to haunt us.

DECEMBER 2016

In April 1862, Emily Dickinson wrote to a stranger, initiating a fervent twenty-four-year correspondence, in the course of which they managed to meet only twice. Thomas Wentworth Higginson, thirty-eight, was a man of letters, a clergyman, a fitness enthusiast, a celebrated abolitionist, and a champion of women's rights, whose essays on slavery and suffrage, but also on snow, flowers, and calisthenics, appeared in *The Atlantic Monthly*. "Letter to a Young Contributor," the article that inspired Dickinson to approach him, was a column addressed to literary debutantes and—despite his deep engagement with the Civil War—a paean to the bookish life: "There may be years of crowded passion in a word, and half a life in a sentence," he wrote, evoking Dickinson's poetry without yet having seen it. "Mr. Higginson," she began, with no endearment. "Are you too deeply occupied to say if my Verse is alive?"

Dickinson was a spinster of thirty-one, birdlike in habit and appearance, with fine chestnut hair and abnormally wide-set eyes, whose color she compared to sherry. She lived in Amherst, Massachusetts, with her parents and her sister, Lavinia, next door to her brother, Austin, and his difficult wife, Susan, whom she adored. Her father, Edward, a prominent lawyer and the treasurer of Amherst College, had a heart that was "pure and terrible," she told Higginson years later. (He found the old man more remote than forbidding.) Her mother, née

Emily Norcross, was recovering from a nervous breakdown that had lasted several years, during which time the poet herself had become reclusive. The room where she worked, and spent much of her life, was furnished with a sleigh bed, a cast-iron stove, a bureau, and a writing table.

Dickinson came to Higginson in the guise of an unpublished novice, though by this point—middle age (she died at fifty-five)—she had composed hundreds of poems. Among them are some of the greatest ever written in English, but an English unique to her—an unworn language. It revives sensation at the extremities of feeling that, in most lives, habit and cliché have numbed. Few voices are more solitary than her first person, yet few are more intimate: she writes I to I. Richard B. Sewall, whose critical biography, *The Life of Emily Dickinson*, is still unsurpassed, classed her with George Herbert, Wordsworth, the author of the Psalms and of Job, and, in her eerie genius for metaphor (a comparison that isn't impertinent), Shakespeare.

It is hard to believe that Dickinson didn't know who and what she was, even if no one else did. She kept her poems in a bureau drawer, sewn into bundles. But she had shared a few with her closest friends, among them her sister-in-law and Samuel Bowles—a driven man, famously attractive, like her new pen pal, and the editor of an influential newspaper, the Springfield *Republican*. Bowles had already printed three lyrics anonymously. She enclosed one of them in her note to Higginson (who then lived in Worcester) with three others:

Safe in their Alabaster Chambers—
Untouched by Morning—
And untouched by Noon—
Sleep the meek members of the
Resurrection—
Rafter of Satin—and Roof of Stone—
Grand go the Years,
In the Crescent above them—
Worlds scoop their Arcs—

And Firmaments—row—
Diadems—drop—
And Doges—surrender—
Soundless as Dots,
On a Disc of Snow.

Higginson, the radical, was a pious man. Dickinson, the dormouse, was a heretic who dared to call the dead suckers, conned of their heaven. Her sweetness of tone makes it easy to miss her bleak audacity. She didn't, it seems, take much of Higginson's advice (which we can only infer from her replies—his half of the correspondence disappeared), except for his suggestion that she delay publishing. But, lost at an anguished crossroads, she needed a Virgil. He had once risked his life to rescue a fugitive slave, and she was, in her way, also a fugitive.

Dickinson's letter concluded with a request not to "betray" her. Higginson never did, but many scholars, including Sewall, consider that, through an excess of caution and a deficit of imagination, he betrayed her art. His first and perhaps instinctive reaction to her verse was a tough critique, though she thanked him for the "surgery." In her next letter, she confided her inner turmoil: "I had a terror—since September—I could tell to none." After that, he was more reassuring. On June 7, she told him, "Your letter gave no Drunkennesss, because I tasted Rum before." Baffled by the poems, beguiled by the woman, but, as a pastor, alarmed for the estranged soul, Higginson suggested that she find a friend. She actually had many, but she asked him to be her "Preceptor" (although he wasn't the only man she flattered with that honorific). An invalid wife and the war, among other imperatives, preempted his attention, but, fitfully, he and Dickinson stayed in touch. "Sometimes I take out your letters & verses, dear friend," he wrote in 1869 (one of only three messages to her that survived), "and when I feel their strange power, it is not strange that I find it hard to write . . . If I could once take you by the hand I might be something to you; but till then you only enshroud yourself in this fiery mist & I cannot reach you, but only rejoice in the rare sparkles of light."

In the course of their friendship, Higginson tried to lead this "wayward" sport of nature, whose rhymes were off, whose rhythm he called "spasmodic," whose lines were strung tensely between dashes, and who claimed the modern privilege of refusing to signify what others expected her to mean in "the direction of rules and traditions." (Her credo was "Tell all the Truth but tell it slant.") After Dickinson's death, in 1886, Lavinia asked Mabel Loomis Todd, Austin's beautiful and ambitious mistress, to edit the poems, and Higginson to help her, lending the project his prestige. (Only ten brief lyrics had appeared in her lifetime, grudgingly surrendered, and without a signature. One was attributed to Emerson.) Todd sometimes went further than Higginson would have liked in taking liberties with Dickinson's syntax, punctuation, and even her choice of words. He approved and took part in the cleanup, however. Their anthology was published in 1890, and reviews were mixed (some ecstatic, more disdainful), but almost immediately Dickinson acquired a cult following, mostly among women. They showed up in Amherst, asking directions to the Homestead, the Dickinsons' Federal manor on Main Street, which has since become a museum. The collection quickly went through eleven editions and was followed by seven others, a memoir by Mabel Todd's daughter, four volumes of letters, endless speculation about the poet's secrets, and the rise of a myth. By the 1950s, Dickinson was part of the canon (almost no one graduates from high school without having read her). Her complete works—nearly eighteen hundred poems, edited by Thomas H. Johnson, and letters, edited by Johnson and Theodora Ward, three volumes of each—were enshrined in annotated editions that restored their formal integrity, revealing the magnitude of her power but also the depths of her strangeness.

Until Higginson held the first anthology in his hands, he had doubts about the wisdom of exposing to the world the runes of a protégée whom he had described as "my partially cracked poetess." Yet the telling ironies in a relationship often aren't the apparent ones, and in a trenchant new book, *White Heat: The Friendship of Emily Dickinson and Thomas Wentworth Higginson*, Brenda Wineapple sets out to discover what these two people saw in each other, and what they couldn't see. In her view, Higginson's epithet wasn't dismissive, not to a romantic idealist who, into old age (he died at eighty-seven), kept searching for the portal to transcendence.

Wineapple is an astute literary biographer with a feisty prose style and a relish for unsettling received ideas. Social history—the taproot of character—is her forte, although one might also say that she has specialized in repatriating fugitive Americans: Janet Flanner, Gertrude and Leo Stein, and, most recently, Nathaniel Hawthorne. (He fits the mold if one agrees with Dickinson in defining the intellect as a patriot's "Native Land.")

Dickinson's experience, or what we know of it, has been so thoroughly archived, interpreted, and reimagined in every genre (Sewall is exhaustive, and, before him, Jay Leyda, the modernist filmmaker and film historian, produced a monumental chronology, *The Years and Hours of Emily Dickinson*) that a contemporary scholar needs a good excuse to exhume the picked-over bones. In rehabilitating Higginson—dispatching the caricature of a tin-eared pedant—Wineapple finds one, and, through him, brings Dickinson into focus for a new generation. The poet's impulse to seek sanctuary in isolation, and the militant's to seek justice through intervention, should, she suggests, feel familiar to us in 2008. It's an enduring schism in American history.

Wentworth Higginson, as he was known to his familiars, was the youngest of ten children, descended from a Puritan divine who had arrived in Massachusetts in 1629. A Dickinson landed in New England the following year. There was wealth, eminence, and political influence on both sides; a symmetry in the families' associations with leading colleges (Wentworth's father was a benefactor of the Harvard Divinity School); and a shared culture of civility and introspection. As Emerson's friend Samuel Ward observed in a letter to Higginson after reading Dickinson's poems:

She is the quintessence of that element we all have who are of the Puritan descent *pur sang*. We came to this country to think our own thoughts with nobody to hinder . . . We conversed with our own souls till we lost the art of communicating with other people. The typical family grew up strangers to each other . . . It was *awfully* high, but awfully lonesome.

Wentworth and Emily came of age, however, during a period of humanist ferment in politics, theology, and the arts—an American Enlightenment described by those who lived through it as "the Newness." The young Higginson had dreamed of becoming a great poet, but Emerson, whom he revered, rejected his submissions to *The Dial*. He married a patrician cousin, Mary Channing, whose crippling ailment seems to have been rheumatoid arthritis. Wineapple describes this interesting character as "tart" and "cantankerous." (Apropos of Dickinson, she once blurted out, "Oh why do the insane so cling to you!") They were both devoted to the radical feminism of Margaret Fuller. A woman "must be a slave or an equal," Higginson declared. "There is no middle ground." To secure a livelihood, he became a minister, but, after two years, he resigned his pulpit, under pressure (he was too much of a reformer for his congregation), to militate for abolition. Dickinson would surely have followed his exploits in the Springfield *Republican*: his failed run for Congress; his arming of anti-slavery homesteaders in Kansas; his collusion with John Brown; his storming of the Boston federal courthouse to liberate Anthony Burns, the fugitive slave who faced rendition (a brave but inept fiasco). In November 1862, Higginson took command of and began training one of the initial regiments of Black soldiers to do battle for the Union—the 1st South Carolina Volunteers. Henry James, who sat out the carnage in Newport, Rhode Island, but whose brother Wilky was wounded in the massacre at Fort Wagner, in Charleston Bay, fighting with the 54th Massachusetts—the most famous Black regiment—had the gall, years later, to mock Higginson's "agitations on behalf of everything, almost, but especially of the negroes [*sic*] and the ladies."

There was nothing obviously cracked about the young Emily, a brilliant student and a saucy gadabout with a streak of vanity that she never outgrew. She wrote for the humor column of her school magazine, and her letters, also full of gaiety and wit, often cartooned her family. (The Dickinsons, Emily included, were never quite as proper as they seemed; beneath their clannish façade of stiff-necked gentility roiled a soap opera of mad scenes, quarrels, and illicit passions. All of them, Wineapple writes, "loved with greedy ardor.") She "rode out" with suitors, and, at fifteen, after a trip to Boston, declared to a classmate, "The world holds a predominant place in my affections."

Emily disparaged her education to Higginson, and, compared with his (at Harvard), it was rudimentary. But she spent the last year of her schooling as a boarder at the female seminary in South Hadley, Massachusetts, that became Mount Holyoke College. The classical curriculum (Greek, Latin, sciences, and literature) included strong doses of evangelical Christianity. A religious revival was sweeping New England, and the girls were urged by their headmistress to profess "hope." Dickinson resisted defiantly, calling herself a "pagan." Belief in God, and in salvation, always tempted her, as flesh tempts a saint, but the real perdition, as she saw it, was renouncing her freedom not to conform.

Dickinson's life has a before and an after, separated by an invisible catastrophe, or perhaps by a critical mass of cumulative blows— spiritual concussions that contributed to her fragility, but also to the release of her creative powers, which came in a tremendous gush in her late twenties. She corresponded with a wide and diverse circle of friends—some ninety people we know of—but as she aged her world contracted like the footage of a blast reversed. By the time she was forty, she refused to leave the Homestead, except to see a doctor, even hiding on the second floor from acquaintances she had received for years; writing and reading after the household was asleep; tending the garden; and, until she gave up music, too, playing the piano. On several occasions, Higginson invited her to literary events in Boston, once to hear a talk by Emerson. But, much as she longed to see him, she was firm in "shunning" society. People, she explained, "talk of hallowed things, aloud—and embarrass my Dog—He and I dont object to them, if they'll exist their side." Bowles called her the "Queen Recluse," but in reality she saw whom she chose: him, her brother, Higginson, some children, and a few others. Austin told Mabel Todd,

with amusement, that his sister had "posed" in many letters. Her studied unworldliness—the virginal or bridal habit of a white dress; the
lily proffered breathlessly to an exceptional visitor; the elfin figure
fleeing at the sound of a doorbell; the pretense of "insignificance"—
was also a form of camouflage:

> The Soul selects her own Society—
> Then—shuts the Door—

Dickinson's father, respecting her seclusion, didn't oblige her to
attend church with the family, although he asked a local clergyman
to examine her theological "soundness." She apparently passed the test
of faith the way her poems did, by seeming chaste and biblical, if you
weren't paying attention. Steeped in devotional literature, she drew
upon its language and cadences to record (and to dissemble) her solitary effort to accept that death *is* absolute. But death is also a metaphor
for something even more fearful to Dickinson, the loss of self that
often occurs in the delirium of infatuation and in the aftermath of a
rejection. Higginson justly called her mist "fiery": her work scintillates
with erotic tension, and even in the letters she wrote him her lowered
eyes seem more geisha-like than maidenly. When Dickinson loved,
she was capable of shameless, imperious, wanton rapture and abjection.
Anyone down to earth was apt to recoil at the totality of her demand.
Most of us, however, know what she means by "a pain—so utter—

> It swallows substance up—
> Then covers the Abyss with Trance—
> So Memory can step
> Around—across—upon it—
> As one within a Swoon—
> Goes safely—where an open eye—
> Would drop Him—Bone by Bone.

Dickinson cultivated passionate friendships—complicities—with
both sexes. One of her beloveds was Susan Gilbert, the lovely, com-

bative orphan who married Austin and was Emily's most trusted reader for some thirty years. The theory that Dickinson was a lesbian shares a Dewey Decimal Classification with a raft of other case studies—Emily the sufferer, performer, healer, seducer, victim, hysteric, dog lover, mystic, feminist paradigm, vestal daughter, consumptive, agoraphobic. But, in the absence of God, Dickinson never ceased hoping for a savior in a mortal guise—indeed, in a virile guise, paternally enfolding. That, in part, may be why she sought out Higginson, and why he kept his distance, despite her importunity, confessing to his wife after the first of his two visits to Amherst, in 1870, "I never was with anyone who drained my nerve power so much. Without touching her, she drew from me. I am glad not to live near her."

The Homestead struck Higginson as a house "where each member runs his or her own selves." Emily told him, "I never had a mother. I suppose a mother is one to whom you hurry when you are troubled." The daughters of depressive women often feel a propitiatory impulse to make some sacrifice of their own aggression and desire, perhaps because they are afraid to overwhelm an unstable figure on whom they depend; because they feel guilty about their own vitality; or to disguise rage—as much from themselves as from their parent. In Dickinson's case, Wineapple observes, mother and daughter both "exercised power in refusal."

Her mother's mental illness coincided or overlapped with three major markers in Dickinson's biography: the "terror" she confessed to Higginson; the period of her greatest creativity; and a debacle that inspired her to draft at least three letters of heart-wrenching eloquence and infantile neediness to a lover, or a phantasm, whom she addressed as "Master," imploring him to "open your life wide, and take me in." Master's identity is one of the most tantalizing enigmas of Dickinson's story. There are two leading candidates. One is the dashing Bowles; the other, Charles Wadsworth, was a preacher famous for his oratory, who lived in Philadelphia but is known to have visited Dickinson at least twice. After his death, in 1882 (Bowles had died four years earlier), Emily described him as "my closest earthly friend." Higginson, in many ways, fits their mold: an object of fantasy to many women;

prominent in the world; and married. Dickinson told him several times that he had "saved her life" in 1862, though he never knew how. Perhaps it was enough that he picked her up, albeit gingerly, when she felt discarded. But she, in turn, gave him the immortality that his own good deeds and modest gifts as a writer wouldn't otherwise have earned.

White Heat is written with a dry heat that does justice to its impassioned protagonists, but, as Wineapple's pendulum shifts back and forth between them, it loses its momentum. Both lives wind down, their drive sputters out, and their paths diverge—the Newness was over. Higginson remarried after Mary's death—a proper sort of wife this time, dainty and much younger. He finally fathered a much-longed-for child (and, one gathers, enjoyed a long-deferred sex life).

During Dickinson's final two decades, her poetic torrent was reduced to a trickle. She developed Bright's disease, the kidney ailment that may have killed her. Her doctor also gave her a diagnosis of "nervous prostration," and she told an old friend, "I do not know the Names of Sickness. The Crisis of the sorrow of so many years is all that tires me." She, too, however, enjoyed a requited passion. Her elderly beau, Judge Otis Lord, of Salem, was a member of her father's inner circle, and she had known him all her life. While it's not clear whether their romance began before Lord was widowed (a late poem suggests that it had), it sparked an astonishingly candid, erotic correspondence that shows Emily expertly, if belatedly, playing hard to get. ("'No' is the wildest word we consign to Language," she teased him.)

At the end of a poem about solitude, possibly composed during the "terror," Dickinson, describing the wind, plants one of her most self-defining lines, and one that is, typically, desolate and triumphant in the same breath:

> He visited—still flitting—
> Then like a timid Man
> Again, He tapped—'twas flurriedly—
> And I became alone—

Becoming alone is the description of a task that none of us escape, and it is the drama that gives Dickinson's poetry its suspense. She expresses that suspense in all the seemingly random and eccentric dashes in her work that Higginson corrected. (He always wanted to make things right.) But they were her cracks, cracks through which the wind slipped in, and those other disembodied visitors, her metaphors and intuitions, and through which she evaded the necessity of putting a period to their mystery—or to her own.

AUGUST 2008

MOTHER COUNTRY

L   ast February, Alison Bechdel was invited to give the annual
         Paumanok Lecture on American Literature and Culture at
         Long Island University's Brooklyn campus. The series is spon-
sored by the English department, and previous speakers have included
Alfred Kazin, Elizabeth Hardwick, Irving Howe, and Edward Said.
Bechdel was introduced as "the daughter of two English teachers"—to
polite laughter. Her work is not yet part of the Western canon. She is
the author of *Dykes to Watch Out For*, a cartoon strip that ran for twenty-
five years, between 1983 and 2008, in more than fifty alternative news-
papers, and of *Fun Home* (2006), a bestselling graphic memoir of her
father, Bruce. *Fun Home* was the first and only work of its kind to be
a finalist for the National Book Critics Circle award. The subject, as
Bechdel noted, isn't exactly "a laugh riot." She described it to the audience as the story of "how my closeted gay dad killed himself a few
months after I came out to my parents as a lesbian."

     Bechdel's lecture, which she illustrated with snapshots from her
family albums, discussed the latest installment of her autobiography,
Are You My Mother? which will be published next month. Helen Fon-
tana Bechdel, the author's mother, who plays a supporting role in *Fun
Home*, is the star here. Not even Henry James, the master of the page-
long sentence, could have traced the memoir's arc in one line—it is like
a DNA molecule. The title, however, gives you an idea of what Bechdel
is up to. She borrowed it from a beloved but unsettling children's book

by P. D. Eastman, published fifty years ago, in which a baby bird, which hatches while its mother is off catching worms, leaves the nest in an anxious search for the missing parent it has never seen, asking a variety of creatures—a cow, a dog, a kitten, and, finally, a power shovel—if they are she. But even the youngest reader has lived enough to grasp the true question, which is "Who am I?" Without its mother, a baby has no reflection.

When I got to the university's Kumble Theatre, it was full, and Bechdel was surrounded by fans. She lives in the Vermont woods, and usually dresses accordingly, but that evening she was wearing pressed jeans with a dark sports jacket and a crisp striped shirt, both from a men's resale shop, accessorized by designer eyeglasses. "Glasses are my only jewelry, so I splurge on them," she had told me on a visit to Vermont, when we had driven into Burlington so that she could shop for frames, go to the gym, and see her shrink. ("I do egregious things," she told the audience, of her new memoir, "like taking you into my therapy sessions and telling you my dreams.") Anyone who has read *Dykes to Watch Out For* could have spotted Bechdel in the crowd, and not only because she was being lionized. She looks just like her cartoon avatar, Mo, a geeky bundle of nerves with a butch haircut (minus the equine forelock), a slight physique, a furtive air, and the general appearance of a teenage boy. At fifty-one, Bechdel is still sometimes mistaken for one.

Cartoonists generally focus on a specific gene pool or cultural type, and the characters in *Dykes to Watch Out For* are a motley crew of more or less radical lesbians, living in a Midwestern city and striving to achieve a state of alternative normality. But the Brooklyn audience was strikingly mixed. Same-sex couples chatted with tweedy academics, and pierced students, their pale arms sheathed in tattoos, sat beside regally poised people of color. *Fun Home*, Bechdel noted, has "cross-over" appeal, although she always brackets in quotation marks anything that might sound even remotely like bragging or pretension. This is partly because she worries that she is on the gods' hubris watch list, and partly because the tragicomedy of narcissism is her big subject. *Are You My Mother?* is "extremely intimate and self-absorbed," she said.

"But by looking inward deeply I'm trying to get outside myself and connect with other people."

Bechdel lives with Holly Rae Taylor, a forty-four-year-old painter, and their cat, Donald, a plump female named after the British psychoanalyst Donald Winnicott, at the top of a steep country road near a rustic ski resort, but not much else, about half an hour from Burlington. Their modest house, built in the 1980s, has cedar siding and a pitched roof. Tibetan prayer flags flutter from the woodshed porch. A mudroom leads to a double-height living space rimmed by a narrow mezzanine. There are cables dangling from its balcony railings which Bechdel, who used to be a martial artist—she has a black belt in karate—uses for suspension yoga.

On my first visit, Bechdel and Taylor were trying to figure out how or if they could rearrange their scant furnishings to make room for an heirloom piano, a Steinway parlor grand, that Helen had offered to give her daughter. It came from the house where Bechdel grew up—where most of *Fun Home* unfolds—and where it occupied a conspicuous place, physically and psychically. The piano also figures in *Are You My Mother?* Helen was a gifted amateur musician, but everyone in the family played. (Bechdel's younger brother John is a well-known keyboardist with the heavy-metal band False Icons; he has also toured and recorded with Killing Joke, Prong, Ministry, and Fear Factory.) The last time Bechdel saw her father alive they sat on the bench, side by side, pounding out "Heart and Soul."

To reach Bechdel's studio, you descend a flight of creaky stairs off the mudroom, then thread your way through a glade of two-by-fours and skis. It is a long, burrowlike hideout, partially below grade, that she added to the house when she bought it, in 1996. (She helped a carpenter friend do the construction work, taping the Sheetrock.) A small inheritance covered the down payment, but she had never owned property before, and the commitment, not only to a mortgage but to an adult life, "terrified" her. The success of *Fun Home* was ten years away, and she was earning a meager living from *Dykes*, and from selling product spinoffs, such as mouse pads and T-shirts. The last *Dykes* strip appeared in 2008, the year that Taylor, whom she had met at a bike swap, then ran into again at a food co-op in Burlington, moved in with her. Solitude, Bechdel told me, is her default mode, "but I like having someone around at the same time that I want to be alone. It's a contradiction that I don't know how to reconcile."

Ambivalence is also a default mode for Bechdel. When she draws herself as a child or a young woman, the figure often has a worried air: eyebrows tilted or raised; eyes as wide as saucers, slightly popping or crossed; hunched shoulders; a cowlick that seems to embody various failed efforts to achieve self-mastery. The voice that narrates the traumas and the conflicts of her younger self both yearns for and mistrusts closeness, strives for detachment yet suffers from too much of it, and is offhandedly confessional but wary of its own sincerity.

Taylor, an earthy woman of uncensored warmth, who is impressively hardy—she runs and bikes in the mountains—added several more contradictions to the list. "Alison has a love-hate relationship with fame," she told me one afternoon, as she was doing chores—chopping wood for the stove that heats the house and tending the compost heap. "She craves it, but thinks that's a bit pathetic. To some extent, her self-deprecation is a public shtick, yet she's a genuinely humble person." On another occasion, a lunchtime talk that Bechdel gave in February, at the New York Institute for the Humanities, which was attended by a number of graphic-world luminaries—Art Spiegelman, Peter Kuper, Gabrielle Bell, and Jessica Abel among them—Taylor marveled at her girlfriend's appeal to both eggheads and buttheads. "Alison's work," she concluded, "has a weird effect on your brain. It sparks both your high lobe and low lobe."

I had met Bechdel and Taylor a year earlier, on one of their infrequent forays to Manhattan. They had come to see *In the Wake*, a new work by the playwright Lisa Kron which was in previews at the Public Theatre. Kron's plays are, like Bechdel's memoirs, black comedies that mine her experience as an outsider: a Jewish lesbian—the daughter of a Holocaust survivor and a community activist—growing up among straight Christians in the Midwest. Kron and the composer Jeanine Tesori had recently optioned *Fun Home* for a musical version.

Helen had met them in the city. After her husband's death, in

1980, she had sold the family house, in Beech Creek, Pennsylvania, the small town where Bechdel grew up, and moved to Bellefonte, a less provincial small town, near State College, where she taught high school English for twenty years. Her middle child, Christian, who lives on disability (he has an obsessive-compulsive disorder), has an apartment close by, and so does her longtime partner, Bob Fenichel, a retired psychiatrist.

Bechdel had planned a program of activities that she thought her mother would enjoy: visits to museums, dinner at the Union Square Cafe, and tickets for *Mrs. Warren's Profession*, by George Bernard Shaw. As a young woman, Helen had dreamed of a stage career, and she took a year off from college to apprentice at the Cleveland Play House. Marriage sidelined her ambitions, but even with three children and a teaching job, she had acted, and sometimes starred, in summer-stock productions. (Kron has since written a scene into the *Fun Home* musical in which Helen plays Mrs. Warren.) Alison, as a child, had run lines with her mother, watched with fascination as she applied her "face," admired the courage with which she transcended her stagefright, and wondered at her decision to sacrifice such a passion. Both parents, in fact, had managed to convey the same message: Don't let children or domestic life interfere with your art. "The drama between my mother and me has partly to do with her bad luck coming of age in the 1950s," Bechdel said. "We were on opposite sides of women's liberation, and I got to reap its benefits. With Dad and me, same story: opposite sides of Stonewall. If only my parents had been born later, they might have been happier, and I wouldn't exist."

The mother of *Fun Home* is a scowling, smoking, brooding character with "dark hair and pale skin," and when Alison asks her, as she sits at the piano, practicing a Chopin nocturne, why she never goes outside she replies, "I told you, I'm a vampire." I was thus a bit surprised to meet a rosy, cheerful, soignée woman in her seventies, who was dressed for the city in a smartly tailored pin-striped suit and a fedora. "Mom has always been crazy about fashion," Bechdel had told me. "Our attic was filled with fifty years' worth of *Vogue*."

Bechdel was eager to see the abstract expressionism show at the

Museum of Modern Art. In the next gallery, there was a design installation with a model kitchen. While mother and daughter were inspecting it, Taylor and I stood at a distance, watching them. "Helen is a fascinating, smart woman, but she has oblique ways of expressing her feelings," Taylor said. "She brags about Alison to other people, for example, but won't praise her in person." Helen had cooed to and petted her sons, but, as Alison tells it in *Are You My Mother?*, one night when she was seven Helen told her abruptly that she was "too old" for a good-night kiss. In another scene, Bechdel's therapist spontaneously hugs her. "I had never fully understood this custom before," she writes. In her early twenties, she sent a composition to Helen, who returned it without a word about its content, though the pages had been lavishly corrected in red ink. (Bechdel's theme was her mother's refusal to touch her. Helen's implicit comment was apparently "No comment.") Over lunch, our cordial conversation steered clear of personal subjects. Mother and daughter circled each other formally, like partners in a minuet.

Bechdel is an intellectual populist and a pioneer, as a woman, in a genre that is not only largely male but macho. She is one of the five key figures, with Aline Kominsky-Crumb, Marjane Satrapi, Phoebe Gloeckner, and Lynda Barry, in *Graphic Women*, a scholarly study of gender in the comics culture, by Hillary Chute, an assistant professor of English at the University of Chicago, where she and Bechdel are co-teaching a course this term. When Bechdel first started drawing *Dykes*, she said, "I didn't think of myself as an activist or a lesbian separatist, though many of my friends were. I just felt the vital importance of seeing an accurate reflection of me and us in the cultural mirror, so I decided to create one."

Graphic narratives for adults, by a single author, unlike comic books, which are often produced by a collective, began to appear, Chute writes, only in the early 1970s, when a Catholic outsider artist named Justin Green, who was obsessed with evil "penis rays" emanating from his sex organ, published *Binky Brown Meets the Holy Virgin Mary*. The genre, from its inception, has been raunchy and anarchic. Bechdel, with many of her peers, shares Green's impulse to commit sacrilege. They treat a serious subject—abuse, persecution, pathology—with crude humor and raw imagery, and subvert a form of entertainment associated with the childhood thrill of defying parental strictures about "good" and "bad" books. "I sometimes think I became a cartoonist because my mother simply doesn't get comics," Bechdel said. "They're like the ultrasonic ringtone on a teenager's phone."

As a graphic memoirist, however, Bechdel is anomalous. She started cartooning with an "anti-elitist" bias that was common in the lesbian community. "Comics were a loser thing to do, and that was the beauty of it. I liked being an outsider. It gave me an objectivity that I thought I would forfeit if I was normal." In *Fun Home*, though, she came around—or home—to the Parnassus where both her parents had once hoped to reside (Helen as an actor, Bruce as a novelist). The "bubble" language spoken by her characters is the vulgate of modern America, and she illustrates her life's most private moments, including some that most people wouldn't want to share—sitting on a toilet with her pants down, performing cunnilingus, masturbating—with what feels, at times, like the gleeful exhibitionism of a streaker. But Bechdel's narration, printed in the white banners that float like skywriting above her images, has a quality that one of Flaubert's biographers, writing of his letters, describes as "lucid comic anguish." Her prose reflects an arduous struggle for dispassion. Each of her memoirs is a "bad" book, with pictures of its author doing egregious things, embedded in a "good" book—a work of literature.

The Paumanok Lecture commemorates the name given to Long Island by its indigenous inhabitants, but it also refers to Walt Whitman's autobiographical poem "Starting from Paumanok," in *Leaves of Grass*, which opens with two lines that seemed apropos of Bechdel's subject:

> Starting from fish-shape Paumanok where I was born,
> Well-begotten, and rais'd by a perfect mother . . .

She confessed to the audience, however, that she had missed out on Whitman's "queer, radical, lunatic companionship" when she was growing up, because "my dad ruined him for me," along with many other great writers. "I didn't want to read the books he loved, because he was always stuffing them down my throat," she told me. Those books, by Proust, Joyce, Fitzgerald, Camus, and other modern masters, frame the chapters of *Fun Home*.

Bruce Bechdel, who was born in 1936, in Beech Creek, was a part-time mortician and a high school English teacher who had once dreamed of a glamorous bohemian life in Europe. He and Helen met in 1956, as cast members in a student production of *The Taming of the Shrew* at the State Teacher's College in Lock Haven, near his hometown. They did live abroad, early in their marriage, when Bruce was a soldier, stationed in Germany. But in 1960—Helen was pregnant with Alison—Bruce's father had a heart attack, and he was called home to help his mother run the Bechdel Funeral Home.

The title of *Fun Home* officially refers to the family's nickname for this venerable establishment, founded by Bruce's great-grandfather. But, from the book's opening panels, the old clapboard house on Main Street—where Bruce embalmed bodies, Alison vacuumed the viewing parlor, and she and her two younger brothers, John and Christian, played "corpses"—tends to merge, in a reader's mind, with the Bechdel homestead, a short walk away. Fun Home II was a derelict Gothic Revival mansion, and Bruce took a "manic, libidinal," but also funerary approach to its decor. He ripped its rotting guts out, then filled the void with simulacra of Victorian grandeur. The effect was less of a living space, perhaps, than an undead one. "Early on," Bechdel writes in *Fun Home*, "I began confusing us with the Addams Family."

Fun Home is the story of a man possessed—a mad "artificer"—who has noble qualities, but a violent temper and isolating secrets. Helen took refuge in her music and her acting, and Bechdel experienced her parents' "rapt immersion" in their solitary pursuits as abandonment. Yet "from their example," she writes in *Fun Home*, "I quickly learned to feed myself," and she admitted to the audience in Brooklyn that she "would rather possess the ability to tell these stories than to have had better parents."

There are no monsters in Bechdel's work—certainly none like the gargantuan Pentecostal Fury who raised Jeanette Winterson, another distinguished lesbian memoirist in her early fifties for whom writing is an act of self-redemption. And Bechdel's brothers take polite issue with her portrait of Bruce. John was "a bit shocked," he told me in an e-mail, "at how miserable Alison portrays herself growing up," and he described an almost idyllic regimen of wholesome family activities: playing chess or croquet, canoeing the local waterways, going on moonlit walks. Christian, Alison's junior by a year, is planning to write his own family memoir, which, he said, will be "much different" from his sister's. "Alison is much harsher on my father than I would be," he wrote in an e-mail. "He did have a temper, though."

Birth order changes the experiences, sometimes radically, of siblings growing up under one roof, and neither of Bechdel's brothers is homosexual. "My father was as uncomfortable with the gayness that he intuited in me as he was with it in himself," she told me. "He wanted me to conform," and he bought her frilly clothes that he forced her to wear. They had a fight over the wallpaper for her room—Bruce insisted on hanging a fussy print, with pink flowers, that Alison despised.

Bruce, like Helen, was capable, on occasion, of "incandescent" tenderness, and *Fun Home* opens with an image of Alison and her father playing "airplane" on the floor. It ends with Alison poised to dive into a swimming pool, where Bruce has his arms outstretched to catch her. "He favored me," she said. "We had a special bond." But the memoir also contains a haunting scene that suggests a streak of sadism reserved, it would seem, for his only daughter. One day, while he was prepping the cadaver of a young man, he asked Alison to help him in the embalming room. The body was laid out on the table, and, in her drawing of it in *Fun Home*, it resembles the fallen statue of a centurion: marbly and muscular, with imposing genitals. But what most disturbed her was the gaping, vulva-shaped red hole where Bruce had started to extract the viscera. She was, at the time, about nine.

Bruce's own funeral took place at the Fun Home in July 1980. It was four months after Alison, then a junior at Oberlin, had announced, in a letter, that she was a lesbian. Her parents got the news, she writes, "on the day that I bullshat my way through the *Ulysses* exam." Bruce's reaction was unexpected, given his hostility to any signs of queerness in his daughter. "At least you're human," he told her. "Everyone should experiment." But he added, "Do you have to put a tag on yourself?" Helen was silent at first, then disapproving, but several weeks later she breached a lifetime of reticence to confide in Alison that Bruce was gay, too. She told her that he had slept with men and boys, including the family babysitter. He had also made at least one sexual overture to a student, after which he was sentenced to six months of "counseling" at a mental hospital. The house had become a "tinderbox," Helen said. As the rare acknowledgment of a painful truth from an inveterate denier who had never before addressed her as "one adult to another," her mother's unbosoming was precious to Bechdel, on both counts.

Bruce was forty-four when he died. He had been renovating another old wreck of a house to resell, and while crossing the highway that ran past its front door he had been struck by a Sunbeam bread truck. Helen had finally asked him for a divorce, and Bechdel believes that, with his past—and perhaps a bipolar disorder—catching up with him, her father had jumped into its path.

Modernity was conceived in deviance, and in the introduction to *Graphic Women*, Hillary Chute quotes a particularly apt remark by a colleague at the University of Chicago, the critic W. J. T. Mitchell: "The decorum of the arts at bottom has to do with proper sex roles." Propriety and decorum are alien to Bechdel. "My artist role and my outsider sexual role are bound up," she said. "They have been from childhood. I saw myself in Harriet the Spy"—the precocious heroine of the children's novel by Louise Fitzhugh, who dreams of becoming a secret agent and practices for her future vocation by spying on her classmates. She records their tics and foibles in a notebook, and when the notebook is discovered she becomes a pariah. "I read Harriet as a lesbian character before I knew there was such a thing," Bechdel said. Unlike Harriet, however, she never set out to write. "I started drawing at the age everyone does—when they pick up a crayon," she said. "But most people stop, and I didn't. When I was little, I either wanted to be a cartoonist or a psychiatrist—they were conflated in my mind by all the analyst cartoons in *The New Yorker*."

At Oberlin, Bechdel took a double major in studio art and art history, but she also studied German, Greek, semiotics, and French, and she gravitated toward her fellow intellectuals. When she came out, however, "I abandoned my old friends," she said. (One of her early loves, a garage mechanic, typified her new friends.) After graduation, she moved to New York, where she worked as a word processor in an accounting firm, a job that gave her time to draw. She specialized in musclemen. "It bothered me a lot that I never drew women," she said. "I have always had a thing about strength. I was a skinny kid who read the Charles Atlas ads in comic books." But in *Fun Home* she speculates that she "became a connoisseur of masculinity" because that is what her father was. After his death, for reasons of gender politics, but also out of self-respect, she "made a project" of drawing lesbians, and of studying karate at an all-woman dojo.

The first *Dykes to Watch Out For* appeared in 1983, in the alternative newspaper *WomanNews*. Bechdel joined the feminist collective that produced it, in SoHo. She wrote book and film reviews, in addition to producing a monthly, then bimonthly, cartoon strip, and learned to do layout and design. In 1985, she and her then girlfriend moved to Minneapolis, where they shared a house with another couple. *Dykes* was by now being widely syndicated, and, in 1991, by which time Bechdel was single again, one of her readers sent her a "flirtatious" fan letter, to which she responded in kind. "I was pathetically vulnerable to other people's attention," she said. Her admirer lived in Vermont, on an island in Lake Champlain, which sounded romantic to Bechdel, and, on a whim, she moved east to join her. The affair ended after six months, but she has now lived in the "Freedom and Unity" state for twenty years.

When Bechdel and I first started talking, in late 2010, she was four years into *Are You My Mother?*, a year past her deadline, and she had just jettisoned half her manuscript. She thought she could still finish in a few months if she turned the heat up (it actually took her another year). But, despite her sense of urgency, she let me sit in a corner of her studio while she drew.

The most prominent piece of art on her studio walls is a gigantic poster of Tintin, who looks like a twin of Mo, so I presumed that he had inspired Bechdel's avatar. "I can see it," she said, though it wasn't conscious. "Mo is me, not Tintin. In fact, all the characters in *Dykes* are more or less me. All I've ever written about is myself, and this book, if I finish it, may be the most solipsistic piece of insanity ever published. But the thing about Tintin is that he's not androgynous and not masculine—he's asexual. That aesthetic neutrality appeals to me. I'm always striving to be a generic person."

During a break—she was printing out the first chapter—Bechdel talked me through the stages of the book's evolution. ("When I see your eyes glaze over, I'll shut up," she said.) She starts by creating the grid of panels on her Mac, in Adobe Illustrator. I hadn't realized how much the form of her work, not only its imagery and emotions, relates to her experience of home: The architecture of the blank pages is distinctly houselike. Its square or rectangular frames, of different dimensions, are walled off by gutters, the white spaces between them; they are stacked vertically, like stories, but entered horizontally, like rooms. "The whole thing about a graphic book is that it's a 3-D object," Bechdel said.

Hanging on a long wall facing the windows is an old wooden desktop plastered with colored index cards. Bechdel doesn't outline her stories, which jump back and forth in time, so much as map them, using the cards as placeholders for her scenes. Her untidy blueprint reminded me of yet another kind of house: a memory palace. This ancient mnemonic device was used by orators in Greece and Rome, and is still a trade secret of modern memory-contest champions. A practitioner visualizes a large edifice with a warren of rooms that she furnishes with familiar objects. She then attaches the items or thoughts that she wishes to recall to the objects. As she walks mentally through the edifice, they act as prompts.

Once Bechdel is satisfied with her grid, she begins writing. She types the narration and dialogue into text boxes or balloons. "Every millimeter of space counts," she said. (The visceral economy of her style is, to an extent, a product of that squeeze.) "I don't start drawing until I've finished the storytelling"—i.e., for years. When she is finally ready to draw, Bechdel begins by sketching the images in pencil, on tracing paper, making several overlays, which she refines each time. Some of the figures—a blissfully happy baby Alison, for example, gazing at Helen—were copied from snapshots. For most of them, though, Bechdel is her own model. She sets up her camera on a tripod, assumes the posture of a character, then takes a photograph. "I spend a lot of time posing as myself," she joked. But she also spent a lot of time posing as her mother.

After she has made a "tight sketch," she puts it on her light box and uses it as the guide for her "final pencil." Then she moves to her drawing board and inks over the pencil lines. She scans this page into her computer, fixes her mistakes, and prints it out. Using Magic Markers, she indicates the areas that need spot color, then returns the drawing to the light box. Working with a brush, on a sheet of watercolor paper, she adds a wash of India ink. The separate elements of the composition—text, line art, spot color, and ink wash—are combined in Photoshop. This is her protocol for every page.

The seven chapters of *Are You My Mother?* all start with a dream, and the first one is a nightmare that Bechdel had shortly after embarking on *Fun Home*. She is trapped in a basement by an avalanche of lumber from a home-improvement project, and she has to crawl out through a small window fretted with a spiderweb (she suffers from arachnophobia). In order to finish the memoir, she also had to conquer a stifling sense of claustrophobia. It was caused, in part, by "a surfeit of autobiographical material"—a family archive of letters and news clippings that Helen had collected in a carton for her. But she was also "drowning" in forty years' worth of her own diaries.

Bechdel started recording the minutiae of her own life at the age of ten, when she developed an obsessive-compulsive disorder. It involved counting and ordering rituals, but as it worsened she was compelled to qualify every statement in the diary—"Dad got a dead person," "We watched cartoons"—with the phrase "I think." "My simple declarative sentences began to strike me as hubristic at best, utter lies at worst," she writes in *Fun Home*, and she inserted "I think," in a deranged scrawl, after every line, then replaced the phrase with a symbolic caret, and eventually she became so consumed with her corrections that she couldn't write at all. At that point, Helen began taking dictation for her "until 'my penmanship' improved." Bechdel writes that "getting her undivided attention" was a fleeting but exquisite triumph, "like persuading a hummingbird to sit on your finger."

At the end of *Are You My Mother?*, Bechdel gives another instance of Helen's ability, however oblique, to comfort her. Alison, about eight, is lying on the floor, pretending to be paralyzed. The two of them call this "the crippled-child game." Helen mimes the act of lacing up her daughter's "special shoes" and hands her two make-believe crutches. "My mother could see my invisible wounds because they were hers, too," Bechdel writes, and she felt, in retrospect, that Helen was sanctioning her imagination, thus her future life as an artist.

For some women, however—creative spirits like Helen—who have been suffocated by domesticity and crushed by the weight of their own disappointments, a child's obvious helplessness may stir the instinct to give succor, but if the child dares to assert her will, or to manifest her vitality—which is to say, her otherness—the mother, who feels deprived precisely of those freedoms, can't abide the affront.

Bechdel punctuates Helen's story with citations from the work of three writers—Virginia Woolf, the psychoanalyst Alice Miller, and Donald Winnicott—who have explored that dilemma. Woolf was the daughter of a tyrannical father and a martyred mother who died when she was thirteen. Her mother "obsessed" her until she was forty-four, when, "in a great, apparently involuntary rush," while walking through Tavistock Square in London, she had the vision of a novel that became *To the Lighthouse*. Woolf noted in her diary—in an entry that Bechdel reproduced by hand (all the quotations in the book are drawn, not scanned or retyped from a printed page)—that once the novel was written her obsession ceased: "I no longer hear her voice; I do not see her."

Alice Miller is the author of *The Drama of the Gifted Child*, a study of parental narcissism and its effect on children who are not necessarily "gifted" with artistic talent or superior intelligence but are unusually attuned to the needs of others. A fragile or depressive mother may use such a child as a mirror, but only to mirror what she wants to see. The child is obliged to disguise the full range of her own feelings behind a mask of compliance. She is rewarded with love for wearing it and punished by rejection for trying to take it off. Bechdel "stumbled upon" Miller's book in 1987, in a Minneapolis bookshop, whose cashier predicted its effect on her: "Kiss life as you know it goodbye." (The working title of *Are You My Mother?* was *The Drama of the Gifted Mother*.) Miller draws heavily on the theories of Donald Winnicott— "and that is how I discovered him," Bechdel said.

Winnicott, who was born in 1896, and whose work was published by the Woolfs' Hogarth Press, was a master prose stylist and a supremely humane pediatric clinician. With Melanie Klein, his mentor, he pioneered the psychoanalytic school of object-relations theory, which by now has largely supplanted orthodox Freudianism as a way to understand a child's earliest experiences of selfhood. An infant, according to Winnicott, doesn't need a perfect or a selfless mother but just, in his famous phrase, a "good enough mother," which is to say, a flawed but empathetic maternal figure whose "ordinary devotion" supplies the essential experience of mutual attunement.

Winnicott's writings spoke to Bechdel in a voice of authority, playfulness, complicity, and profound kindness, which breached her solitude. Every chapter of *Are You My Mother?* relates to a concept from his essays on the mother-child bond. His life as a man also inevitably intrigued her. She imagines a scene in which Winnicott and Woolf cross paths in Tavistock Square—he on his way to a session of analysis with the doctor who trained him, James Strachey, Freud's translator and disciple. Bechdel draws Winnicott on the couch in Strachey's consulting room, recalling that his own mother (like Alison's) "stopped breastfeeding him very early." And she weaves his poignant sexual history (he was married but celibate until the age of forty-eight, when he met another woman, his true love) into her own. Winnicott is Helen's foil—and her rival.

Showing Helen her reflection in *Are You My Mother?* was the final impediment to Bechdel's release from her dream of captivity. It was a daunting prospect. There was not only the risk that Helen would feel hurt and exposed at the way she was represented. There was a risk for Bechdel that her book would have failed to achieve one of its prime objectives: making herself visible to the one living person by whom she most longed to be seen.

Helen's piano arrived in Vermont on February 3, the day, by coincidence, that Bechdel finished her book. She had, by then, sent her mother five chapters. Bob Fenichel had read them first, so that he could warn Helen if they contained "anything too upsetting." Bechdel told the audience in Brooklyn that her mother "wasn't thrilled" with the book but was stoically "resigned" to it. I hoped that Helen might say a bit more, so I wrote to her. "I believe that any writer has an obligation to be true to her story," she replied. But she added, "Alison's story is hers, not mine." Her response to her daughter was even more laconic: three words on six years of work and five decades of shared experience. Yet they were, in their way, a critic's, if not a mother's, blessing. "Well," she said, "it coheres."

APRIL 2012

CLOSET ENCOUNTERS

———— ⟨∞⟩ ————

B efore there was Marie Kondo, who taught us the magic of tidi-
ness, or Hillary Clinton, who made a white pantsuit into a mantra, there was Sara Berman, whose frugal all-white wardrobe is
the subject of a new exhibit at the Metropolitan Museum of Art. You
have probably never heard of Berman, who died, peacefully, at the age
of eighty-four, thirteen years ago. Born in Belarus, in 1920, she lived
the sort of family-oriented life that is celebrated in a paid obituary. Her
parents immigrated to Palestine when Sara was twelve, and lived in a
beach shack near the Mediterranean. She married a landsman, who
became a diamond merchant; in the early 1950s, the couple resettled in
the Bronx, and some fifteen years later, as empty-nesters, they went
back to Israel. Berman was sixty when she made an unsparing triage of
her possessions and got rid of most of them. More radically, she shed
her husband after thirty-eight years of unhappy marriage.

Berman's boldness was inspiring to her daughter, the artist Maira
Kalman. It suggested, Kalman said, on a recent morning at the Met,
that "nothing in life has an expiration date. You are free to change at
any age." Maira's son, Alex Kalman, is the co-founder of Mmuse-
umm, a museum tucked into a freight-elevator shaft in Tribeca that
specializes in poetically composed micro installations of prosaic objects. *Sara Berman's Closet*—the Kalmans' joint tribute to Sara's minimalist elegance, ruthless self-editing, and passion for order—had its
debut there before graduating to the Met's American Wing, which is

typically devoted to domestic arts of the seventeenth to nineteenth centuries. Amelia Peck, a curator of the wing, said of the exhibit, "This is as modern as we get here." As modern and as modest, she might have added. The exhibit consists of a wooden cabinet the size of a flea-market stall, with two hanging racks of well-worn tops and bottoms, and a few shelves whose sparse contents are reminiscent of the ghostly porcelain assemblages of Edmund de Waal.

It was at the time of her divorce, when Berman moved into a studio in Greenwich Village, that she restricted her wardrobe to shades of white. "I can't tell you why," Kalman said. "None of us liked to talk about things—a film we saw, a feeling we had, a decision we made—and Mom, in particular, lived in the moment." White is an emblem of purity and renunciation, but, as the uniform of the suffragists, also of sisterly solidarity. In the Jewish faith, it is the color of the bridal gown that becomes a burial shroud. To Berman, it recalled the sun-bleached laundry flapping on her clothesline by the sea in Tel Aviv, and her tropical wardrobe as a young beauty there. There is nothing like white, at any age, if you aspire to dazzle. A fetching snapshot in the gallery shows the old Berman in a dandyish ensemble of white trousers and a double-breasted jacket under a white trenchcoat, accessorized with a man's tie. "She looks like Marlene Dietrich," Kalman said fondly.

Berman's studio, pictured in a wall note, was mostly white, too. It was furnished with a bed, a low table, where she did her fastidious ironing of the white clothes, and a few tiny chairs that might have come from a kindergarten. Her floor was strewn with beach-ball globes—thirteen of them, which she tossed around after dinner with the Kalmans and their kids, who lived down the block. One of those globes rests on a shelf in the closet, along with a few essential possessions: a small stack of biographies (Greta Garbo, Oscar Levant), the only books Berman read; some immaculate lingerie and house linen; a packet of handwritten letters from her sister; and a battered piece of faux Louis Vuitton luggage—a jewelry travel case that alludes, perhaps, to her displacements. There is nothing of value in the closet, if you reckon value in material terms. But Berman's greatest luxury was her belated freedom.

Women who reinvent themselves are as varied as their ambitions for distinction. Where Sara Berman divested, Arabella Worsham acquired. Her dressing room is also on display in the American Wing, adjacent to—or, as the curators conceived it, "in conversation" with—Berman's closet. Worsham was an obscure Southern belle who married the railroad magnate Collis Huntington, in 1884, at the age of thirty-three, a promotion from mistress to wife that would make her America's richest woman. The dressing room—from a mansion on West Fifty-fourth Street that Worsham sold to John D. Rockefeller when she became Mrs. Huntington—is "one of the best preserved New York interiors from the nineteenth century," according to Amelia Peck. It was created exactly a century before Berman's closet, in 1882, and there is nothing *not* of great luxury in this richly patterned, gorgeously appointed boudoir, with its lavish woodwork and its painted frieze of frolicking putti. A dress from Paris hangs in the armoire, and drawers hold exquisite underthings. Worsham was a connoisseur whose appetite for peerless objects and pictures rivaled J. P. Morgan's, and her estate seeded several museums. But if you read Edith Wharton or Henry James, you know that the grandes dames of New York society weighed a woman's worth on the scale of virtue; they judged Worsham by the lightness of her morals, not the ballast of her splendor.

It is fun to imagine how Berman and Worsham would have sized each other up. One was a courtesan, the other a divorcée; both flouted the conventions of their milieux. They were both humbly born, dependent on men, and, one suspects, frustrated artists. Yet each woman fashioned a sovereign identity using the only materials she had to work with, the same in both cases: clothing and decor. A preacher of almost any faith might extract a sermon from this "conversation," and a therapist might mine it for a study of interiority. But the real test of character is for the beholder. Whom do you envy? The apostle of worldliness, for all she amassed, or the apostle of simplicity, for all she could do without?

In April 1932, an unlikely literary debutante published her first book. Laura Elizabeth Ingalls Wilder was a matron of sixty-five, neat and tiny—about four feet eleven—who was known as Bessie to her husband, Almanzo, and as Mama Bess to her daughter, Rose. The family lived at Rocky Ridge, a farm in the Ozarks, near Mansfield, Missouri, where Wilder raised chickens and tended an apple orchard. She also enjoyed meetings of her embroidery circle, and of the Justamere Club, a study group that she helped found. Readers of *The Missouri Ruralist* knew her as Mrs. A. J. Wilder, the author of a biweekly column. Her sensible opinions on housekeeping, marriage, husbandry, country life, and, more rarely, on politics and patriotism were expressed in a plain style, with an occasional ecstatic flourish inspired by her love for "the sweet, simple things of life which are the real ones after all." A work ethic inherited from her Puritan forebears, which exalted labor and self-improvement not merely for their material rewards but as moral values, was, she believed, the key to happiness. Mrs. Wilder, however, wasn't entirely happy with her part-time career, or with her obscurity. In 1930, she sat down with a supply of sharpened pencils—she didn't type—to write something more ambitious: an autobiography.

Laura Ingalls was born in the sylvan wilds near Pepin, Wisconsin, in 1867, and she grew up on the frontier, in the various log cabins, claim shanties, sod dugouts, and little frame houses that her inveterately restless father, Charles, built for his wife and daughters each time he bundled them into a covered wagon and moved on, mostly westward, in search of an elusive prosperity. While the Ingallses were living outside the town of De Smet, in what is now South Dakota, Laura met her future husband, a laconic homesteader ten years her senior. Almanzo Wilder, whom she called Manly, had raised horses as a farm boy in Malone, New York, and he owned the finest team in town—two beautiful brown Morgans. When De Smet was cut off from supplies by a winter of record cold and relentless blizzards that buried the railroad tracks, he and a friend had risked their lives to buy grain from an outlying farmer who was rumored to have a reserve. They barely made it back, in a whiteout, but they saved their neighbors from starvation.

Almanzo and Laura started courting when she was fifteen. By that time, she was helping to support her family by teaching school (she was younger than some of her students) and working as a part-time seamstress. Her elder sister, Mary, had gone blind after an illness diagnosed as "brain fever," which may have been caused by measles or meningitis. Carrie, the third-born, was thin and sickly. Grace was the baby. Laura had always been the sturdy one, pleasant-looking but no beauty, her father's favorite, and something of a tomboy who occasionally showed flashes of defiance. Almanzo was the town hero, and Laura had a rival for his affections, yet she treated him coolly. After her death, in 1957, Laura's qualms about a life like her mother's surfaced in an unpublished manuscript. Caroline Ingalls was a woman of some education and gentility who had also taught school before marrying a pioneer. (The only relics of her former life were a treasured figurine—a china shepherdess—and her love of fashion and poetry.) "Sweet are the uses of adversity" was, perhaps by default, her working motto. She rose before dawn to stoke the fire and boil the bathwater. She fed her family with whatever she had. She made all their clothes and linens, recycling the scraps for her patchwork quilts. She baked the bread, churned the butter, blacked the stove, and restuffed the pallets that they slept on with fresh hay. Even when it was twenty below, she did the washing for six people, pressing with heavy flatirons laundry that had frozen stiff. When her husband was away on some urgent survival mission (Laura recounted how he once walked three hundred miles to find work as a field hand), she fetched the wood and pitched feed to the horses, then waited up for his uncertain return, knitting in her rocker. Informed summarily that she would be packing up, yet again, to start over in a new wilderness, she protested feebly but acquiesced.

Laura waited until she was eighteen, in 1885, before she agreed to marry Almanzo. Their daughter arrived a year later. She was named for the wild roses on the prairie where she was born.

The book business, hard hit by the Depression, was cutting back drastically, and a first draft of Wilder's memoir, "Pioneer Girl," was passed over by several agents and publishers, who felt that it lacked drama. But she persisted—less interested, she later said, in the money than in the prestige of authorship—and when Virginia Kirkus, an editor of children's books at Harper & Brothers, received a new version of the material, now recast as a novel aimed at readers between the ages of eight and twelve, she bought it. That "juvenile" (as such chapter books were quaintly called), *Little House in the Big Woods*, was the first volume of an American family saga that has since sold about sixty million copies in thirty-three languages. During last year's presidential campaign, when a journalist from the *New York Times* asked Heather Bruce, Sarah Palin's sister, about the candidate's reading habits as a child in Wasilla, she mentioned only one book, *Little House on the Prairie*, the third and best known of the eight novels that Wilder published in her lifetime. It describes the Ingallses' migration from Wisconsin to Kansas, where they build an illegal homestead on land reserved for the Osage tribe, and suffer a series of Job-like tribulations: predation by wolves and panthers, a prairie fire, malaria, blizzards, menacing encounters with the Indians, and a near-fatal well-gas accident. None of it crushed their spirits or shook their belief in self-reliance, although the story ends on a bitter note—one that Governor Palin might have recalled. Charles learns from a neighbor that federal troops are coming to evict the settlers. The "blasted politicians in Washington" have betrayed them, and, without waiting to be run off "like an outlaw," he abandons the little house in a rage. In the last scene, with his family camped by its wagon in the high grass, he gets out his fiddle. "And we'll rally round the flag boys," he sings. "We'll rally once again / Shouting the battle-cry of Freedom!" Ma shushes him—it's too martial a song for the girls, who are half-asleep, but "Laura felt that she must shout, too."

In 1974, *Little House on the Prairie* was loosely adapted as a television drama, which ran for nine seasons. It was said to be Ronald Reagan's favorite program. After it went off the air, the actors reunited to make three Little House films. Melissa Gilbert, who played the young Laura, grew up in the role from the age of ten to eighteen, and last year she played Caroline in a musical based on the books. The farmhouse at Rocky Ridge now receives some forty thousand visitors annually. It is one of seven historical sites and museums—in New York, Iowa, Minnesota, Wisconsin, Missouri, South Dakota, and Kansas—devoted to the series and its lore. (Last autumn, the Kansas museum, which bills itself as "The Little House on the Prairie," was sued for trademark dilution by the company that produced the series. A spokesperson for the museum—which is owned by the television personality Bill Kurtis and his sister—says that it declined a cash offer to change its name. The case is pending.)

Wilder scholarship is a flourishing industry, particularly at universities in the Midwest, and much of it seeks to sift fiction from history. The best book among many good, if more pedestrian, ones, *The Ghost in the Little House*, by William Holtz, a professor emeritus of English at the University of Missouri, explores a controversy that first arose after Wilder bequeathed her original manuscripts to libraries in Detroit and California. It is the work of a fastidious stylist, and, in its way, a minor masterpiece of insight and research. Holtz's subject, however, isn't Laura Ingalls Wilder. It is her daughter and, he argues, her unacknowledged "ghost," Rose Wilder Lane.

By the time that Laura published her first book, Rose was a frumpish, middle-aged divorcée, who was tormented by rotten teeth and suffered from bouts of suicidal depression, which she diagnosed in her journal, with more insight than many doctors of the era, as a mental illness. For more than a decade, she had earned a good living with what she considered literary hackwork for the San Francisco *Bulletin*, its rival, *The Call*, various magazines, and the Red Cross Publicity Bureau. She had published commercial fiction, travelogues, ghostwritten memoirs, and several celebrity biographies. Charles Ingalls's granddaughter had inherited his wanderlust, and her career had given her a chance to indulge it. Much of her reporting had been filed from exotic places. She had lived among bohemians in Paris and Greenwich Village, Soviet peasants and revolutionaries, intellectuals in Weimar Berlin, survivors of the massacres in Armenia, Albanian rebels, and camel drivers on the road to Baghdad.

In 1928, she had come home to Rocky Ridge for an extended visit with her aging parents, whose income she subsidized. They were so used to denying themselves basic comforts that they threatened to have their electricity cut off, even though they no longer needed to live so austerely, and Laura's martyrdom, as Rose saw it, was a reproach to her own way of life. "My mother cannot learn to have any reliance upon my financial judgment or promises," she wrote to a sometime lover. "Where is perseverance, thrift, caution, industry—where are any of the necessary virtues? Simply not in me." She grandly spent eleven thousand dollars to build Laura and Almanzo a new fieldstone house—an "English cottage"—which they didn't want, and she bought them a Buick, which Almanzo drove into a tree.

The transformation of a barefoot Cinderella from the Ozarks into a stylish cosmopolite who acquired several languages, enjoyed smoking and fornication, and dined at La Rotonde when she wasn't motoring around Europe in her Model T is, like the Little House books themselves, an American saga. Rose's published writing was sensationalist, if not trashy, but her letters and her conversation were prized for their acerbic sophistication by a diverse circle of friends which included Dorothy Thompson, a leading journalist of the day; Floyd Dell, the editor, with Max Eastman, of *The Masses*; Ahmet Zogu, who became King Zog of Albania; and Herbert Hoover, despite the fact that he had apparently tried to suppress an embarrassing hagiography that Rose and a collaborator had cobbled together in 1920. (He hadn't yet entered electoral politics, but he was widely admired for his postwar relief work in Europe.) Hoover was not unique among Rose's subjects in deploring her fabrications. Charlie Chaplin was so incensed by them that he threatened legal action, as did Jack London's widow. Henry Ford repudiated a portrait of himself that he couldn't recognize. Laura, who publicly (and disingenuously) insisted that her stories were pure autobiography, also sometimes balked at the liberties that her daughter took with factual detail. Fidelity to a subject, or to history, was of less importance to Rose, as she implied in a placating letter to Chaplin, than a "corking" tale. But perhaps she didn't understand the principle at stake: she had reinvented herself just as brashly.

The Wilders' life on a shrinking frontier was considerably bleaker than even the Ingallses' had been. The first decade of their marriage, as Laura later recalled, was a period of almost unrelieved calamity and failure. Their infant son died. Drought and hail destroyed their crops, and they struggled to pay the interest on their heavily mortgaged house and equipment. Then the house burned down. Almanzo had a stroke, brought on by diphtheria, and he never fully recovered from the paralysis. Virtually destitute, they embarked on a series of futile peregrinations, by train and wagon, across the Midwest, with a wretched interlude on the Florida Panhandle. In 1894, they were uprooted by one of the worst depressions in American history, and headed for the Ozarks, which had been touted by promoters as yet another promised land. They struggled for years to eke out a living from the rocky soil.

Rose was, in essence, the child of refugees. The girls in Mansfield laughed at her for her patched clothes and bare feet. The family sometimes went hungry, and Rose blamed the condition of her teeth on early malnutrition. She later recalled her parents' outward show of courage and gaiety and her own sullen pride in defying her humiliations. But she confided them to her journal, where she also complained bitterly about her mother. "No affection" heads the litany of her privations. "She made me so miserable as a child that I never got over it." Even as a grown woman, Laura belittled her, Rose said: she "hesitates to let me have the responsibility of bringing up the butter from the spring, for fear I won't do it quite right!"

William Holtz points out that Laura had been so harried by poverty and hardship—doing some of the man's work that Almanzo couldn't manage, in addition to her own—that she might not have had much left to give, except the example of self-denial. Rose herself could be grandiose and domineering. There is nothing explicit in their letters (few of Laura's survive, one a belated paean of gratitude) to suggest that Wilder merited the accusations, even though she accepted Rose's extravagant gifts and literary labors on her behalf with a sense of entitlement that was more like a child's than like a mother's. Rose, in her less aggrieved moments, could admit that Mama Bess, through no fault of her own, had the wrong daughter. Whatever their disappointments, they kept them from each other.

After high school, Rose left home to work as a telegraph operator, and in 1908 she took a job in San Francisco. Holtz isn't sure whether she had already met her future husband, Claire Gillette Lane, a newspaper reporter her own age—twenty-two—but they married a year later. She became pregnant only once, and lost the infant, a boy. (Later in life, she informally adopted a series of protégés whom she considered foster children; she could be a needy and controlling benefactor, but she lavished upon her wards the gifts of maternal warmth and of faith in their potential of which she herself had felt cheated.)

If Rose had reckoned on her husband as a cultivated soul mate and provider, she was quickly disabused. Gillette Lane was full of schemes for making a fortune in advertising and promotion. The young couple went on the road for several unhappy years. Back in San Francisco, in 1915, she "got rid of Gillette" ("my attitude toward men has always been essentially exploiting," she later remarked), and was hired as an assistant at *The Bulletin*. The editor, Fremont Older, a legendary newsman and anti-corruption crusader, became Rose's mentor and a "model of integrity" to her, Holtz writes, if not a surrogate father. She failed to absorb his ethics, although under his tutelage she learned not only to rewrite her copy but to accept being rewritten. In that sense, one could say that the career of Laura Ingalls Wilder began there.

Rose saw her mother as a literary apprentice, not as an artist, even though she had always encouraged Wilder's writing—first the journalism, then the juveniles; they were a less strenuous and more profitable source of income for an elderly woman than chicken farming. But, whatever art may be, the Little House books fulfill its purpose as defined by Horace: "to entertain and to inform." Mother and daughter essentially divided that labor. One has to suspect that the delicious minutiae of the books' famous how-to chapters on molding bullets, pressing cheese, digging a well, making a rag doll, drying plums, framing a house, and smoking a ham, among dozens of daily activities, were mostly Laura's contribution. (In my favorite of many Christmas scenes, little Grace gets an elegant new coat and hood, trimmed in swan's down; her father shot the bird, her mother cured the skin and did most of the sewing, and her older sisters pieced out the lining from scraps of blue silk.) It was what Laura knew, loved, and had proved, in her columns for the *Ruralist*, that she could write about.

Rose had proved that she could romanticize whatever material she was given. She did some minor tinkering with "Pioneer Girl," but, once it was decided to fictionalize the memoir as a children's story—the idea had come from an editor who rejected the memoir—she took a more aggressive role. It varied in intensity from book to book, but she dutifully typed up the manuscript pages, and, in the process, reshaped and heightened the dramatic structure. She also rewrote the prose so drastically that Laura sometimes felt usurped. "A good bit of the detail that I add to your copy is for pure sensory effect," Rose explained in a letter.

John Miller, a thorough biographer and historian who, like Holtz, compared the manuscripts with the published texts, came to a different conclusion about the collaboration. In the introduction to his book *Becoming Laura Ingalls Wilder*, he writes, "Wilder demonstrated a high degree of writing competence from the beginning, and her daughter's contribution to the final products, while important, was less significant than has been asserted." (The four pages of manuscript that he reproduces arouse more questions than they settle, however. In Laura's scribbled margin notes to Rose—points of fact about geography—she misspells definite as "deffinite" and remarks that her husband "don't remember" the distance between two towns.) A concise, recent biography by Pamela Smith Hill, *Laura Ingalls Wilder: A Writer's Life*, is more overtly partisan. Hill accuses Rose of insensitivity to her mother's "imaginative vision," and, at times, of arrogance, condescension, bullying, self-aggrandizement, and even plagiarism. (Rose secretly wrote an adult novella of her own, *Let the Hurricane Roar*, which was widely admired and sold briskly. The substance and characters were pillaged from "Pioneer Girl." Laura apparently never read the book and considered it a betrayal.)

The cumulative evidence suggests that sometimes Laura stood her ground and sometimes she was cowed into submission, but most often she solicited and welcomed Rose's improvements. When Rose left the farm, in 1935, the editing of the five books yet to come was done by correspondence. "I have written you the whys of the story as I wrote it," Laura told her in a letter that accompanied a draft of volume four, *On the Banks of Plum Creek*, "but you know your judgment is better than mine, so what you decide is the one that stands." Rose, for her part, could be an insufferable didact. She played down her authority, even as she hammered it home: "I'm trying to train you as a writer for the big market," she had told her mother in 1925. (Laura had written an article about her Ozark kitchen, which, heavily revised, had appeared in the magazine *Country Gentleman*.) "You must understand that what sold was *your* article, *edited*. You must study how it was edited, and why . . . Above all, you must *listen* to me."

Little House in the Big Woods was a great success, critically and commercially. Seven months after it was published, Franklin Delano Roosevelt defeated Herbert Hoover. His victory bitterly dismayed the Wilders—Rose, in particular. Shortly after the inauguration, she noted in her journal, "We have a dictator."

At the turn of the twentieth century, the Wilders, along with other disillusioned pioneers, had briefly rallied to the incendiary populism of William Jennings Bryan. By the middle of the decade, Rose had become a follower of Eugene Debs, the union organizer and Socialist candidate for president. In her days as a bohemian, she had flirted with communism. Laura was a Democrat until the late 1920s; after the First World War, she served as the local secretary of a national loan association that dispersed federal money to farmers, and as the chairwoman of her county's Democratic Committee. But, ultimately, both women's experience of adversity—or their selective recall of it—made them less sympathetic to the homeless and the jobless. "The Greatest Good to the Greatest Number," Rose argued in a letter to Dorothy Thompson, "will obviously be reached when each individual of the greatest number is doing the greatest good to himself."

Laura had kept in touch fitfully with her sisters, and when she began to research her childhood, they sometimes provided details that she'd forgotten. Mary had died in 1928, but Grace, a farmer's wife, and Carrie, a journalist, were both still living in South Dakota—Grace and her husband receiving welfare and surplus food. Nevertheless, from Rocky Ridge, the predicament of the urban poor was a remote abstraction, and the Wilders blamed rural poverty on the Democrats' support, as they saw it, of industry at the expense of agriculture. They opposed legislation that compelled farmers to plow crops under as a strategy for price support. Miller writes that, according to Rose, Almanzo was ready to run off an agent from the Agriculture Department with a shotgun, telling him, "I'll plant whatever I damn please on my own farm." In 1943, the year that Laura published *These Happy Golden Years* (the final installment of her saga), she told a Republican congressman from Malone, New York, "What we accomplished was without help of any kind, from anyone."

The Wilders had, in fact, received unacknowledged help from their families, and the Ingallses, like all pioneers, were dependent, to some degree, on the railroads; on taxpayer-financed schools (Mary's tuition at a college for the blind, Hill points out, was paid for by the Dakota Territory); on credit—which is to say, the savings of their fellow citizens; on "boughten" supplies they couldn't make or grow; and, most of all, on the federal government, which had cleared their land of its previous owners. "There were no people" on the prairie, Laura, or Rose, had written. "Only Indians lived there." (Hill writes that Wilder agreed to amend the sentence when an outraged reader objected, calling it "a stupid blunder." It now reads, "There were no settlers.")

In 1936, *The Saturday Evening Post* published Lane's own "Credo," an impassioned essay that was widely admired by conservatives. Her vision was of a quasi-anarchic democracy, with minimal taxes, limited government, and no entitlements, regulated only by the principle of personal responsibility. Its citizens would be equal in their absolute freedom to flourish or to fail.

Everything that Lane wrote after "Credo"—fiction or polemics—was an expression of that vision. She may have been the first to invoke the term "libertarian" (it dates to the eighteenth century) to describe the agenda of a nascent anti-statist movement of which she has been called, with Isabel Paterson and Ayn Rand, "a founding mother." To the degree that she is still remembered for her own achievements, it is mainly by a few libertarian ultras for whom her tract of 1943, *The Discovery of Freedom: Man's Struggle Against Authority*, is a foundational work of political theory. (It was written "in a white heat," she said.)

The struggle against authority defined Rose's life. She railed against a mother who had infantilized her (even though she returned the favor), and at a president who, she believed, was infantilizing a free republic. ("I hoped that Roosevelt would be killed in 1933," she wrote to her agent, George Bye, who also represented Eleanor Roosevelt.) She fought a valiant losing battle for the psychic freedom necessary to write something authentic, yet she was beholden to her parents for her greatest literary successes. In 1938, Rose serialized *Free Land*, a novel set on the Dakota plains, whose central character was modeled on Almanzo. It reached the bestseller list, and a reviewer in the *Times* recommended it to the Pulitzer Prize committee. But once Rose had exhausted her family history, her creative life was finished. Her last attempt at fiction, in 1939, *The Forgotten Man*, is the story of a working-class hero whose ingenuity has been thwarted by the New Deal. When it was rejected by an editor as artless propaganda, Rose, according to Holtz, argued that she "could not write it otherwise."

By then, Lane had moved east. In 1938, at fifty-one, she bought three suburban acres near Danbury, Connecticut, and a clapboard farmhouse—her first real home. (Remodeling, she told a friend, was "my vice.") As she aged, her inner and outer worlds both contracted. She abandoned her journal and, with it, Holtz concludes, her introspection. Old friends were alienated by her increasingly kooky and embattled militance. (One of them described her as "floating between sanity and a bedlam of hates.") The FBI took notice of her "subversive" actions to protest Social Security, and she made headlines by denouncing the agency's "Gestapo" tactics. She talked about reducing her income to a bare minimum, so that she wouldn't have to file taxes. During the Second World War, she found an improbable new pulpit—a column, "Rose Lane Says," in the *Pittsburgh Courier*, a progressive African American weekly. In 1943, convinced that wartime rationing would lead only to inefficiency, she denounced it to her readers, and, to make the point that a determined individualist could live off the grid, she arranged with her neighbors to share a cow, a pig, and some chickens, and she canned the produce from her garden. Two hours from Manhattan, she was re-creating her parents' life.

The Wilders were a long-lived family. Almanzo died in 1949, at ninety-two; Laura in 1957, at ninety; and Rose in 1968, at eighty-one. She bequeathed her literary estate to Roger Lea MacBride, her "adopted grandson" and political torchbearer. (He ran for president on the Libertarian ticket in 1976.) Among the papers of mother and daughter was the draft of a novella that Wilder had mentioned in a letter of 1937: "I thought it might wangle a little more advertising for the L. H. books if I said I might write the grown up one," she told Rose. "You could polish it and put your name to it if that would be better than mine."

At some point soon afterward, Laura did set down the story of her experience as a bride and a young mother, but she abandoned it. That was the manuscript found after her death; in 1971 MacBride published it, without revisions, as *The First Four Years*, and it is now marketed as volume nine in the Little House series. But Laura's instincts were right. The writing is prissy and amateurish; the heroine is bigoted and obsessed with money. It is too simplistic for an adult reader, and too mature for a child. In slightly more than a hundred pages, there isn't even a glimmer of the radiant simplicity that draws one to the Little House books.

Last June, Anita Clair Fellman, a professor emerita of history at

Old Dominion University, in Norfolk, Virginia, published *Little House, Long Shadow*, a survey of the Wilders' "core" beliefs, and of their influence on American political culture. Two streams of conservatism, she argues—not in themselves inherently compatible—converge in the series. One is Lane's libertarianism, and the other is Wilder's image of a poster family for Republican "value voters": a devoted couple of Christian patriots and their unspoiled children; the father a heroic provider and benign disciplinarian, the mother a pious homemaker and an example of feminine self-sacrifice. (In that respect, Rose considered herself an abject failure. "My life has been arid and sterile," she wrote, "because I have been a human being instead of a woman.")

Fellman concludes, "The popularity of the Little House books . . . helped create a constituency for politicians like Reagan who sought to unsettle the so-called liberal consensus established by New Deal politics." Considering Obama's victory in November, and the present debacle of laissez-faire capitalism, that popularity may have peaked. On the other hand, it may not have. Hard times whet the appetite for survival stories.

AUGUST 2009

WORLD OF INTERIORS

In Rachel Cusk's most recent novels, *Outline* and *Transit*, an English writer named Faye encounters a series of friends and strangers as she goes about her daily life. She is recently divorced, and while her new flat is being renovated her two sons are living with their father. There is something catlike about Faye—an elusiveness that makes people want to detain her, and a curiosity about their pungent secrets. They tell her their histories, and she listens intently. As these soliloquies unspool, a common thread emerges. The speakers suffer from feeling unseen, and in the absence of a reflection they are not real to themselves. Faye shares their dilemma. "It was as if I had lost some special capacity to filter my own perceptions," she says. But she lends herself as a filter to her confidants, and from the murk of their griefs and sorrows, most of which have to do with love, she extracts something clear—a sense of both her own outline and theirs.

Critics have hailed these books, which are the first volumes of a trilogy, as a "reinvention" of the novel, and they are certainly a point of departure for it, one at which fiction merges with oral history. Each witness has suffered and survived a version of the same experience, but uniquely, and the events that are retold don't build toward a revelation. The structure of the text, a mosaic of fragments, mirrors the unstable nature of memory. It is worth noting that *Outline* was published in 2014, a year before Svetlana Alexievich won the Nobel Prize in Literature. (*Transit* was published two years later.) Alexievich interviews women and men who have lived through cataclysms—the Second World War, Chernobyl, the Soviet gulags—and she distills their testimony into what the Swedish Academy cited as a "history of emotions." Cusk has been chastised for ignoring politics and social inequities, and the central catastrophe in her fiction is family life. But her imaginary oral histories are exquisitely attuned to the ways in which humans victimize one another.

Late in *Transit*, Faye listens to a palaver about clothes and sex by a friend named Amanda, who works in fashion and has "a youthful appearance on which the patina of age was clumsily applied." "No one ever tells you the truth about what you look like," Amanda says of her profession, to which Faye responds, "Perhaps none of us could ever know what was true and what wasn't." At the end of their conversation, which is mostly about Amanda's affair with her contractor, she stands up to leave the café, "darting frequent glances at me," Faye observes. "It was as if she was trying to intercept my vision of her before I could read anything into what I saw."

When I met Cusk, last winter, at a hotel in New York, I imagined that she might be similarly deflective, but she wasn't. "You've caught me in a pliant conversational state," she said, tucking her long legs under her. Cusk is tall and elegant, with the features of a ballerina: an expressive mouth and eyes in a finely molded small face. Frankness on intimate subjects seems to be a credo of both her life and her work. She had just finished a multicity book tour, and she was flying home to London the next day, eager to see her two teenage daughters, Albertine and Jessye, and to resume work on *Kudos*, the last volume of her trilogy. "I'll celebrate my fiftieth birthday in the air," she noted. When I asked what the milestone meant to her, she paraphrased D. H. Lawrence: "Some people have a lot farther to go from where they begin to get where they want to be—a long way up the mountain, and that is how it has been for me. I don't feel I am getting older; I feel I am getting closer."

One way to measure the gifts of a writer, particularly a prolific one like Cusk, who has published twelve books in twenty-four years, is by the distance between her early work and that of her maturity. Cusk made her debut in 1993, at the age of twenty-six, with *Saving Agnes*, a down-from-Oxford bildungsroman about a grandiose, tormented girl finding her way in London, which won the Whitbread First Novel Award. Her subsequent novels include *The Country Life*, a parody of a gothic romance between a bratty invalid and his au pair, written in the ornate syntax of a Victorian moralizer; *In the Fold*, set in a bohemian manor house rife with sexual and dynastic intrigue; and *Arlington Park*, interlocking stories of suburban anomie. The chaste prose of her current trilogy seems almost like a reproach to the self-conscious virtuosity that preceded it. Before she wrote *Outline*, Cusk was a wickedly clever stylist, who fired off aphorisms like a French court diarist and made up the sort of metaphors—"cauliflower-haired old ladies"; the "floury haze" of a dry summer—that you flag in the margin. A woman's gray teeth are "a bouquet of tombstones." But Cusk sometimes bared her own teeth: her power to dazzle and to condemn.

Cusk judges several of her early books harshly: they were, she said, "bedevilled by a lack of benevolence." By the time she published *The Bradshaw Variations* in her early forties, that devil was behind her. Like its predecessors, but more humanely, the novel tells a conventional story of family rivalries and marital ennui (particularly wifely ennui). In retrospect, however, it was the end of a line. The Bradshaws' real malaise, which wasn't clear to Cusk yet, is the tyranny of conventional stories: the fates and the characters that we inherit, and to which we surrender our desires, along with our lives in the moment. Cusk was about to upend the plot of her own life—to break up her family, then to lose her house and her bearings. The ensuing turmoil would force her to question an old core principle of the writer's vocation, to presume authority, and of woman's vocation, to sacrifice herself for others.

As it happened, Cusk didn't celebrate her birthday on the plane. She and her third husband, Siemon Scamell-Katz, who had traveled to America with her, were grounded in the Ramada at the Newark airport. Cusk was "looking from the window at a Hopperesque landscape of freight trains and telegraph poles and feeling an entirely unfounded sense of optimism!" she e-mailed me gaily.

Cusk has felt more stranded in less alien environments: Los Angeles, where she spent the early part of a childhood she described as purgatorial; the "mediocre" Catholic boarding school where she was bullied and ostracized; provincial society in Brighton and Bristol, where she lived with her second husband when their daughters were young, struggling to reconcile the demands of motherhood with those of art and autonomy—the subject of her memoir *A Life's Work*; and that marriage itself, which ended in a draft of bitterness that she purged like a poison in her memoir *Aftermath*.

Cusk's former husband Adrian Clarke, who is nameless in *Aftermath* and virtually dematerialized—he haunts the text like a ghost—was a prominent civil-rights lawyer who quit his job when they left London, in 1999, shortly after the birth of their first daughter. He was a legal scholar at Oxford University for a while, then took up photography. They agreed that he would assume the primary burden of childcare while she worked on her books. "My notion was that we would live together as two hybrids, each of us half male and half female," she writes. Many modern couples negotiate such an arrangement, but for Cusk it was more than a pragmatic bargain, or even a matter of justice—she staked her identity on it. "The child goes through the full-time mother like a dye through water," she writes. "To act as a mother, I had to suspend my own character."

In the thirteen years that she lived with Clarke, Cusk published seven books, including *The Last Supper*, a memoir of the family's three-month sojourn in Italy which deserves a place in the canon of irritably highbrow British travelogues. "Consider the pizza," she writes. "It is like a smiling face: it assuages the fear of complexity by showing everything on its surface." On an ill-timed visit to Assisi—it is an overcast Sunday, and the city is teeming with tourists—the family has a long wait for a space in one of the parking lots. The hordes have come to see not the sublime early frescoes of Giotto but the dry bones of St. Francis, which reside in his basilica. "The mania for the tangible is the predictable consequence of the intangibility of religious belief," she writes.

The most deeply felt passages in *The Last Supper* are reserved for the artists of the Renaissance; the most unforgiving, for any group, pastime, or individual that Cusk perceives as philistine. As in the case of the poor pizza, a lack of depth, or of an appetite for the dark and the visceral, never fails to disappoint her. But Cusk saves her fiercest scorn for the English middle class, and that animus has caused trouble for her, not only with critics who consider her an unreconstructed elitist. One of the British expats whom she encounters in *The Last Supper* disputed Cusk's depiction of him, and sued her when the memoir appeared. Her publisher settled the suit without fighting it, then recalled and pulped the first edition. A revised text has been reprinted several times.

Clarke figures as an obliging fellow traveler in *The Last Supper*. His presence is subsumed in the marital "we." So, it would seem, was Cusk's sense of entitlement to a stand-alone "I." *Aftermath* is evasive about the reasons that the marriage ended. This was partly for the children's sake, Cusk told me. In the book, however, she alludes to an "important vow of obedience" that was broken, and to her resentment of the fact that "I did both things, was both man and woman, while my husband—meaning well—only did one." Clarke, she writes, "believed that I had treated him monstrously," perhaps because he discovered that he had surrendered his male prerogatives to a feminist ideal only for his wife to regard him as desexed. A passage in *Arlington Park* may shed some light on Cusk's view of this transaction. A woman who has uprooted her family from London and moved to the suburbs deeply regrets it. She and her husband are like deportees "with no access to the things that brought them together." He, like Clarke, was a prominent lawyer, but he takes a job at a sleepy local firm, and only at her urging: "He wouldn't have moved an inch if she hadn't borne him along with her," though she fears that in bearing him along she "had damaged him, so that she could no longer love him."

Whatever blame Cusk assumed for the debacle, she was outraged by Clarke's demand for "half of everything, including the children," she writes in *Aftermath*. "They're my children," she tells him. "They belong to me." "Call yourself a feminist," he retorts. (Clarke declined to comment on Cusk's portrayal of their life, except to dispute any implication that she had paid him alimony or supported the family single-handedly.) But perhaps he is right, she reflects later. Perhaps a feminist true to her convictions wouldn't be "loitering in the kitchen, in the maternity ward, at the school gate." And the deluded creature who thinks that she can be both a person and a woman is like an alcoholic with the "fantasy of modest social drinking."

Aftermath is a mystifying book if you read it as an elliptical, one-sided account of a divorce. And even a reader sympathetic to Cusk's iconoclasm is perplexed by her illogic. She takes on the role of a bread-winning husband, but, when her spouse claims the rights of a stay-at-home wife, she expects him to revert to ancestral form—to cede the kids to her and go make some money. (Clarke has since become a psychotherapist.)

Cusk's drive for separation, however, is a struggle with the paradoxes of a primal attachment being played out in an adult relationship. Marriage, in her work, is oppressive on two counts: as a patriarchal institution and a maternal body. A child attacks a controlling mother with the intent to "destroy" her, but also to prove that she can't—that the mother's love can survive the attack. If the mother surrenders or retaliates, the child feels abandoned. She is separate, yes; she has succeeded; but she is powerless to console herself. After the breakup, Cusk stops eating, "and soon my clothes are too big for me . . . just as my mother's clothes were when long ago I opened her wardrobe and curiously tried them on." Looking at her daughters, she recalls that "once I was pregnant with them, and the memory is too strange to tolerate for long. My body is . . . drifting and fading toward a blank vision of its own autonomy."

In *A Life's Work* and *Aftermath*, Cusk risked a form of exposure that has an element of indecency to it. Like D. H. Lawrence, whom she calls her mentor, she sides with instinct against propriety, despite the cost to herself and others. "I haven't hidden anything," she told me, "not my aggression or my anger." Later, she added, "Wanting people to like you corrupts your writing." But her streak of valor was largely lost on critics in Britain. The memoirs' merits as literature took a back seat, in reviews, to personal attacks on the author's perceived arrogance and narcissism, and on her ambivalence toward maternity, about which *A Life's Work*, in particular, is radically honest, and at times self-excoriating. Book reviewing can be a blood sport in the UK, and there was until recently even a prize, the Hatchet Job of the Year award, for the most savage critique. Camilla Long, a columnist for *The Sunday Times*, won it for her vivisection of *Aftermath*, in which she described Cusk as "a brittle little dominatrix." ("Bizarre" and "whinnying" were some other epithets.) Cusk was nearly annihilated by this reception. It was "English cruelty and bullying," she said. "I was depleted to the point of not being able to create anything." A teaching job kept her afloat financially. When she returned to her vocation, in 2013, she was "another writer," and a consciously "obscured" one. "A journalist recently told me that she had been sent to find out who I was," Cusk said. "There seems to be some problem about my identity. But no one can find it, because it's not there—I have lost all interest in having a self. Being a person has always meant getting blamed for it."

At seven o'clock on a Sunday evening, ten weeks after Cusk's birthday, we listened to the French-election news at the Red Lion, a pub in the village of Stiffkey, on the Norfolk coast. The weather was golden, and Cusk had gone for a long walk by herself on a path that runs through the salt marshes. When she arrived at the pub, wearing a pair of overalls, Scamell-Katz was waiting with a chilled bottle of Chablis. A few local friends—a fishmonger, a livery driver, a landscaper, a set builder—joined us with their pints. The talk, at first, was of electoral upsets on both sides of the Atlantic. Norfolk voted for Brexit, despite the fact that its farmers depend on immigrant labor. It wasn't clear what the consensus of our group was, and Cusk tactfully turned the subject to children and roses. She calls herself "antisocial," though the adjective didn't jibe with her warmth and animation in that company. Having recently quit smoking, she vaped discreetly, drank with relish, and joked about her gardening skills. The only time that I saw a flash of aloofness was when the subject of nicknames arose. (The fishmonger's was Fishy.) It bothered her, she admitted, when people shortened "Albertine" to something cuter, like "Bean" or "Bibi." "It's a noble name," she said. "'Noble' is its literal meaning."

Cusk and Scamell-Katz divide their time between Norfolk and London, where she owns a flat and her daughters go to school. "We spend most of our life in the car," she said, "though at least we get to talk all the way." They have been a couple for four years, and married for three. Their romance began one Christmas, when they were both without their children, and Scamell-Katz took Cusk to a wild Scottish peninsula, in the middle of a storm. I had the impression that their complicity still surprises them daily.

Sunday nights at the Red Lion are a ritual of the couple's country life, though they are otherwise homebodies. "You lose your power by living the wrong way," Cusk said. She isolates herself to write, then works "around the clock"; Scamell-Katz, who is semiretired, protects her from intrusion, reading her manuscripts and vetting her reviews. The actual composition of a book, as opposed to the long period in which Cusk thinks about it, makes notes, and works out the structure, is relatively brief. "I don't want to live a writer's life," she said, by which she meant one shackled to a computer, "so I'm unemployed most of the time. My process is very uncomfortable. The hardest stage is to overcome the fakery, and I can't associate with people while I'm doing that. But the writing part is pure technique. It's a performance, like getting on a stage, and before I start I have to have rehearsed everything I want to say, and to know what's in my sentences." In Cusk's recent novels, it isn't the drama of the events but their specificity that keeps you riveted. Many experimental writers have rejected the mechanics of storytelling, but Cusk has found a way to do so without sacrificing its tension. Where the action meanders, language takes up the slack. Her sentences hum with intelligence, like a neural pathway.

At the beginning of *Outline*, Faye flies to Athens, where she teaches a summer writing workshop. She accepts an invitation from her seatmate on the plane, a Greek businessman, to go out on his speedboat, where she gets a sunburn and fends off his advances. Her students are asked what they noticed on their way to class, and, later, assigned to write about an animal. Local friends entertain her, though mostly with their travails, and, on the morning that she is to leave, Faye finds a playwright named Anne, her replacement at the school, eating honey with a spoon in her living room. Anne confides that, following a mugging, she discovered that a word or two—"jealousy," for example—would sum up the idea she had for a new piece of work, and there would then be no reason to go on with it. This had even happened to her with people, and since "Anne's life" summed up her daily existence she could no longer see its point.

In *Transit*, whose title refers to the predictions of an Internet astrologer "too obviously based on a human type to be, herself, human," Faye buys the top floor of a derelict house in a choice location and renovates it with the help of contractors from Poland and Albania. Her downstairs neighbors, longtime residents of the gentrifying neighborhood, hate her with a vengeance, and try to sabotage her. She visits a beauty salon, where she changes her hair color, and a boy in the next chair, furious at being shorn, explodes into violence. Two best-selling male memoirists, with whom she shares the stage at a rain-sodden reading, dominate the event. A kind man with bad teeth takes her out and tells her the story of his adoption.

Faye's encounters are orchestrated like a fugue, with each voice taking up the theme: the quest for freedom from a false self—a stock character one has been forced to play by parents who extort compliance, or by a mate who imposes submission as the price for love. By resigning oneself to those terms, Faye tells the kind man, one stops being alive; living becomes "merely an act of reading to find out what happens next."

Rachel Cusk was born in Saskatchewan, on February 8, 1967, to a British couple who had moved to Canada. She was the second of their four children, with an older girl and two younger boys. Carolyn, her mother, came from a large Catholic family in Hertfordshire. Peter, her father, a Protestant from Yorkshire, converted to Catholicism before their marriage.

The Cusks met at a tennis club, in the early 1960s. Peter had trained as an accountant, but "he was driven and aggressive," Cusk said, and he hankered for adventure. In Canada, and later in Los Angeles, he moved up the corporate ladder, and the perks of success—"the Mercedes and so on"—were, Cusk felt, of unseemly importance to him. Carolyn, she told me, was a "very pretty," "extraordinarily vain," and "priggish" girl who "wasn't educated, though she should have been." She had a "powerful personality," but no channel or ambition for it outside the family. (Carolyn Cusk said on the phone that she studied at Central Saint Martins, one of England's premier art schools, and that at one point she had a successful interior-design business.)

Cusk's feelings about her parents are still raw, and she seems to harbor wrath at past wrongs that no triumph of literary sublimation has been able to propitiate. On certain birthdays, she told me, "I would get a call from my mom reminding me of the torment she had gone through on that date." Cusk's birth, in an understaffed hospital during a blizzard, was long and difficult. Cusk suggested that her father blamed her for the trauma his wife had suffered, because he always seemed angry with her. When she reached puberty, she began to feel that her developing body was "disgusting." "I always felt repellent," Cusk said. "That has come out in my work, unfortunately, as disgust for the repellent qualities of other people." Both Peter and Carolyn were firstborn children and perhaps, Cusk said, their birth order caused them to favor her older sister. Only once in her life did she believe that they loved her: in the period of anguish and self-starvation when her first marriage ended. (The Cusks were shocked by Rachel's view of them, which they consider distorted.)

Cusk's parents had also "divorced" her, as she put it, although, as in the narrative of her breakup with Clarke, there are two sides to the story. She tells of a loveless and repressive childhood, in which her parents, she claimed, "blamed me for everything," and she often felt like an outcast. Her mother's prudishness and conformity were, by Cusk's account, stifling not only to the young Rachel. On the morning after she and Scamell-Katz were married—in "a fantastic party on the beach," she said—"I met my father in the kitchen. 'I didn't realize there were men like that,' he said of Siemon and his friends, who had been dancing wildly around a bonfire in knee-high boots. And he wished he could have been like them, boots and all. Because his own wildness had been domesticated by my mother."

In "Coventry," an essay in *Granta*, Cusk describes how her parents would stop speaking to her completely, for long periods of time, to make her pay for "offenses actual or hypothetical." "Being sent to Coventry," she explains, is an English expression that means, essentially, getting frozen out. "It is the attempt to recover power through withdrawal, rather as a powerless child indignantly imagines his own death as a punishment to others . . . My mother and father seem to believe they are inflicting a terrible loss on me by disappearing from my life." Cusk often had no idea what her offenses had been, even as an adult, though one has to wonder if some of them weren't related to the fact that a woman like the mother whom Cusk described to me—a perfect storm of narrow-mindedness, seething resentments, and vituperative retaliation—figures in several of her novels.

The last of these Coventries began on a winter Sunday in Norfolk, two years ago, and Scamell-Katz thought that something he said had provoked it. "We heard they were having some troubles," he explained, "so we asked them up for the weekend and looked after them. Rachel's father seemed grateful that she was on more solid ground with me" than she had been with Clarke. "But, at the end of the dinner, I put my arm around Rachel, and asked them why they thought she was so honest, and how they thought they had influenced her work." They seemed to stiffen a little, he said. After they left, there was no call or thank-you note, and six months passed without contact. Cusk eventually decided that her life was better with her parents out of it. Her daughters were free to see their grandparents, she writes in the essay, but "I myself don't wish to re-enter that arena. I don't want to leave Coventry. I've decided to stay."

Like Clarke, Peter and Carolyn had some objections to Cusk's account of their parting ways. Peter could not recall any conversation about masculinity in his daughter's kitchen, or any men in knee-high boots. He did, however, remember that at the dinner in Norfolk he had made some disparaging remarks about *Wolf Hall*, a novel by Hilary Mantel, who had encouraged Cusk's work, and that his daughter had lashed out at him. The words had stung, he said, so he had remembered them: "'You know nothing, and no one cares what you think anyway.'"

When Rachel was a baby, her father accepted a new job, in Los Angeles. Cusk imagined, she told an interviewer, that, as "stuffily brought-up people," they had wanted to "let their hair down," but that the hedonism of Southern California had been "frightening" to them. (What was more frightening, according to the elder Cusks, was the fact that the Manson family's murder of Sharon Tate took place three hundred yards from their house.) They moved to rural Suffolk when Cusk was eight, and three years later, in 1978, she followed her sister, Sarah, to a convent boarding school, St. Mary's, in Cambridge. The heroine of *Saving Agnes* is an alumna of such an institution: a hotbed of "female cruelty."

Sarah went on to Cambridge, and Rachel to Oxford, where for the first time, she said, "I had the experience of people treating me kindly and sharing my interests." On a shelf in her office, there is a snapshot of her from that period. The girl in the picture has a dreamy gaze, and thick, badly cut hair; she is holding a cigarette in an elongated hand. There is a lot of smoking in Cusk's fiction, and she started at a young age, despite the fact that she suffered from severe asthma—perhaps, she suggested, as a result of her ordeal at birth. "Being in control of my own destruction," she said wryly, "has always seemed like a solution for it."

Cusk and Clarke met at Oxford, but she had a very brief first marriage before they reconnected. If her parents had been afraid to let their hair down, she wasn't. "I equated sexuality with truth," she said of her libidinous twenties. "Inhabiting my body powerfully was the key to it. Sex has always been incredibly interesting to me, and it becomes more so. Which is strange, because my self-consciousness is so extreme."

Albertine was conceived when Cusk was thirty-one. Some women are never happier than when they are pregnant. For others, a swelling womb threatens their integrity—their literal self-possession. And becoming a mother raises the specter of becoming your *own* mother. One of Cusk's beefs with Carolyn is that "no one taught me how to be a woman"—though, actually, she was taught, and she rejected the lessons. "What do I understand by the term 'female'?" she asks in *A Life's*

Work: "A false thing; a repository of the cosmetic . . . a world in which words such as 'suffering,' 'self-control' and 'endurance' occur, but usually in reference to weight loss; a world steeped in its own mild, voluntary oppression, a world at whose fringes one may find intersections to the real: to particular kinds of unhappiness, or discrimination, or fear." In getting pregnant, she writes, "I have the sense of stepping off the proper path of my life."

A Life's Work is at once a cri de coeur, a prison diary, and a repudiation of Catholic Mary-worship (even though she prays "superstitiously" to the Virgin in a moment of "madness"). The memoir is heretically funny, though its humor is driven by dread. When Cusk has trouble nursing, she takes her newborn to a breast-feeding clinic, where the "babies boil like a row of angry kettles." Her daughter's "pure and pearly being requires considerable maintenance. At first my relation to it is that of a kidney." Albertine suffers colic, and Cusk reads Dr. Spock—a gift from Carolyn, of all people. "Spock's babies," she writes, "are cheerful souls in spite of . . . their constant gastroenteritis and chronic excrescences of the skin." Still, she notes, "in their anomic, tyrannical hearts they like to know who's boss, for weakness drives them to enslave and dominate."

At the outset of the memoir, Cusk warns the reader that she is writing in "the first heat" of the transformation from active subject to passive vessel. But as she gets used to the climate of maternity her own piercing wail abates. There are no sudden paroxysms of beatitude, just a subtle shift. She reads a poem by Coleridge, "Frost at Midnight," and notices, for the first time, that there is a baby in it. "It is a poem about sitting still," she writes, "about the way children act as anchors on the body and eventually the mind." The love it expresses "is a restitution." Reality begins when an infant gazing at her mother first intuits the existence of a self beyond her own, but for a mother it can begin at the same moment. Cusk told me that she would have been a different writer if she hadn't had children: "I would have been a minor lyricist." The compromise of motherhood, she continued, is an essential aspect of female reality, "and if you design an uncompromised life for yourself" you sever a vital artery. "Something has to be sacrificed."

Cusk is Scamell-Katz's fourth wife. (He appended his first wife's surname to his when they married.) His third wife, a yoga teacher with whom he has a teenage son, Foiy, lives near them in Norfolk, and their relations are amicable. After that divorce, he bought some land in Stiffkey, and he and Cusk have been building a house there together. Their property is semi-secluded, off a winding lane, with a distant view of the North Sea. Scamell-Katz, who has a background in design, acted as their architect, and, with his owlish glasses and dandified clothes, you might mistake him for one. In a neighborhood of manses and cottages, the house makes, as its owners do, a statement of nonconformity. The façade is a patchwork of corrugated metal and raw slate, and the interiors are austerely modernist. Cusk found the industrial windows on eBay—they had been fabricated for a school that was never built—and she scoured the site for bargain fixtures and furnishings. "There is a certain type of vendor you can always trust," she said. "She's a materialist who buys too much, then feels guilty and gets rid of her mistakes at a loss." (An oversized sofa, which barely fitted through the doorway, arrived while I was there.)

Family houses have a central place in Cusk's fiction, perhaps because she has lived in, fled, fixed up, envied, hated, yearned for, abandoned, and been dispossessed of an unusual number, along with the promises of happiness that they represented. "Freedom," Faye says, toward the end of *Transit*, "is a home you leave once and can never go back to." In an essay for *The New York Times Magazine* on remodeling her flat, Cusk describes how she gutted the rooms and threw away "decades' worth of clutter," but then missed the abandon sanctioned by shabbiness, in which no one had to worry about defiling a pristine sofa or scratching the floor. Men she knows are as obsessive about housekeeping as women, but their decor doesn't define them in the same way. On one hand, they don't have the feminist's temptation to prove that she isn't trivial by not caring about appearances; on the other, they "never seem quite so trammeled or devoured by domesticity . . . It may be the last laugh of patriarchy that men are better at being women than women are."

Her own marriage may be a case in point. When Cusk and Scamell-Katz told me about their trip to Scotland, she recalled the beauty of their conversations, and he recalled having brought emergency provisions—a goose and wine—on the train with them. Where she is conscientious about domestic chores, nurture seems to give him unguilty pleasure. He does much of the cooking (he left the pub early to start dinner), and it's easy to see how the tenderness of a virile man would appeal to a woman as conflicted as Cusk is about femininity. "I'm a bit in awe of Siemon's patience and self-control as a parent," she said.

Scamell-Katz, like Faye's date in *Transit*, was adopted as a baby by a modest family, and when he was still a child his birth mother wrote to his parents asking for a photo. His father tore up her letter in a fit of rage, but then, feeling remorseful, he taped the pieces back together, and handed them to Siemon on his eighteenth birthday. Until he sold his company, eleven years ago, at the age of forty-one, Scamell-Katz made his living as a marketing guru. He wrote a book on the subject, *The Art of Shopping*, and he still does some consulting. (His alimony, Cusk noted crisply, has dented their income.) Marriage and fatherhood are now his prime occupations, along with painting: a long-deferred passion. His studio, however—a ramshackle quonset hut—suggests a certain self-abnegation, particularly compared with the office that he built for Cusk, in an annex to the main house. Her two-room study is paneled in blond wood and skirted by a private deck; light streams through the windows, which look out on the garden; there is a wall of bookshelves, mostly still bare, except for some essential volumes, and among them was a novel I didn't know, *In Love*, by the British screenwriter Alfred Hayes, which was published in the 1950s. It speaks intimately to Cusk, and she wanted me to have it. Hayes, she said, "gives you an amazingly precise representation of what the world looks like if there's no love in it."

After the weekend, I went back to London. I was reading *In Love* on the train, and from time to time I looked up to see the green fields of Norfolk receding in the window. Hayes's novel is set in postwar

New York, and it opens in a hotel bar. What follows is the story of a hardboiled writer who thinks he has no illusions about love, and a pretty girl who just wants to be happy. Their fatal error is to mistake each other for their fictional avatars—the sexy artist and the appealing waif—and truth takes its revenge.

During my visit, Cusk's daughters had been staying at their father's house, in part so that their mother could work but also because Albertine had wanted to be in London. During the Easter weekend, there had been an argument over their living arrangements, which had brought Cusk to tears, and they'd had a "seminal" conversation to hash things out. "All I want," she told her husband, "is for them to treat me as conventional people treat their mothers." Scamell-Katz pointed out that she hadn't raised them to be conventional people, she had raised them to be free women, so she shouldn't complain when they brandished that freedom at her.

Later that week, I met Cusk and her daughters in Highgate for a quiet early dinner in an empty trattoria. Cusk and Jessye were there when I arrived, and Albertine came a little later—she was taking a walk to clear her head from the stress of schoolwork. The girls are so close in age (eighteen and seventeen) and in appearance (small, sturdy, and beautiful, in a different register from their mother) that you might mistake them for fraternal twins. But when I asked Jessye if she would miss Albertine, who leaves for university in the fall, she said that she wouldn't—she'd have more room in the flat—and Albertine burst into tears. Cusk, who was tenser than I had seen her—alert to every nuance of her daughters' moods—delicately set about repairing the damage.

I saw Cusk once more, at home in Tufnell Park. After she met Scamell-Katz, he persuaded her to sell the fixer-upper that Faye buys in *Transit*—the one with the vile neighbors. Her current flat is the upper duplex of a Victorian row house on a pleasant street, with bedrooms on the top floor, off a small terrace, and an open living area beneath them. The apartment makes up in flair what it lacks in scale, with interesting modern art, a smart orange kitchen, and IKEA furniture. It is homier and more bohemian than the house in Norfolk.

Cusk was still struggling with *Kudos*. (She finished the book last week.) "It feels like I'm pregnant with a lawn mower, something large and sharp that I have to expel," she said. Last year, she interrupted her work to help Albertine with her university applications. "For the first time, I found myself tinkering with a manuscript. In some ways, that was interesting. There was a funny freedom to having less control. But the messing around also annoyed me, and the work wasn't as good."

"Kudos" is the ancient Greek word for "honor" or "glory." "Female honor is the burnish of having survived your experiences without being destroyed by them, and female glory has to do with moral integrity," Cusk said. She cited Medea as an example of both. Medea is an early antiheroine in literature, and the progenitor of all the *alienées* whose crimes are a reproach to the hypocrisies that underpin civilization. (Camus's Meursault is her direct descendant.) She is a princess with magical powers who betrays her homeland for an ambitious Greek—Jason—in exchange for his promise to marry her. They escape to Corinth, where Medea bears Jason two sons, and they supposedly live happily for a while, though one rather doubts it. Jason is a congenital opportunist, and when he is given a chance to marry Glauce, the beautiful daughter of his host in exile, he tells Medea that, unfortunately, he has to leave her—but it's nothing personal. Medea sends her boys to Glauce with a wedding gift, a golden cloak steeped in poison. She dies horribly, along with her father, who tries to save her. You can't really begrudge Medea these murders, but there is one last cord to cut, and she agonizes over it. In the end, she decides to break Jason's heart, though it means breaking her own, and she kills their children.

Two years ago, the Almeida Theatre, in London, commissioned Cusk to adapt Euripedes' *Medea* for the contemporary stage. She had thought deeply about Greek tragedy, but other plays had meant more to her. If she'd had any notions about *Medea*, she wrote in an essay on the adaptation, they were that "the play's premise—the murder of two children by their mother—had attained a troubling sort of autonomy that exposed it to all sorts of cultural misuses," misogynistic ones. "'Medea' seemed to operate as a byword for maternal ambivalence."

Cusk read it differently—as a play about a feral divorce, and about an "entirely familiar" woman who "broadcasts both her own pain and the larger injustices" of which women were victims 2,500 years ago, and still are, in her view, despite the "lip service" that society pays to equality.

One thing that has changed is the audience for *Medea*. In 431 B.C., when it made its debut, at the festival of Dionysus, the crowd was largely male (Greek women were cloistered from the public sphere), and men didn't like the fact that a barbarian sorceress who defies patriarchal authority escapes her comeuppance in a winged chariot. Critics of the Almeida production had a few qualms, but not about what Susannah Clapp, in *The Observer*, called the "coruscating" power of the writing. Clapp continued, "It is Cusk's skill to show both a compendium of grievances and a woman whose grief exceeds them— who cannot be reconciled. This makes her play a true tragedy." Cusk's Medea doesn't kill her children—in part, she explained, because in modern terms the act would make her a psychotic, and Cusk sees her as "an ultimate realist," who is "determined to honour the logic of her own conclusions."

Medea, Cusk's first play, also gave her an opportunity to explore some of her own conclusions, especially about feminism. You can trace their evolution in her writing, from *Saving Agnes*, where she describes feminism as "a placebo of self-acceptance," and *A Life's Work*, which rejects the pieties that make a woman's biological "destiny" to bear children seem sacred, through the argument with herself about gender in *Aftermath*, and, finally, to the last scene of *Transit*. Faye has been invited to a dinner party by her cousin. He and his new wife own a fancy country place. The other guests are traditionally married couples, and their squabbles are a throwback to Cusk's earlier fiction. At first, you wonder why she would resurrect this milieu; then you realize that she has to revisit her revulsion for the doll's house before leaving it forever. A fog closes in; the next morning, Faye feels a change stirring beneath her. Silently, she lets herself out.

Cusk's phone beeped with a text, and she excused herself for a minute. When she returned, she looked upset—she had forgotten an appointment, she would have to rush off, and she apologized profusely for ending our talk so abruptly. There was a last question I had hesitated to ask: Why, given her history, did she risk remarriage? She thought for a minute as we gathered up our things. "I'm very strong," she said. "The strongest thing about me is my honesty. Not that it has helped me to be better at living. I have used my strength for the purposes of destruction. But now I can use it to build something that will last."

JULY 2014

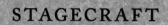

STAGECRAFT

Birthdays are important to Marina Abramović, the performance artist who was born in Belgrade, the capital of what was then Yugoslavia, on November 30, 1946. The body is her subject, time is her medium, and birthdays mark the moment that the performance of living officially begins. Abramović has never been shy about her age—when she turned sixty, she celebrated with a black-tie gala at the Guggenheim Museum—and age has been kinder to her than she has ever been to herself. You would recognize her today from the grainy photographs of her earliest performances, forty years ago, when she was a dark, offbeat girl with sad eyes and chiseled features in a pale face. Perhaps it was too expressive a face to be pretty—the obdurate and the yielding at odds in it. But some charismatic women, like Abramović, or her idol Maria Callas, are beautiful by an act of will.

At sixty-three, Abramović radiates vitality and seduction. Her glossy hair spills over her broad shoulders. When she isn't dressed for exercise or the stage, she is likely to be wearing designer clothes. She is fleshier than she used to be, and her body has a different kind of poignance than it did in her waifish youth, but she still has no qualms about subjecting it to shocking trials. In 2005, thirty years after she first staged *Thomas Lips* in an Austrian gallery (Thomas Lips was a Swiss lover whose androgyny had fascinated her), she revived the performance, protracted from two hours to seven, in the Guggenheim rotunda, as part of a show called *Seven Easy Pieces*. The program notes for the original read like the recipe for a banquet dish that would have pleased de Sade:

> I slowly eat 1 kilo of honey with a silver spoon.
> I slowly drink 1 liter of wine out of a crystal glass.
> I break the glass with my right hand.
> I cut a five-pointed star on my stomach with a razor blade.
> I violently whip myself until I no longer feel any pain.
> I lay down on a cross made of ice blocks.
> The heat of a suspended heater pointed at my stomach causes the cut star to bleed.
> The rest of my body begins to freeze.
> I remain on the ice cross for 30 minutes until the public interrupts the piece by removing the ice blocks from underneath me.

Last August, Abramović invited me to observe a five-day retreat that she held at her country home in the Hudson Valley. The main house, built in the 1990s, sits on a rise overlooking some twenty-five acres of meadows, orchards, and woodland. Its design was inspired by a star-shaped castle on the Baltic. Abramović bought the property in 2007. Even though the star has six points, and the red star that dominated her childhood, and which figures prominently in her iconography, is a pentagram, she felt that destiny had led her to it. The decor is minimal—a few modern sofas and chairs in bright colors—and the walls are bare. Until recently, she spent weekends here with her second husband, Paolo Canevari, an Italian sculptor and video artist seventeen years her junior. They met in Europe in 1997, and divided their time between her canal house in Amsterdam and his apartment in Rome. In 2001, they moved to a loft in SoHo. After twelve years together, two of them married, they divorced last December. For the first time, Abramović has learned to drive. "I did it to be independent," she explained. Her timidity and ineptitude behind the wheel seem incongruous in the character of a daredevil, but, she added, "I have always staged my fears as a way to transcend them."

The retreat was an intensive workshop in hygiene and movement

that Abramović calls "Cleaning the House." She has taught performance art on several continents, and she has often used Ayurvedic,
shamanistic, Buddhist, Gurdjieffian, and other holistic or ascetic practices to initiate her students. The participants were thirty-two of the
thirty-nine mostly young men and women whom she had chosen to
participate in a full-scale retrospective at the Museum of Modern Art,
Marina Abramović: The Artist Is Present—the first such honor for a performance artist—which opens on March 14. They will be reenacting
five of the approximately ninety pieces that she has created since 1969,
including three that were originally performed with the German
artist Ulay (Frank Uwe Laysiepen), her former lover and collaborator.
Imponderabilia, a joint work of 1977, will include live, indeed interac-
tive, nudity—another first for the museum. It involves a naked couple
planted like caryatids on either side of a narrow doorway at the entrance to a gallery, their backs to the frame. Everyone who enters must
sidle past them, deciding which body to face. MoMA will provide an
alternative access to the space, an accommodation that Abramović
thinks is a pity. Her role as an artist, she believes, with a hubris that
can sound naïve and a humility that disarms any impulse to resent it,
is to lead her spectators through an anxious passage to a place of release from whatever has confined them.

Abramović's career falls into three periods: before, with, and after
Ulay. He was the son of a Nazi soldier, born on November 30—Marina's
birthday—in 1943, in a bomb shelter in Solingen, an industrial city in
Westphalia that has always produced Germany's famously superior
cutting implements: first swords, then knives and razors. By fifteen,
he had been orphaned and was fending for himself. Abramović met
him on November 30, in 1975. A gallerist in Amsterdam asked Ulay
to drive her in from the airport, and to help with the logistics of film-
ing *Thomas Lips* for Dutch television. Their chemistry was immediate.
Her first impression was of a tall figure, rock-star skinny, and flam-
boyantly strange. "He has a heart face," she recalled, alluding to its
double-sidedness. "Half is a tough guy, unshaved, short hair; half has
makeup, long hair, and, like me, he wears chopsticks in it." Ulay's art,
until then, had consisted primarily of Polaroid self-portraits that

documented his experiments with mutilation—piercing, circumcision, tattoos—and an obsession with twinship: a male/female duality. That night, after a Turkish dinner—he showed her his diary at the restaurant, she showed him hers; they had both torn out their birthday page, which she took as a karmic sign—she told me, "We go straight to his house and stay in bed for ten days." She added, "Back at home, I get so lovesick I cannot move or talk." She was married, at the time, to a former fellow-student from the Belgrade Academy of Fine Arts, but it was an oddly slack union. Both spouses still lived with their parents, and Abramović had a strict curfew: ten o'clock. (They divorced in 1977.) Her mother called the police when Marina "ran away" a few months later, at twenty-nine, to rejoin her soul mate.

Abramović and Ulay made art symbiotically for twelve nomadic years, from 1976 to 1988. They spent one of them living with Aboriginal people in the Central Australian desert. Amsterdam was their base, but their home on the road, in Europe, was a black Citroën van, which figured in their performance of ideal couplehood. It miraculously survived the beatings it took, and is part of the MoMA retrospective. Their union was also much battered and repaired, though it ultimately couldn't survive the demands of such intense proximity, of primal wounds, or a discrepancy in ambition that Ulay suggested in an e-mail. "It is very important to understand how much Marina invests in her artistic career, it being her life," he wrote. That is "one of the reasons why she never wanted to have children." Their parting was wrenching for Abramović, whose nerves can defy almost any blow except for abandonment. She still believes in true love, and she dispenses affection with a lavishness as intense as her craving for it. But, she reflected, "people put so much effort into starting a relationship and so little effort into ending one." On March 30, 1988, they embarked on their last performance. She started walking the Great Wall of China from the east, where it rises in the mountains, and Ulay set off from the west, where it ends in the desert. After three months, and thousands of miles, they met in the middle, and said goodbye.

Grace and stamina were prime criteria for the "reperformers" Abramović had chosen for the retrospective, and, judging from their looks, so was the kind of ethereal shimmer that painters once looked for in models for sacred art. Many are dancers; some teach yoga or Pilates; others are performance artists eager to debut at MoMA, and to work with a master. They arrived on a chartered bus, and Abramović greeted each of them with a maternal kiss, then confiscated their cell phones. They had signed a contract that obliged them to observe complete silence; to fast on green tea and water; to sleep on the hard floor of an old barn; and to submit to her discipline, which is partly that of a guru, partly of a drill sergeant. (Her drills included practice in nostril flushing and tongue scraping, and a health-food cooking lesson, complete with recipes, which the fasting disciples copied dutifully into their notebooks.) The weather was perfect for a New Age boot camp—hot and dry—and, after breathing exercises in a circle, the troupe filed down to the banks of an icy kill that runs through the property, where all its members, including Abramović, stripped for a communal swim. Divestment in a larger sense—of comfort, modesty, impatience, habits, and attachments—seemed to be what she was after. One afternoon, everyone assembled in an orchard behind the house to await her instructions. She told them to begin moving in slow motion; she would let them know when three hours had elapsed, but until then they couldn't stop. I watched from a window for a long time as the sun elongated their shadows, and they seemed to become part of the landscape. My own metabolism slowed down with them, and things hidden from a restless eye revealed themselves. I could almost see the apples ripening.

While Abramović's stand-ins are performing, in rotating shifts, on the sixth floor of the museum, she will present a new work, *The Artist Is Present*, in the Donald B. and Catherine C. Marron Atrium. From opening time to closing—eight to ten hours a day—for seventy-seven days, until the show ends, on May 31, she will sit immobile at a bare wooden table, gazing fixedly into space. Her original concept for the piece involved an elaborate scaffold and props, but as she refined it with Klaus Biesenbach, a close friend and MoMA's chief curator at large, its showy elements and verticality were discarded. "I made a huge mistake in *The House with the Ocean View*," she said, referring to her performance at the Sean Kelly Gallery in Chelsea, eight years ago—"to put myself up on some kind of altar." For twelve days, Abramović confined herself to three stark, open-sided cubes, cantilevered to the walls, about five feet above the floor. She could walk between them, and each one had a ladder that she never used—the rungs were knives with the blades upturned. Towels, fresh clothing, water, and a metronome were her only provisions. The gallery was dim, but the "house" was spotlit. Here she sat, lay, stood, stared, stretched, slept, showered, urinated, and fasted in silence, always on view. Some spectators came to ogle her through a telescope she had set up near a back wall, others to keep a reverent vigil. "In every ancient culture," she went on, "there are rituals to mortify the body as a way of understanding that the energy of the soul is indestructible. The more I think about energy, the simpler my art becomes, because it is just about pure presence."

The Artist Is Present will be the longest durational work ever mounted in a museum. (The artist Tehching Hsieh spent a year caged in his Tribeca studio.) Members of the audience may participate by sitting in a chair opposite Abramović's. She is hoping for an "emotional connection with anyone who wants to look at me for however long," but Biesenbach is worried about the show's unique unpredictability. "It's an experiment that has never been tried before, and we don't know what will happen," he said. If past performances are a guide, some spectators will accept Abramović's invitation to "exchange energy" with her as they might line up for Communion, although Biesenbach hinted that "people from Marina's past" might be plotting to surprise her. "What you can and can't control is part of the piece," Abramović said. "Electricity fails, nobody shows up—doesn't matter. If you are not one hundred per cent in the now, the public, like a dog, knows it. They leave."

The one given is the "enormous bodily pain" that Abramović knows she will suffer—"especially at the beginning. Motionless performances are the hardest." Pain is the constant in her art. (Only rarely has she aborted a performance, although once the audience intervened to save her life. This happened in 1974, at the Student Cultural Center in Belgrade, where she performed a piece called *Rhythm 5*. She lost consciousness inside the perimeter of a burning star and was dragged to safety.) She has screamed until she lost her voice, danced until she collapsed, and brushed her hair until her scalp bled. In an early piece, she ingested anti-psychotic drugs that caused temporary catatonia. She and Ulay traded hard slaps, hurled themselves at solid walls, and passed a breath back and forth, with locked lips, until they fainted. He pointed an arrow at her heart as she tensed the bow. These performances were works of dynamic sculpture, with a formal rigor and beauty, but what, I asked her, distinguished their content from masochism? "Funny, my mother asked the same question," she replied. "All the aggressive actions I do to myself I would never dream of doing in my own life—I am not this kind of person. I cry if I cut myself peeling potatoes. I am taking the plane, there is turbulence, I am shaking. In performance, I become, somehow, like not a mortal. All my insecurities—having a fat body, skinny body, big ass, long nose, a guy, being abandoned, whatever—aren't important." What makes it art? Context and intention, she said: "The sense of purpose I feel to do something heroic, legendary, and transformative; to elevate viewers' spirits and give them courage. If I can go through the door of pain to embrace life on the other side, they can, too."

Some people inflict pain upon themselves in order to replay— and to master—cruel treatment that they once endured helplessly. Abramović's mother, Danica Rosić, was born into a clan of great wealth, power, and piety; her uncle was the patriarch of the Serbian Orthodox Church. Marina's father, Vojin Abramović (known as Vojo), came from a large and poor family. He and Danica, both Montenegrins, joined the Communist partisans, in 1941, and fought on the front lines. After the war, their service was rewarded with high positions in Tito's government. Vojo was appointed to the marshal's elite guard, and Danica to direct an agency that supervised historic monuments and acquired art works for public buildings. (In the sixties, she headed Yugoslavia's Museum of Revolution.) The perks of office included foreign travel, a seaside villa, and a huge apartment in the capital, which had been confiscated from Jews during the Nazi occupation.

Danica furnished it ornately, and her maids, her husband, and her children (Marina's brother, Velimir, a prominent philosopher, was born in 1952) were strictly prohibited from touching a thing. "We were red bourgeoisie," Abramović said.

Marina's relations with her mother were always fraught. Danica and Vojo were a volatile couple who slept with loaded pistols and quarreled violently over his philandering. Danica, who beat Marina for willful, attention-seeking behavior, lived by a Spartan code of "walk-through-walls" Communist determination, as her daughter has put it. "I learned my self-discipline from her, and I was always afraid of her," she told me. In an interview with her mother that Abramović filmed for a theater piece titled *Delusional*, Danica reflects on the experiences that steeled her character. "As for pain, I can stand pain," she concludes. "Nobody has, and nobody ever will, hear me scream." She demanded the same ostentatious stoicism from her daughter, and she was indifferent, if not unsympathetic, when Marina developed the kind of incapacitating migraines that she herself suffered. An astute new biography, *When Marina Abramović Dies*, by James Westcott, who was once Abramović's assistant, suggests that these bouts of agonized solitary confinement in her body are a taproot that she draws on both to create and to endure her performances.

Danica, however, nurtured her daughter's art. Despite her severity, she had a penchant for the kind of genteel "cultural grooming" that a girl of her class would have received before the Communist era. ("My father hates opera, hates Russian ballet, likes to drink with old partisans," Abramović told me. "My mother is everything about education. I have a piano teacher, English teacher, French teacher, all books are like Proust or Kafka.") On June 11, 1963, Marina was looking forward to her first foray from home without a chaperone—a trip to Paris. She was a lonely sixteen-year-old chess champion with Coke-bottle glasses, a gangly frame, and flat feet (she wore orthopedic shoes) who cried all the time, she said. But she was painting seriously, and Danica, who had cleaned out a spare room in the family apartment so that she could have a studio, arranged the trip as an introduction to French culture. (Marina entered Belgrade's Academy of Fine Arts two years later, and in the late sixties she was a leader of student demonstrations that resulted in a concession from Tito: the social club for the wives of his secret police was converted into an arts center for avant-garde experiment, where she gave her first performances.)

Half a world away, on a street in Saigon, Thich Quang Duc, a sixty-six-year-old monk, folded his legs in the lotus position and immolated himself to protest the persecution of Buddhists by the Diem regime. His death was photographed by Malcolm Browne, and reported by David Halberstam, who was, he wrote, "too shocked to cry" as the flames consumed the body. Self-martyrdom as a public spectacle had precedents in Asian culture, but Thich's composure, as he lit the match, and sat serenely for ten minutes of masterly staged agony, rocked the West and burrowed into its collective dream life. "No news picture in history has generated as much emotion around the world," President Kennedy said.

Abramović says that she never forgot that "terrible image of devotion to a cause," and in a recent interview Ulay noted that the photographs and film footage streaming out of Vietnam politicized his generation of artists. Thich's auto-da-fé coincides with the moment that a new genre—an art of the ordeal, spawned by the generational conflicts and social upheavals of the 1960s—began to gather momentum. Those who practiced it did so, at first, in the name of sabotage and refusal. They were, like the Romantics and the Dadaists before them, assaulting bourgeois complacency, redefining obscenity (as the news did), and rejecting materialism—the production of theatrical illusion, and of art objects that could be commodified. "The knife in a play is only an idea of something that can kill, but a knife in my work is always real," Abramović said to me. Audiences were asked to witness extreme and sometimes life-threatening rituals that involved self-harm, or that violated deeply ingrained taboos. Performer and beholder shared an aesthetically stylized yet visceral experience in actual time. The more puerile efforts of this school, which was called "body art" ("performance art" or "time-based art" are now the preferred terms), generated a prurient thrill, or just revulsion. The best of them reminded one that there is no voyeurism with impunity.

In 1969, Valie Export (née Waltraud Lehner—she took her alias from a brand of cigarettes) stormed a porn theater in Munich wearing a pair of crotchless trousers, and brandished a machine gun at the startled patrons, challenging them to engage with "a real woman." In the early and middle seventies, the Franco-Italian artist Gina Pane lacerated her flesh with thorns and razors. Chris Burden, a Bostonian, arranged to have a friend (an expert marksman) shoot his arm with a rifle at close range, and to be crucified to the roof of a Volkswagen. Vito Acconci, of Brooklyn, masturbated in a crawl space under a ramp at the Sonnabend Gallery, as its patrons walked over him. In another New York gallery, Joseph Beuys, a German who had served in the Luftwaffe, cohabited for three days with a coyote. Across the Atlantic, Abramović invited an audience in Naples to probe, soil, bind, tease, disrobe, penetrate, or mark her body, "as desired," for six hours, using any of seventy-two implements arrayed on a table. They included nails, lipstick, matches, paint, a saw, chains, alcohol, a bullet, and a gun that was, at one point, aimed at her head. "I am the object," she declared in her program notes. "During this period I take full responsibility." As the hours passed, she remained utterly impassive, though she couldn't hold back her tears. A few spectators wiped them away, and, as others began toying with her body, two factions emerged: vandals and protectors. It wasn't entirely a division by gender. "The women didn't touch me," she said, "but some of them egged the men on." Photographs of this performance, *Rhythm 0*, show Abramović being laid out like a corpse, posed like a mannequin, pinned with slogans, stripped to the waist, kissed, showered with rose petals, doused with water, and hooded like a captive. Someone used the lipstick to write "end" on her forehead.

Abramović's feminism has always been a mythical, rather than a political, understanding of women's oppression—and of their power. RoseLee Goldberg, a leading curator and historian of performance art, noted that for American women of Abramović's generation "being a feminist meant joining the party. That kind of solidarity—or of conformity—signified something different to Marina. By the time she became an artist, she wanted freedom on her own terms. And I always saw her in the pieces with Ulay as being in charge."

Abramović has often commented on the irony that her birth certificate bears a red star, while Ulay's has a swastika. That is the conflict—between communism and fascism—that shaped her worldview. But in 1997, twenty-three years after her ordeal in Naples, she returned to Italy for an act of engagement with contemporary history. It was two years after the Dayton Peace Accords, and the Montenegrin minister of culture had invited Abramović, the child of national heroes, to represent their native country at the Venice Biennale. Sean Kelly, her gallerist, advised her to decline, on the ground, Westcott writes, that "she shouldn't risk the perception" of complicity with Slobodan Milosević. (Serbia and Montenegro were then a federation; they are now independent.) She, however, was determined to participate. Even though "she recognized Serbia's role as an instigator of the violence," Westcott continues, "she saw aggression on all sides," and the invitation was "an opportunity to perform an act of mourning" for the dead on all sides. But when the minister learned of the performance she was planning, and its price tag—about a hundred thousand dollars—he rescinded the invitation with an insulting letter: "Montenegro is not a cultural margin and it should not be just a homeland colony for megalomaniac performances."

Outraged, Abramović and Kelly asked Germano Celant, a curator of the Biennale, to find her a venue. The only space left was a fetid basement with low ceilings and a concrete floor, in the Italian pavilion. It was perfect for her purposes. The performance that Abramović staged there, *Balkan Baroque*, which won the Golden Lion—the award for best artist—was an expression of her complex shame for, and her attachment to, her identity not only as a Yugoslav but as the daughter of Vojo and Danica. Equipped with a bucket and brush, she spent six hours a day, for four days, abjectly scrubbing fifteen hundred raw cow bones that, in the summer heat, were crawling with maggots. The interview with Danica from *Delusional*, and one with Vojo, waving a gun and telling grisly war stories (they were both filmed in Belgrade in 1994, when the city was still an armed camp), were projected on the walls at angles to a video of Abramović, in a white lab coat, explaining a sadistic Serbian technique for killing rats. She, meanwhile, wept as she scrubbed, and sang folk songs of her homeland. The stench, Biesenbach said, was unbearable, but so was the intensity.

Most of Abramović's peers among the pioneers of what might be called "ordealism," to distinguish it from tamer or more cerebral forms of conceptual and performance art, have long since retired from their harrowing vocation, and some died young. Acconci, who stopped performing in 1973 (he turned to architecture), told me, "What I loved about performance was the contract. You say you are going to do something and you carry it out. What I hated about it was the display of self—the personality cult." He saw Abramović's *The House with the Ocean View*, he said, "and I had no idea how to enjoy it. Why did she need an audience to validate a private experience? Are the people really into it with her?" He also questions the principle of reperformance, a contentious point in the art world. One party holds that the integrity of time-based art is inseparable from its transience, and that no performance can or should be resurrected. In an app-happy age, this radical embrace of loss has its nobility.

Abramović has been a prominent target for the purists. Even Ulay recently remarked, "I don't believe in these performance 'revivals.' They don't have the ring of truth about them. They have become a part of the culture industry." The credo that he and Abramović lived by in the seventies, "art vital," called for "no rehearsal, no predicted end, no repetition, extended vulnerability, exposure to chance, primary reactions." Acconci told me, "Marina now seems to want to make performance teachable and repeatable, but then I don't understand what separates it from theater." (In keeping with his principles, however, he lets things go. He gave Abramović permission to reperform a version of *Seedbed*, his masturbation epic, as part of *Seven Easy Pieces*, which also included homages to Beuys, Pane, Export, Bruce Nauman, and her younger self—the martyr of *Thomas Lips*.)

For Abramović, this debate is too esoteric. "In the seventies, we believe in no repetition," she said. "Okay, but now is a new century, and without reperformance all you will leave the next generation is dead documents and recordings. Martha Graham also didn't want her dances reinterpreted by other choreographers. I think it is selfish of the artist not to let her work have its own life." She hopes to raise several million dollars to convert a derelict movie theater that she bought three years ago in Hudson, New York, into the Marina Abramović Foundation for the Preservation of Performance Art, with a study and media center, a café, and a hangar-size performance space. At the moment, it is a temporary warehouse for a lifetime's worth of documents. (The purgative ethos of the retreat does not, apparently, apply to her archives.) In addition to prints, books, and correspondence, she has held on to posters, ticket stubs, yellowed news clippings, props, and souvenirs of her travels. It is quite a payload for a nomad, and the retrospective is adding to it. There is the 224-page MoMA catalogue; a book of essays by the art critic Thomas McEvilley, *Art, Love, Friendship: Marina Abramović and Ulay, Together and Apart*; and a documentary directed by Matthew Akers, who has been following Abramović since last summer and has filmed hundreds of hours. (He will record every second of her performance.)

The publication of Westcott's biography also coincides with the show. It tells a riveting story with composure and autonomy, and it gives perspective to a tortured, myth-laden narrative that Abramović herself can't stop retelling. *The Biography*, created in the early nineties with the videographer Charles Atlas, and its sequel, *The Biography Remix*, with the stage director Michael Laub, are a grandiose unfolding self-portrait. It takes the form of elaborately scripted multimedia spectacles that call for supporting actors, live pythons and Dobermans, colored lights, bondage costumes, a Callas soundtrack, a rehash of old performances, and a voice-over in which Abramović recounts, sometimes in Serbian, the milestones of her life. This extravaganza seems at odds, to say the least, with her ideals of abstinence and spontaneity. Initially, though, it helped Abramović "to get over" Ulay, she told McEvilley, and every few years she adds a new chapter. The next installment, a theater piece directed by Robert Wilson, *The Life and Death of Marina Abramović*, is in the works.

On November 30, Abramović invited a group of old friends to her sixty-third-birthday dinner, in her SoHo loft. It is a luxuriously spare, open space with a fashion plate's dressing room off the master bath— Abramović's gift to herself after Paolo Canevari moved out. She likes to cook homey meals, and, in the country, she had gathered vegetables from her organic garden to make a soup for the reperformers when they broke their fast. But on this occasion she had hired a chef, a young artist whose menu had an unusual concept: It was dedicated to the victims of Hurricane Katrina. Rum and bourbon were served in paper cups, and after a lengthy cocktail hour the doors to the kitchen were folded back to reveal sixty-three quarts of gumbo in plastic containers. The guests looked somewhat stricken when a posse of couriers arrived to distribute the gumbo to the homeless. While they were wondering when or if something to eat would appear (eventually, it did—okra doughnuts), David Blaine, the magician, did card tricks, and changed the time on Laurie Anderson's watch from across the room. He is planning his own next feat of ordealism—he will seal himself in a super-sized glass bottle and have it tossed into the ocean. "Marina is one of my greatest inspirations," he told me. She was in glamour mode, in a clingy black dress and artful makeup, with her hair down. "I want you to meet someone," she said, and led me to a corner where a giant cherub with a soft, sad face and a disheveled pageboy was leaning against the wall. "This is Antony. He will, I hope, be singing at my funeral."

Antony Hegarty, of Antony and the Johnsons, is famous for his otherworldly voice. But it is not just his music, I surmised, that Abramović finds so compelling. His fragility is transparent, whereas she has to suffer in public to make hers visible beneath an Amazonian guise. The song he will sing, when she dies, "if all goes well," she said, is "My Way." Then she outlined the program for her farewell performance. It will take place simultaneously in three cities: Belgrade, Amsterdam, and New York. All the mourners will wear bright colors. And in each city, there will be a coffin. "No one will know," she said, "which has the real body."

———— ∞ ————

In 2006, Nicolas Sarkozy, who was then the interior minister of France, agreed to let the playwright and novelist Yasmina Reza follow him, as part of his inner circle, while he campaigned for the presidency. The proposal came without any pretense on her part of servility or of discretion in how she would portray him. Reza is an adversarial writer even in her tender moments, which are infrequent, and she has a gift for derision that Flaubert might have admired. One has to wonder what Sarkozy was thinking. But he gamely countered with his own dare. "Even if you demolish me, you will elevate me," he boasted to her at the outset. "I don't think I did either," Reza told me, in January, in Paris, "but I might have wounded his amour propre. The truth does that."

Dawn, Dusk or Night was published in France shortly after Sarkozy's victory, in 2007. (Their last interview and, Reza wrote, their only attempt at a real conversation took place at the Élysée Palace.) It created a sensation, selling some 300,000 copies, although reviewers could not agree what to make of it: it was "too close," "too detached," "cruel," "savory," "photoshopped prose," "lucid," "like pictures from a spy satellite," "caustic," "a literary curiosity," and a "literary monument." "Sometimes," one commentator remarked, "the hunter is more interesting than the prey."

Reza distilled her notes from an intermittent year on the campaign trail into a collage of fugitive impressions and vignettes, some poetic

and penetrating, others a bit cavalier, and at least a few naïvely conceited. (Sarkozy and his then wife, Cécilia, attend one of Reza's plays,
and Reza reports that, on the plane to a rally, he recites from memory
a short "essential" bit of monologue.) Sarkozy introduced Reza as a
"genius" to Tony Blair, and invited her to sit in on his first meeting, in
Washington, with the then junior senator from Illinois. The concentration of so much political talent and presidential ambition in one
room impressed her, but, on the whole, she found politics a bore—"a
dumb job for smart people," as a friend of hers puts it in the book. A
journalist warns her that she is out of her depth. "Don't do it, Yasmina," he says. Politicians "are stronger than us." But, she reflects defiantly, "To be threatened by someone's strength, you have to be in
competition with him. Or weakened by sentiment."

"The Ballad of Yasmina and Nicolas," as a headline referred to
Dawn, Dusk or Night, does have a model in French letters: the private
journals that courtiers of the eighteenth century wrote by candlelight
to edify an unworldly child, or to amuse a paramour. Reza's aphoristic
style has some of the same elegance. (When the polls show Sarkozy in
the lead, she observes, "To be the favorite: how disappointing for a
lover of adversity.") Beneath its disenchantment, it also has some of
the same yearning for sincerity. As the title suggests, Reza, too, was
hiding something from the glare of day. The book is dedicated to a
man whom she calls G, and of whom she gives tantalizing but mysterious glimpses. One infers that he is an important politician, perhaps
a rival to Sarkozy; that she is courting him with this bravura performance of lèse-majesté; and that he eludes and therefore compels her as
Sarkozy does not. (After a speech that Sarkozy felt was particularly
bold and clever, he asked Reza familiarly, *"Ça t'a plu?"*—"Were you
pleased?" The presumption of the question—that she, "of all people,"
would be pleased by his self-infatuated rhetoric—insults her.) Yet Sarkozy, she told me, not without admiration, also "understood better
than anyone else what I had done." In a way, she conceded, she had
betrayed him. It wasn't that she had exposed his vanities—he had
signed on for the scrutiny. But he had once chided her, half-jokingly,
"You're not here to admire others!" And, without his knowledge, she

had spent a uniquely privileged year in his company writing, as she put it, "a chronicle of love" whose true subject was another man. (G's identity has aroused speculation but has never been revealed.)

A talent for ingratitude is often a prerequisite for great achievement. Few creative artists have the gall of Yasmina Reza, and few have her powers of invention. In the past two decades, she has produced three novels of literary distinction; three screenplays; a translation of Kafka's *Metamorphosis* for Roman Polanski; two memoirs in the laconic style of the Sarkozy book; and seven works of theater that have earned her a controversial celebrity. (Six of her plays have been translated for the English-speaking stage by Christopher Hampton.) On March 22, her latest play, *God of Carnage*—a comedy of manners, or, perhaps more accurately, a debacle of manners—opens on Broadway. "I always refuse to change the setting for foreign productions," she said, "but in this case I made an exception. The characters work so plausibly as New Yorkers." (They are two well-off couples who meet with civilized intentions to discuss their sons, eleven-year-old schoolmates. One boy has bashed the other's teeth in.)

Reza made her debut with *Conversations After a Funeral*, which won the Molière Award (France's most prestigious drama prize) for Best Author in 1987, when she was twenty-eight. It was followed by *Winter Crossing*, in 1989, which also won a Molière. Her third play, *Art*, won two in 1995, but they were perhaps the least noteworthy of its honors. *Art*, which describes an episode in the friendship of three men who come to blows over a minimalist painting and end up vandalizing it and the friendship, has been translated into more than thirty languages, and, according to Reza, no other contemporary play in the world is performed as often or as widely. (Gross receipts have been estimated at more than $300 million, making Reza one of the most successful contemporary dramatists in any language.) The London production, with Albert Finney, Tom Courtenay, and Ken Stott, won a Laurence Olivier Award for Comedy, and ran for six years. ("The category surprised me," Reza said dryly. "I thought I had written a tragedy.") The New York production, in 1998, starring Alan Alda, Victor Garber, and Alfred Molina, won a Tony for Best Play.

The argument among the friends, about the white-on-white canvas for which one of them has paid an exorbitant sum, is really a debate about the way that people value, or overvalue, the attributes, relations, and received ideas in which they invest their identity. But the play itself became a screen upon which beholders projected their view of Yasmina Reza. Few quibbled with her stagecraft or her dialogue. She has a mynah bird's ear for the coded preening, casual profanity, and calculated self-deprecation by which her protagonists—upper-middle-class professionals, for the most part—dissemble their fragility. Some critics, however, perceived *Art* as the polemic of a closet philistine who was mocking modernism, if not modernity. Others dismissed Reza as a boulevard crowd-pleaser with art-house pretensions: "the queen of 'big ideas, lite.'" The French were disdainful of her triumphs abroad, and Reza was scathing to me on the subject of "left-wing journalists in whose opinion success is right-wing." To the degree that she will consent to define herself—and escaping definition is one of her central preoccupations—it is not only as a writer who doesn't traffic in big ideas but as one with a profound antipathy toward intellectualizing. "I'm not cerebral," she said. "I never theorize about human nature. My work is visceral and subjective. I'm interested in the banal, unguarded moments and the hairline fractures in a character that let the light through. Sarko has a fracture, that's why I have a tenderness for him—his surface isn't impermeable." Reza, who is a first-generation French citizen—her parents were both Eastern European Jews—likes to consider herself an outsider to the cultural establishment. "I have *never* wanted to join a coterie. But my reserve and my ferocity are mistaken for arrogance by journalists, so I give them the strict minimum. If they sense that I don't care about their opinions, they're right." (In part because she is so loath to be branded, Reza followed *Art* with *The Unexpected Man*, a small, beautifully nuanced study of character in which two strangers on a train—played, in New York in 2000, by Alan Bates and Eileen Atkins—fantasize about each other without speaking until the end.)

God of Carnage was written on commission, in 2006, for the Berliner Ensemble, and directed by the legendary Jürgen Gosch. Reza herself directed the Paris production, which starred Isabelle Huppert. (Ralph Fiennes headlined the cast in London, last year.) The Broadway production, directed by Matthew Warchus, stars James Gandolfini, Marcia Gay Harden, Jeff Daniels, and Hope Davis as the two couples, one earthy, the other patrician-looking. The action takes place in a long, uninterrupted scene in the Cobble Hill living room of the victim's parents (the earthy ones). A discussion of the boy's dental work—implants will have to wait until his jaw matures—and of the penitence that his mother feels is appropriate are the first items on the agenda, but goodwill quickly evaporates. The ensuing fracas follows an arc that Reza has perfected: fraudulent politesse gives way to toxic caviling that degenerates into a brawl in the course of which all bluffs are called. (Some of the comedy, which involves projectile vomiting and annoying phone calls, and some of the irony, which relates to Darfur and a hamster, are atypical for a satirist of Reza's finesse.)

Actors love Reza's work more reliably than drama critics do. She writes for an ensemble of equals—there are almost no minor roles—and the volatile mixture of wit and resentment in a tight structure ignites with a spark. She herself started out as an actress. After college, at Paris X Nanterre, where she studied sociology and theater—"I was just really passing time"—Reza auditioned for the National Conservatory of Dramatic Art. She thought that she had given "a very original performance, but I didn't get in, and the rejection left me with an enduring sense of injustice." (Eight years later, she noted, "I was a judge.") On the rebound, she enrolled at the International Theatre School Jacques Lecoq, where the training stresses movement, gesture, pantomime, and spatial awareness. Reza said, "Lecoq played to my forte—a physical language that you are born with or not. I think, write, and direct with my body. French actors trained at the Conservatory tend to work with less spontaneity. I had to liberate Isabelle Huppert from her classical education. I had to get her to use her body more capriciously." (Huppert's character in God of Carnage pins her husband to the sofa and pummels him like a Fury.) For a few years, when Reza was in her twenties, she did "all kinds of parts, from Sacha Guitry to Arrabal, and quite a few that were avant-garde—my physique is modern." But she thought that she wasn't beautiful enough, or beautiful in the right way, for the leading roles that she aspired to. (She is beautiful in an exotic way, small and waifish, with dark hair that frames sensuous features—the face of a houri.) "So I had to find something else," she said. "Acting, finally, is a disastrous profession. You are at the mercy of others, and you spend your life waiting, which is intolerable to me. I am very impatient." She has described time as a "curse," "Hell," and as an enemy "I can't bow to."

Reza did not have to wait long for fame; she was thirty-five when *Art* had its première. But the scope of her success brought her a notoriety that was, she said, "destabilizing, and even devastating. You can't pretend to not give a damn, but you have to try to forget about it. In order to regain my balance, I turned down all the offers and invitations that poured in and spent my time with real friends who don't give a shit about my celebrity. I wrote *The Unexpected Man* and *Hammerklavier*"—a memoir of fragments in a terse, dreamy present tense. "And I went off to the seaside with my daughter"—Reza has two children—"for three weeks, where I wrote a key section of *Desolation*," her first novel. "They satisfied the need to create something intimate, and to repossess myself. By then, I was forty, and I felt free again."

Desolation is an eloquent howl at the grotesque fatuity of a tame life, and a work of exceptional virtuosity. In a novella-length monologue delivered with a murderous glee, Samuel Perlman, a retired clothier, addresses his absent son, a thirty-eight-year-old beachcomber whom, his wife tells him, he has "crushed." When his daughter reports that her brother is, finally, "happy," Perlman unleashes a diatribe about all the therapeutic clichés with which people who aspire to be civilized console themselves for having compromised their vital obsessions. Mellowness, tolerance, self-acceptance—they are, in his view, "the peace of dead souls." As Perlman takes stock of his losses—of the few friends who nobly "embraced frivolity"; of the mistress who, despite being a "complete nothing," had a genius for abandon; of the wife who charmed him until she began "neglecting futility"; of the children whose laughter had once been free and defiant—he recognizes that he, too, has been "tragically humanized."

Reza's fiction is the deep end of her talent—a reservoir of buoyant anguish and pessimism. The protagonist of *Adam Haberberg* (2003), her next novel, is an obscure writer sitting on a bench in the Jardin des Plantes, feeling the first chill of mortality, who realizes that he can no longer bear to be Adam Haberberg. The central character in *Dans la Luge d'Arthur Schopenhauer* (2005), Ariel Chipman, is a suicidally depressed academic who has sacrificed real living to an idea of what his life should be. (The three other characters are his long-suffering wife, Nadine; an ex-colleague whom he despises; and a psychiatrist.) *Luge* was staged in 2006, with Reza playing Nadine. She tells the psychiatrist, "You're going to say, but I don't care, that I'm arrogant to think I've done well by keeping my distance from these so-called brainiacs who have ruled my husband's life, for his whole life my husband has been crazy about these so-called brainiacs who desert him at the crucial moment . . . to a terrible solitude." Reza was accused of sharing Nadine's contempt for intellect (Louis Althusser and Gilles Deleuze are also mentioned in passing; the former, it is noted, strangled his wife, and the latter jumped out a window)—a version of the charge leveled at *Art*. But Reza told an interviewer, "There is nothing useless about philosophy. On the contrary, I would like philosophy to recover its original function: as an art of living." Spinoza's theory that "one should put aside hope, and concentrate on joy" is, she believes, admirable in principle, but all theory "has to be confronted by lived experience." (If her work had a house philosopher, it would probably be Thomas Hobbes.)

I was introduced to Reza in New York, late in December, at a reading at the Strand Bookstore. "The first thing I noticed about you was your trousers," she said. "I thought they were something that I might wear." Reza, the connoisseur of frivolity, finds fashion interesting, knows what suits her (a trim little skirt, high heels), and makes it a uniform. Her literary persona has a whiff of machismo that is at odds with the intensely feminine woman, a bit uncertain despite her bravado, that she seems in person. There are not many women writers whose work, like Reza's, is a theater of cruelty—though it's a festive cruelty, like the bullfight. "The actress is the female part of me, and as a female I am an idiot, archaic, a slave of instinct who can't exercise her intelligence," she says wryly. "I write as a man." The archaic woman finds questions about her date of birth impertinent, but Reza will turn fifty on May 1. I asked her if age hadn't cured her of some of her idiocy, and she laughed. "The only wisdom I've acquired is how not to be too wise."

Our conversation continued a couple of weeks later in Paris. I arrived on a mild, overcast Sunday in the middle of the couture shows, and the Rue Saint-Honoré was mobbed with Americans stimulating the French economy. Reza had invited me for tea, and to shake my jet lag I walked through the Tuileries, crossed the river, and meandered around Saint-Germain. Half the magazines at the news kiosks seemed to have a radiant Carla Bruni—Sarkozy's new wife—on the cover. I thought about the passages on love in *Dawn, Dusk or Night*. Reza had marveled at the inanity of a sentence in Sarkozy's autobiography: "Today, Cécilia and I are back together for good, for real, no doubt, forever." Another day, he had said, "Love is the only thing that counts." Returning from a trip, he had confided, "I can only love a landscape if I'm in it with someone I love." "A vain formula," Reza wrote, "like all those in which he brandishes the banner of love." At least once, though—at his most endearing—she lets him catch her in flagrante with a romantic platitude:

> Flying to Toulouse.
> I say I still love the men I have loved.
> He shrugs as if I had uttered something incredibly stupid.
> —Yes, I assure you. I have never stopped loving the men I've loved.
> —Oh, please!
> —I still love them, but differently.
> —It's all in the "differently," my pretty one. Don't take me for a moron. Once you qualify love, it ceases to exist.

The author of *Art* could afford the grandeur of a private house, or an aerie on the Seine, but she lives in a writerly apartment in an old building in a Left Bank cul-de-sac. A narrow dining room with a marble fireplace adjoins a big, square salon. Shelves lining a long wall are filled with art books and a few small heirlooms. There are two dark paintings on varnished wood that look antique but were done by Reza's best friend, Moïra Paras, a Romanian artist who is, Reza says, her severest and most trusted critic. "We are opposites in almost every respect, but very alike," she told me. Moïra, she writes in *Hammerklavier*, "couldn't care less how the rest of the world sees her."

Reza does her writing in an office, but she checks her e-mail at an old rolltop in a corner of the dining room. A mass of papers and purple tulip petals from a disheveled bouquet littered the dining table. (Two vases of tulips figure in *God of Carnage*. They are part of the drama. Reza's stage directions sternly forbid superfluous props or detail. They invariably read, "No realism," "The barest decor possible," "Maximal abstraction.") We settled in the salon, on two deep white sofas covered with tribal rugs. An untidy stack of classical sheet music sat on top of an upright piano that Reza had bought with her first royalties—she is a passionate amateur musician—and under an etching of Beethoven. French doors opened onto a little balcony whose potted orange trees were shrouded for winter. The balcony overlooked an unkempt but charming park, with a crumbling stone wall at one end, where an old woman was feeding birds, and a playground at the other. It was almost empty at that hour, but a few children were making the noise of a dozen.

Reza's own children—her daughter, Alta, a twenty-year-old law student, and her sixteen-year-old son, Nathan—were both at home. Reza had made Sunday lunch for them, and their father, Didier Martiny, a filmmaker, had come over to help Nathan with his homework. Martiny was Reza's companion for twenty-three years. They met in college, and he has directed three films from her screenplays. They never married (there are no happy marriages in Reza's work— "Conjugal life," Nadine says in *Luge*, "kills everybody"), and they separated years ago but remain close friends. Nathan is learning Spanish, he told me, and Reza is relearning it. This spring, she will direct her first film, which is partly set in Málaga. It is the story of three

sisters—one a movie star, one a housewife, one a struggling actress—
and of their widowed mother, a Spanish hairdresser who, improbably,
has become engaged to a younger man, her building manager. Em-
manuelle Seignier plays the movie star. The story is drawn from an
episode in *A Spanish Play* (2004), a drama about the profession of acting that is more self-consciously literary than most of Reza's playwrit-
ing. (In 2007, *A Spanish Play* had a brief Off Broadway run, in a
production directed by John Turturro.)

Reza's protagonists tend to be dangerously wounded middle-aged
or old men, like Samuel Perlman and Adam Haberberg. (A mature,
infuriated bull makes a compelling menace on the stage, to himself
and to others.) Her film will focus on women—"on their failed dreams
and their solitude." The character of the hairdresser is inspired by
Reza's mother, Nora. "It has taken me a lot of time, maturity, and
daring to examine our relationship," she said.

Nora Reza is a former violinist who abruptly ceased to play when
she had children. (Yasmina never heard a note.) She was born in Hun-
gary, and immigrated to France in 1950. On a trip to Budapest with
Yasmina in 1997, she pointed out the elegant building on Vörösmarty
Square where her family had lived on an entire floor. Her father was a
rich wool merchant, and Nora went to school with the children of
"the Jewish aristocracy." Of all the girls, she told Reza, she was the
prettiest. For several days, mother and daughter wandered through
the city, and Nora, Reza wrote in *Hammerklavier*, reminisced "about
her resplendent past without emotion, without apparent regret." But
she never lost her Hungarian accent: "My father must have liked it."

Reza's father, Elias, was a Russian Jew of Iranian nationality whose
parents came from Samarkand. As a way to deflect anti-Semitism, his
ancestors, when they were living in Persia, had changed their name,
Gedalea, to Reza, a common Persian patronym. Fleeing the Bolsheviks, the family arrived in France sometime in the 1920s. Elias earned
an engineering degree but later went into the import business. He was
interned at Drancy, the camp from which French Jews were shipped
east for extermination, but his name and his Iranian passport, Reza
said, saved his life. She is the eldest of her siblings; she has a brother

who is a film producer and a sister who is a psychotherapist. Yasmina is actually Reza's middle name. "I won't tell you what my parents called me," she said. "It's too absurd, and very French." When she was seventeen, she embraced the sense of foreignness and singularity that she has always felt, by becoming Yasmina Reza.

Neither of her parents mentioned their experiences living under the Nazis ("The past is very vague in our family"), and Elias became observant only in old age. But one evening, after the Six-Day War, in 1967 (Reza was eight), her father suddenly "introduced the word 'Jew' into the house in an uncompromising, mythical way," which is how she still uses it. She will often pause to reflect that a trait she is describing in herself or a character is "typically Jewish." Her grandparents' escape route from Russia to France was "a typical Jewish circuit." Her sense of humor is a "typically Jewish distancing device that laughs at catastrophe." "Jews don't have much affinity for modesty," she writes in *Dawn, Dusk or Night*. (Sarkozy's maternal grandfather was a Greek Jew, and his father was Hungarian; those points of ethnic kinship with Reza have been widely noted.) Perhaps her most constant refrain touches upon her "Jewish anguish about assimilation"—a feeling that she has no roots, no native soil, no sense of place, no nostalgia for one. Even to establish the bare facts of her life in a conversation, like the one we were having, stirs her fear of captivity. "I am not what I say about myself," she warned me later. "Writers inevitably return to their childhoods," she remarks in *Nulle Part* (Nowhere), an autobiography composed in 2005 from vivid shards of memory and sensation. But a skittish name changer who comes from nowhere "has nowhere to return to."

Any place, however, can be nowhere if, like Reza, you grew up, as she put it, "estranged from reality." Her childhood home was a middle-class apartment in the suburb of Saint-Cloud. (She has admitted to giving journalists the impression that her background was much grander—"gilded youth, travels, cosmopolitanism, etc.") Her father, she said, worked day and night, and her mother's beauty was a similarly full-time vocation. (Reza was afraid that Nora would recognize herself in a passage of complacent prattle by the mother in *A Spanish Play*, "but luckily she didn't.") "It was a terrible childhood," Reza said lightly, as if she were saying "a terrible haircut." "My parents were too busy doing other things to bring up their children." The most poignant sentence in *Nulle Part* evokes a memory of being lost as a little girl: "In this public park where my parents showed up to look for me—they who never looked for me anywhere—I ran toward them with so much joy that its lack of all proportion was a chagrin."

Reza's father was a self-made man with a reverence for French culture who recited Paul Valéry to his children. Like his daughter, he was a passionate amateur pianist, always furious at his own mediocrity. "At the piano, we are rivals," she writes in *Hammerklavier*, where she also recounts a dream in which her father comes back from the dead to tell her that he has met Beethoven, who scolds him for presuming to imagine that he could ever play the Adagio from Opus 106. When Elias was dying of cancer, she writes, he did in fact massacre that movement, which he and Reza both loved. (He sits at the keyboard in his nightshirt, and "the waning light lays bare all the evidence of decay." Reza's reaction is to laugh uncontrollably at the catastrophe.) Yet for all his refinement and his intelligence, and for all her ironic tenderness in his regard, Elias, she said, was a brutal man who "didn't know how to be a father. Yet his brutality wasn't malicious. He was violent but loving. And I understood from our relations that human beings can't be reduced. Without that revelation, I couldn't have become a writer."

If you read Reza closely, you realize that she almost never uses the past tense. There are also certain words that recur like an incantation both in her writing and in her speech. In *Desolation*, she is everywhere at pains to distinguish "joy" from "happiness," and to exalt "frivolity" as an art of living but also as a form of unrepentant fatalism. *Devenir*, "to become"—in Reza's sense, to become oneself—is ubiquitous. "To keep becoming is the obsession of everyone to whom I have given a name and voice," she writes in the Sarkozy book. And then there are the nouns "*chagrin*" and "*fêlure*." "*Chagrin*" can mean pain, grief, or suffering. A *fêlure* can be the crack in a hard surface—Flaubert describes human speech as a "cracked iron kettle." But Colette uses "*fêlure*" as an essential rift in her being. It is the split between a male and a female seeking reunion in the act of love, and between a parent and a child who have lost their primal connection. I suspect it has that meaning for Reza.

I had hoped to meet with Reza once more, in New York, at a preview performance of *God of Carnage*, but she e-mailed to say that, with her film starting to shoot in a few days, she was too anxious and tired to come. "I would ideally love to make a film the way I write," she had told me, "fast, no script, improvising as I go along, not thinking too much. *Art* was written in six weeks. But I need more experience."

On one of my last days in Paris, we drove to the muddy countryside with Reza's art director and her assistant to scout locations, and tramped through several dilapidated châteaux. They were looking for a winding staircase with wooden risers and light from above; an old-fashioned bedchamber with a single window to the right of a long wall that was big enough for a piano; and a quality of soulful gloominess. Reza's decisions—"yes," "no," never "maybe"—seemed to come, like her prose, from a well of mysterious assurance. "I know just what I want," she said, "but the minute I've answered a question I feel like changing my mind."

MARCH 2009

I f you had an hour in a hotel suite, alone with Charlotte Rampling, to talk about sex, what would you ask her? For forty years, the British actress, whose name has become a verb ("to rample"—ensorcell with an enigmatic gaze) and the title of a rock song by Kinky Machine ("I always wanted to be your trampoline," they sing to her), has specialized in fatally obsessed, perverse, smoldering, reckless, and unmoored women. She has played the survivor of a concentration camp who engages in sadomasochistic sex with her former torturer, in *The Night Porter*; a waifish "basket case," in *Stardust Memories*; and a widow in pathological denial of her husband's death—a probable suicide—in *Under the Sand*. "I generally don't make films to entertain people," Rampling said. "I choose the parts that challenge me to break through my own barriers. A need to devour, punish, humiliate, or surrender seems to be a primal part of human nature, and it's certainly a big part of sex. To discover what normal means, you have to surf a tide of weirdness."

Rampling, who has lived in France since the early seventies and has become, in essence, a French movie star, was in New York to promote her latest film, *Heading South*, directed by Laurent Cantet. In it, she plays Ellen, a brittle, sardonic fifty-five-year-old spinster (Rampling herself is sixty) who teaches French literature at Wellesley, and spends long summer vacations at a Haitian resort shacking up with a beautiful local beach boy named Legba. It is a story about sexual tourism—Legba is a gigolo—set under the squalid regime of Baby Doc Duvalier, and the hotel is a swingers' club, of sorts, for well-heeled white women. Ellen is their "queen bee," a gossip and a manipulator who pretends serenely that it costs her nothing to share Legba's favors with a harem. "None of the deeply disturbing characters I've played were as unnatural to me as this one," Rampling said. "I find it infuriating that a beautiful, smart woman like Ellen is—at any age—so invisible to the men of her own world that she has to pay."

Rampling was having a wraith's breakfast—an espresso and a glass of water—when she answered the door, without makeup or a minder, primly dressed in a white shirt, black trousers, and flats. Age has softened the feline planes of her face, though there is nothing slack about her self-possession. The patrician reserve that serves as a foil for her carnal rapacity in so many roles is a legacy of her upbringing—her father was a British colonel and an Olympic athlete (he won a gold medal in swimming), and her mother was an heiress—although Rampling's personal life has been anything but unperturbed. She suffered, for decades, from the burden of keeping her sister's suicide a secret from their mother; from a breakdown, in the late 1980s; from a long period of clinical depression; and from the shock of her second husband's betrayal after a marriage of twenty years (she discovered his infidelity with a younger woman in the French tabloids). A new companion, ten years her junior, and critical praise for the films of her middle age helped to restore her equilibrium.

Heading South seems to an American like a quintessentially French conceit about colonial predation with the conventional gender roles reversed, though Rampling disagrees. "The women involved are almost all Anglo-Saxons who go south looking for young Black or Hispanic men, and it's a huge industry," she said. "The French don't indulge in those kinds of desert-island fantasies"—an assertion that might come as a surprise to the clientele of Club Med. "A vast generation gap between lovers is hardly unheard of in France, but their intimacy is more complex. Watching Jeanne Moreau play the old Duras in *Cet Amour-Là*, for example, you understand the mutual fascination of a mature woman and a much younger man: she is attracted to his devotion, he to her deep wisdom.

"Age teaches you to accept that you can't share your erotic wisdom," Rampling said. "But on the screen you can open a door to the games and secrets that we hide from each other. Then we're not all so alone."

JULY 2006

THE CLEOPATRIAD

A ccording to *The Onion*, a group of "leading historians" has announced that the culture of ancient Greece was "entirely fabricated" between 1971 and 1974 by a team of scholars working "nonstop" to forge the relevant evidence. "We just started making things up," a spokesman explained at a recent news conference—"Homer, Aristotle, Socrates, Hippocrates, the lever and fulcrum, rhetoric, ethics, all the different kinds of columns, everything." (Euclidean geometry, for example, is actually the work of a grad student named Kevin.) The group did not claim credit for the biography of Cleopatra—a product of Greek civilization, like all the Ptolemaic pharaohs—although perhaps it should have. Legions of others have conjured her from a void.

Cleopatra VII, a living deity to her subjects, was the second of five or six children in a murderous royal family that ruled the richest country in the Middle East. Her older sister, Berenike IV, had seized the throne while their father, Ptolemy XII, nicknamed Auletes ("the flute-player"—an allusion to licentious tastes), was away in Rome, mortgaging his kingdom for military aid. Pompey the Great propped up his regime, and on his return Auletes got rid of Berenike and her second husband—she had already killed her first.

In 51 B.C., when Cleopatra was eighteen, she inherited the crown jointly with a younger brother, Ptolemy XIII, and, in accordance with dynastic custom, they were married. The boy king was not yet old enough for conjugal relations, but his counselors conspired to seize sole power on his behalf. Cleopatra went into exile, and late in 48 B.C., while she was abroad, rallying her partisans and raising an army, Julius Caesar arrived in Alexandria, flush with victory over Pompey in Rome's civil war. Caesar had a strategic interest in Egypt's wealth and stability, but no personal investment in which of two quarrelsome siblings sat on the throne. To win his confidence, Cleopatra needed to act boldly. She stole back into Alexandria under cover of darkness and smuggled herself into Caesar's quarters in her own palace (though probably not rolled up in a carpet). However she finagled her nocturnal job interview, she seems to have aced it. The next morning, her brother, learning that he had been outplayed, dashed into the streets and nearly persuaded a mob to rise against the usurpers. Caesar's Praetorians dragged him back inside, but his handlers rallied their forces.

In the ensuing war against Caesar and Cleopatra, which the world's greatest general nearly lost (until reinforcements arrived, he was severely short-handed), Ptolemy drowned. The victors celebrated with a leisurely Nile cruise, a visit to the pyramids, and some whistle-stopping in the heartland. This public honeymoon demonstrated an inspired gift for mixing business with pleasure, and both with stagecraft, which Cleopatra would perfect by the time she met Mark Antony. Perhaps somewhere on the sacred river, she conceived her first child. The birth of Caesarion ("little Caesar") consolidated her bonds with his father, and with her own people and their priests, who rejoiced at a male heir.

With a son as her symbolic co-regent and Caesar as her protector, Cleopatra had no need to remarry. She henceforth governed alone—uniquely so among female monarchs of the period. Her autonomy depended on the fickle goodwill of Rome, and her exchange of favors with two Roman leaders has defined her for posterity. But accounts of her sexual politicking are maddeningly one-sided. If she employed a court historian, his chronicles have been lost; so has her correspondence. Her palace compound in Alexandria, which contained the greatest library of the ancient world (including, perhaps, medical texts she is said, in the Talmud, to have written), was swept away by a tsunami in the fourth century. The lascivious fury who corrupted Caesar and unmanned Antony was largely an invention of the man who vanquished her—Octavian, the future Augustus—and his apologists.

Among the writers who actually met Cleopatra, Cicero said of her, "I detest the queen"; Nicolaus of Damascus, her children's tutor, defected to her archrival, Herod, and then to Octavian. Of first-century writers, Josephus, a Jewish historian writing for a Roman audience, based his account on Nicolaus's; Plutarch, Antony's biographer, had access to some firsthand testimony, but admitted to cherry-picking. Lucan is the most fun to read. He concentrates on the queen's barbarian splendor and depravity, but can one take the word of Nero's protégé? Suetonius and Appian, historians of the second century, and prolific Dio, of the third, have been flagged for complacency in their errors and biases. Theirs and many other ancient texts exist only in fragments. What survives of them, two thousand years after Cleopatra's death, is still the primary source for biographers.

Perhaps the tomb where Antony and Cleopatra were buried together by Octavian (a suspiciously tender mercy from a pitiless foe) will one day be discovered and will yield a jewel that graced her ear, her handwriting on onyx tablets, a death mask—some intimate remains. Franck Goddio, a French marine archaeologist, has been trolling for that tomb for eighteen years off the coast of Alexandria, and Zahi Hawass, an Egyptian archaeologist, has been digging for it since 2005 at Taposiris Magna, the site of an ancient shrine to Osiris, some thirty miles from Cleopatra's capital. Their grail is elusive, but a trove of the artifacts they have recovered is part of a new show, *The Search for the Last Queen of Egypt*, at the Franklin Institute in Philadelphia. The pièce de résistance is the figure of a headless woman so eloquently chiseled that her flesh seems to breathe. Petite, voluptuous, and nude beneath sheer draperies knotted between her breasts, she wears the costume of Isis. The figure is too old, by several hundred years, to represent Cleopatra, though after the queen gave birth to Caesarion she began to style herself as a New Isis. Dressed in raiment like the statue's, she appeared to her subjects at religious festivals—a fertility goddess incarnate. Sailors carved Isis on their prows and spread her cult to Greece, Rome, Persia, North Africa, Asia Minor, and Iberia; it even reached Germany and Britain before dying out about four hundred years into the Christian era. But her avatar lives on, an inexhaustible source of fascination about the first and greatest mystery to man: the sexual power of woman.

For the most part, however, the Franklin show promises occult revelations—secrets from the crypt—that it can't deliver. Instead, music from the deep (a soundtrack of harps and violins) plays in the dark galleries. A video projection shows Cleopatra's courtiers reveling in a hot tub. Museumgoers with impatient toddlers can bypass the coins from Cleopatra's mints, which don't agree about her profile, and go straight to the film clips. (In those, at least, the image of the queen is fairly consistent, from Theda Bara to Liz Taylor: a black wig, snake arm bracelets, lurid eye makeup, lots of bosom, and a smoldering glance.) In a triumph of inanity, the wall notes dwell on the queen's beauty while conceding that no one knows what she really looked like.

Just after the show opened, it was announced that the producer Scott Rudin expects to cast Angelina Jolie as Cleopatra in a 3-D biopic, possibly to be directed by James Cameron. (A rock musical starring Catherine Zeta-Jones and directed by Steven Soderbergh is also in development.) Jolie's casting sparked a new round of the old debate about the queen's DNA. It is widely accepted that she was ethnically Greek; the pharaohs of her house were caste-proud Macedonians ("Cleopatra" is Greek for "glory of her race"). They descended from Ptolemy I, a general who had served with Alexander the Great in his conquest of Egypt, and they had practiced sibling incest for some three hundred years by the time their last dynast was born. Inbreeding had consolidated their power, but also, one presumes, their traits. They tended to be fleshy, if not obese, with prominent cheekbones and hawkish noses. Effete men and ferocious women recur in their genealogy; several able, autocratic queens had set a precedent for Cleopatra. But her grandmother may have been a concubine, and the identity of her mother—presumed to be Auletes's full sister, but perhaps an

Egyptian of the native aristocracy—is disputed. An editorial in *Essence* protested that Jolie was stealing a role that should rightfully go "to a Black woman," while a chorus of bloggers argued for Snooki.

Rudin's film is based on the exceptionally artful new biography *Cleopatra*, by Stacy Schiff, which joins two other worthwhile lives of the queen published in the past few months, by Duane Roller and by Adrian Goldsworthy. Reading them side by side is an experience that proves the justice of Shakespeare's tribute: "Other women cloy / The appetites they feed, but she makes hungry / Where most she satisfies." Roller's *Cleopatra*, part of a series of brief lives, Women in Antiquity, gives a rich account of late Ptolemaic culture, and surveys the queen's history—without any "post-antique material," but with a nimble use of "she may have" and "presumably"—in fewer than two hundred pages. The author is a professor emeritus of Greek and Latin at Ohio State University, so he had access to the ancient sources in their original languages, as well as to the scholarly literature in German and French. His voice is donnish and impartial, albeit a bit flat, like the daylight in his black-and-white photographs of modern Tarsus and Jericho, and his assertion that one really can't hope to know Cleopatra. This volume should appeal to readers who prefer an aerial view of the subject to the seething congestion of its ring roads.

Goldsworthy is a distinguished biographer of Julius Caesar, and his somewhat mistitled entrant to the lists, *Antony and Cleopatra*, is a four-hundred-page work of Roman military and political history. The density of detail about plots and battles often overwhelms the narrative, yet it reproduces the claustrophobia of a brutal culture dependent on slavery and enslaved to ambition. The prose itself has a martial rhythm. Goldsworthy covers his bloody terrain with the brusque authority of a centurion, demolishing myths and smashing idols. Bluff, bibulous, depressive Antony doesn't impress him. Women may have adored Antony, as did his troops, but "he was not an especially good general." His family claimed descent from Hercules, and he cultivated the resemblance, but the virility of his appearance—chiseled features, bullish neck, a tunic rakishly girded up to show off well-muscled legs—belied the weakness of his character: "There is no real trace of any long-held beliefs or causes on Antony's part" beyond "glory and profit."

In his attitude to Cleopatra, Goldsworthy seems to take his cue from Caesar. The august conqueror, he writes, "would have wanted to bed" this nubile supplicant who owed her throne to his idol, Alexander. The age difference, perhaps, was piquant to both of them. She was twenty-one, and almost certainly a virgin; he was fifty-two, and an expert seducer noted for his taste in spirited women. (He made a specialty of queens.) But Caesar barely mentions Cleopatra in his account of the Alexandrine Wars, and she is likewise offstage for long stretches in Goldsworthy's saga, as the men who matter duke it out. "Whether we like it or not, Cleopatra was not really that important," he writes. She "only became queen because her father was placed back in power by a Roman army. Even after that, she would have been dead or exiled by her early twenties were it not for Caesar's intervention."

Whether we like it or not, biographers bring their experience as men or women to their task. Roller and Goldsworthy both seem determined to resist the temptations of a siren, as if she might corrupt their integrity. Schiff relies on the same venerable Cleophobes and exercises the same caution about them. She takes her epigraph from Euripides: "Man's most valuable trait is a judicious sense of what not to believe." Imaginative attunement with a subject, however, does not have to compromise a vigilant biographer's critical detachment, and Schiff's beautiful writing hums with that tension. This is her fourth ambitious life (her second, of Véra Nabokov, won a Pulitzer Prize). It is an edifice of speculation and conjecture—like every "Cleopatra" ever written. But unlike nearly all of them it is a work of literature.

The great queens of history, Simone de Beauvoir writes in *The Second Sex*, "were neither male nor female: they were sovereigns." That paradox expresses Beauvoir's view, in 1946, of the inequality between a male subject with an identity of his own creation and a female object defined by her relation to men. There is no evidence that Cleopatra felt the slightest sense of inferiority—singularity was her privilege. Yet the coin of her legend has two faces: a subject on one side, an object on the other. In Egypt she commanded armies, conducted foreign policy as an equal with male heads of state, treated the treasury as her private bank account, and administered a bureaucracy that has been compared with Soviet Russia's. Deference was her due, and she exacted it from coffers and flesh. Ruthlessness was her birthright. After Caesar routed Ptolemy XIII, he united her with the next little brother in line for a short life and an unconsummated marriage, Ptolemy XIV; she is said to have poisoned him shortly after Caesarion was born. She also rid herself of a troublesome sister, Arsinoë, who had tried to dethrone her. A teenaged Arsinoë, in golden shackles, aroused the pity of the Romans when Caesar paraded her in his triumph after the Alexandrine Wars. Her life was spared, and she was sent into exile at the Temple of Artemis in Ephesus, where for years she nursed dreams of revenge. Cleopatra eventually persuaded Antony that her last living sibling was one too many. He ordered his men to drag Arsinoë from the shrine and put her to death. It seems fitting that, of all the words the queen must have written on matters of love and state, the only one to survive, "*Ginesthoi*" (found on a scrap of papyrus used to line a mummy case), is the Greek imperative "Let it be done."

In Rome, however, Cleopatra was Caesar's mistress, a scarlet woman who made fashion news: her "melon" hairdo (rows of tight braids gathered into a low bun) launched a new craze. The Romans were used to exotic queens, but certainly not to "the queen himself"— Cleopatra's epithet on a temple stele. There were no hybrid deities in the Roman pantheon, and even common-born Egyptian women were regarded as alien creatures with phallic attributes—Herodotus had claimed that they urinated standing up. They did, however, have the right to do other business—to work, own property, and seek divorce— with a freedom that was scandalous to a culture so patriarchal that every daughter in a Roman family was named for one of its males (Caesar's two sisters, for example, were both called Julia).

The strangeness was mutual. When the queen of Egypt arrived for an extended visit in 46 B.C., with a large entourage, Caesar put her up at his villa in the suburbs. Compared with gorgeous, cosmopolitan

Alexandria, the filthy, ramshackle city of a million people that the queen saw from her perch in the hills "qualified as a provincial backwater," Schiff writes. "Disdain," she observes, "is a natural condition of the mind in exile," and it came naturally to Cleopatra. So did flamboyance. But even if she had tried to temper it she would have been a somewhat lurid curiosity.

Cicero may have spoken for his fellow citizens when he deplored the queen's "insolence." It especially rankled him that she had reneged on (or forgotten) a promise to send him a book from her library. Yet their conversations, he told a friend, were "of a literary kind, not unbecoming to my position—I shouldn't mind telling them to a public meeting." One infers from this grudging compliment that Rome's greatest orator had, despite himself, been impressed with a young woman, some forty years his junior, who could hold her own with him on lofty subjects.

Schiff extrapolates what evidence she can for Cleopatra's princely education—her mastery of rhetoric, study of science, knowledge of the classics, and genius as a linguist. According to Plutarch, she was the only Ptolemy to have learned Egyptian, in addition to seven other Middle Eastern languages, including Hebrew, in which she was fluent. He is equivocal about her beauty, but the music of her voice, the charm of her speech, her arts of persuasion, a beguiling intellect, the power to disarm whomever she chose made her, he concludes, "irresistible."

As for Caesar, Dio claims that he was indifferent to the jealous tattle. He was, of course, married (how many women since Calpurnia have had to listen to an unfaithful husband remind them that "Caesar's wife must be above suspicion"?), and, presumably, he slept at his official residence in town, or pretended to. His son, a toddler, looked just like him, and he recognized his paternity, though not officially. But the soon-to-be dictator for life (he received the title in February 44 B.C.) acknowledged the enlightening influence of his sojourn with Cleopatra in a series of reforms. "He laid the foundations for a public library," Schiff writes. The Nile waterworks inspired him to drain marshes and build dikes. He commissioned a census. (The Alexandrians were obsessive bookkeepers.) He admired the rationality of the Egyptian calendar, which divided the year into twelve equal months, with a five-day coda, and adopted it. His most personal and, in hindsight, reckless gesture of homage was to install a life-size golden statue of Cleopatra/Isis in the temple of his family forum, next to the statue of Venus Genetrix, from whom the Julian clan claimed descent. But, in exalting Cleopatra, an infatuated Caesar also put her in her place—forever, it turns out—as a love goddess.

The quarrel between the ancients and the moderns in the field of Cleopatra studies is, in essence, a face-off between misogyny and feminism, though both sides have sympathies and ideals alien to their subject. (The villainess and the heroine are also two sides of her coin.) Even Schiff, the worldliest of Cleophiles, is, in that respect, typical of the latter-day writers—women in particular—who tend to extoll the queen's virtues while downplaying her sexual opportunism. (Goldsworthy's skepticism is here a good corrective. Cleopatra's benevolence to her subjects, he believes, is "largely wishful thinking.") Schiff takes the view that the men who defamed Cleopatra as a strumpet were discomfited by her intellectual prowess. "In the same way it is easier to ascribe her power" over Caesar and Antony "to magic than to love. We have evidence of neither, but the first can at least be explained; with magic one forfeits rather than loses the game."

Cleopatra clearly aroused the same prurient fantasies in her day that she does in ours. (Herod, too, cast her as a "slave to her lusts." He claimed that she had tried to force herself upon him in the course of a state visit to Jerusalem in 36 B.C. Its purpose was to negotiate land and mineral rights, and when she cut a tough deal that made him look stupid he tried to use her alleged sexual harassment as an excuse to assassinate her.) But there was no shame from Cleopatra's perspective—that of a woman for whom nothing was taboo—in exploiting her effect on men, or, for that matter, in relishing it.

Caesar's murder on the Senate floor, by forty assassins, on March 15, 44 B.C., led to the civil war that ultimately destroyed the Republic. Antony and his fellow-triumvir Octavian, Caesar's posthumously adopted son, led the party of avengers that emerged victorious. They divided the world between them, with Octavian as the imperator of the West and Antony of the East. Cleopatra had hedged her bets, during the conflict, by helping Dolabella, an ally of the assassins, then sending a fleet to Octavian, which never reached him. There were few luxuries she couldn't afford, but acting on principles was one. The victors had cause to mistrust her.

By 41 B.C., Antony was ensconced at Tarsus in central Turkey, settling scores and gorging on adulation (much of it female). He sent his go-between, Quintus Dellius, to Alexandria, summoning his client monarch to explain herself. Dellius sounds, in Schiff's description, rather like a Roman Rosenkrantz: an obsequious courtier of "acrobatic loyalties" who today might have been a talent agent. That, in a sense, is the role he tried to play when he met Cleopatra. Whatever preconceptions he had arrived with, Schiff writes, "he quickly grasped that he would not be delivering up a sorry, subdued queen for arraignment." Either Dellius "melted in Cleopatra's hands, realized Antony would, or both." Urging the queen to come abroad with him posthaste, he coached her on what to pack: regal clothing, dazzling jewels, and heady oils for her body. She took notes, but dismissed him.

Perhaps Cleopatra's preconceptions about Antony also changed in the presence of a winking messenger who implied that his master was an easy mark. She, like any goddess, had no scruples about using her powers to assume a guise, and by now, at twenty-eight, her instincts for male vanity were exquisite. When she finally did stage her fabulously kitsch entrance at Tarsus, that summer, sailing down the Cydnus River in a gilded barge with purple sails, wreathed in incense and reclining on a divan attended by nymphs and cupids—"Venus was come to revel with Bacchus," she announced, "for the good of Asia"— Plutarch describes it as an act of mockery.

Cleopatra, Goldsworthy asserts, "only had importance in the wider world through her Roman lovers," but the seduction that assured her immortality was that of a Greek writer. Without Plutarch, there would probably be no Cleopatra industry. His *Life of Antony* was contemporary with another ancient biography based on scant evidence and hearsay: the Gospels. Its portrait of Cleopatra may have been col-

ored by the intemperate heroines of classical tragedy, and perhaps by
the Eve of Genesis. Yet, in the absence of certainty, one has to judge
what not to believe by the standards of literary justice, and the master manipulator who steals Plutarch's stage the minute she appears
on it, midway through the narrative, is vibrantly plausible in her
contradictions.

"It was difficult for anyone to come into contact with Ptolemaic
Egypt and not contract a case of extravagance," Schiff writes, and
Antony did. After Tarsus, he followed Cleopatra home, where she
kept him in style, indulged his laddish pranks, hunted and gambled
with him, cheered him at sports, and shared his binges. They reveled
as Venus and Bacchus, but they also went on rowdy slumming parties,
in the alleys of Alexandria, disguised as slaves. According to Plutarch,
the queen, her lover, and some congenial courtiers formed a secret
society—the Inimitable Livers—dedicated to hedonism, if not debauchery. (Cleopatra wore a ring engraved, perhaps mockingly, with
its motto: "*methe*"—intoxication.) She had, it would seem, two full-
time jobs: her kingdom and Antony.

After the long idyll that followed their summit at Tarsus, Antony
returned to Rome. He soldiered quite a bit, made a politic marriage to
Octavian's sister, Octavia, and fathered two daughters. Three years
passed. In 37 B.C., he made preparations for an expedition (funded by
Cleopatra) to conquer Parthia. When he failed ignobly on the battlefield, he behaved like a disgraced celebrity: he threatened suicide, succumbed to alcoholism and depression, mistreated a wife whom all
Rome loved for her beauty and virtue, and went back to his mistress.
If one believes Plutarch, Cleopatra used all her wiles to reclaim the
prodigal—especially touching is the detail that "she reduced her body
by slender diet"—though it proved to be a Pyrrhic victory.

Early in their liaison, Cleopatra gave birth to Antony's twins, a
boy and a girl, and later to a younger son. "Given the way she was
stockpiling successors," Schiff writes, she was "arguably doing more to
unite East and West than had anyone since Alexander." The children
were deified and invested with titles and kingdoms. Antony, who also
began appearing as a god, enlarged their mother's domain with vast

territorial bequests that restored Ptolemaic Egypt to its former glory. In Syria, Cleopatra minted coins with her profile on one side and her consort's on the other, in which they, too, look like twins. These grandiose gestures announced a dynastic union and, what was more provocative in Rome, an imperial strategy.

In 32 B.C., Antony sealed his fate by formally repudiating Octavia. Her brother pried his ex-in-law's will from the Vestal Virgins and read it to the Senate. It stipulated that he be buried with the queen. Antony had enjoyed great popularity, but he never returned to defend it against Octavian's machinations. Posterity would blame Cleopatra for her lover's abdication of his city, his party, and his senses when so much was at stake.

Once Octavian declared war on the "harlot queen" of Egypt, both sides made preparations for an epic confrontation at Actium, on the west coast of Greece. But the lovers dallied on their way north, staging a theater festival at Samos and neglecting their supply lines. Even modern accounts of the debacle hold Cleopatra at least partially responsible for their cavalier miscalculations, but this presumes that a lucid, unfettered Antony could have saved their cause by resisting her hubris. Goldsworthy's judgment of his blinkered venality seems, in the end, sounder than Plutarch's more doting view of a simple, big-hearted hero undone by an "evil" love. That hero panicked in the heat of battle and abandoned his men to follow Cleopatra's treasure-laden flagship when he saw her take flight. Then he withdrew into a state of petulant despair.

About four hundred years separate us from Shakespeare's lustful "gipsy" with the "immortal longings" that have been so well requited. About the same span of time separated Cleopatra from Euripides, Aeschylus, and Sophocles. As a supremely well-tutored Greek princess, she would have read their plays with a sense of kinship to the noble characters. She may have thought of them again when Octavian offered her a (false) promise of mercy in exchange for Antony's life. A Ptolemy's first loyalty was to survival, and it was simple enough to kill a trusting man who had loved her—she conned him with a message that announced her suicide, and he hastened to follow.

Until the end, on August 10, 30 B.C., Cleopatra believed that her gifts of eloquence could save her from Arsinoë's humiliation. But when she realized that Octavian was immune to them, and that he intended to parade her through the streets of Rome, she sat down to a splendid banquet. Afterward, having bathed and dressed, she called for her diadem. There may have been a delivery of figs and, buried in their basket, a tool of death, but even Plutarch doubts that the fangs of a serpent delivered the fatal poison. Years of experiments in toxicology had prepared her for an elegant demise. It spared her from the knowledge that Octavian would murder Caesarion, and that Octavia would adopt her orphans. The murder, at least, wouldn't have surprised her.

NOVEMBER 2010

SKIN DEEP

━━━∞∞∞━━━

On October 22, 1949, *The New Yorker* published a report by Lillian Ross on that year's Miss America Pageant. It begins,

> There are thirteen million women in the United States between the ages of eighteen and twenty-eight. All of them were eligible to compete for the title of Miss America in the annual contest staged in Atlantic City last month if they were high-school graduates, were not and had never been married, and were not Negroes.

Ross makes no further comment on the exclusion of more than a million young Black women from the pageant, although her allusion to them was provocative for its time. Until 1948, their fathers and brothers had been serving in a segregated military. It was five years before the Supreme Court, in deciding *Brown v. Board of Education of Topeka*, ended legal segregation in American schools. And while the Miss America Pageant abolished the ban on Black contestants in 1950, none would compete until 1970, and none would win until Vanessa Williams took the crown, in 1984.

Six years later, *People* magazine launched an annual issue devoted to "The World's Fifty Most Beautiful People." The most beautiful of the beautiful gets the cover. (There are currently about seven billion lovely and unlovely humans on the planet; *People*'s short list, however, is restricted to celebrities.) The honors for 2014 went to Lupita Nyong'o, who won an Oscar this year for her supporting role in *12 Years a Slave*. Nyong'o, thirty-one, was born in Mexico to Kenyan parents while her father, a college professor, was teaching there. They returned to Kenya when she was three, where they lived, she has said, a comfortable "suburban" life. She was educated in the United States at Hampshire College and at the Yale School of Drama. Her poise, like her chic, is striking, and her beauty is classically African. Two "most beautiful" stars of mixed African ethnicity, Halle Berry and Beyoncé, preceded Nyong'o, in 2003 and 2012, respectively. They are both notably lighter-skinned.

There is nothing critical to say about Nyong'o's new title except, perhaps, that it should seem so radically newsworthy. It is nearly fifty years since Malcolm X published his autobiography, in which he describes the mortifications that Black people endured "to look pretty by white standards." For Black soldiers, those standards still have the power to oppress. They are currently contesting the Pentagon's new rules for "appropriate" grooming, rules, they object, that would force them to straighten their naturally wooly locks, and which limit braiding—a tradition with deep cultural symbolism in Africa and its diaspora. (Braids, ironically, are emblems of valor.) In an article for *The New Yorker* on the Black hairdressing industry, I wrote about Malcolm's efforts, as a young man, to "dekink" his hair with homemade "congolene": half a can of Red Devil lye mixed with two sliced white potatoes and two well-beaten raw eggs, then worked through the scalp. This excruciating procedure gave him a head of "shining red hair . . . as straight as any white man's." And here, perhaps, it is worth noting that, since 1985, only one Black man, Denzel Washington, has won another of *People*'s celebrity beauty contests—for "The Sexiest Man Alive."

Unlike Beyoncé's hair, which was blond on her *People* cover, or Halle Berry's hair, worn in a feather cut, Nyong'o's short do looks unprocessed. But a hairstyle is hardly the issue. Women with strong African features and jet-black skin are, even today, with a Black family in the White House, scarce in the pages of mainstream fashion magazines, or as sponsors of upscale beauty products. (Nyong'o has recently been signed as the "face" of Lancôme cosmetics.) The super-model Alek Wek, a member of the Dinka ethnic group, who was born in what is now South Sudan and fled to Britain as a refugee from her country's civil wars, was one of the first, and is still an exception.

Nyong'o has cited Wek as an inspiration. Growing up, she said, she "dreamed" of having light skin; Wek, who has skin the color of polished obsidian, was the first mirror in which she could see her own beauty. Oprah Winfrey has noted that if Wek had appeared on the cover of a magazine when she was a girl, "I would have had a different concept of who I was." But, around the world, Nyong'o's selection has generated an outpouring of praise and gratitude, especially from younger women of color, for the "validation" it represents—a validation tainted by its rarity.

Agunda Okeyo, writing on Salon.com, raised another objection to Nyong'o's apotheosis. She writes, "Media outlets from the Daily Mail to Forbes to the Hollywood Reporter have described Nyong'o with one particular word: 'exotic.' This is basically a coded way of saying she is beautiful despite being black *and* dark-skinned." Nyong'o, she argues, is no more exotic than Meryl Streep, a Yale alumna who had a similarly middle-class upbringing.

But the epithet "exotic beauty" has been used for centuries to characterize almost any colonial woman whose allure is heightened by her otherness. She has taken the form, real or fictional, of Salome, Cleopatra, a geisha, a Creole, a Jewess, an odalisque, an Arab dancing girl. She wears a sari or an *ao bai*. She refills her Western lover's opium pipe and inspires his art. The phrase is redolent of an alien hypersexuality, and it doubly objectifies the woman it describes: as a fetish and as a primitive. (Patsey, Nyong'o's character in *12 Years a Slave*, is raped repeatedly by a brutal master who fancies himself in love with her.)

Unlike most Miss Americas, Nyong'o has shown exemplary dignity and a certain reticence in interviews about the *People* hoopla: she refuses to gush. She has also not mentioned a recent image of her role model Alek Wek, now thirty-seven, and a human-rights activist, who has lived in the West since she was fourteen. Last October, Wek was featured on the cover of *Forbes Life Africa* magazine wearing nothing (visible) but a thick golden collar that resembles the rigid neck-stretching rings of tribes in Burma and South Africa. The tribes would seem to have little in common, except, perhaps, that their maidens and matrons, like billions of women everywhere, suffer to be thought beautiful.

MAY 2014

REGIME CHANGE

—∞∞∞—

The news that Karl Lagerfeld had died came as a shock—a bit like hearing that the Queen of England is dead. Like many of his clients, Lagerfeld was coy about his age, though it seems that he was eighty-five, and one shouldn't be surprised when an elderly person expires peacefully. But then Lagerfeld wasn't, as the Queen isn't, really a person. Each made a decision early on—Lagerfeld's willful, Elizabeth's imposed by tradition—to renounce being an individual. Monarchy will not be the same after Q.E. II, in part because we know too much about her successors, their ordinary faults and desires. And the realm of fashion won't be the same after Karl I.

But Lagerfeld's regime as a designer was more significant than his legacy will be. A supreme technician and workhorse, he didn't change the way we dress. His sketches, like his speech, were rapid-fire, but their dazzle concealed a lack of originality. In 1983, some thirty years into Lagerfeld's career, the owners of Chanel hired him to jazz up the brand, and he succeeded wildly, though, unlike its creator, he never reimagined womanhood. Decades earlier, Fendi had brought him on board to make fur fun again, and he did that, too, dyeing and distressing it with his singular insouciance. Lagerfeld liked to play at being a desecrator. "You have to treat an institution like a whore," he said, referring to the decorous house that Chanel built. "Then you get something out of her."

Well-bred aesthetes have a long history of mocking the proprieties with one hand and enforcing them with the other. Compared with the iconoclasm of Rei Kawakubo, or of Alexander McQueen, Lagerfeld's work was old-fashioned. He prided himself on staying relevant, but I suspect that in his heart—a well-defended safe room—he revered beauty too much to despoil it by radical experiment. His real audacity was reserved for his aphorisms. "I am like a caricature of myself," he admitted, in an atypically sincere moment. "For me, the Carnival of Venice lasts all year." If his ready-to-wear for Chanel often felt intentionally superficial, perhaps it, too, was a form of caricature.

Just as most of us have never known an England without Elizabeth, few of us can conceive of the fashion world without Karl. They are both unique in their longevity, and neither ever allowed personal considerations—age, fatigue, grief, self-doubt, or criticism—to interfere with duty. For sixty-five years, Lagerfeld churned out collections, while pursuing parallel careers in photography and publishing. He read voraciously, and boasted of owning a library of some quarter million volumes. He also found time to write a bestselling diet book, cautioning readers that, if they didn't care about getting skinny for the sake of fashion, they shouldn't read it. Having virtually given up bodily nourishment, he took comfort in the bulimic acquisition of fabulous dwellings, objects, and people, nearly all of them disposable. ("The most important piece in the house," he said, "is the garbage can.") This great Stakhanovite was contemptuous of those peers—especially his chief rival, Yves Saint Laurent—who caved to the pressures that he seemed to thrive on. Perhaps their breakdowns aroused a sentiment—fellow feeling—that he had ruthlessly cauterized in himself.

There was, of course, a man behind the carnival mask, who had once been the child of a terrifying mother, and the lover of a fickle Adonis, the "perfect," "odious" Jacques de Bascher, who betrayed him with Saint Laurent, and died of AIDS, leaving Lagerfeld bereft of the desire for another intimate. Despite his professional schadenfreude, Lagerfeld was generous to friends. He doted on a godson, and loved his cat, a creature with her own Instagram account, modeling career, full-time maid, and diamonds.

He also paid homage to Colette, a predatory feline soul who never felt the need to reconcile her contradictions—greed and discipline, reticence and flamboyance—which were Lagerfeld's, too. It is unlikely that they met, but at the end of *The Pure and the Impure* Colette details her requisites for a friend: "They have lost their solemnity and have acquired a sane notion of what is incurable and what is curable— for instance, love." In sum, she wrote, "they have become frivolous the hard way." Lagerfeld, I imagine, would have passed muster.

The notion of majesty depends on the taboo against lèse-majesté: treating one's sovereign as a familiar. But that taboo has been negated by social media. In the past decade, populism democratized fashion; styles changed by referendum, rather than by diktat. Lagerfeld's death underscores the demise of an archaic operating system whose code was written by Louis XIV. The Sun King consolidated his power by turning his court into a hotbed of status anxiety, calibrated in degrees of chic, of which he was the arbiter. The runway shows that Lagerfeld staged for Chanel, at obscene expense, seemed drawn from Louis's manual. Lagerfeld, too, used spectacle to reinforce his image as a divinity: trucking in an iceberg from Sweden; launching a spacecraft. He, like Louis, made an art of wowing his subjects as a way of cowing them. His passing is more than "the end of an era," as the headlines put it. It is the end of a three-hundred-year autocracy, headquartered in France. The king is dead; long live the Web.

DECEMBER 2016

SCENES FROM A MARRIAGE

TWO FOR ONE

There are some clothes, like cars, that pique your curiosity, and you just have to know (or, if you are a child of the quiz-show era, to show off by guessing) their make and model. About ten years ago, I startled a grande dame by asking her if the cocktail dress she was wearing, hands down the chicest in the room, wasn't a Dior, from 1948. It looked perfectly contemporary, but Dior did some of his greatest work in the same fabric: a glossy, malleable black satin that held its shape like meringue. "Yes," she admitted, "but please don't tell anyone that I've been wearing it for half a century."

Not long afterward, at a party downtown, I saw another black dress, which was equally worthy of reverence, but this one I couldn't place, even after I had examined it from every angle. It belonged to a youthful woman who carried herself without the sense of preciousness that often marks a couture client like the grande dame. The material was unpretentious—cotton or rayon matte jersey—so not couture, I thought, yet like couture the cut had a mandarin inscrutability. Softly pleated, overlapping swags fell from the shoulders and were molded to the body like the leaves of a corn husk, tapering to a narrow V that should have hobbled the woman's ankles, but she moved gracefully. I was just about to tap her on the shoulder when she turned and, reading my intentions with a look of amusement, uttered two words: "Isabel Toledo."

My first encounter with Toledo's work was an upscale parody of a commercial that fashion lovers of a certain age will remember. The commercial—for the Anne Klein budget line, Anne Klein II—ran in the 1980s and made a deeper impression than the sportswear it advertised. There were several spots, all a version of the same scenario. In one, a handsome cowboy notices a cool, urban-looking woman in a fast car who has stopped to make a phone call at a gas station. As she strides toward the booth with a jacket tossed over her shoulders, then juggles her Filofax with the receiver, she catches the cowboy sizing her up but pays no attention. He seems mystified, as much by his own attraction as by her independence. (That wishful notion—that independence is attractive to he-men—lives on as a plot staple of cable television.) Just as he is mustering the courage to address her, she utters three words: "Anne Klein Two."

In 2006, Isabel Toledo, of all people, was hired as the creative director of Anne Klein. She has always been her own woman, so the choice seemed apt demographically, if for no other reason. But Anne Klein makes clothing for the office and for suburban weekends, and is sold largely in malls, whereas Toledo, a forty-seven-year-old, Cuban-born avant-gardist, is virtually unknown outside the fashion world, and initiates speak of her talent with the kind of awe generally reserved for a chess prodigy. She is often mentioned with Geoffrey Beene and Charles James as a designer's designer, someone whose cutting has an ingenious rigor not obvious to a layman. "I think one can fairly call Isabel a genius," Valerie Steele told me recently. (Steele is the director of the museum at the Fashion Institute of Technology.) "She has an ability to do the kind of spatial modeling in her head that a computer does. By pulling a drawstring through the fabric, or folding it like origami, though also using more conventional techniques—seaming and draping—in innovative ways, she transforms a geometric plane into a poetic volume that you couldn't have imagined." (Toledo has described her craft as "romantic mathematics.")

Toledo's surprise appointment to her position at Anne Klein, and her abrupt dismissal from it, one year and three well-received collections later, got more press than her own line has ever generated. She has worked outside the mainstream, without much fanfare or capital (yet always with the interest of an elite—she won a Cooper-Hewitt National Design Award in 2005), for the past quarter of a century, and her longevity in a fickle business that eats its young and abandons its old on the ice floes of oblivion is a rare feat. "Maybe I've survived because I'm *not* a fashion person," she told me. "I don't like the disposable culture fashion feeds into—I see myself as a maker of great hand-me-downs. Objects or clothes last because they function, and because you've found the most rational solution to a design problem." (Despite her beauty—huge eyes in a pale, angular face with a regal forehead—Toledo doesn't look much like a fashion person, either, or, at least, not in her working uniform: a pair of clogs, white carpenter pants, and a sweater, with her old-fashioned hair cascading down her back like the tresses of a Gothic Magdalene from Galicia, where her mother's family originated.)

Since 1984, when she opened her house, working out of a tenement next to the Port Authority and doing all the sewing herself, Toledo has been married to her business partner, Ruben Toledo, an artist, set designer, filmmaker, and one of the fashion world's leading illustrators. (In the introduction to *Style Dictionary*, Ruben's affectionately scathing cartoon glossary of fashion's absurdities, Richard Martin, the late curator of the Met Costume Institute, compared his work to the caricatures of Daumier and Grandville.)

The Toledos are an inseparable couple—a collective of two. He is the impetuous, outgoing one, a wiry man with a trim mustache who cuts the figure of a bohemian dandy and does most of the talking. They have a long lease on four floors of a loft building in the Flower District, which houses her workrooms, and they live upstairs, in a garret penthouse they renovated on the cheap, fifteen years ago. A dining room, furnished with a marble drafting table at which they eat and work, opens onto a listing balcony that overlooks a former lithography studio. They sleep on a mezzanine, under a ceiling splotched by a century of water stains—yellow scabs that sometimes reopen. Ruben covered two of the walls with a graffiti-like frieze of faces. The decor is, as he puts it, "a crazy quilt" of found objects—puppets, a birdcage, hula hoops—some hanging from the rafters. A cactus from Woolworth's is now, thanks to Isabel's "insane green thumb," fifteen feet tall. Friends contributed eccentric furniture, and, surrounded by art books, canvases, and stylized dress forms that Ruben designs for Pucci Mannequins (including the refreshingly well-padded "Birdie," 38-32-44), a woodworm-ridden Buddha sits on an odd-shaped table. A week before Christmas, the drafts rattling the safety glass of a big skylight in the main room, which frames a view of the Empire State Building, were so icy that I asked Isabel to lend me a sweater—the Toledos sometimes have to wear the matching ski suits that hang on pegs in the bathroom. She does the cooking in a tiny alcove, and he brews the Cuban coffee. They have Sunday brunch together, lingering over it for hours, and at night, if they don't feel like going out, Ruben said, "we put some cha-cha or rumba music on and boogie around by ourselves. We're both great dancers."

Ruben's well-paid commercial art has seen them through hard times, and, in the beginning, he did the cutting for her designs, pressed the samples, and delivered the orders by taxi to the few outlets in Manhattan—Bendel's uptown, and Patricia Field on East Eighth Street—that were adventurous enough to carry them. The Toledos are no longer struggling artists (although the romantic ethos of authenticity and creative struggle is part of their identity), but they still operate on an artisanal scale. Their company employs about a dozen people, most of them Chinese—former sweatshop workers whom Toledo retrains—and a few brainy interns, generally from the top of their classes at Parsons or FIT. When Isabel has puzzled out a design in her head, she describes it to Ruben, mostly with gestures, and he does sketches that their part-time pattern cutters translate into muslins. Three times a week, Ruben's eighty-year-old father, Vitellio, a retired tailor who once had a carriage-trade clientele in Old Havana, comes in from New Jersey to help. (On the morning I met Señor Toledo, he arrived with a neatly wrapped "present" for Isabel—the lid of her pressure cooker, which he had taken home to repair.) "We're like a big family," Ruben said, "and to work here you have to be comfortable as part of an organism." This cozy hive can produce, at most, only three hundred pieces a season, which are retailed at Barneys in New York;

Ikram in Chicago; Nordstrom in Dallas; Colette in Paris; Joyce in
Hong Kong; and a few other high-end department stores.

The Toledo boutique at Barneys consists of a rack or two opposite
the up escalator on the second floor (where Prada and Lanvin occupy
the corner salons). On a recent visit, four big drawings by Ruben and
a few samples from Isabel's minuscule 2008 Cruise collection were on
display. An ingenue's charming dance frock with a fifties silhouette
was sprinkled with embroidered pinwheels, in peppery colors, and it
came with a little bolero that tied under the bosom. For a more classical taste, there were a couple of modern chitons—soft dresses with
Grecian pleating, a Toledo signature—in pewter or black rayon jersey,
which you could wear barefoot or to lunch at the George V. The most
striking piece was one of Toledo's future great hand-me-downs. It was
a short, champagne-colored gown with a fitted waist and a full skirt,
constructed entirely of narrow, hand-shirred silk bands seamed into
tiers. That kind of demi-couture is not for the bargain hunter, and
Toledo's prices range from twelve hundred dollars to ten thousand (for
a "coat of armor" in metallic lace). But Julie Gilhart, Barneys' fashion
director, told me that the line reliably sells out almost as soon as it
appears. "Most of my clientele," Isabel said wryly, but without resentment, "seems to be manufacturers buying the clothes to copy."

The Toledos reckon that in twenty-four years of marriage they
have spent, at most, a week apart—when he flew to Japan, ahead of
her, for a "fashion opera" whose sets he had designed. As photogenic
newlyweds who were fixtures of the downtown club scene and at Studio 54, they gave an interview to *Paper* magazine in which they expressed their desire to have "ten children as soon as possible." They
have never had any. ("Not yet," Isabel said, when I asked them about
it, to which Ruben objected, with some alarm, "I don't want to share
you.") But they are so enmeshed with each other that it's hard to imagine them making the compromises, or dividing the prosaic labors, of
parenthood. "I think we don't know which one of us is which," she
admitted.

It's obvious, however, that their differences are part of their chemistry. Ruben, who was born in Cuba a year after Isabel, described

himself as "a typical street-smart Havana mutt for whom anything goes, while the Spanish side of Isabel loves rules and order." He is a "pack rat," and she hates clutter. His extroverted, Latin gallantry leaves one with a first impression that she, by contrast, is profoundly shy, and even friends call her "unreadable." But her reticence is of a piece with her economy as a designer, and in both cases, she has plenty to say, especially to her husband. They go back and forth about art and life, debating how alike and unalike they are, as if they were exploring the paradoxes of a thrilling new acquaintance. "We always know we can get through to each other," she said, "and that's so sexy." He paints her obsessively ("It's really because I'm always handy"), and their symmetry as a dyad appeals to photographers, among them Karl Lagerfeld. He posed them on giant stools for a portrait that appeared in the catalogue of a joint exhibition in 2000, at Kent State University Museum. They are about the same height—five and a half feet; both slight and dark (one of their oldest friends, Joey Arias, the performance artist and drag star, describes them as "salt and pepper shakers"); and their weights in the marriage also seem evenly balanced.

West New York, New Jersey, where the Toledos grew up, was a blue-collar barrio with a vibrant Latin culture where thousands of Cuban exiles settled in the 1960s. Ruben's family arrived on a "freedom flight" in 1967, and he still recalls the white cowboy boots and leopard-skin jacket that he was given by the Salvation Army. "They were my first American clothes, and when everyone stared at me I thought it was because I looked so cool," he said. Isabel's father, Felix Izquierdo, who bore a striking resemblance to Clark Gable (he died three weeks before her wedding), was born in Cuba to parents from the Canary Islands. He went to work, at twelve, as a clerk in a hardware store whose owners eventually gave him a share in the business. He lost it when he emigrated, and took a job operating knitting machines in a textile factory. Eventually, he scraped together enough money to open a clothing shop in Union City. "I loved the no-nonsense way my father dressed," Isabel said. "Menswear has such authority. The only clothes that I ever wear, besides my own, are Ruben's."

Bertha Izquierdo, Isabel's mother, had once been employed at a rich uncle's shoe factory in Camajuani (the provincial town where Isabel was born), selecting leathers. "Cuban women didn't work outside the home, but she wanted to," Ruben said. "It was a modern family, unlike mine, and it seemed like an ideal family, unlike mine—we're solitary people who love each other but fight a lot—and Bertha played the catcher on a women's baseball team." (Spherical skirts or sleeves, seamed with contrasting thread, like a baseball, are among Toledo's leitmotifs.) Isabel recalls an idyllic early childhood in an extended family. Even after the revolution, her resourceful mother managed to dress her three daughters—Isabel is the youngest—"like little princesses." But when they started over in New Jersey, in 1968, Bertha also got a factory job, assembling airplane ignition parts, and the girls were sent to a babysitter after school. "I've always been bull-headed," Isabel told me, "and I refused to go. So my mother had to bribe me with the promise of sewing lessons." At first, she practiced on little pillows or stuffed animals, but soon she started sewing for herself. "I was always so skinny that I hated shopping," she said. She often stayed up late into the night making her school clothes, and she also sewed for her sisters. Ruben recalled seeing one of the Izquierdo girls, whom he didn't yet know, at a local dance hall wearing "an amazing dress of white gauze that everyone admired." It was the era of *Saturday Night Fever*, and the dress came from a store-bought pattern that Isabel had reworked. Even at the babysitter's kitchen table, she was engrossed by laying out a pattern. It wasn't merely the paper-doll template for a cute outfit or a toy but an abstract puzzle whose multiple solutions were governed, like music, by mysterious laws.

Having met her dress before he met Isabel, Ruben found himself sitting near her in a ninth-grade Spanish class. He was thirteen and she was fourteen, and for him "it was love at first sight." But one afternoon, when Isabel and I were, exceptionally, by ourselves, she told me, "I was a wild girl at that age, wild but innocent. All I cared about was getting dressed up and going dancing. I figured out how to get rides into the city with older boys from the neighborhood, who were glad to take me, because I had the 'look' you needed to get into the clubs—a cross between Lolita and Keith Richards." Hoping to calm her down a bit, Isabel's father got her a summer job in a bridal shop. There was a rush order to fill, and she helped out with the bridesmaids' dresses. "But when they were finished, I quit, and I wouldn't take any money, which the owner couldn't understand," she said. "By then, I knew that sewing was my vocation, though not that kind of sewing, and I was afraid of being trapped, for life, catering to Bridezillas. That's pretty funny," she concluded, "because catering to Bridezillas in one form or another is the fate of most designers."

Ruben, in the meantime, contrived to fail both Spanish and art, his mother tongues. "That's because you were already an artist," Isabel said, but she also suggested that his "crush" on her had played a part. "Please don't insult me by calling it a crush," he retorted. "True love isn't a 'crush,' as time has proved."

They started dating when they finished high school, and if Toledo's work had a narrative—which it doesn't, she said vehemently: "I don't need images or fantasy to express emotion through design"—it would surely be that of their romance.

Like their parents, Ruben and Isabel were driven by a desire to assimilate. "That's what makes our work so American," he said. After a semester at the School of Visual Arts, he dropped out and sold used cars, hung out at the Mudd Club, met Andy Warhol, Klaus Nomi, Keith Haring, and other "not great models for good behavior," and eventually got a job as a salesman at Parachute, an edgy boutique in SoHo. (By that time, he was supplementing his income by selling photographs of Isabel, colored with food dye, to the postcard buyer at Fiorucci.) Joey Arias and Kim Hastreiter, the editor of *Paper*, used to drop by. They both remember Ruben talking nonstop about his beautiful girlfriend. Isabel, in the meantime, enrolled at FIT, then transferred to Parsons. She dressed for the clubs in bubbles of tulle with fishing-wire straps, and "wearable sculptures" of pulled thread. But in 1979 she quit her studies for a chance to intern with Diana Vreeland at the Met's Costume Institute. "Mrs. Vreeland was fascinated by Isabel's footwear," Ruben noted. "One day she'd be wearing combat boots, and the next granny shoes."

Conservation was not yet the esoteric province of experts in hazmat suits that it has become, and Isabel had few credentials beyond her gifts as a seamstress. She began by working on the institute's old buckram dress forms, reshaping them with cotton batting and surgical mesh, but one day she was handed a gown by Madame Grès that had started to tear, and was told to mend it. "The name meant nothing to me," she said. "I had no idea who all these mythic figures were. I looked at the technique, not at the label, and figured out, from the structure, how it should be repaired. Couture is a language, and I learned it the way a child does, by immersion. Another time, I was restoring a Vionnet, and when I turned it inside out, and saw the seams, I thought, Wow. I knew that the curators were wrong about it. It wasn't, as they said, the bias cut that gave it its shape, but the weight of the fabric."

Toledo spent five years at the Met, which were in essence an apprenticeship with the twentieth century's greatest couturiers. In 1985, during Fall Fashion Week, she mounted her first runway show for buyers and the press. (She had been selling her creations on consignment at Fiorucci, and her "pre-collections"—part of chaotic spectacles at Danceteria, where Joey Arias hosted a monthly revue called *Mermaids on Heroin*—had won her an underground following.) At her official debut, Toledo presented a collection pieced together from denim wedges in primary colors, which caused a stir and made the windows at Bergdorf's. Harold Koda, who had worked at the Costume Institute as an exhibition assistant when Isabel was an intern (he is now the chief curator), was in the audience. "Isabel's early work challenged the notion of what clothing could be," he said. "She wasn't a militant, like Rei Kawakubo, but her approach struck me as aggressively conceptual in that it asserted the primacy of the pattern over the garment. I have always loved the purity of her ideas—nothing she does is superficial—and her clothes are fascinating as design objects. But, as the artist evolved and the woman matured, she invested the clothes with a cryptic sensuality in which, I think, you can read Ruben's influence, and that of their marriage. I still remember a dystopian-looking but very beautiful cocoon jacket of rusty-brown organza—the color of a cockroach—lined with what seemed to be the filter of an air conditioner. It was constructed like a T-shirt pulled over the head backward, and it reminded me of late Balenciaga."

Toledo says that she doesn't channel other designers, though her admirers tend to invoke canonical figures in making a case for her place in the pantheon (besides Charles James, Geoffrey Beene, Vionnet, Claire McCardell, and Bonnie Cashin, contemporaries such as Alber Elbaz, of Lanvin, and Azzedine Alaïa are frequently mentioned). "In terms of invention and of blurring the boundaries between art and fashion, Isabel is like a modern-day Schiaparelli," Kim Hastreiter said. Compared with Schiaparelli, a stormy, protean figure who enriched the vocabulary of fashion more than any of her peers, Toledo is, or still is, a minor—and democratic—deity who doesn't seek to dictate the way women should live.

Yet she, too, has a mischievous side, and has always enjoyed testing the limits of what clothing can be. In 1988, she created the "Packing Dress," a flat white circle with four holes—for the legs, arms, and head. (On the body, it resembles a Surrealist lampshade.) Ten years later, at one of her last runway shows (their expense, in relation to the business they generated, had become prohibitive), she unveiled the "Hermaphrodite," an ethereal confection of droopy pouches, in topaz chiffon, lashed with bias tape, which can be turned inside or out, suggesting either an orifice or an appendage, depending on your hormone levels that evening. ("When you wear something for the first time," Isabel said, "it should surprise you with a rush of feeling you weren't expecting"—the ephemeral feeling, perhaps, of being happy with yourself.) But her archives are also full of deceptively straight-looking lace and ruffles; ladylike shirtwaists with a New Look flare; minimalist sheaths cut on the bias; and dress-and-coat ensembles in lavish brocade that flirt with propriety, or even with mumsiness, until you perceive the ironic detail that subverts them. As a woman designer (and her own guinea pig), Toledo thinks about body parts—and flaws—that a man might overlook. "I have a pointy chin," she said, "so sharp lapels make me look witchy if they're not set properly." I have a dictator's jaw, so I was very surprised that when I put on a gendarme coat of rubberized silk (it looked like the skin of a wet otter), with a high collar, which Toledo designed at Anne Klein, you would not have mistaken me for Mussolini.

The announcement that Toledo had been hired to create some excitement at Anne Klein heartened the professionals who considered her the rightful heir of Cashin and McCardell—women with an original perspective on American style in a landscape dominated by male designers, many of whom are, today, boy wunderkinds. Anne Klein herself was more of a trendsetter than an artist, but she sensed the nascent feminism of a new generation. A former sketcher on Seventh Avenue, who founded the company in 1968, she liked to say, "Clothes aren't going to change the world, the women who wear them will." She dressed the baby boomers just then beginning to enter the workforce in separates that they could "mix and match"—a novel concept for the time. In 1974, when Klein died of breast cancer, at fifty-one, Donna Karan inherited her mantle and wore it for a decade with panache. (She and her old schoolmate Louis dell'Olio did much of the work on Anne Klein II.) Karan left the year that the Toledos went into business, and, under a series of successors, the brand fell into the doldrums.

Shortly before Toledo joined Anne Klein, its parent company, Jones Apparel, a conglomerate with $5 billion a year in sales, had been looking for a buyer or for bids from private-equity firms, but had received a low valuation from analysts. The chief executive, Peter Boneparth, was betting that he could reinvigorate a sluggish corporate metabolism from the top down with an injection of charisma. "It wasn't about getting the name who was the biggest," he told *The New York Times*, "but the person who had the best perceived talent"—perceived, that is, by the fashion press (which helped to build suspense for Toledo's debut) rather than by the moneymen. At her first outing, Fall-Winter 2007, she showed clashing plaids in a smart walking suit, and mixed chunky knits with fluid trousers. There was a confident swagger to the leather and charmeuse. Even though the clothes were designed for production in China ("I was expected to pick out the buttons before I had thought about the clothes," Toledo said) and she adapted her standards of tailoring to a mass market, some critics felt that the collection fell short of the revelation they had been expecting, or that it was too cerebral for the target audience. "The Anne Klein lady wants a nice red blazer," an industry expert told me, "but a customer for Isabel's clothes has to be literate in fashion to read their subtlety, and even then it's only fully apparent in a dressing room." As Koda noted, "There is sometimes a tongue-in-cheek primness to Isabel's work—the sex appeal isn't explicit." For the sort of woman who dresses at Gucci, or even at Donna Karan, the spirit of the clothes was probably a bit too impeccable. But for Spring 2007 Toledo let her hair down. Ruben hand-painted a bouquet of gossamer shirtwaists, and transparent layers drifted down the runway like a cloud of milkweed on a June day. You could feel a collective surge of appetite from the front row, and the bees and butterflies left buzzing.

Just as Spring was being shipped, and it seemed that a well-loved Cinderella, superior to her rivals yet toiling in obscurity, had been liberated, Jones backed out, without notice or explanation. A corporate shakeup had ousted Boneparth, and a new management team apparently balked at the commitment necessary to launch a designer with far-reaching ambitions—especially one whom it hadn't hired— and decided, in a dismal retail climate, to focus on lower-end brands. Toledo is officially still under contract to Anne Klein, and she won't be at liberty until next year to discuss her experience, except to say that she's "sad and disappointed, and we brought some of our best technicians to Anne Klein, but we're regrouping."

At one of our last meetings, the Toledos and I went out for lunch at a French bistro near their loft building. (Ruben does an excellent imitation of wounded macho pride if a woman reaches for the check.) It was raining, and I saw that Isabel was staring intently at the umbrellas in a stand near our table. I asked her why. "If you had never seen an umbrella," she said, "and you had no idea what it was for—if it just looked like a dying lily—could you imagine its shape open?"

MARCH 2008

—◦◦◦—

L ast June, Men's Fashion Week in Milan took place a few days after Miuccia Prada and her husband, Patrizio Bertelli, who runs the business end of their empire, had raised $2.1 billion with a long-delayed, much ballyhooed initial public offering on the Hong Kong Stock Exchange. Both the IPO and Prada's runway show—a collection of Day-Glo floral prints and nerdy plaids— inspired complaints from Giorgio Armani. "Fashion today is in the hands of the banks and of the stock market and not of its owners," he told the press. He went on to scold Prada for "bad taste that becomes chic." Her clothes, he added, are "sometimes ugly."

Armani's perception was hardly novel, and Prada might not have disagreed—"I fight against my good taste," she has said—though she also might have pointed out that when bankers want a fashion insurance policy they buy one of Armani's suits. He is the champion of the risk-averse, and Prada has always slyly perverted the canons of impeccability that his brand embodies. Only in the dressing room do you discover that her ostensibly proper little pleated skirts, ladylike silk blouses, and lace dinner suits are a test of your cool. If you can't wear them tongue-in-cheek, as Prada herself does—thumbing her crooked nose at received ideas about beauty and sex appeal—they can make you look like a governess.

Invincible female self-possession is a central theme of the joint retrospective that opens in May at the Met Costume Institute, *Elsa Schiaparelli and Miuccia Prada: Impossible Conversations*. Its subjects were born six decades apart (Schiaparelli in Rome, in 1890; Prada in Milan, in 1949), and they never met, though some of their affinities seem almost genetic. They both had strict Catholic girlhoods in upper-crust families, with traditional expectations for women, and they both took heart from maternal aunts whose feistiness defied the mold. Schiaparelli is the more patrician—her mother descended from the dukes of Tuscany—but her father was a university professor, and so was Prada's. Neither woman set out in life to design clothes, or even learned to sew. They were both ardent rebels and feminists who came of age at moments of ferment in art and politics that ratified their disdain for conformity. Schiaparelli was involved with the Dada movement at its inception in Greenwich Village, after the First World War; Prada was a left-wing graduate student in Milan during the radical upheavals of the 1970s.

These heady adventures delayed their careers. Schiaparelli was thirty-seven and Prada was thirty-nine when they delivered their first collections. But experience of the real world, which was a man's world for both of them, made them intolerant of female passivity and desperation. They don't really care what makes a woman desirable to men. Their work asks you to consider what makes a woman desirable to herself.

Andrew Bolton and Harold Koda, the curators of the Costume Institute, originally conceived of the retrospective as "an imaginary conversation," Bolton told me. But, as they began to compile quotations from Schiaparelli and to interview Prada, they realized that this conceit was too tame. It is doubtful that the notoriously touchy Schiaparelli would have been happy about sharing a double bill, even with such an illustrious compatriot, or that Prada would have submitted to comparison with a contemporary. She is widely considered the most influential designer in the world today partly because her enigmatic code is so hard to copy: she changes the password every season.

The title of the show alludes to a famous column in the *Vanity Fair* of the 1930s—"Impossible Interviews"—which was illustrated by the

Mexican artist Miguel Covarrubias. Among the mismatched sparring partners whom he caricatured with impious glee (the fan dancer Sally Rand and Martha Graham; Adolf Hitler and Huey Long; Sigmund Freud and Jean Harlow) were Joseph Stalin and Schiaparelli:

STALIN: Can't you leave our women alone?
SCHIAPARELLI: They don't want to be left alone . . .
STALIN: You underestimate the serious goals of Soviet women.
SCHIAPARELLI: You underestimate their natural vanity.

Her "interview" with the dictator appeared in 1936, when she was at the height of her glory, and had recently returned to Paris from a French trade fair in Moscow, where her presence made news. No other couturier had been willing to risk the censure that Schiaparelli received—and shrugged off—for consorting with the Bolsheviks, and, while she was there, she presented a capsule collection of Soviet-friendly fashions suitable for mass production. One of the ensembles was a simple black dress with a high neck, worn under a red coat, with outsize pockets, and a beret. (It wasn't, apparently, what the commissars of chic had in mind. They rejected it as too "ordinary.")

As a moderator for the imaginary conversation between Schiaparelli and Prada, the curators turned to another provocative Italian— the novelist and semiotician Umberto Eco. In the last chapters of *On Ugliness*, his lavishly illustrated iconography of the repulsive, the obscene, and the bizarre, Eco suggests how the worship of beauty, like any established religion that turns reactionary, is vulnerable to attack by freethinking apostates. Until the twentieth century, physical monstrosity was an almost universal metaphor for sin, disease, corruption, greed, inferiority, and, in the features of a witch, the primal fear of female carnality. But when the modernist avant-garde revolted at the pieties of academic art, and the bourgeois complacency that it flattered, it embraced what Ezra Pound called "the cult of ugliness." (It was also the cult of dissonance, as in Stravinsky's music, and of fragmentation, as in Picasso's Cubist portraits of his lovely muses in which he smashed their features into shards.) "There is no more beauty,"

Marinetti exulted in *The Founding and Manifesto of Futurism.* "No work without an aggressive character can be a masterpiece."

Schiaparelli was a nineteen-year-old student of philosophy at the University of Rome when Futurism erupted, and she later heeded its call in the swagger of her broad-shouldered suits, the rawness of her furs and embroidery, and a tough attitude toward any simpering or mincing in fashion which her contemporaries described as "hard chic." Prada took up the mantle, literally, in her abrasive collections of the 1990s, which used, among other materials, wallpaper prints, nasty fabrics, bottle caps, and broken glass. In 1999, she showed a Teflon wool hiking skirt. "Brown is a color that no one likes," she told Bolton, "so of course I like it because it's difficult." She has often said that when she hates something herself—crochet, for example—she works out her antipathy in a collection: it gives her the space "to be intrigued." (She also hates golf, apparently—a theme of her June menswear.) Last year, she designed a collection, in cheap cotton, inspired by hospital scrubs. "If I have done anything," she told British *Vogue*, "it was making ugly cool."

"Hard Chic" and "Ugly Chic" are two of the seven categories (with "Naïf Chic," "The Classical Body," "The Surreal Body," and "Waist Up/Waist Down") into which Bolton and Koda group the examples of Schiaparelli's couture and Prada's ready-to-wear (which is mostly from her runway shows) at the Met. The exhibits are juxtaposed with quotations from both subjects, who seem to agree that nothing is dowdier than solemnity. Prada has obviously studied Schiaparelli closely, and whether or not she has channeled her through Saint Laurent, as Bolton suggests, the kinship between many of their designs seems almost mimetic. Yet Prada's citations of Schiaparelli—a peekaboo raincoat in transparent vinyl, empire-waist dresses with trompe-l'oeil pleats, deadpan mourning-wear, draped ombré gowns, whimsical appliqués, and the ubiquitous motif of disembodied lips—are an exercise in sampling, not imitation. They enrich and complicate, rather than merely translate, her models, and they illustrate the way that critics and artists of every generation reinvent the formal languages that they inherit.

Schiaparelli and Prada are most alike—indeed, nearly identical—in their ambition to be unique. (Prada dominates the runways and the fashion press season after season mostly by pleasing herself; the Prada style is a distillation of her personality.) But, in at least one respect, they bear no comparison. Even the Devil wears Prada, and millions know her name. Schiaparelli presented her last collection of couture in 1954, and if she is remembered at all outside the fashion world it is mostly by association with a color that she made her signature, an electric pink still known in France as *le shocking*, or with a once-famous perfume, also called Shocking, which was introduced in 1937. Its droll bottle—the hourglass torso of a female nude, sculpted by the Surrealist Leonor Fini, whose model was Mae West—caused a minor scandal that has also been long forgotten.

The capricious force of nature known as "the great Schiap," however, was once the reigning queen of couture. In 1934, *Time* ran a business story on her prodigious success and put her on the cover. The flattering photograph softens her austere features, and the furtive glamour that she projects hints at erotic secrets. (But the young Elsa, as a daughter and a sister of beautiful women, "was always being told," she wrote, "that I was ugly," and her only marriage—an elopement, in her early twenties, with a faithless cad who abandoned her in New York—may also have been her only experiment with love.) Between 1927 and 1940, she generated a meteor shower of ideas that revolutionized the way women dress. In the column of her practical innovations are wraparound dresses, culottes, overalls, the jumpsuit, mix-and-match separates, and those Futurist power suits whose linebacker shoulders and tapered cut minimized the padding on a female body. Her radical experiments with fabrication produced paper and plastic clothes, fantasy furs, Plexiglas accessories, camouflage prints, and bark-like crumpled silks. In 1935, she became the first designer to stage a fashion show as entertainment, with a set, music, and the skinny models who quickly supplanted all other native species.

Comedy had a niche in fashion before Schiaparelli, though much of it was unintentional. When she embellished a cotton summer dress with seed packets, or an evening bolero with dancing elephants, she

stole the flame of irony from her comrades in the avant-garde. Cocteau, who sketched some of her embroideries, commissioned her to
create his film and theater costumes, but Salvador Dalí was her prime
accomplice, and their surreal couture, which strips away the veils that
have always disguised fashion's romance with fetishism, are the first
true hybrids of clothing and art. Among their collaborations were
a belt buckle in the form of lips; cocktail hats in the shape of a
lamb chop, a high-heeled shoe, and a vagina; and a white muslin evening gown that Wallis Simpson chose for her trousseau. Dalí had
painted the skirt with a bright-red lobster, which matched its cummerbund, and Cecil Beaton photographed the future duchess wearing
it serenely, despite—or perhaps to mock—her reputation as a scarlet-
clawed predator.

The last of Schiaparelli's duets with Dalí is also the most troubling,
and it is hard not to read it as a work of protest art. The women who
could afford her couture, and the men who paid their bills, had ridden
out the Depression in Paris, Saint-Tropez, or New York, but, wherever
they lived, it was a Shangri-La, sealed off from the blizzards of violence and misery howling around them. The masterpiece in question—
a simple sheath known as "the tear dress," from 1938—was a warning
salvo from the outside world, meant, perhaps, to breach their sense of
inviolability. Trompe-l'oeil incisions on the pale blue silk (a print by
Dalí) represent wounds inflicted on the skin of a living creature. The
cuts have been folded back to reveal bloody sinews. Appliqués on a
matching mantilla reproduce the incisions. In 1940, Schiaparelli fled
Paris for New York, and spent the war years volunteering for the Red
Cross and raising money for pro-Allied French charities.

In 1973, the year that Schiaparelli died, Miuccia Prada (whose
given name is Maria) was a twenty-four-year-old graduate student at
the University of Milan. Having earned a doctorate in political science, she abruptly changed course and spent the next five years training as a mime at Milan's Piccolo Teatro, under the legendary director
Giorgio Strehler. Mime, like fashion, is a silent art, and in both cases
a practitioner has to imagine how the language of a body will translate
the message that she wishes to convey.

Like many of her classmates, Prada was caught up in the fervor of a radical period that was particularly volatile in her native city. At the opening night of La Scala in 1968, protesters hurled rotten eggs at patrons in evening dress, and the city was still in turmoil a few years later, when Armani's slouchy, neutral new brand of chic opportunely made its appearance. Prada joined the Communist Party, and—or but—according to different reports, she wore Saint Laurent to distribute leaflets. ("But" seems to imply that if she sniffed the noxious weed of Marxism she didn't inhale.)

Prada doesn't like to discuss politics, but she has never disavowed her youthful idealism, and, in 2006, she says, "a party of the left" had asked her to run for parliament. She declined the invitation, noting that she likes her day job—and that it would also be impertinent for a billionaire to represent working-class Italians. (Her crocodile handbags can cost twice as much as a small Fiat.) As for wearing a little something from the Rive Gauche boutique on the front lines of the people's struggle for hegemony, she prefers to recall having costumed herself in vintage dresses from a thrift shop and high heels. A French fashion curator has called her style "a collage of intuitions," though Prada simply says, "I didn't want to resemble anyone." She has also shrewdly managed not to alienate potential customers on the left or the right. The bohemian impudence of her clothes is offset by their conservative opulence.

The young Prada, however, did resemble thousands of her peers in Europe who flirted with militancy or even married it, then got divorced, with no hard feelings. And joining the Communist Party in Italy or France has never meant renouncing the perks of your class— you can carry your card in a Prada wallet. Those wallets have now been around for almost a century. Prada's family owned a luxury leather-goods business founded, in 1913, by her grandfather Mario, who had opened a little shop of lugubrious elegance in the Galleria Vittorio Emanuele II, a glass-roofed arcade near Milan's Duomo. The company's beautifully hand-tooled suitcases, handbags, and steamer trunks were popular with a patrician clientele, and Mario received a warrant for his goods from the Italian royal family. When Prada was a little girl—her nickname was Miu Miu (she gave it to her secondary label)—the shop was off limits to the females of the family. It was Mario's conviction, Prada has said, that women belong at home. But after his death, in the late 1950s, her mother, Luisa, took over the business, and in the mid-seventies the flame passed to Miuccia.

She started out by updating the stuffy merchandise with her own designs, and in 1985 she introduced a line of lightweight backpacks, in a fine-gauge parachute nylon trimmed with leather, that pretty much transformed urban life for the kind of woman who walks everywhere, has a lot to carry but likes her hands free, and sees the point of spending hundreds of dollars on the platonic ideal of a schoolboy's satchel. By then, Prada was living with her future husband. Bertelli, who started out in the handbag business, joined her company; as it grew (according to *Forbes*, in the late seventies its annual sales were about $400,000; in 2010, they were about €1.6 billion), he insisted that she start doing women's wear. "I often think that to be a fashion designer, you must give up your brain," Prada told a British interviewer, and for a while she refused. But her first collection debuted on a runway in 1988—a year after her wedding. Her bridal outfit was an "ugly chic" cotton day dress in army gray that she wore with a man's camel overcoat.

Prada and Bertelli, who have two adult sons, live in the apartment where she grew up. (She has a separate apartment for her old clothes; she never throws anything out.) Her style is both deeply rooted in the sartorial conventions of bourgeois Milan—the drab palette and sober luxury of tailored clothes that are meant to convey substance and respectability—and incorrigibly irreverent about the ideals of womanhood (the virginal convent girl, the virtuous matron) that her class held dear. But her collections also evoke the men whom those wives and daughters dressed to please, placate, arouse, make proud, and sometimes deceive.

One of Prada's formative influences, she told Andrew Bolton, was Luis Buñuel's *Belle de Jour*. The film, with costumes by Saint Laurent, came out in 1967, when Prada was eighteen. It was a watershed moment for the well-brought-up girls of her generation, especially, perhaps, girls like Miuccia—cerebral but impetuous—who were just emerging from their cocoons of docility to discover feminism. "I have nothing against super-sexual fashion. What I am against is being a victim of it," she has said. "To have to be sexy? That I hate. To be outrageously sexy? That I love."

Buñuel's heroine, Séverine, a society woman slumming in a brothel, was played by Catherine Deneuve, and Saint Laurent's most memorable costume for her was a long-sleeved black dress with a white collar and cuffs which was nunlike in its severity. ("I'm always happiest when dressed almost like a nun," Prada says. "It makes you feel so relaxed.") Prada's heroines also seem to have double lives, if not split personalities. They are often fastidious from the waist up—in a classic turtleneck or a pin-striped shirt; a Peter Pan collar; a military jacket that belies the existence of a bosom—but wanton from the waist down, in lamé or sequins (worn for day); faux-python scales; a phallic print of lipstick tubes on white silk; a peacock-feather kilt; exotic skins; see-through lace; or embroidered gauze. Skirts have always been Prada's specialty, in part because the bottom half of a female body is all about birth and sex, she explained to Bolton. Too much attention to the "spiritual" top half makes her "uncomfortable," and so does being pigeonholed as an "intellectual."

Prada's paradoxes have often been qualified as "postmodern," but her style—or perhaps she herself—isn't anxious enough. Her gift for generating anxiety, on the other hand, is one of her trade secrets. For Fall 2011, she showed a series of short coatdresses in pancake-makeup colors, belted at the waist, with panels and sleeves of mangy faux fur. The models looked as if they were swagged in roadkill. Were these outfits fabulously ugly, or inexcusably hideous?

There may be only one designer more absolute in her confidence than Prada: her fellow honoree at the Costume Institute. Schiaparelli did more than any of her peers to promote fashion's status as an art, and she would no doubt have found it natural to mingle at the Met with Phidias and Vermeer. Prada's statements about art suggest that she must find her own enshrinement somewhat ironic. Her fortune has financed an adventurous private collection, an exhibition space outside Milan, and a foundation that supports cultural experiments. In 2010, she was invited to present the Turner Prize at Tate Britain, partially in recognition of her prominence as a patron. (She wore a pair of plastic banana earrings with a stark black coat.) She has also worked with the Dutch architect and urbanist Rem Koolhaas on the design of her major retail spaces, which she calls "epicenters," in New York and Los Angeles. Yet Prada insists that her vocation and her avocation are unrelated. She has refused to collaborate on limited editions of Prada merchandise with any of the art stars in her collection. ("Anything that doesn't sell," she once said dryly, "is a limited edition.") In her somewhat heretical view of a profession that often hankers after transcendence, fashion design may be a creative enterprise, concerned, as art is, with culture and identity, but it isn't what artists do.

Prada's useful notion of "ugly cool" may finally solve the problem of finding an English equivalent for the French epithet "*jolie laide*." The literal translation, "pretty/ugly," and the dictionary definition, "a good-looking ugly woman," both fail to convey the feat of self-transformation that it represents. The nerve, the will, and the ardor of a *jolie laide* make you forget her homeliness. Maria Callas and Amy Winehouse both epitomize the type, and one of the most memorable *jolie laides* in France was Schiaparelli's muse María Casares, the great Spanish actress who played the role of Death in Cocteau's *Orphée*. Their charisma as performers gave a radiance to their witchy features that makes the prettiness of a perfect face seem insipid by comparison.

One of the ensembles in the category of "Ugly Chic" is a three-piece Prada suit from 1996, with a wraparound skirt, a boxy jacket, and a shapeless, high-necked shell. The fabric is a stiff synthetic, digitally printed with a smudgy grid. Each piece is a different awful color (mustard, chartreuse, mold green). It was modeled on the runway by a young Kate Moss, and even she couldn't pull it off.

It isn't that Prada undervalues beauty's power—both she and Schia-parelli have dozens of ravishing ensembles in the show. But the old radical, you suspect, resents it as an unearned asset of the one percent, and the brainy feminist wants you to understand its pathos as a love charm doomed to expire. You shouldn't need it if you love yourself.

MARCH 2012

SILENT PARTNER

—⊗⊗⊗—

Véra and Vladimir Nabokov were married for fifty-two years—
a record, apparently, among literary couples—and their intimacy was nearly hermetic. When they were apart, he pined
for her grievously. She was his first reader, his agent, his typist, his
archivist, his translator, his dresser, his money manager, his mouthpiece, his muse, his teaching assistant, his driver, his bodyguard (she
carried a pistol in her handbag), the mother of his child, and, after he
died, the implacable guardian of his legacy. Vladimir dedicated nearly
all his books to her, and Véra famously saved *Lolita* from incineration
in a trash can when he wanted to destroy it. Before they moved from
a professor's lodgings in Ithaca, New York, to a luxury hotel in Swit-
zerland, she kept his house—"terribly," by her own description—and
cooked his food. She stopped short of tasting his meals when they
dined out, but she opened his mail, and answered it.

According to Véra's biographer, Stacy Schiff, her subject had such
a fetish for secrecy that she "panicked every time she saw her name in
[Vladimir's] footnotes." It seems inapt to call Véra's love selfless,
however: the two selves of the Nabokovs were valves of the same
heart. And extravagant devotion may sometimes be the expression of
vicarious grandiosity. Schiff's biography won a Pulitzer Prize in 2000,
and Véra's name has since entered English as an eponym. Last year, an
article on *The Atlantic*'s website concluded that the luckiest scribes are
those married to "a Véra," a spouse of either sex who liberates them

from life's mundane chores; the less fortunate long for a Véra between loads at the laundromat. There is also the option of a paid Véra, for writers of means—or of scruples.

Letters to Véra, the first complete volume of Nabokov's letters to his wife, was published this month. A lifetime of scholarship informs this massive tome, which was edited and translated from the Russian by Olga Voronina and Brian Boyd, Nabokov's definitive biographer. Its heft, however, is grossly lopsided. The period between 1923, when the couple met, and 1940, when they escaped with their six-year-old son, Dmitri, from France to New York, generated four fifths of the correspondence. The remaining thirty-seven years, until Nabokov's death, fill barely eighty of five hundred pages. (There are 268 additional pages of appendices and endnotes.) Because all but one of his novels in English were composed in America—"I'm an American writer," he insisted when he was asked to define his literary identity— the most fertile decades of his career, and of Véra's midwifery, play out offstage.

We do get a self-portrait of the young Vladimir unvarnished by Nabokovian irony. The earliest letters, intoxicated with language and desire, are intoxicating to read. A ball rolls under a chair, the only furniture in a room: "things seem to have some sort of survival instinct." Trying to quit cigarettes, Nabokov imagines the angels smoking in Heaven like guilty schoolboys. When the archangel passes, they throw their cigarettes away, and "this is what falling stars are." From Paris, he describes the Métro: "It stinks like between the toes and it's just as cramped."

Nabokov's ambition, as a young man, was to give Véra "a sunny, simple happiness," a rare enough commodity for Russians of their generation. They were born three years apart—he in 1899, she in 1902— and they spent their youth outrunning the murderous upheavals of the twentieth century. Many of their compatriots lost their bearings and would never recover. But each of them found a lodestar in the other.

Véra Evseevna Slonim was born into a rich Jewish family that fled St. Petersburg during the Revolution and settled in Berlin, the de facto first capital of the anti-Bolshevik diaspora. She was pale and fine-boned, with the huge eyes of a waif. Her elegance in speech and dress rivaled that of her husband. He liked to joke that he had turned her hair white prematurely; it gave her an ethereal aura that belied her toughness. Véra's character, Vladimir told her, was made of "tiny sharp arrows."

After the Slonims reached Berlin, Véra's father, a lawyer, founded a publishing house. It was one of eighty-six that served a community of half a million émigrés who were religious about their Russianness. Véra worked in the office. She and her two sisters had been polished and educated to a high standard, mostly at home. "They were raised to be perfect," a nephew recalled. To be perfect was to marry well. In the meantime, she taught English and translated from several languages. Some of her work was published in the journal *Rul*, the most prestigious of the outlets for writers in exile. One of its star contributors was a young aristocrat, ladies' man, chess player, dandy, and lepidopterist who was earning his living as a private tutor. He signed his poetry with the pseudonym V. Sirin, but literary insiders, including Véra, knew his real name.

On May 8, 1923, Véra Slonim and Vladimir Nabokov met at a charity ball, or so he recalled. Schiff sets their meeting on a bridge, "over a chestnut-lined canal." All accounts, including Véra's, agree that she was hiding her features behind a black harlequin mask that she refused to lift as they meandered through the city to the Hohenzollernplatz, rapt in conversation. The mask suggests audacious premeditation. Had Véra "accosted" Sirin, as Boyd describes it? Was this an audition for which she had studied the role? And had she come with the "venerating expectation" that George Eliot attributes to Dorothea Brooke before her first meeting with Casaubon?

Nabokov later told his sister that Véra had indeed arranged the encounter. Véra refused to speak for herself to posterity. But she did admit to having memorized Sirin's verse, including his love poems to another woman, and she recited it to him in a voice that he found "exquisite." The writer was seduced with his own words. They were married two years later.

On the evidence of these letters, no couple ever enjoyed a more perfect complicity. In his very first sentence, Vladimir tells Véra, "I won't hide it. I'm so unused to being—well, understood." In 1924, he reflects, "You know, we are terribly alike." And a few months later: "You and I are so special; the miracles we know, no one knows, and no one loves the *way* we love." He was ready to give her "all of my blood." Through their decades of vicissitudes, he referred to their marriage as "cloudless"—even to his mistress.

As the years pass, however, and the "radiance" of his passion dims, Nabokov is increasingly consumed with practical matters. By the 1930s, he seems too preoccupied to take pains with his style. For a writer who labored over his prose, that negligence—hasty sentences full of repetition—may be just a little luxury, like his cigarettes, that he knew Véra would indulge. But the substance has changed, too. There is less about his art, except for the effort to publish it, and more about his digestion. He struggles as a stateless person to obtain visas, and "our letters," he laments, degenerate into "bureaucratic reports." Long passages are devoted to his social rounds, a recitation, for the most part, of obscure Russian names. Perhaps Nabokov did not wish to trouble his "Pussykins" with unpleasantries like the rise of fascism; he mentions Hitler exactly twice. On April 7, 1939, the day Mussolini invaded Albania, Nabokov is strolling in a London park, where the yellow pansies "have Hitler faces." A few days later, he spends a morning with a fellow lepidopterist. "We talked about everything, starting with the genitalia of Hesperiidae"—a family of butterfly— "and ending with Hitler."

Boyd and Schiff both drew upon these letters for their biographies, so they contain few surprises, except for the revelation—a disconcerting one, for a lover of Nabokov's fiction—that he could be a bore. Here, for example, he prepares for a reading in Paris:

I had a great shave and began to dress. It turned out that the sleeves of my tuxedo were too short, that is, that the cuffs of the beautiful silk shirt of the same provenance stuck out too far. Besides, the belt was peeking out from underneath the vest when I stood up straight. So Amalia Osipovna quickly had, first of all, to make me those, you know, armbands, out of elastic and Zenzinov had to give me his suspenders . . . When all of that had been sorted, I looked very smart.

He goes on to relate his dinner with Amalia and Zenzinov, his consumption of an eggnog, their arrival, by cab, at the "packed" hall on the Rue Las Cases, and the fatigue induced by having to smile at so many admirers. He loses track of their names, but he does record the gratifying presence of important writers and "thousands" of ladies—"in a word, everyone." When the reading finally gets under way, he opens his briefcase—a "very nice" one borrowed from a friend—and spreads out his papers. After a sip of water from a handy carafe, he begins to recite. The acoustics are "magnificent," and every poem is greeted with rapturous applause. The account continues for four pages.

There is little doubt that Mrs. Nabokov took a keen interest in her husband's every triumph, toothache, and fried egg. But it is also possible to imagine that, in bleak moments, she tired of his endearments ("my little sunshine"), bridled at his pet names ("lumpikin"), and resented the ostentation of a love that can be hard to distinguish from self-infatuation ("It's as if in your soul there is a prepared spot for every one of my thoughts").

We will never know, however, what Véra felt. She systematically destroyed her own letters to Vladimir, and even blacked out the lines she had added on their postcards to his mother. At best, she was a fitful correspondent. Vladimir's frustration with her epistolary reticence is a constant theme—"Pussykins, you write disgustingly rarely to me." Boyd marvels at Nabokov's tolerance "of what many in his position might have seen as a failure of . . . reciprocity."

Failures in a marriage, however, tend to be reciprocal. "When I think about you, I get so happy and light," Vladimir exults to Véra in 1926, "and since I think about you always, I am always happy and light." He surrenders to this trance of buoyancy at a moment when Véra, a newlywed, has been sent to a sanatorium—against her will, it seems—to recover from depression and weight loss. In response to a "sad little letter" in which she seems to have begged for release from her incarceration, he tells her, "Understand this, my love, none of us wants to see you till you're completely well and rested. I beg you, my love, for my sake shrug off all that gloom . . . Think what I must feel knowing things are bad for you."

Nabokov's uxorious complacence reaches its low point in the spring of 1937, the "darkest and most painful" year of the marriage, as Boyd puts it. Vladimir's sexual charisma was legendary, and Véra was aware of his womanizing before she married him, thanks, in part, to a list of some thirty paramours he had provided, on her father's letterhead, early in their courtship. She had caught him on the rebound, four months after the end of his engagement to a rich beauty of seventeen. (The girl's parents had become alarmed at Nabokov's prospects and, evidently, at his morals; he had shared his diary with their daughter, who hurled it across the room.)

Earlier that year, Schiff tells us, Véra had received an anonymous letter, written in French but "patently from a Russian." She was in Berlin with Dmitri while Vladimir was in Paris, romancing publishers, and the letter informed her that her husband was besotted with a blond divorcée named Irina Guadanini, a vivacious flirt from St. Petersburg who earned her living as a part-time dog groomer. Véra confronted her husband with the rumor, and he shrugged it off. "*I forbid you to be miserable*," he tells her in March. "There's no power in the world that could take away or spoil even an inch of this endless love." (He has recently mentioned a rendezvous with Irina at La Coupole; he wants Véra to know that in the course of their meal he misplaced but recovered the top to his precious fountain pen.)

As spring approaches, the couple spar over vacation plans, she insisting on a Czech resort and he on a beach house in the South of France. "*You make me anxious and cross*," he scolds—she is being intransigent. And a little later: "My dear love, all the Irinas in the world are powerless . . . *You should not let yourself go like this*." And then in April: "My darling, your muddle-headedness is absolutely killing me. What's really going on?" What's going on, we learn from Schiff, is that Nabokov is enjoying torrid sex with his worshipful mistress while lying to his wife about ending the affair. He suffers not a little shame, yet tells Irina he can't live without her. He even hints that he will leave Véra—given time. And, in letters that might have made a fascinating appendix, he extolls his and Irina's uncanny compatibility in suspiciously familiar prose. "For the more mortal among us," Schiff observes, "there is cold comfort in the idea that even Nabokov could not coax two entire vocabularies out of reckless passion."

"It is the work of the artist," Nietzsche wrote, "that invents the man who created it. 'Great men' as they are venerated are subsequent pieces of minor fiction." Biographers do well to heed this caution, and so do Véras. It might have been the epigraph for *Pale Fire*.

Boyd calls Véra "an expert at blanket denial." In the late 1960s, Andrew Field proposed to write Nabokov's biography. Vladimir and Véra both welcomed the project, though they were wary of Field's prying, and Boyd speculates that she destroyed her letters to protect their contents. When Véra read a manuscript of the book, in 1973, she objected to what she considered a lifeless and distorted portrait. "After close to 48 years of life together," she told Field, "I can swear that I have never once heard [Nabokov] utter a cliché or a banality."

But how much did she deny to herself? In that regard, it is worth quoting a letter that Schiff found in the Nabokov archives. Véra wrote it, in 1959, to her older sister, Princess Hélène Massalsky. Lena, as she was called, had stayed in Berlin and barely survived the war. She left her husband, who then died. At some point, she converted to Catholicism. She had a son of twenty-one, Michaël, whom she had struggled to raise on her own. Véra was planning to visit them, but on one condition: "Does Michaël know that you are Jewish, and that consequently he is half-Jewish himself?" If he did not, she continued, "there would be no sense in my coming to see you, since for me no relationship would be possible unless based on complete truth and sincerity."

At the end of this volume, you have to wonder what Véra's qualms were as she disposed of her letters. She must have had some. The truth of her past would never be complete without them. Was it the act of a morbidly private woman refusing to expose herself—and thus, consciously or not, enshrining her mystique? Or an auto-da-fé that destroyed the evidence of wifely heresy? These questions reverberate in the echo chamber of *Letters to Véra*. "You are *my* mask," Nabokov told her.

NOVEMBER 2015

In 1965, Ingmar Bergman ferried a film crew to the island of Fårö, a Swedish military outpost in the Baltic Sea, to shoot the exteriors of *Persona*. The island is a place of harsh beauty and isolation; there is no respite from either in Bergman's masterpiece. He was working, as usual, with a close-knit company of Swedish actors and technicians, but, for the first time, he had looked abroad for an actress to play opposite Bibi Andersson, a veteran of eleven Bergman films. The newcomer had to resemble her co-star closely enough to suggest a confusion of identities, and to possess a supremely expressive face—her character is a mental patient who refuses to speak. The little-known Norwegian whom he cast was the twenty-six-year-old Liv Ullmann.

Ullmann will be seventy-five on December 16, three days after a documentary about her life with Bergman, *Liv and Ingmar: Painfully Connected*, opens in New York and Los Angeles. The director, Dheeraj Akolkar, is an Indian filmmaker in his thirties; when he first approached Ullmann, she turned him down. But she is famous for saying no to directors—Brian De Palma, Steven Soderbergh, Bergman himself. In 1981, she declined the role of Emelie Ekdahl in *Fanny and Alexander*, which Bergman had written for her. "I still don't know why I did that," she said recently, over brunch in a midtown hotel. (She was taking little bites of her toast, as she does at the breakfast table in *The Passion of Anna*.)

Liv and Ingmar suggests why Ullmann denied herself a part she likened to a "birthright": it took her decades, after her five years with Bergman, to escape her thralldom. They fell in love on the set of *Persona*. He was almost twice her age, forty-seven, and both were married. Before they met, Ullmann had felt invisible. "I paid school friends to go to the movies with me. I barely spoke until I was thirty. Ingmar and I recognized each other as born outsiders."

Ullmann quickly became pregnant (their daughter, Linn Ullmann, a successful novelist, was born in 1966), and, forsaking all others, who were not welcome to visit, moved into the house that Bergman built for them on Fårö. He was the auteur of their relationship, which she tried to live according to his direction, but their cloistered life alone with a toddler left her, she said, "insatiably hungry" for connection. "Needing to please has always been my weakness," she said. "My father died when I was six, so I sought a reflection of myself from wise older men." (God is one of them, she said—she is a believer—but James Stewart was another. She met Stewart in Hollywood, after she left Scandinavia, in the 1970s. "The first thing I blurted out was 'I always wanted you to be my daddy.'" She smiled ruefully at the recollection.)

There is no mystery to what Bergman saw in Ullmann: it is on the screen, in the ten films they made together, during and after their relationship. "He called me his Stradivarius," she said. "I can see today that I was beautiful, but I never felt so." She supplied him with a vital missing element, one that also eludes most of his characters: "I was normally neurotic, but Ingmar liked to say that, unlike him, I was born in one piece."

Bergman would not be the first artist to seek reunion for his fragmented psyche in the embrace of a whole woman. Yet Ullmann made a startling assertion: "People assume that I was the muse for Ingmar's female characters, and that Max and Erland"—Max von Sydow and Erland Josephson, Bergman's chief leading men—"were his alter egos. In *Scenes from a Marriage* the wife is me, and parts of her dialogue were stolen from my diary. But otherwise I was his alter ego. I was Ingmar. He translated himself into a woman's voice."

Ullmann's voice dominates *Liv and Ingmar*; Akolkar intercuts his interviews with the actress, and readings from her memoir *Changing*, with clips from the Bergman archives. She speaks in a golden autumnal tone that contrasts with the Gothic romance the film narrates, and a self-acceptance at odds with the disillusionment that both lovers suffer. But would the Master have approved the happy ending: old wounds healed, cruelties forgiven, serenity achieved? Ullmann believes so. He encouraged her independence once she had wrested it from him, and took pride in the directing career that she launched in middle age. (Her film adaptation of Strindberg's *Miss Julie*, starring Jessica Chastain, Colin Farrell, and Samantha Morton, will be released next year.) "I am always quoting a sentence of Kierkegaard's," Ullmann concluded, "even though he may not have written it. 'We come into this world with sealed orders.' Ingmar believed that, too."

DECEMBER 2013

EYE OF THE NEEDLE

T wo years ago, at an auction in Paris that set new records for couture, the Met Costume Institute acquired twenty-six ensembles by Paul Poiret that his granddaughter had put up for sale. They had belonged to the couturier's wife and muse, Denise, and hadn't been seen in public since she wore them at the turn of the twentieth century. Even though the couple divorced, with bitterness on both sides, in 1928, Mme. Poiret reverently preserved her legacy, and kept a diary of the occasions—a ball, a fête, a première—for which each garment was created. Harold Koda and Andrew Bolton, the curators of the institute, were stunned, Bolton told me, "by the revelation of Poiret's modernism." As Janet Flanner wrote eighty years ago, Poiret was one of those "pirates" who "steal ideas from the future and force them on their own generation." There hadn't been a Poiret retrospective in America since 1976, and the Costume Institute almost immediately began planning one.

Poiret: King of Fashion occupies a special exhibitions gallery on the main floor of the Met. In addition to most of the new acquisitions, there are twenty-two Poirets from the archives or on loan; a display of accessories, decorative objects, and graphic art; and flacons of his perfumes. (He was the first couturier to brand himself by building an empire that purveyed, in addition to scents, home furnishings, "genuine reproductions" for the mass market, and a lifestyle.) Jean-Hugues de Chatillon, a scenographer for the Paris opera and ballet, has designed an installation of lush, hand-painted backdrops that, like a whiff of opium, evoke the fantasy life of the Belle Époque. Projected digital animations illustrate the ingenious construction of a brown silk-velvet opera coat from 1919 and a pink satin evening gown from 1923. The beauty of the show is of a piece with its contents. It invites you to discover what Poiret's contemporaries saw in him—and what they couldn't yet see.

Poiret was a rarity among couturiers: a native Parisian. He was born in 1879, the son of a draper whose family lived above the shop. His parents sent him to an elite lycée, where he felt out of place, until that feeling—a mixture of shame, yearning, and defiance—mobilized his ambition. In part to deflate his pretensions, his father apprenticed him to an umbrella maker. But Poiret stole time to dress a wooden mannequin that his sisters gave him, using scraps of parasol silk, and to make fashion sketches. Their originality recommended him to the courtly designer Jacques Doucet, who became his idol and mentor, giving him the opportunity to dress Réjane and Sarah Bernhardt, onstage and off. Among his costumes for Bernhardt were the breeches that she wore, at fifty-six, to play Napoleon's adolescent son in Rostand's *L'Aiglon*—her most famous trouser role. But she got Poiret fired when, within earshot, he made some sarcastic remarks about the production.

In 1900, Poiret served ten months in the army, then was hired by the Worth brothers to design casual daywear—"fried potatoes," as opposed to the "truffles" of their court gowns. But a marvelous kimono cloak, his earliest masterpiece (a later version is in the show), horrified an elderly Russian princess, who declared it a monstrosity. Jean Worth himself objected, perhaps jealously, to what he called Poiret's "dishrags," including a novel dress that fell vertically in a cascade of pleats, prefiguring the flowing neoclassic columns that would make him famous. According to Palmer White, Poiret's biographer, he "was tired of antagonism and wanted to strike out on his own." His mother lent him some money and, in 1903, he opened a modest establishment on the Rue Auber, behind the Opéra. With some prodding from Doucet, Réjane paid him a visit. She ordered a suit of marine-blue serge edged in bright red that, White reports, "she wore everywhere, and to greatest effect when, with regard to her divorce, she held press conferences to express her strongly feminist views."

Poiret was the apostle of comfort and simplicity who invented the sheath and the sack dress (both usually ascribed to Balenciaga, who streamlined them in the 1950s). He proposed the first couture trousers—a pantaloon gown or suit for day and a lamé dhoti worn under a lampshade tunic for evening. Most notably, he abolished the corset, inviting women to brave the streets, and sometimes the hostile mobs that attacked them with hisses or even blows, in the silhouette of a new century. The audacity of the clothes, which were more suggestive of an attitude—an uncorseted mind—than an erogenous zone, and the youthful charisma of their creator (he was not yet thirty) attracted such rebels as Isadora Duncan, Peggy Guggenheim, and Nancy Cunard. Their meeker sisters in Europe and America were emboldened by example.

Yet Poiret also perpetrated the hobble skirt, which makes him a problematic candidate for a feminist Wall of the Righteous. (There are no hobble skirts at the Met.) "I freed the bust," he liked to boast, "but I shackled the legs." And, like so many of his contemporaries, he was enthralled with the barbaric splendor and the hyper-refinement of an imaginary Orient. He styled his own persona after that of a sultan from *The Thousand and One Nights*, the theme of a bacchanal ("The Thousand and Second Night") that, in 1911, the Poirets threw in the garden of their eighteenth-century mansion on the Right Bank. Three hundred guests consumed nine hundred liters of champagne, while parrots and monkeys screeched in the shrubbery, and semi-nude Black houris and jinns circulated with platters of exotic delicacies. Scheherazade's tales had recently been translated into French by the Arabist Joseph-Charles Mardrus (whose bride, the bohemian writer Lucie Delarue, wore a cycling outfit to their wedding that may have inspired Poiret's harem pants), and she was, in many respects, his paradoxical ideal woman: the slave girl as free spirit.

Poiret was a master of synthesis and invention, but, like most autodidacts, he was also a sponge who soaked up inspiration and was loath to acknowledge it. It isn't a coincidence that the earliest Poiret in the show is dated 1905—the year he married Denise. The purity and assurance that radiate from her photographs, even in the most outré setting or creation, were always his best advertisement. The Fauves suggested Poiret's palette, and the Ballets Russes his gestalt. He commissioned Raoul Dufy to design his exuberant textiles and wallpapers, and hired the unknown Man Ray and the young Edward Steichen to take his fashion photographs. The artist Paul Iribe (a lover of Coco Chanel) sketched Poiret's trademark, a rose, and worked with Georges Lepape on the stylized, deliciously colored stencils that illustrated his collections. Earlier revolts informed Poiret's iconoclasm. His shift was modeled on the Empire chemise—a homage to the republican fashions of Greece and Rome that came into vogue with the French Revolution and reappeared as a challenge to Victorian conformity in the Artistic Dress of the pre-Raphaelites. Indian, Japanese, and Islamic robes taught him to construct a garment of rectangular panels, without a pattern. His virtuosity as a draper was unrivaled except perhaps by Madeleine Vionnet, and, more than fifty years before Issey Miyake, Poiret, who couldn't sew, created minimalist coats and dresses by twisting one continuous length of fabric into a three-dimensional volume.

If Poiret was one of the boldest innovators and self-promoters in fashion history, he was also one of its most spectacular casualties. There was no hyperbole to the epithet bestowed upon him by the American press—"the King of Fashion"—which Poiret repaid, on his return from a tour of the United States, with a pontifical tirade on the pathetic sameness and puritanism of American women. But the revolution that Poiret had set in motion caught up with him in the twenties, in the form of his nemesis, Chanel, and what he contemptuously called her *"misère de luxe."* He dissipated his creative forces striving for novelty and refused to understand that the women of a fast new generation weren't nostalgic for harem life, and didn't have the patience to reinvent themselves every time they got dressed—they wanted a uniform. Even before Denise left him, his profligacy had plunged him into debt, then into ruin. He lost his collection of modern paintings;

the mansion, and a villa in Saint-Tropez; several opportunities for a comeback; and, as the years passed, sixty pounds of his lordly heft to disease and poverty. Evicted from a series of ever humbler lodgings, Poiret died in 1944, in occupied Paris, nearly destitute. Chanel was living at the Ritz.

There will always be a market for little black dresses, but in recent seasons Milan and Paris have rediscovered the charm of a turban, feathers, a kimono sleeve, graphic filigree, tiered Empire sheaths, harem pants, scarf dresses slipping from a shoulder, and fur-trimmed cocoon opera coats. They speak to a free spirit with the means and the leisure to reinvent herself. "For whom, Madame, do you mourn?" Poiret is said to have asked Chanel, alluding to her favorite color. "For you, Monsieur," she replied. The ghost is risen.

MAY 2007

THE EMPIRE'S NEW CLOTHES

S omething funny happens to puritanical republics. After a while, they begin yearning for the glamorous, immoral ways of the aristocracy they overthrew. This yearning seems especially keen in China, where state television serves up feudal soap operas with the regularity of daily meals. Last November, 700 million people streamed the first installments of a typical saga, *The Legend of Mi Yue*. The story follows the fortunes of an orphaned princess who is exiled to the harem of an aging emperor, where she gives birth to his son but has to outwit malevolent rivals—warlords, concubines, her own sister—to become the Middle Kingdom's first female ruler. Women fans, especially rural ones, who don't get much chance to dress up, relish the fabulous costumes. Nolan Miller, who dressed the catfighting consorts of a later dynasty—the House of Carrington—might have admired them.

China's patrician culture, unlike its avatars on TV, had an ethos of supreme refinement based on *xiushen*, the Confucian notion of self-cultivation. Its arts, writing, and dress were imported to Japan millennia ago, and Kyoto, in particular, attracts throngs of Chinese tourists. Whether they are nostalgic for their lost imperium or just having fun, they kit themselves out to visit the temples in head-to-toe Edo style: men in gray cotton kimonos, women in brightly flowered ones. As a guide explained recently, during a selfie break, the reenactors were renting their finery by the hour. "It's a booming business here," he said. "With a package deal, you also get accessories and a hairstyle."

The kimono is a national costume for which China has no equivalent. When most Westerners picture Chinese dress, they think of the Mao jacket, or of the *qipao*, a sexy sheath with a mandarin collar and frog closings. Even these garments exist in dialogue with the West: the "Mao" jacket was actually introduced by Sun Yat-sen, to Occidentalize Chinese menswear, and the *qipao*, based on a gown for male scholars, was adapted for women by French-inspired tailors in Shanghai. The Han dress movement, which started a decade ago to protest the dominance of Western fashion, encourages its followers to post pictures of themselves in period costume. But you can't rent Han clothing for an outing to the Great Wall, and sartorial fantasy of any provenance is scarce in Beijing. When I visited, in early January, everyone seemed to be wearing jeans and puffers. Even in the Dashanzi Art Zone, a former factory complex where galleries and design companies are concentrated, there is little of the fashion street theater that enlivens comparable neighborhoods in Tokyo, Berlin, and Brooklyn.

"Drabness has been a kind of camouflage we're only just sloughing off," my young friend Luhan remarked. We were walking through a residential hutong—an alleyway that had not yet been gentrified—where sooty wash hung from clotheslines. "Dark colors are practical for a filthy climate. But in a climate hostile to personal expression both sexes wore the same shapeless clothing as a badge of patriotism." Her mother, she said, once passed a barefoot woman on the sidewalk surrounded by a crowd that was shouting insults at her. They had thrown her shoes—a pair of high heels—up into a tree.

High heels made in China are now widely available in Beijing's discount malls, but high fashion is still the province of a few designers who earned their cachet in the West, and in most cases trained there. Qiaoran Huang studied at Parsons in New York, and Grace Chen at the Fashion Institute of Technology. The radically original Ma Ke, who dresses China's First Lady, graduated from Central Saint Martins in London.

Ma Ke's couture dignifies the harshness of proletarian life with garments of mud-caked homespun, but she is an exception. China's rich think of themselves as a new aristocracy. They are impatient with drabness and proud to assert their national identity—not to say their buying power. Their court dressmaker, who was unknown in the West until recently, and to whom the West was virtually unknown until sixteen years ago, is Guo Pei. Mandarin is Guo's only language, and her clothes speak it, too. Chiu-Ti Jansen, the stylish founder of China Happenings, a media company, describes her as the country's "first 'homegrown' master couturier." Guo's aesthetic, she says, expresses "a visually deprived nation's pent-up longing for imperial grandeur." Her feat is the more remarkable in an environment "where the majority of nouveaux riches worshipped Western luxury brands."

There are two Guo Peis, however. Guo A is a counterrevolutionary—a conservative whose work rejects not just the austerities of Maoism but also the youthquake of the 1960s. She borrows her silhouettes from the pages of Eisenhower-era *Vogue*, in which socialites of indeterminate age, with arched eyebrows and a slouch, wore tailored sheaths under a matching coat, or boxy little Chanel jackets with braid and gold buttons. Guo's ensembles are distinguished by Chinese embroidery of exquisite quality, but their fusion of East and West feels superficial. It's exportware, reimported.

Guo B is a fabulist of sovereign fancy. She samples images of dress from Renaissance art, opera, Gothic fairy tales, or wherever she finds them in pre-*Sputnik* fashion history, and recombines their hallmarks—a sleeve, a ruff, an apron, panniers—with fantastical decoration that alludes to her own heritage. Porcelain is a recurring theme, especially blue-and-white. So are filigree and cloisonné. Fans or scrolls become part of a garment's postmodern architecture. Her appliqués mushroom magically on the slope of a skirt. A mermaid gown that Charles James might have made for Gypsy Rose Lee is crossbred with a Ming vase; a cascade of ruffles evokes the waterfall in a brush-painted landscape.

Guo A dutifully supports Guo B, because her art pieces, which may take thousands of hours of hand labor, can't pay for themselves. They do, however, advertise her talents on the runway and on the

Internet. Lady Gaga coveted one for a music video, then found that she couldn't move in it. Rihanna asked to borrow a coronation cape of sunflower-yellow satin, trimmed in matching fox, with a sixteen-foot train and some fifty pounds of 3-D embroidery. "I had never heard of her," Guo said of the diva. "And I don't like lending big things to celebrities." But then Rihanna, who has 57 million Twitter followers, wore the cape to the Met Gala, last May. Resplendent and impassive, she took the stairs like a temple idol ascending to her altar, and the image went viral. (So did photoshopped versions of it lampooning the cape as an omelette.)

The gala inaugurated *China: Through the Looking Glass*, the most ambitious show the Met Costume Institute has ever mounted. The installation sprawled across three floors, taking over the Astor Court and the Chinese galleries and juxtaposing their contents—devotional sculpture, masterpieces of calligraphy, Qing ceramics—with several centuries of couture inspired by Eastern exoticism. Andrew Bolton, who curated the show, described Guo's decoration of Western silhouettes as a unique form of "auto-Orientalism." The millennial history of Chinese dress, he observes, has no precedent "for this kind of synthesis."

In a high-ceilinged gallery, encircled by great Buddhas, a gown by Guo had pride of place. Long tongues of brocade sheathed an armature shaped like the dome of St. Peter's. Each tongue was so densely embroidered with gold thread that its surface looked chased.

Some of the pairings of sacred art and decadent couture gave off a whiff of sacrilege. Yet the dress, like the show, asked you to suspend your prejudice toward fashion as a vain pursuit and consider it as the mandarins did: an aspect of self-cultivation. Guo was pleased with the attention, though unawed. The honor, she said, belonged to China.

Guo A is the one you meet. She is a gracious woman of forty-nine, pretty and petite. There is nothing of the fashion priestess about her—no exaggerated chic. She exudes naturalness and a conventional femininity. Her husband and partner, Cao Bao Jie, known as Jack, is a rugged-looking businessman from Taiwan—an importer and converter of luxury European textiles. His wealth staked Guo to her career, and his devotion has nurtured it since they met, in the late 1990s. Jack and Guo have two daughters, eight and sixteen; they live in a northern suburb of Beijing, in a private house whose massive chandeliers, white leather sofas, and plush media room would not seem out of place in an upscale enclave of Houston. Guo has a collection of teddy bears, and Jack has one of batiks.

Nearly everything about Guo A is anomalous in the Western fashion world, not least her indifference to it. "Changing your look every season to please a fickle customer isn't how I work," she told me. "I aim to create heirlooms that a woman can pass down." Her couture is handmade to order, and her "demi-couture" is hand-finished. (She doesn't do ready-to-wear.) Guo's dressy fabrication heightens the formality of her daywear, and there is no hint of irreverence to her embroidery. She sticks with traditional talismans—a phoenix, a dragon, butterflies—of good luck or longevity.

The house specialty is wedding and evening wear of delirious opulence, with five- or six-digit price tags, and here the gap closes between Guos A and B. "The Chinese prize intricacy," Guo told me, in describing the ideal of her needlework. Yet her virtuosity is mysterious, considering that she has only ever seen haute couture in a museum. Jack took her abroad, for the first time, in 2000, partly to acquaint her with the antique Chinese textiles in overseas collections. When I asked her about mentors or models, she hesitated. "Well, I admire Chanel and Rei Kawakubo," she said, "but more as career women than as designers." Balenciaga was the only other couturier she cited, for his technique. He retired in 1968, as the May uprisings in Paris threatened to disrupt the old order. Guo has a similar distaste for youthful insurrection. Older women, she said, inspire her more than younger ones. The house muse, Carmen Dell'Orefice, is a leonine model of eighty-four.

Brides are an exception, however. Last year, according to the BBC, the Chinese wedding industry generated revenues of some $80 billion. The average expenditure per couple is a third greater than the average wage. Angelababy (Angela Yeung), China's Kim Kardashian, spent $31 million on her recent wedding to the actor Huang Xiaoming.

(The white gown for the vows was by Dior, but to the tea ceremony the bride and groom wore traditional red-and-gold costumes by Guo Pei.) At the other extreme, Guo once made a wedding dress for the daughter of a woman living on unemployment, who invested her life savings—eight thousand dollars—in it, even though Guo begged her to save the money "for necessities."

Eight thousand dollars does not go far at Guo's bridal boutique, on a posh street in Shanghai. Many of her patrons might spend as much on dinner. They are the consorts of oligarchs, women entrepreneurs, and, reportedly, the wives and daughters of Party officials. (When I asked Guo about the nomenklatura, she held her finger to her smile and said, "It's better not to discuss them.")

Last September, in New York, I met a cadre of Guo Pei stalwarts who had underwritten a luncheon benefit at the Pierre hotel. Her golden gown was on display in a ballroom, and during the meal she presented a runway show for First Ladies, in town for the United Nations. A businesswoman named Lucy Liu chaperoned her fourteen-year-old daughter, Alice, who wore a Guo Pei party dress smothered in tulle roses. ("Is it too much?" she asked.) Liu's line of work, she said, was "water conservation." Other guests were involved with "industrial packaging," "finance," and "the Internet." A beauty with the classy pallor of Mi Yue owned cosmetic-surgery clinics. Major jewelry was ubiquitous—at 1 p.m.

I was curious about a dapper tough guy in a porkpie hat who arrived by limo with a female entourage. "Guo Pei is a genius," he whispered confidentially. "But it's hard for common people to understand her." He claimed to be a Manchu prince—"though princes of old didn't have my panache." His wife owned "thousands" of Guo Peis, and they lived in a "royal palace," or at least a copy of one, on the grounds of a water park. Their collection of Chinese ceramics, he boasted, was "better than the Met's." I asked him how he'd made his fortune, and the short answer was "profiteering."

"We're all part of the club," Liu said gaily, which wasn't a metaphor. Jack and Guo have a shrewd business plan. "You can't trust Chinese people to pony up," Jack told me, "and we can't afford to spend months on a dress if they don't." So patrons of the house pay an annual fee, from which their orders are deducted. The club has four tiers of membership, with subscribers in the top tier spending roughly $800,000. There are about four thousand subscribers.

Rose Studio, Guo's showroom in the Chaoyang district of Beijing, occupies three floors of a low building in an industrial park near her house. From the outside, it might be a factory; on the inside, gold-speckled mirrors line the walls and ceilings, and the reception area is furnished with baroque divans. Tall vitrines hold an archive of runway pieces, including Rihanna's cape, which have been scaled down to fit a collection of Barbies. Like the teddy bears, they speak to Guo's taste for girlyness.

On the top floor, out of sight, a few dozen tailors, pattern cutters, shoemakers, and needlewomen work on the orders. Guo eschews machines and computers. A decorative pattern is copied from a book, transferred to tracing paper, stenciled on cloth, cut out, and pasted onto a muslin, then painted to see how the colors harmonize. Beading or crystals may then be overlaid on consecutive layers of embroidery, which acquire the surface of a bas-relief. Guo employs another five hundred people at three locations outside the capital. Most learn their craft on the job. "I'm a good teacher," she said.

A spiral staircase, with a bronze dragon coiled around its banister, leads to the VIP fitting rooms. There, one afternoon, I met a client named Jade Zhu—a svelte woman of fifty-one who was about to take her IT company public, and had flown in from Hong Kong to order a wardrobe for the celebrations. Western socialites need a deep closet of gowns for black-tie charity events, but there isn't much charity in China, hence no tradition of galas. Corporate parties, foreign travel, and state receptions are, with weddings and the lunar New Year, the primary occasions for dolling up. "I've been a couture client at Chanel for years, but now I wear only Guo Pei," Zhu said. "As you age, your traditions become more important, and I'm ready to embrace a more Chinese style."

"A more Chinese style" is, for a certain class, both a statement of pride and a strategy of caution. Christine Tsui, a scholar at the

University of Hong Kong, who often writes about the nexus of Chinese fashion and politics, noted recently that when Xi Jinping launched his anti-corruption campaign, in 2012, Western luxury brands saw a drastic reduction of their mainland sales. The nomenklatura capitalists, whose Vuitton bags and Rolex watches were suspiciously incommensurate with their official salaries, began to patronize native-born designers. This shift coincided with a government effort to alter the perception of "Made in China" as a synonym for "cheap and shoddy." The new buzzword was "Designed in China," and the Party encouraged its faithful to adopt "neo-Chinese dress."

Guo's loyalty to her country, both as a citizen and a creator, is part of her appeal to its governing elite. She has often been chosen to costume stars at state-sponsored events, such as the Beijing Olympics and the New Year's Gala, which has a television audience six times that of the Super Bowl. (This year's gala was widely derided online for its egregious propaganda.) "My generation is the most patriotic, because during our lifetime we have seen such an increase in prosperity," she said. "I really don't care about ideology, or who's in power, as long as the economy keeps growing."

Zhu's time was short, so she slipped behind a screen to try on a selection of samples. The first was a tailored sheath. (Mrs. Kennedy wore its prototype.) "I'd like it embroidered with my daughter's horoscope," she told Guo, without asking what the work would cost. "Clothes aren't a major budget item for me," she said lightly. The next number she tried on had the silhouette of a Victorian morning dress, with leg-o'-mutton sleeves and a prim collar. "We'll jewel the cummerbund," Guo told her, and she knelt at Zhu's feet to sketch a design directly on the muslin. Old colleagues told me that Guo's "people skills" have been crucial to her success. There is no servility to her manners in the studio, yet she treats her clients with a warmth that conveys the impression they are part of the family. "My mother also did beautiful embroidery," Zhu told me wistfully as she was leaving, in a cloud of scent and fur. "She made our clothes of cast-away scraps."

Homemade clothes were the norm in China during Guo Pei's childhood; her mother, like millions of other women, sewed for her family. Guo was precociously dexterous. She could thread a needle by the age of two, and since her mother had bad eyesight she was proud to be useful. "That's where my ambition came from," she said. "I wanted to be a tailor, to support my mother when she couldn't see." Her childhood coincided with the Cultural Revolution, which she doesn't remember, except that her family had enough to eat and that both parents earned a salary, "so we didn't feel poor." But life in Beijing was constrained and monochrome; paranoia ran high, as citizens were encouraged to inform on their neighbors, or even on their parents, if they saw any seditious behavior.

Guo was lucky that no one overheard her bedtime stories. Her mother's mother, who lived with them, was born in the twilight of the Qing dynasty. Her prosperous family had lost its wealth before the Communists came to power, but Empress Dowager Cixi—whose passion for Peking opera shaped her epoch's florid style—was a mythic figure to her. "My grandmother taught me about elegance," Guo said. "She was my first teacher. Every night when I was four or five, she described the dresses that women wore in the old days, and I pictured them before I fell asleep."

If Guo's mother inherited any precious keepsakes, she destroyed them. (The self-styled prince at the Pierre told me that he got started as a collector by scavenging objects that families were frantic to get rid of.) All Guo inherited was a reverence for storytelling, heirlooms, and old ladies. Her grandmother's bound feet didn't repel her. An upper-class woman would have been proud to hobble on her "flowerpot-sole shoes"—embroidered slippers on tall pedestals—and Guo pays homage to them in vertiginous chopines that are lashed to the ankles with satin ribbons. "I'm not a feminist," she said emphatically. "I think women should be like water: it looks soft and tender, but it's very powerful."

Guo makes clothes for special male clients like the self-styled prince, but she disapproves of gender fluidity for either sex. Her father joined the army as a young man, and during the revolution he captained a militia. In those stark years, when Mao's wives wore Mao suits, the dandyism that the Party suppressed was invested in parades of hardware. Guo's own taste for martial splendor complements her penchant for ornamental femininity. The inspiration for her golden dress came to her in a French war museum. "They had a portrait of Napoleon dressed for battle. Everything about his appearance—down to the buttons of his uniform—spoke of a respect for beauty, even in the face of death."

The same could not have been said for the Chairman, who died when Guo was nine. He purged China of the "Four Olds"—ideas, culture, customs, and habits. Artisans were "reeducated," and their skills were lost. At the Beijing Institute of Clothing Technology, I visited a costume museum that preserves a collection of antique clothing which escaped the Cultural Revolution's bonfire of the vanities. The Han and Manchu garments make modern embroidery, even Guo's, look coarser by comparison, like a second-generation image.

Wang Yi, an associate professor of fashion design, was my guide at the museum. In the early eighties, Wang and Guo were fellow students at the institute, then known as Beijing No. 2 Light Industry School. "Before the revolution, all upper-class girls were educated in needlework," she said. "They spent years on their trousseaus, and the emphasis was on finesse." (Embroidery has a distinctive "hand," like the brushstroke of a calligrapher, which a connoisseur can identify.) "Guo is trying to reinvent imperial style. But there's a gap of a century in Chinese history, and her patterns, colors, and techniques have all been improvised in a vacuum."

The institute has an inviting shop on the ground floor—a loftlike space with raw-pine floors—that sells work by the students. Transparent bomber jackets hung on one rack; roomy linen shifts on another. You could buy a bubblegum-pink fur chubby to wear over a campy sequined cocktail dress. There was plenty of cheek, and no chinoiserie. Wang introduced me there to Bobo Zhang, a thirty-four-year-old professor of fashion design and communication. Zhang, skinny and chic, was all in black: a turtleneck over leather jeggings. "I don't have any interest in Guo Pei," she said. "It's a good thing that she trains technicians from ethnic communities, who would not otherwise be employed in industrial Chinese fashion, but there is no new style or concept to her clothes. On the other hand, foreign fashion people are curious about China, so maybe she can attract their attention, even just as a novelty."

"Bobo represents the younger generation," Wang pointed out. But I heard a similarly blunt assessment of Guo from Huang Hung, who publishes a lifestyle magazine and promotes the work of up-and-coming designers through her company and boutique, Brand New China. "Our young people are looking for a cultural identity," she said. "Guo Pei's notion of identity isn't contemporary. While I can see her as a great costume designer, her clothes tend to reinforce a Western stereotype—*The World of Suzie Wong*." Huang, a robust woman of middle age who was educated at Vassar, told me that her own taste runs to Eileen Fisher. "Chinese people, like Americans, prize comfort," she said. "We want clothes that we can move in, and that are easy to care for. The kids who work for me buy Lululemon online. You get upward mobility with Guo Pei, but not the forward kind."

Guo and Wang were fifteen when they won coveted places at the institute in Beijing, joining the first four-year design program offered by a Chinese vocational college. It was 1982, six years into the Reform era; the government wanted to expand industrial clothing production and encourage foreign investment in it. "But it wasn't about the art of fashion," Guo explained. "That notion didn't yet exist. They just taught us how to sew."

The girls studied sketching, painting, and anatomy, under professors from the Central Academy of Fine Arts, and then moved on to cutting, tailoring, and pattern making. They aspired to hipness, as art students do. "Everybody got an afro," Wang said, and she showed me a picture of a teenage Guo with a nimbus of permed hair. "Outside Beijing, on a school trip, people stared at us." Their rebellions were modest. Wang laughed at the memory of a summer dress, mass-produced by a Chinese company, that they all rushed out to buy because the color—chrome yellow—was so daring. "Then we discovered that gnats loved it, too," she said.

Guo was a popular student, Wang said. "She was just so cute, and always smiling." But the boldness of her graduation project impressed the class: a bouffant white wedding dress with tiers of ruffles. Guo has recalled that she asked a professor for help with the skirt, but he had no idea how to construct it. He referred her to a costume designer, who showed her how to make a pannier of bamboo. "Today, it might seem kitschy, but it put the other projects to shame," Wang said. "The rest of us did ordinary street wear. Only she had the nerve to dream."

When their class graduated, in 1986, every student was assigned to a job in a state-owned garment business. But, after eighteen months at a factory that produced children's clothes, Guo was hired as a designer by one of the new companies funded by the first wave of private investment. She spent the next decade anonymously turning out women's wear, mostly for office workers. "In those days, we didn't know what high style looked like," Guo said. "China had only one fashion magazine, with a few color inserts. I once paid a month's salary for an illustrated book from Hong Kong."

Paola Zamperini, a scholar of Chinese dress who chairs the department of Asian languages and cultures at Northwestern University, was a student in Beijing in the early nineties. She pointed out that, even during the Cultural Revolution, there was one realm where flamboyance was the rule. "The theater kept color and eroticism alive in China," she said. "Mao himself married an actress." (The current First Lady, Peng Liyuan, used to be a popular singer.) "Dancing girls in revolutionary operas wore shorts like hot pants; men showed off their physiques in tight trousers and tapered shirts." Every year, Guo told me, a few old movies from the West reached Beijing and gave her a glimpse of "the outside world." She is still wedded to the ideals of glamour that they purveyed.

The first costume dramas on television were imported from Korea and Japan, and by the late nineties the Chinese were making their own. Guo's boyfriend at the time worked in the nascent film industry, as a stage and set designer. He introduced Guo to actresses and singers who commissioned her to make gowns for public appearances, and she designed the costumes for *The Palace of Desire*, a *Mi Yue*-esque epic whose heroine was a Tang princess. "Those were her first art pieces," Wang said. "She put her heart into them, though she didn't get paid much. Friends told her she was being exploited."

By then, many pent-up Chinese appetites were straining for release. The Party's planners realized that fashion had commercial potential, and in 1995 the state-funded China Fashion Association sponsored a competition to name the country's ten best designers. That radical notion—of an auteur whose signature confers cachet—gained currency for the first time since the revolution. Guo made the ten-best list two years later. She had proved herself as a connoisseur of collective desire, even though she had no ownership of her designs; in one case, Wang told me, a boss ordered six inches cropped from the hem of a "daring" maxicoat, to save money on fabric. Yet she had conjured chic from cheap materials and unskilled labor. And even though her style was "still immature," Guo said, her clothes were often back-ordered. It thrilled her to see women wearing them on the street.

In 1997, Guo left the security of a steady job and founded Rose Studio. "There's a Chinese saying," she told me: "'Timing makes the hero.' Chanel came along at the right time, and so did I—at the moment of China's ascendance." That was the year, after two decades of gradual opening, that capitalism made its great leap forward: the government privatized large swaths of the nation's industry. Jack's luxury goods now had a mainland market, though, he said, "I was very picky. I chose to work with only ten designers." Guo was one of them, and when they decided to marry, several years later, he gave her two choices: an expensive ring or sixty thousand meters of fabric. She took the fabric. "One reason I'm sentimental about wedding dresses is that I never got to wear one," she said. "It was my busiest season."

On a frigid morning just after New Year's, Guo and her staff were putting the finishing touches on a spring collection that she would show in Paris at the end of January. A local model walked back and forth in the showroom so that the designer could study the clothes in motion, and Guo snipped a tassel here and there. "This girl isn't quite thin enough," she whispered to me.

Partly as a result of the Met show, the Chambre Syndicale de la Haute Couture had admitted Guo as a guest member, which entitled her to a slot on the calendar for Paris Couture Week. "Haute couture," like "Champagne," is a legally controlled French appellation, zealously protected by the Chambre. Few applicants are admitted. "I got the acceptance letter a day before the terrorist attacks," Guo said. "I'd been told I had no hope of getting in, and I'd been feeling really depressed about it." By the time she heard, she had to scramble to meet the requirements. A guest member needs a Paris atelier and a certain number of petites mains—a house's skilled artisans, most of them women, who do the hand sewing that defines haute couture. Jack had rented the ground floor of an old mansion off the Rue Saint-Honoré, with the idea of opening a boutique in the courtyard. He and Guo were shocked by the red tape that governs the alteration of a historic property in Paris. "You can't even change a single tile!" Guo marveled. In China you can raze almost anything.

Guo was not going "all out" with this show, she told me, in part because she lacked the prep time. She was waiting until couture week in July to "pull out all the stops." But she seemed ambivalent about her goals. Expanding into ready-to-wear, a move she is considering, would be a challenge, because her reputation rests on craftsmanship, and she risks cheapening it. For most designers, couture is a loss leader that helps to sell scents and accessories; Guo has none of her own to hawk.

At times, Guo speaks frankly about her ambitions: "I want to make clothes that sell in order to finance clothes that don't sell but which speak to my soul." But could she sell them in Paris? "To succeed in the West, Guo has to understand its zeitgeist," Andrew Bolton said. "Couture today is much closer to ready-to-wear than it used to be, and she may have an outmoded notion of it. The work of designers like Karl Lagerfeld or Raf Simons is relevant to the lives of contemporary women." The French PR firm that Jack hired to promote the show seemed to take Bolton's view. It advised her to focus on "wearable" designs that would appeal to an "international" clientele. The couture I saw that morning did not strike me as international, though I could imagine its appeal to women from Russia or the Middle East, who are less shy about displays of wealth and who share Guo's notions of feminine mystique.

But Guo has succeeded in the global economy's biggest market on her own terms. When I asked how the current financial crisis would affect her, she serenely predicted that it wouldn't: her core clientele was recession-proof. "I am confident about my work, and I don't care what people think about it," she said. And perhaps that was her point in bringing it to Paris. Her show wasn't an audition—she was throwing down a gauntlet. Zhang Qinghui, an industrial economist who serves as a vice president of the China Fashion Association, phrased Guo's challenge to the West diplomatically. "The French couture industry has rigid high standards and its own history," he said. "But it will have to get used to a new world."

Guo's Paris debut proved to be more of a dessert course than an entrée. There were dresses for a thé dansant, dainty and frosted, in a macaron palette. Sabrina might have worn them. A chiffon poet's blouse with embroidered cuffs was paired with the only trousers on the runway. Tabards were a theme, gorgeously bejeweled, but they seemed extraneous to the clothes they decorated, and one of them looked like a lobster bib. The first number that Guo sent out, however, announced what she can do when she pulls out all the stops. It was a strapless gown of distressed guipure—with scorched edges, stiffened and gilded—that looked like a giant sea sponge. Salt crystals glistened in its pores. It had the idiosyncratic "hand" of a great artisan.

This ravishing excrescence reminded me of a shipwreck-themed Alexander McQueen show from 2002, which opened with a video of a drowning girl. McQueen worked the way a dreaming brain does, transmuting suppressed instinct into images that can trouble, mystify, and elate. Guo B has often been likened to him, but when I mentioned the comparison, I evoked a rare flash of temper. "We are like night and day," she said, "because I love life, and I want my clothes to send a positive message." (McQueen committed suicide at forty.)

In that respect, she may have more in common with McQueen's successor, Sarah Burton, who designed Kate Middleton's wedding dress and is one of her favorite designers. There are many versions of nomenklatura chic, but their common purpose is to telegraph "positivity"—rapt support for a man, a brand, a party, or a message. Burton's clothes for the Duchess of Cambridge are one example. The shapely pink sheath that Melania Trump wore to a rally in South Carolina is another. With a few silken tassels, it could have been a Guo Pei.

These clothes are an exalted form of livery, a uniform for women performing an old-fashioned role, and Guo's club members also seem content to abide by its protocols, at least in public. But stylish women of the twenty-first century try on and cast off many guises, and their clothes echo the dissonance among them.

The Chinese runway, like the Chinese theater, is a place where fantasy and eroticism have a freedom that is repressed elsewhere. Guo censors her prodigious imagination in her lucrative clothes for rich ladies, and it isn't clear that she or they see any need to embrace an alien notion of idiosyncrasy. Yet Jack said something telling about his wife, and perhaps prescient about her prospects in the wider world. He was describing their first encounter, as a merchant of European luxury goods and a young designer raised under communism: "She had never seen cloth like that before, and its beauty staggered her. But she didn't buy it just to use. She bought it to learn from."

MARCH 2016

I have never met any of the lucky women who owned a dress by
Charles James. A college friend, though, had an aunt who wore a
James to her engagement party, in the late 1950s. It must have
been one of his last creations, since he went out of business in 1958.
"Imagine that! A James in the family!" my friend said, as if she were
speaking of a Vermeer. "I've always wondered what happened to it."

I've always wondered what happened to James. His name draws a
blank outside the fashion world, although Christian Dior called him
"the greatest talent of my generation," and Balenciaga, a miser with his
enthusiasms, considered James "the only one in the world who has
raised dressmaking from an applied art to a pure art." But by the time
this compliment reached James's ears he was living at the Chelsea Hotel, nearly destitute, and estranged from all but a few devotees. They
were mostly members of a wild younger generation that included
Halston, a former protégé, who briefly gave James a job and, in 1969,
produced a retrospective of his work in an East Village nightclub.
James turned on him, though, as he had on so many friends and bene-
factors. He was demanding at his best, and substance abuse heightened
his volatility.

Like Proust, who gave his mother's furniture to a brothel, James
sometimes lent a couture outfit to a club kid. But he also liked to
model the clothes himself; his physique was elfin. Diana Vreeland
recalled meeting James in the late 1920s, when he was voguing on a

beach in the Hamptons in women's hats of his own creation and "beautiful robes." He was about to make his debut as one of those boy wonders who have played an outsize role in the history of fashion. And there always was something of the boy wonder about him: a puerile sense of entitlement that did him in, a prodigious imagination that never gave out, and a conviction that he was immortal. James died at seventy-two, and at the end of his life he was wizened and frail, but he still had the luxuriant dark hair of a matinee idol. His grudges were luxuriant, too. He had so much bitterness to discharge, so much glory to recall, and such philosophy to impart—a whole science of couture— that he talked through the night to whoever would listen.

James's years of obscurity never shook his confidence that posterity would give him his due, and, sure enough, the largest James retrospective ever mounted, *Charles James: Beyond Fashion*, opens on May 8 at the Met Costume Institute. The show's curators, Harold Koda and Jan Glier Reeder, and its conservators, Sarah Scaturro and Glenn Petersen, have, in effect, rescued, restored, and annotated a lost gospel. Reeder, a James expert, spent three years demystifying a biography that James embroidered. Her catalogue essay is the first reliable chronology of the life and the work, and James's range will astonish anyone who knows him only through a few photographs by Cecil Beaton. One of those images—a classical frieze, in which eight swanlike beauties are posed in a grand salon—is on the cover of the catalogue. Each ball gown is a pearly cascade of satin or taffeta, undergirded by an armature of bone, padding, or tulle.

Beaton's picture, however, plays to received ideas about James that Koda and Reeder otherwise take pains to dispel. The mature James lacks the irony of a postmodernist, yet his samplings from the past (bustles, panniers, and crinolines) have the same nerve. The young James was a leader of the avant-garde, whose ingenious tailoring— "off-grain" cuts, displaced seams, asymmetric draping that eliminated darts—is hard to read in a photograph. (Fashion history has a prejudice for the photogenic, and the tour de force of simplicity is often slighted.) James designed several outfits with an adjustable fit, so that two sizes accommodated most figures. The infinity scarf and the wrap dress were his inventions, as was the down jacket—a puffer for evening in ivory satin, which Dalí admired as a "soft sculpture." One of James's novelties was a proto sports bra.

By rights, he should be remembered, like Chanel, as one of those revolutionary pragmatists who changed the way that women dress. But James was often too early to get credit for his breakthroughs. He introduced an A-line coat ten years before Yves Saint Laurent, who had just taken over at Dior, made headlines with the Trapeze dress. It must also be said that Chanel and Saint Laurent focused on women's lives, while James fixated zealously on their proportions. "The feminine figure," he believed, is "intrinsically wrong," i.e., not platonically ideal by his standards. His mission to correct its flaws with a nip and a tuck, an arcing seam, a buckram implant, a cushion of air between skin and cloth diminished his relevance, even as it enhanced his prestige as an anatomist. The young find remedial fashion intrinsically uncool.

Charlie James, as he was known to his familiars, was born on July 18, 1906, at Agincourt House, not far from the Royal Military College in Sandhurst, England, where his father, Ralph, was an army staff officer. The baby was named in honor of his late maternal grandfather, Charles Wilson Brega, a Chicago shipping and real-estate magnate. His daughter Louise had met Ralph on a world cruise with her family; he was returning from a posting in China.

In 1910, the Jameses moved into a sixteen-room mansion in London. At five or six, Charles began composing for the piano. He was sent to boarding school at eight, and, at fourteen, enrolled at Harrow, though he left before graduation, with dismal grades. He later suggested that his departure was precipitated by a "minor escapade," although Reeder found no official record of it. James was openly gay from his late teens, she notes, and for the friends in his clique—Beaton among them—beautiful manners and bad behavior were the essence of chic. They shared a taste for fancy dress, makeup, and dramatics. (In the 1930s, James became a successful costume designer.) Ralph James considered his son a disgrace, and the antipathy was mutual. James turned to fashion, he explained to a correspondent, "out of a compulsion to be involved in a business of which my father disapproved."

By 1924, James was living in his mother's hometown, and working for Commonwealth Edison, in a desk job arranged by the company's president, a family friend. When the flamboyant teenager staged a fashion show—of batik beach wraps—at the office, he was reassigned to the architecture department, where he absorbed some of the technical concepts that he would apply to couture. In 1926, however, he did something unthinkable for a member of his class, male or female: he opened a millinery shop. Ralph forbade his wife and daughters (one older, one younger than their brother) to patronize it. Louise sent her friends, however, and the doyennes of Chicago society loyally helped to underwrite the ventures of her prodigy. James shaped his hats directly on clients' heads, cutting, twisting, and scrunching the felt or straw into whimsical shapes. A red cloche had a Jack Russell's cocked earflap; a turban molded to the skull suggested Amelia Earhart's flight helmet.

Most American couturiers have had middle- or working-class backgrounds. Adrian was the son of a milliner, Norell of a haberdasher; Mainbocher worked in the complaints department at Sears, Roebuck; Galanos's parents ran a Greek restaurant in New Jersey. Debonair Bill Blass, the son of a traveling salesman, could recall a time when he and his lowly ilk were asked to use the service elevator. James's connections gave him a ready clientele for the couture business that he launched in 1928, when he added a line of clothing to his hats and opened a salon in Manhattan, on the second story of a former stable owned by Noël Coward. Beaton promoted his work in *Vogue*, and James, who had considerable flair as a huckster, seduced the fashion press on both sides of the Atlantic.

In 1929, he was back in London, preceded by his reputation. Lady Ottoline Morrell became a client, and Virginia Woolf first heard of "the man milliner who was dropped by Heaven" through her friend Mary Hutchinson, a cousin of Lytton Strachey. "So geometrical is Charlie James," Woolf reported to her lover Vita Sackville-West, "that if a stitch is crooked, Vita, the whole dress is torn to shreds, which

Mary bears without wincing." Hutchinson wore a James blouse for her portrait by Matisse, at the artist's request. But, she later recalled, "Charlie was sometimes so entranced by the shape he was 'sculpting' over one's own" that when a dress arrived "it was impossible to get into."

James's entrée to Bloomsbury was sponsored, in part, by his Harrow schoolmate Stephen Tennant, the gay aesthete who was a model for eccentric characters in novels by Evelyn Waugh and Nancy Mitford. James ran up a fetchingly polymorphous wardrobe for him that included slinky beach pajamas. Tennant gushed in a letter to Beaton about an "ineffably limp" dress shirt in creamy satin and the "stunningest" black trousers, which "seem glued to every fissure & ripple of thigh & bottom." Yet, if James flirted with cross-dressing, he didn't let his female clients take the same liberty. He claimed to prize character above beauty in a woman, but he was an absolutist in his reverence for an old-school ideal of femininity.

Between the two world wars, James owned exclusive salons in Paris, London, and New York. He tacked between them, stretching his resources (which is to say borrowed resources) thin. Financial improvidence eventually destroyed his business, and his artistic scruples—the only kind he possessed—routinely jeopardized his deadlines and contracts. Balenciaga's couture ateliers produced some three hundred ensembles a year. James managed to create fewer than two thousand in the course of four decades. He once reworked a sleeve so many times that the labor and the materials invested in it supposedly amounted to twenty thousand dollars. The cost of such obsessiveness couldn't be recouped, even at the astronomical prices that the world's best-dressed women were happy to pay, while his opportunism strained their goodwill. The Countess of Rosse, a devoted patron, once brought a rich friend to James's atelier. He told her, "I couldn't possibly make anything for a frump like you."

No one, least of all James, has ever accounted for his artistry as a tailor. Apparently, he spent time in Paris studying his trade, though where or under whose aegis is uncertain. He thought of his vocation as sartorial engineering, but Harold Koda believes that there was more instinct than science to James's craft, and Richard Martin, the late fashion historian, dared to suggest that James "pretended to give serious thought to the structural elements of the dress, but a study . . . shows that he simply applied more and more layers until he achieved the needed density and shape."

Instinct and reason, however, are both aspects of spatial intelligence. James could visualize a complex pattern in three dimensions, then wrap or drape it directly on a body. The manipulation of material was one of his signatures, and he had no qualms about distressing it, or combining classic luxury fabrics with funky synthetics, like a fuzzy white plush that resembled wet feathers. The architect of the Pantheon's dome would have admired his cantilevered skirts, one of which, belonging to the Petal dress, had a circumference of nearly eighty feet. James's masterpiece, by his own just assessment, was the famous Clover Leaf ball gown. I tried but failed to follow the cutaway drawings that illustrate its construction—it had thirty pattern pieces and weighed ten pounds—or Reeder's description of "the semi-bias in the asymmetrical outer layer" and the "sequence of undulating curves, that work in symphony . . . with top and bottom curves undulating in opposite directions." For a 2011 James show at the Chicago History Museum, the curators resorted to CT-scan technology to expose the bones of a James under its flesh. A photograph shows three bemused-looking technicians grappling with what looks like a supine debutante who wound up in the ER after the ball. It is actually James's Swan dress strapped to a gurney.

Koda told me that "to really understand" a James "you have to take it apart." But his catalogue essay, "The Calculus of Fashion," does an excellent job of noninvasive deconstruction. And if you strip a James to its foundation what you find is sex. The true function of fashion, James said, is to arouse the mating instinct. The Broadway star Gertrude Lawrence was quoted as saying that she had never bought anything more respectable than a James—or as "utterly indecent." His Taxi dress, of the early thirties, spiraled seamlessly around the body and clasped at the hip. (Later models zipped across the torso on a rakish diagonal.) The dress got its name, James explained, because he wanted to design a garment that a woman could slip into—or out of—in the back of a cab. A deceptively austere sheath, such as the Coq Noir of 1937, swaddled the figure like a mummy's wrapping, but James bunched the excess silk at the back, forming an obscenely gorgeous labial bustle. A James gown invites you to imagine the lobes and crevices of the nude body beneath it, and it wasn't for the faint of heart. "Elegance," he wrote, "is not a social distinction but a sensual distinction." Gypsy Rose Lee, the queen of burlesque, was a favorite client.

Upper-class life carried on during the Depression with an insouciant disregard for the general misery. Vreeland and her husband, a banker, who were living abroad, kept a liveried chauffeur for their Bugatti. By the end of the decade, James was juggling fully staffed couture ateliers in London and in Paris, where he stayed at the venerable Hôtel Lancaster. His friend Jean Cocteau lived across the hall, and Cocteau's influence is apparent in a series of grosgrain opera coats that Beaton photographed against a background by Christian Bérard. The coats were an experiment in using humble materials for exalted purposes, and they have an aura—stark, dreamy, faintly vampiric—of costumes for a Surrealist chatelaine.

Cocteau also allegedly saved James from a suicide attempt, which was not his first. In Chicago, James had tried to kill himself over an unrequited love, having taken pains with the decor of his death scene: flickering candles, gilded mirrors, an ether-soaked handkerchief. "Racked by the pain in his nose," Reeder writes, he was rushed to a hospital that his grandfather had funded. In some respects, however, James had an unusually robust survival instinct. He decamped from Paris for London in August 1939, then sailed for New York.

The Second World War was a golden age for American fashion. Stylish women who had shopped in Paris were forced to become locavores. James opened a couture salon on East Fifty-seventh Street, but he also established relationships with leading retailers. In 1941, B. Altman mounted a show of his trouser skirts. Wearing pants was still largely taboo for middle-class women—slacks were acceptable on the factory floor and for the construction jobs that women had stepped up to fill—but James devised a clever solution for the conflicting demands of comfort and propriety. The skirt was essentially a bifurcated sarong, threaded between the thighs. It freed the legs and their stride, but a crossover front panel dissembled their separation. A sporty knee-length version anticipated the culotte; a resort-wear evening ensemble came with a midriff-baring top. The respectable and the indecent were never far apart.

New York was tonic for James. He liked to deplore the vulgarity of garmentos, but he was nothing if not a man on the make. He found a kindred spirit in Florence Nightingale Graham, a former nursing student and makeup salesgirl from a small town in Ontario who had re-invented herself as Elizabeth Arden. James was her walker in New York and Chicago, although his mother failed to get her into the society pages—she was "trade." When Arden became engaged to a Russian prince, James designed her trousseau. She shared James's ambition to correct women's flaws, and in 1943, when she decided to expand her beauty business to include custom-made clothes, she hired him to head the department. Their partnership ended in bickering over money and credit for his designs (she was not the first or the last of his associates whom he accused of piracy), and she was incensed by a backlit red vase that he had placed prominently in the window, giving her tony establishment, she felt, the air of a bordello. But, thanks in part to Arden's patronage, James met Millicent Rogers, Babe Paley, Marietta Tree, Slim Keith, and Austine Hearst, among other glamorous clients, who inspired and subsidized some of his greatest work. Hearst commissioned the Clover Leaf gown for Eisenhower's inaugural ball, though she had to wear something else—it wasn't ready.

When the war ended, James hired Japanese Americans recently liberated from internment camps to staff his new atelier, on Madison Avenue. They worked, he wrote, on "my most important bigger clothes, ball dresses and such"—including the sumptuous baroque gowns in an advertising campaign, photographed by Beaton, for Modess sanitary napkins. The idea was "that any woman at a difficult moment can imagine herself a Duchess," although, at a difficult moment, you could never have squeezed a James gown into the stall of a ladies' room. The Japanese had "a special quality of precision" that James found lacking in the New York labor pool. Harold Koda, however, told me that James was a selective perfectionist. He violated the integrity of his fabrics, and, Koda said, "I was shocked to discover how shoddy some of his seams are."

After the war, French fashion regained its predominance, which is to say its American market. Although James was among the world's most expensive couturiers—he charged seven hundred to fifteen hundred dollars for a dress—he fulminated at the disproportionate profits and the obsequious coverage that his counterparts in Paris were reaping. The problem, as he saw it, was partly a lack of competition from an American fashion industry enfeebled by mediocrity and rife with plagiarism. To encourage native talent and originality, he joined forces with Michelle Murphy, of the Brooklyn Museum, and he created the prototype for a dress dummy whose figure held the promise, he thought, of transforming the fit of American sportswear. The Jennie was a slim but realistic modern Eve, with a small bust, a convex tummy, and a slouch. It never caught on commercially, though James's advocacy did have a lasting consequence: He persuaded Millicent Rogers to donate twenty-four of her James gowns to the Brooklyn Museum. Her bequest set a precedent for treating couture as art—and as a tax deduction.

James's career was approaching its zenith. In 1950, he won a prestigious Coty Award, the first of two, and, in 1953, the Neiman Marcus Award—fashion's Oscar. (He startled the black-tie audience by appearing in jeans at the ceremony. "The blue jean is the only art form in apparel," he explained.) He also branched out into other fields. The philanthropists Dominique and John de Menil hired James to decorate their house in Houston, designed by Philip Johnson. James's voluptuous biomorphic furniture and hot color scheme—fuchsia, crimson, and tobacco halls; pewter, gold, and chartreuse upholstery—eroticized the modernist architecture. Johnson excluded the house from surveys of his work.

But no departure was more radical for James than his church wedding, in 1954, to Nancy Lee Gregory, a wealthy divorcée from Kansas, twenty years his junior. Some of their friends suspected venal motives, though James insisted he had married for love. "My wife knew I was homosexual," he said in an interview years later, adding that "all of society is double-gaited." When a son, Charles Jr., was born in 1956, James celebrated his new status with a collection of children's wear. One of the pieces was a baby's cape, in robin's-egg blue, eccentrically cut, like the carapace of a tortoise, with front-set armholes designed to limit an infant's "flailing." Princess Grace of Monaco ordered eighteen items for the layette of her daughter, Caroline.

A late marriage and fatherhood sometimes mellow a restless bachelor, but they seemed to exacerbate James's disaffections. The fine print of his financial dealings, documented by Elizabeth Ann Coleman, the curator of an important James show at the Brooklyn Museum in 1982, traces the death spiral of a grandiose enterprise out of control. The business had been diversified into a labyrinth of corporations that handled contracts for couture, ready-to-wear, faux furs, costume design, maternity fashions, the children's wear, prom dresses, accessories, and other projects, many unrealized, including a foundation. In the first year of the marriage, when the couple was living at the Sherry-Netherland Hotel, and James had just leased a sprawling new atelier, Charles James Manufacturers recorded revenues of $112,963, against expenditures of $310,266.

Bitter litigation with his licensees contributed to the brewing debacle. For much of the next four years, the couple lived on the run from their creditors—a list of their addresses includes more than a dozen hotels in New York, New Orleans, Kansas City, and Chicago. In 1957, days before the birth of their daughter, Louise, the Internal Revenue Service seized the contents of James's showroom; a year later, city marshals raided his office, and the business sank under its debts. Nancy's money was gone, and Charles was using amphetamines prescribed by Max Jacobson, the infamous Dr. Feelgood. "I do not know," James said, "if I did right to marry and ruin Nancy, but . . . the necessity of success and achievement came first." Nevertheless, their mutual tenderness survived divorce, and Nancy helped to preserve the James legacy. But she took the children and moved back to Kansas.

James landed at the Chelsea in 1964. The maids refused to clean his squalid rooms, which he shared with a beagle named Sputnik. He continued to produce custom clothing for the occasional client, but, fueled by speed, he indulged in an orgy of blame. James ended his fifty-year friendship with Beaton over a perceived disloyalty, accused the Brooklyn Museum of stealing materials that he had left there for storage, returned his awards in a fit of pique, and denigrated Vreeland for a long list of slights.

Yet, in destitution, James discovered a talent for generosity as a teacher. He embarked on a series of projects focused on "fashion engineering" with the Art Students League and Pratt Institute, and he won a Guggenheim Fellowship to write a textbook on the same subject. His young friends saw him as a link to the heroic age of couture. Antonio Lopez, the illustrator, preserved a record of James's work in hundreds of drawings. Homer Layne, a Pratt student from Tennessee, became his chief assistant and the steward of his archives, which he gave to the Met last year. The photographer Bill Cunningham documented the late-night "seminars" at which James held forth on "the fine points of couture, the follies of the rich, and 'the plagiarists of Seventh Avenue.'"

James never produced the textbook, and he never finished a memoir he was writing, which he intended to call "Beyond Fashion." But in 1974 a British magazine published his autobiographical sketch, "A Portrait of a Genius by a Genius." That is how he had lived—with a messianic faith in his uniqueness—and that is how he left the scene. On Friday, September 22, 1978, the day before he succumbed to pneumonia and heart disease, an ambulance was called to the hotel. "It may not mean anything to you," James told the medics, "but I am what is popularly regarded as the greatest couturier in the Western world."

Layne spent the weekend clearing out the rooms before the hotel could seize their contents. James owed six months of back rent.

APRIL 2014

EYE OF THE NEEDLE

⎯⎯∞∞⎯⎯

In 1953, Jacqueline Lee Bouvier married John Fitzgerald Kennedy in one of those "weddings of the century" that seem to occur every few years. She was a twenty-four-year-old former debutante who had been working for a Washington newspaper as an "Inquiring Camera Girl" while prospecting for a husband. He was a freshman senator from Massachusetts with his eyes on the White House. But you know all that, and what ensued. You may even recall the pictures of Jackie's dress—one of the most photographed bridal gowns in history.

Jackie was the architect of her own myth, and pretty much everything she wore after her marriage was chosen to enhance it. Her Gallic ancestry, embellished in the retelling, was a central motif. In that regard, her wedding gown was a disappointment to her. According to Kennedy historians, the young Miss Bouvier had lobbied for something svelte and Parisian. But Joseph Kennedy, the groom's father and impresario, overruled her. He was wary of sending the wrong message: decadent foreign glamour.

The dress that Jackie got was a chaste confection of ivory silk taffeta with a portrait neckline, a daintily tucked bodice, and a parasol skirt appliquéd with frilly rosettes. She wore it with regal aplomb, though her pique may have simmered. In 1961, Mrs. Kennedy's first year in the White House, a writer who interviewed her for the *Ladies'*

Home Journal reported that the gown had been made by "a colored woman dressmaker" and was "not the haute couture."

That "colored woman dressmaker," Ann Lowe, was in fact a consummate couturier. Her work was admired by Christian Dior and by the legendary costumer Edith Head. Jackie's formidable mother, Janet Auchincloss, was a faithful client. Jackie and her sister, Lee, had both made their Newport debuts in a Lowe dress. Marjorie Merriweather Post, the heiress and philanthropist (Donald Trump bought Mar-a-Lago from her estate), chose a silk-faille *robe de style*, attributed to Lowe, for her portrait by an artist who had painted Queen Elizabeth. Olivia de Havilland accepted her first Oscar in a strapless Lowe number of aqua tulle lavished with hand-painted flowers. Jessica Regan, an associate curator at the Met Costume Institute, compares Lowe with Mainbocher: "She was a brilliant example of the American couture tradition—a sculptural designer whose work was a dialogue with the body of the woman who wore it."

Lowe's evening and bridal wear were sold coast to coast in upscale department stores. She owned salons at several locations on Madison Avenue. In her heyday, the mid-fifties, she claimed that she sold a thousand gowns a year, grossing $300,000. (Her math tends to be inflected by hyperbole. Each gown was an original that required hours of intensive labor; Balenciaga, by comparison, produced about three hundred pieces of couture annually.)

Yet Lowe commuted to the Upper East Side from a ground-floor apartment in Harlem that she shared with her sister Sallie, who did the cooking. The same millionaires who cherished the finesse of her needlework haggled shamelessly over her prices, and she routinely undercharged them, explaining in interviews that the sheer happiness sewing brought her was its own reward. Retailers profited from her label's cachet but didn't advance the costs of her materials or her labor, and the debts she incurred to suppliers helped ruin her. (She was ruined several times but staged more comebacks than Muhammad Ali.) The Kennedy wedding, for which Lowe also dressed the bridesmaids, was a notable debacle for her. A plumbing disaster in her studio destroyed the gowns shortly before the event; toiling sleeplessly, she re-created them at her own expense. She never complained to the family. She did, however, indignantly refuse to use the service entrance at the Auchincloss farm, threatening to take her work back to New York if it and she weren't ushered through the front door.

In 2007, a retired biology teacher from Washington, D.C., Joyce Bailey, made a landmark bequest to the recently established National Museum of African American History and Culture. Bailey's glamorous mother, Lois K. Alexander Lane, is a singular figure in the history of Black fashion. Born in Little Rock in 1916, she dreamed of becoming a designer, but spent most of her life working for the federal government. On the side, she founded a school in Harlem that offered classes in dressmaking and millinery. In 1979, she opened the Black Fashion Museum, in a brownstone on 126th Street, a few blocks from Lowe's apartment.

Lane spent decades building the museum's archives. By the time her daughter donated them to the NMAAHC, they contained about two thousand garments designed, fabricated, or worn by African Americans. The earliest artifacts—a muslin dress, a bonnet—were the handiwork of enslaved women. But Lane also collected the showstopping outfits that Zelda Wynn Valdes created for such stars as Ella Fitzgerald; Geoffrey Holder's costumes for *The Wiz*; and the drab-chic day wear of Arthur McGee, a dressmaker's son, who was the first Black designer to run a studio on Seventh Avenue. In Lane's collection, a simple rayon dress that Rosa Parks had been sewing for herself when she refused to give up her bus seat in Montgomery shared pride of place with the opulent ball gowns of Ann Lowe. "Lane had done something that the great costume collections in the United States had not," Robin Givhan wrote in *The Washington Post*. "She focused on storytelling"—the stories that clothes tell of pride and hardship, triumph and endurance.

Lowe's rediscovery is due largely to the work of Black fashion scholars and curators, beginning with Lane, and including, more recently, Elaine Nichols of the NMAAHC; Elizabeth Way of the Fashion Institute of Technology; and Margaret Powell, a textile historian from Pittsburgh. A draft of Powell's master's thesis on Lowe was published online, in 2012, by the Corcoran School of the Arts and Design, and she was working on a full-scale biography when she died of cancer, at forty-three, two years ago.

Despite assiduous research, however, much of what is known about Lowe's life—especially her youth—comes from interviews that she gave as an elderly woman. One can't discount her lapses of memory, or her genius for embellishment. But one also can't discount the paucity of public records documenting the births, marriages, and deaths of Black Americans, not to mention their accomplishments. Several dozen of Lowe's dresses have been lovingly preserved—out of thousands. The fabric of her biography is an imperfect patchwork.

According to her own chronology, Lowe was born in Clayton, Alabama, in 1898. In the census of 1910, however, she figures as a married woman of twenty-one, living with her first husband, Lee Cone (his name has ubiquitously been reported as "Cohen"), a tailor, in the town of Dothan, about fifty miles from her birthplace.

Clayton is the seat of Barbour County, a center of plantation culture before the Civil War. A Confederate monument still stands in the courthouse square. George Wallace, the infamous segregationist, and his wife, Lurleen, who succeeded him as governor of Alabama, raised their family in Clayton, and racial strife has a long history there. On Election Day 1874, a white supremacist mob carried out a violent coup in Barbour. Its members murdered at least seven Black voters, and wounded scores, while routing hundreds of others at their polling places. Having destroyed ballots already cast, the insurrectionists unseated a Reconstruction judge duly elected by a majority of Alabamians—many of them free men of color.

One of those men was Lowe's grandfather General Cole ("General" was his given name, not a rank), a carpenter who had helped build the original Clayton courthouse. Around 1860, Cole bought the freedom of his wife, a young woman of mixed race: Georgia Thompkins, or Tompkins—Lowe's grandmother. Georgia's father owned the plantation where she and her enslaved mother worked as seamstresses.

Lowe's mother, Jane, was born during the Civil War. At some

point during Reconstruction, she met Ann's father, Jack Lowe, of whom nothing is known. But by the beginning of the twentieth century Jane and Georgia had established themselves as society dressmakers in Montgomery, the state capital, catering to political wives and daughters. Ann's education in the segregated schools of Alabama would have been rudimentary, and she dropped out at fourteen. But her apprenticeship in the family business trained her for one of the few vocations by which a woman could support herself respectably. It also gave her a rare example of female autonomy.

Lowe's driving ambition, she told Mike Douglas, as a guest on his talk show in 1964, was "to prove that a Negro can become a major dress designer." She cut the figure of one, birdlike and soignée. Her uniform was an exquisitely severe black suit or dress, accessorized by a trademark hat, a taut chignon, red lipstick, and dark glasses. By then, Lowe was the tenacious survivor of a game in which most contestants get thrown off the island. Who now remembers Gustave Beer, a contemporary of Charles Frederick Worth? What about posh Carolyne Roehm, a fixture of the Reagan era? Does Bill Gaytten ring a bell? (He briefly replaced John Galliano at Dior.)

From early childhood, Lowe possessed a transcendent self-confidence in her gifts. At five or six, she had started turning scraps of silk into the trompe-l'oeil flowers that became her signature as a couturier. Her husband, she said, forbade her to work—he wanted a stay-at-home wife—and she obeyed him for a while. But when her mother died, in 1914, Ann was recalled to Montgomery to finish four ball gowns for Alabama's First Lady, Elizabeth Kirkman O'Neal. It was, Lowe said, "my first big test in life," and it inspired her to feel that "there was nothing I couldn't do when it came to sewing."

Within two years, Lowe's life was transformed by a chance encounter at a Dothan department store. An out-of-town shopper noticed Lowe's clothes and remarked that she had "never seen a colored girl so well dressed." That lady, Josephine Lee, the wife of a wealthy citrus grower from Tampa, had four daughters, the eldest of whom were twins engaged to be married. She offered Lowe a job as her live-in dressmaker, initially to create gowns for the wedding party.

Lowe, who had recently given birth to a son, Arthur, ditched her husband and leaped at the opportunity: "I picked up my baby and got on that Tampa train."

Lowe recalled her years in Tampa as the happiest of her life. The local press celebrated her work in its accounts of weddings and galas. An "Annie Cone" dress was a status symbol. Jessica Regan noted that Lowe became famous for her surface embellishments—"for tiny carnations with organza petals, each one minutely hand-finished. But the interior structure of a dress was just as important to her. Invisible tacking stitches keep the layers of fabric moving together; a lightly boned bodice holds the bosom stable on a dance floor. Her emphasis on a perfected fit made her clients feel secure."

That security was a luxury that Lowe herself couldn't enjoy. She raised her son as a single mother in the Jim Crow South. They lived in the staff quarters of a rich man's house. Its owners were "sincere" with her, Lowe later recalled, yet she had to navigate boundaries of race and class that neither talent nor affection could breach. As Elaine Nichols noted in a recent e-mail to me, Lowe was "helping young, wealthy white women (and their parents) live in a world of fantasy." In that respect, she belongs to a tradition of Black dressmaking that stretches back before the Civil War. "A dressmaker, in some senses, is a body servant," Elizabeth Way observed. "She works on her knees."

Michelle Obama was the first chatelaine of the White House to champion the work of Black designers—Tracy Reese, Laura Smalls, Duro Olowu, Byron Lars, Mimi Plange, and Maki Oh, among others. But she wasn't the first to wear them. Women of color have been dressing First Ladies at least since 1861, when Mary Todd Lincoln hired Elizabeth Keckley as her personal "modiste."

Keckley was born on a Virginia plantation in 1818. Her father, Armistead Burwell, was its owner. She and her mother, a skilled seamstress, were his house slaves. For three decades, she endured a life of violence and degradation. Burwell "loaned" her to his son Robert (a minister), and when Keckley was eighteen one of Robert's parishioners took it upon himself to "subdue" the girl's "stubborn pride" with a whip. Later, she fell prey to a local shop owner, who raped her for four years. A son, George, was born of those assaults; he would die as a Union soldier.

In 1847, Keckley and George were transported to St. Louis, Missouri, by her white half sister and new mistress, Anne Garland. As the Garlands' fortunes dissipated, they hired "Lizzie" out to sew for ladies of their acquaintance. A few of those ladies grew fond of Keckley, and loaned her the price of her freedom. Her artfulness as a couturier, however, had increased her value as a piece of property. The Garlands demanded twelve hundred dollars for mother and son. (Abraham Lincoln and his wife had recently paid that sum for a house in Illinois.)

Once she was a free woman, Keckley sent George to Wilberforce University, in Ohio, a historically Black institution, where she herself later taught domestic arts. In 1860, she settled in Washington, D.C., and established a dressmaking business, with a bipartisan clientele that included the wives of Stephen A. Douglas, Robert E. Lee, and Jefferson Davis. A daughter of Edwin Sumner, the Union general, arranged the job interview with Mrs. Lincoln.

Mary Lincoln, like Jackie, was a Francophile and a clotheshorse. Her extravagance was notorious. Unlike Jackie, she had a dumpy figure and pretentious taste. (Her sartorial ideal was the Empress Eugénie.) Keckley dressed her with an elegance befitting her station— and her self-importance—but toned down the flamboyance. Volatile women are an occupational hazard of the fashion business, not to say of the plantation house. Stoical, reserved Mrs. Keckley had a gift for talking Mary Lincoln through her bouts of outrage and depression. And when the Lincolns lost their son Willie, at eleven, to typhoid, months after Keckley's son was killed on the battlefield, the two women grieved together.

That companionship, however, had a bitter aftermath. In 1867, the widow Lincoln, short of funds, decided to sell her luxurious White House wardrobe. Keckley traveled to New York to help with the sale. No buyers were found, and their foray was derided in the press. The next year, Keckley donated a trove of Lincoln memorabilia to Wilberforce, including the bloodstained bonnet that Mary had worn to Ford's Theatre. Her gift infuriated the former First Lady, who had wanted the items back. But the worst affront came several months later, when Keckley, seeking in part to raise sympathy for Mrs. Lincoln, published a memoir with the sensational title *Behind the Scenes, Or, Thirty Years a Slave, and Four Years in the White House.* The condemnation it received, especially from the Lincoln family, effectively ended a career that depended on deference and discretion.

Elizabeth Way, who wrote a master's thesis on Keckley and Lowe, was struck by their similarities, she told me. "Their skills were inherited from enslaved ancestors, and they both transformed them into free labor. More remarkably, they were able to build a client network of elite white women who came to respect their professional authority. Lowe represents a transitional figure in fashion history—a bridge between the old-fashioned artisan that Keckley was and the modern designer."

The American South has never been a bastion of modernity in fashion. Even in the North, chic women of Lowe's generation—and of Jackie's—looked to Paris. When Lowe began her career, designer ready-to-wear was five decades away. Mrs. Lee, however, realized that Lowe had the potential to create sophisticated haute couture—at down-home prices. In 1917, the family sponsored her enrollment in an established dressmaking school, S. T. Taylor, on lower Broadway in Manhattan.

Nearly every American designer of the past century gravitated to New York, the capital of self-invention. It was a magnet for Lowe, too. She was unprepared, however, for the prejudice she encountered among northerners. "The whole idea to admit a Negro girl to a high-class fashion school was absurd," she told a journalist in 1966. The school's director, who was French, "didn't believe I had the fifteen hundred dollars for the course—he just laughed. When I showed him my bankbook, he stopped laughing, but he still didn't believe that I could learn what he was teaching there." Here one should note that Harvard's tuition, at the time, was a hundred and fifty dollars, and that S. T. Taylor, according to Margaret Powell, advertised its courses in *The Crisis*, the NAACP magazine. It is entirely plausible, though, that Lowe's fellow students snubbed her—until they were humbled by her virtuosity. She left after a few months, when the dazzled Frenchman acknowledged that there was nothing he could teach her.

Lowe spent the next decade in Tampa. In 1919, she married a hotel bellman named Caleb West, and launched her own business in a workroom behind their house. She trained a staff in her exacting techniques of hand beading and trapunto (a style of quilting that creates an intricate raised design), and some of her protégées went on to prosper independently. Lowe's most treasured creations from that era were her fancy-dress costumes for Gasparilla, a local festival with parties and parades akin to Mardi Gras. The revels included a themed ball; they were dogged by charges of racism until the nineties.

One of the earliest Lowes to have survived, a short flapper-style dress from 1926, is the costume for a Gasparilla courtier that might have come from *les petites mains* of Lesage. "The asymmetrical neckline has one jeweled shoulder strap," Powell writes. "A large jeweled medallion in the upper left of the bodice and a series of small medallions towards the bottom of the skirt are connected with sprays of brilliants . . . in a pattern reminiscent of tree branches or curling smoke." The cloth has decayed, but the embellishment is intact. Each tiny bead was attached individually.

Lowe may have distinguished herself in the South, but she was also stymied there. Her white competitors had an insuperable advantage, Powell writes. A Black dressmaker could not get credit or rent a workspace in the downtown business district; her clients had to visit her in a segregated neighborhood. Josephine Lee, for one, felt that Lowe was "too good to waste herself" in a provincial backwater.

By 1928, Lowe had moved to New York with several assistants and rented a third-floor studio on West Forty-sixth Street. "No one flocked in," she told the *Daily News* in 1965. "I kept afloat for a whole year making the wedding gown and trousseau for Carlotta Cuesta"—a former Gasparilla queen. In the early months of the Depression, Lowe went looking for a job in the garment district. (She claimed to have started her new business with twenty thousand dollars in seed capital, although that figure, more than ten times the average family's annual income at the time, should probably be adjusted for exaggeration.) According to the census of 1930, Lowe was sharing her two-bedroom apartment on Manhattan Avenue with her husband, her son, her assistants, and "a roomer." The marriage didn't endure. Lowe told *Ebony* that Caleb West "wanted a real wife," so he divorced her.

When no one hired Lowe, she offered to make gowns on spec. Her work, as usual, found appreciative buyers. For the next decade, she freelanced anonymously for carriage-trade houses such as Sonia Gowns and Hattie Carnegie. Eventually, she said, she met "the right people." By then, she was using her maiden name. One of the earliest garments with an "Ann Lowe" label is now at the Met Costume Institute: a sublime wedding dress from 1941, with the silhouette of an Erté Tanagra. Embroidered trapunto lilies, bedewed with seed pearls, cascade down the bodice; molten satin bubbles at the hem like a pool of candle wax.

Some of the greatest designers have been hopeless with money. Paul Poiret and Charles James both died destitute. Yves Saint Laurent was a financial imbecile, but his partner, Pierre Bergé, managed their fortune cannily. Lowe never had a Bergé, not to mention a yacht, a country house, or an art collection—common perks of success in fashion. Her son, Arthur, kept her books and paid the bills. But after his premature death, in a car accident, no one capable took over. In 1962, the Internal Revenue Service shuttered Lowe's salon for nonpayment of taxes.

The timing was ironic, since the new First Lady's patronage, or even a public acknowledgment, might have rescued Lowe. But Jackie's reported slight was more painful to her than any lost business, and she registered her chagrin in a letter of heartbreaking dignity. "My reason for writing this note is to tell you how hurt I feel," she wrote. "You know I have never sought publicity but I would prefer to be referred to as a 'noted negro designer,' which in every sense I am . . . Any reference to the contrary hurts me more deeply than I can perhaps make you realise."

Letitia Baldrige, Jackie's social secretary, called a few days later to assure Lowe that the reference to "a colored woman dressmaker" hadn't been approved by Mrs. Kennedy, and to convey an apology for her distress—without, however, taking responsibility for it. Lowe then engaged an attorney and sought "tangible" redress from the *Ladies' Home Journal*, in the form of a story about her career. The magazine never obliged, but Jackie may have tried to make amends. A year later, one of Lowe's eyes was removed—it had been irreparably damaged by glaucoma. While she was in the hospital, someone paid off her debts to the IRS. Lowe always believed that the First Lady was her anonymous benefactor.

Lowe's misfortunes of the early sixties nearly crushed her. "I almost gave up dreaming about beauty and thought only of suicide," she told the *Daily News*. Saks offered her a workroom and a title—the head designer of its Adam Room, creating bridal and debut gowns. She brought Saks her clients, and it touted her collaboration. But Lowe agreed to a disastrous deal: she had to buy her own materials and pay her own staff. "I didn't realize until too late," she said, "that on dresses I was getting $300 for, I had put about $450 into it."

Overwhelmed by debt, Lowe was forced to declare bankruptcy. She went to work for a small custom shop, Madeleine Couture, until cataracts blinded her other eye. In 1964, she underwent a risky operation to remove them. Once she could see again, she opened a new salon. When the cataracts grew back, she dictated her designs to a sketcher and her assistants realized them.

After Kennedy's assassination, Lowe finally got credit for Jackie's wedding dress, and she liked to claim that it was exactly what the bride had asked for: "a tremendous, typical Ann Lowe gown." (The logo on one of her labels is the dainty figure of a court lady in a hoop skirt and panniers.) Her work began to appear in national magazines. *Vanity Fair* featured one of her coming-out dresses in an editorial spread. *The Saturday Evening Post* ran a picture of three insouciant debs, riding the Central Park carousel in their Lowe gowns. It accompanied a profile of the designer, whose headline became Lowe's sobriquet: "Society's Best-Kept Secret." She played along. "I'm an awful snob," she told *Ebony* in 1966. "I love my clothes and I'm particular about who wears them. I am not interested in sewing for café society or social climbers. I don't cater to Mary and Sue. I sew for the families of the Social Register."

There is no evidence that Lowe's society clients invited her to their affairs or their debuts. She heard about them secondhand: "When someone tells me, 'The Ann Lowe dresses were doing all of the dancing at the cotillion last night,' that's what I like to hear." But in 1967 Josephine Lee's granddaughter asked Lowe to contribute a gown to be auctioned at a Junior League fund-raiser in Tampa. She was happy to oblige, though she added that—after fifty years—she was curious to attend the sort of gala that she had so often sewn for. The family brought her as a guest of honor, and she sat at the front table.

Lowe's presence at what Powell called a "historically white event" was an audacious break with tradition. Lowe had defied exclusion countless times in her life. But, unlike Keckley, an activist for the impoverished former slaves who had flocked to Washington in 1862, and unlike Rosa Parks, a dressmaker by trade, she never played a public role in the civil rights movement. Nor did she advertise the fact that she sewed for distinguished Black clients such as Elizabeth Mance, a classical pianist, or Idella Kohke, a board member of the Negro Actors Guild. I found a picture of Kohke in the New York *Age*, a venerable Black newspaper. She was featured in an article on Easter finery, dated April 20, 1957. A caption describes her "fabulous ensemble—a gown of imported French black satin created by Ann Lowe." Lowe's name was unqualified by an epithet. It apparently needed none.

The historically white fashion press never paid attention to Harlem's vibrant fashion scene. Yet Lowe's name had such prestige in the Black community that *The Age* sent her to Paris, at exorbitant expense—an ocean crossing, a stay at the Hôtel Lutétia—to cover the postwar couture shows. A story from 1949 reports that Dior, Balenciaga, Paquin, Molyneux, Dessès, and other *grandes maisons* had received their correspondent graciously. (At one of the *défilés*, Lowe said, she met Mrs. Post, who introduced her as a prominent designer.) One longs to know what she made of the clothes—and of Europe. But perhaps the picture that ran with the story—of an outfit that Lowe had designed for the paper—was a form of reportage. Her "Paris-inspired creation" was a sexy black cocktail dress "with the new sheath skirt which dips very low to the right side. The overskirt is appliqued with cutwork of large dahlias. The wing collar is highlighted by a deep plunging neckline."

There is nothing else so daring in the Lowe archives, and it made me wonder what she might have created had she been freer to innovate. "Her work was overwhelmingly pretty," Elizabeth Way reflected. "It wasn't radical, or meant to be. Even in the sixties, she was still inspired by the nineteenth century, and by a nostalgic ideal of femininity. Yet I also think it's important to appreciate what breathtaking courage she had."

Lowe's career flourished, in part, for the same reason it would decline: she deferred to the proprieties of the women for whom she sewed. They were originally southern belles. Later, they were East Coast patricians, or the daughters of Midwestern industrialists who lived, as Jackie had, in a bubble of gentility. But by the late 1960s society girls were interested in shacking up with rock stars and jetting off to ashrams. Coming out was a charade of purity that many endured to placate their mothers. Lowe made a late effort to evolve: she skimmed her froth; she trimmed her sails; she spiced up her palette. American Beauty—a debutante dress from 1967, smothered in roses—looks virginal from the front, but it's backless to the waist. The *New York Times* fashion critic Virginia Lee Warren pretended to be shocked on behalf of the girl's mother. No scandal was intended, Lowe told her; she just didn't want the "hands of the boys" soiling her creation.

Lowe's mantra might have been an adage attributed to Winston Churchill: "Success is not final. Failure is not fatal. It is the courage to continue that counts." But Churchill wasn't a self-employed Black octogenarian with an eighth-grade education and no savings.

Lowe soldiered on until 1972. Her vision outlived her sight. Only complete helplessness forced her to retire. By then, her sister had died, and she couldn't manage her own care. (Keckley, in a similar predicament—frail and penniless—took refuge in a home for destitute women of color that, in better days, she had helped found.) Lowe moved to Queens, to live with a friend whom she described as her "adopted daughter," Ruth Alexander—one of the assistants from Tampa who had followed her to New York. She died there on February 25, 1981. Her obituaries were a jumble of misinformation. Ann Lowe's real story is her own best-kept secret.

MARCH 2021

F ive years ago, the Metropolitan Museum of Art mounted an exhibition of tapestries from the Renaissance that turned into a spring blockbuster. Its sequel, *Tapestry in the Baroque: Threads of Splendor*, opened last week. Countless New Yorkers have, at some stage (usually around tenth grade), been schlepped up to the Cloisters to see the Unicorn tapestries, and some remember from their *Hamlet* footnotes that when Polonius is stabbed through the arras Shakespeare is referring to a woven hanging from a town in France where great tapestries were made. But the appeal of the show, to both a mass audience and an esoteric one—the contemporary art world—came as a surprise to curators, and the editors of *Tate*, a journal published by the eponymous gallery, asked Elaine Reichek for her take on the phenomenon.

Reichek is a grandmother who does embroidery, but, whatever associations that image has for you, forget them. A conceptual artist with a degree from Yale and a punkish shock of platinum hair, she is a leading figure in the field of mixed-media art. The Museum of Modern Art gave her samplers a solo exhibition in 1999, and her latest show, *Pattern Recognition*, opened last week at the Nicole Klagsbrun gallery. "I think that what makes tapestry so topical is its relation to computer art," Reichek said recently, over lunch at her studio in Harlem. "They both involve patterning, and reducing or enlarging an image to a charted form. A stitch, in essence, is a pixel. With any pixelated surface, whether it's a tapestry or a digital photograph, the more pixels you have, the higher your image resolution."

One assumes, wrongly, that Reichek learned to embroider at someone's knee. "My mother played golf," she said. One also assumes that, for an artist of her generation (she is sixty-four), choosing embroidery was a feminist statement about women's work. "I was one of four women in my class at Yale, which had no women on the faculty," she said. "But what I do isn't about being a 'woman artist.' Men historically did most of the major woven and embroidered pieces. When I started out, in the sixties, we, my peers and I, hated everything that looked like art. Chuck Close purged brushes. Richard Serra was throwing lead. I was looking for a different medium to make marks with, and my early works were minimalist line drawings with thread. But then I got interested in samplers, and that became my endeavor." Reichek's samplers include embroidered reproductions of a Web page, Seurat's portrait of his mother sewing, an Attic frieze, quotations in needlework from Freud and Colette, Charlotte Brontë's favorite collar patterns with a paragraph from *Shirley*, and an extract from Darwin's journals. Her needlework literally gives depth to the texts and images that she translates. "Unlike a pen or a brush," she said, "a stitch pierces the surface that it covers and belies its flatness, becoming part of the supporting structure."

Reichek "shops" for her images on the Internet and plots them on a computer. Until now, her embroideries have been executed by hand, each one requiring months of labor, but for *Pattern Recognition* all except two of the pieces were created by her "latest toy," a digital sewing machine. She calls the show "an alternative art history in swatches," and the swatches—twelve-by-ten-inch rectangles with pinked edges—include miniature versions of paintings by Mondrian, Warhol, Philip Guston, Ed Ruscha, Magritte, Nancy Spero, and Damien Hirst. "Sampling, pastiche, appropriation—all those techniques that we think of as contemporary—have an ancient history," she explained. "Embroidery has been called 'the Hypertext of the Silk Route,' and as local patterns traveled by caravan around the world they were 'downloaded' by people who didn't know where they came from."

The Met's *Threads of Splendor* lives up to its name. At the preview, Reichek noted the affinities between the art world today and the Baroque court culture that produced the masterpieces on display: "Tapestries were the trophies of a gilded age with an overheated art market, and only the super-rich could afford them. A cycle like Rubens's *Triumph of the Eucharist* took thousands of man hours to complete, with the weavers sitting cheek by jowl at a giant loom, each one, like an autoworker, responsible for a separate component of the product—feet or foliage or faces. This, too, is an era of megabuck commissions, and many of the gigantic pieces intended for art palaces are, in whole or in part, outsourced and produced industrially." She stopped in front of *The Battle of the Granicus*, the scene of an epic confrontation between Alexander the Great and the Persian satraps. It was commissioned by Louis XIV, designed by Charles Le Brun, and woven in the workshop of Jean Jans the Younger, at the Gobelins factory in Paris, between 1680 and 1687. The capes and banners of a great horde billow in the wind as trumpets blare, shields flash, flesh yields to spear, and, under a lowering sky, rendered in countless minute ivory and blue pixels, fabulously muscled warriors, human and equine, tangle in the surf. "Wow," Reichek said. "Now, there's a biopic."

OCTOBER 2007

In the first chapter of *Daisy Miller*, Henry James's novella of 1878, a priggish American expatriate, Winterbourne, makes the acquaintance of a shameless flirt from Schenectady in the gardens of a Swiss hotel, where he is visiting his aunt, and she is staying with her dyspeptic mother en route to Italy. James describes what Daisy is wearing: a dress of white muslin "with a hundred frills and flounces, and knots of pale-coloured ribbon," accessorized by "a large parasol, with a deep border of embroidery." Winterbourne has never seen a prettier creature, even if her forwardness unnerves him. "I have always had a great deal of gentlemen's society," she boasts. He is thrilled, but shocked, when she accepts his invitation to go sightseeing—unchaperoned—even before she knows his name.

The discrepancy between Daisy's appearance ("She had the *tournure* of a princess," Winterbourne thinks) and her disregard for appearances is central to the story. She represents a new female of the species that, James suggests, only the brash innocence of an ascendant republic could have produced. In that respect, the refinement of Daisy's taste is a mystery to Winterbourne's aunt, Mrs. Costello, who pronounces her "hopelessly vulgar" even while conceding to her nephew that "she dresses in perfection."

Two complementary shows opening this week, one at the Met Costume Institute, the other at the Brooklyn Museum, are dedicated to American women who have dressed in and to perfection. The former, *American Woman: Fashioning a National Identity*, is curated by Andrew Bolton. The latter, *American High Style: Fashioning a National Collection*, is curated by Jan Glier Reeder. The joint catalogue is written by Reeder, and it commemorates the transfer of Brooklyn's incomparable archives of couture, ready-to-wear, uniforms, folk costumes, textiles, and accessories—more than a century in the acquisition—to the Met, under the terms of an unusually collegial open adoption. (Brooklyn, which could no longer afford the costs of stewardship, will retain permanent access and exhibition rights.)

Daisy's ghost haunts the Met show, and not only because she had "ever so many dresses and things from Paris." Bolton surveys the formative period of modern fashion—the 1890s to the 1940s—and frames it as a face-off between Old World and New World ideals of femininity. He cites the Paris couturier Jean Patou, who decided, in the 1920s, to advertise in *The New York Times* for house mannequins, because "the slender American Diana" was superior to "the rounded French Venus," at least as a clotheshorse. In Bolton's opinion, not only Diana's silhouette but also her attitudes would "triumph" over those of Venus to set the standards of style for the twentieth century. "Fashion intersected with feminism to become a liberating force for women in America," he writes in the show's wall notes.

Last month, in a workroom at the Costume Institute, Bolton showed me a scale model of the installation, which he calls "a time capsule," and some of the eighty ensembles that it contains. They are displayed on faceless mannequins in a pavilion on the Met's second floor, where Nathan Crowley, a film production designer, has conceived a suite of gorgeously hand-painted panoramas, animated by music, lighting, and video projections. Each round chamber is the habitat for an "archetypal" American woman who represents a stage of evolution toward modernity.

The Heiress of the Gilded Age is upholstered sumptuously for a ball in Newport by Charles Frederick Worth, the English-born Paris couturier, whose clientele of aristocrats commended him to the arrivistes. The Gibson Girl, of the same period—America's first pinup—is posed against a backdrop of nature, in a pair of riding breeches, a skating sweater, and a woolen bathing costume that breaks the sensational news that women have legs. A decade passes, and the scene shifts back indoors, and from athletic nubility to the vampish languor of the bohemian. Her habitat is a stylized rendering of Louis Comfort Tiffany's New York studio, where she practices the art of provocation by jettisoning the corset for the Empire shifts of Paul Poiret (the couturier of choice for American iconoclasts such as Isadora Duncan and Peggy Guggenheim), and for the harem trousers of the Callot Soeurs, who took the inspiration for their fluid drapery and exotic embroideries from the East.

A woman of purpose—the Suffragist/Patriot—emerges during the First World War, in a smartly man-tailored walking suit and a military uniform. Archival film footage documents her front-line service as a driver or a nurse and her struggles for equality with the men whose sartorial dignity she has adopted. After the Armistice, the torch of progress passes to a painted girl with bobbed hair, who uses it to light her cigarettes. She is the sylph who beguiled Patou—reckless Daisy reborn as the Flapper. The vertical lines of her figure, in Patou's streamlined daywear, and in short, beaded chemises by Lanvin and Molyneux, are echoed by a mural of the New York skyline. Hemlines fall with the stock market, and fashion during the Depression is an escapist reverie of the high life that Bolton situates in an Art Deco cinema. The wardrobe of the Screen Siren has a lunar sheen. Scenes from *Limehouse Blues* (Anna May Wong in her "dragon dress," by Travis Banton) and from *Dinner at Eight* (Jean Harlow in bias-cut white satin, by Adrian) flicker on the walls.

In the last gallery, a video montage of images relates Bolton's archetypes to the evolving appearance and status of actual women. It includes a tribute to select heroines—his candidates for a Mount Rushmore of Fashion—who, he said, "define American style in all its diversity": Michelle Obama, Lady Gaga, Serena Williams, Grace Kelly, Marilyn Monroe, the Olsen twins.

Fashion cycles are like election years: it is often hard to perceive change for the better unless you take a long view, and some innovation is reaction in disguise. Bolton acknowledges that his archetypes were "mass-media creations" that didn't reflect the reality of the average housewife or co-ed. Yet the archetypes do suggest the way that each ideal makes subtle alterations to the notion of a woman's place, and to the code that determines who is worthy of respect and who isn't.

Bolton has grounded the clothes in more social history, and has invested more imagination in making their perfection intelligible, than is often the case in museum fashion shows, which tend to focus on virtuosity at the expense of context. Yet if one looks too closely at any symbolic antithesis (Diana versus Venus) it dissolves into a multitude of contradictions: Americans did dominate high fashion in the first half of the twentieth century, but only to the extent that haute couture was dependent on dollars and a cabal of Francophile magazine editors in New York. American fashion and feminism have intersected, especially in the past thirty years, but often uneasily, if not as antagonists. And high style wasn't native to the New World. The apostles of what Bolton calls "Americanness" in dress, from Levi Strauss to Ralph Lauren, have often been Jewish immigrants, or their children. (Today, many are Asian and Latinx.)

A more accurate subtitle for the Met show might be "Borrowing a National Identity"; it suggests, ironically, just how successful the French were in exporting their own national identity—"the *tournure* of a princess"—to this side of the Atlantic.

Walking with Reeder last month through the Brooklyn galleries, where many of the mannequins were still shrouded in dust sheets, and accessories had not yet been unpacked, I had a sense of déjà vu. I once helped a friend sort through the wardrobe of her late mother, an ambassador's wife, who had lived in a vast Sutton Place apartment where entire rooms had been turned into closets for a staggering collection of couture. My friend offered me a dress that I had admired, a sheath of pure lines, in black chiffon and organza, by Galanos. It exuded her mother's perfume, and I still associate that scent with a matrilineal endowment—a knowledge of grace and seduction passed down through the clothes that a woman of fashion keeps for the next generation.

That is the emotion that surprised me in Brooklyn. The museum's monumental collection was seeded by bequests from or in memory of such women, and many of the donors were their daughters, sisters, and nieces. Among the heirlooms in the show are Worth's ensembles for Peter Cooper's granddaughters Eleanor and Sarah Hewitt, and his lavish court-presentation gown for Emily Roebling, who supervised the construction of the Brooklyn Bridge after her husband, Washington, its chief engineer, was stricken by caisson disease. There are also the Schiaparellis, Mainbochers, and Charles Jameses worn by the perennially best-dressed Millicent Rogers and Mona Bismarck. And there are masterpieces by the Callots that belonged to Rita Lydig, a dark beauty of the Belle Époque who sat for Steichen and Sargent and was famous for winning one of the largest alimony settlements in American history. They were bequeathed to the museum by her notorious sister, the literary dilettante and lesbian roué Mercedes de Acosta. ("You can't dispose of Mercedes lightly," Alice B. Toklas wrote to Anita Loos. "She has had the two most important women in the U.S.—Greta Garbo and Marlene Dietrich.")

Reeder's approach is less theatrical but more specific than Bolton's, and broader in scope. It is a valedictory, of sorts, that pays homage to the individuals who enriched Brooklyn's collection, and to the designers, many of them women, who, as the collection grew, entrusted the museum with their legacies. Reeder is particularly illuminating about the nineteen-forties, when couture clients were housebound in North America by German U-boats, and a gifted new coterie of designers had the motive and the freedom to articulate a "national identity" without foreign competition, except, perhaps, from Schiaparelli, who spent the war in New York, in exile from the Nazis. Schiaparelli's radical sportswear of the late twenties—divided tennis skirts and trompe-l'oeil sweaters—was an inspiration for Claire McCardell, Bonnie Cashin, Valentina, Elizabeth Hawes, Carolyn Schnurer, and Vera Maxwell. So was her Surrealist whimsy. Among the Schiaparelli trophies in Brooklyn—a Zodiac jacket, one of the first pants suits, her iconic bug necklace (a plastic disk crawling with toy insects)—is a sublimely goofy cotton summer dress randomly appliquéd with large seed packets.

McCardell, in particular, presciently decided that "playclothes" were the future. (In 1944, she used a print of yellow happy faces on a three-piece beach ensemble.) Cashin added a man's suit collar to a Mexican poncho, and reproduced it in a houndstooth plaid, with matching spats and a lap rug. Her clients, like McCardell's, were youthful women with a sense of humor, who prized comfort and informality, and maybe even earned a living. Elizabeth Hawes, who closed her custom dress house during the war to work in a factory and to write a column for the left-wing daily *PM* ("Girls in Slacks Have the Most Fun at Coney Island"), also designed uniforms for Red Cross volunteers. The fashion business, in her Jacobin view (she called it a "racket"), demeaned the women in its thrall. Having learned her trade in France, she viewed haute couture as a vestige of the ancien régime long overdue for a revolution. It was a matter of conscience to her that ordinary women deserved stylish, practical ready-to-wear that they could afford. (After the war, however, Hawes and her husband, the movie director Joseph Losey, were blacklisted in their respective fields, and she was forced to submerge her talent in anonymous designs for boys' overalls.)

The Depression and the Second World War politicized American fashion, which had never before had a serious left wing. Charles James, in the meantime, was proving that an American could produce ball gowns that rivaled those of the French in luxury and finesse. He was a consummate mandarin (his mother was a patrician from Chicago, his father a British officer), with an exclusive following—Babe Paley, Austine Hearst, Dominique de Menil, and Marietta Tree. But in the early sixties he outdid himself for a favorite client—a daughter of the people, as the French would say—who was better known without her clothes than for them: Gypsy Rose Lee.

Henry James never did explain the mystery of Daisy Miller's transcendent chic, and perhaps he couldn't. But Gypsy's wink, in an ad for

Smirnoff vodka, nearly a century later, may hold a clue. Her majestic figure is dressed to perfection by the other James in a swagged and molded gown of taupe satin that doesn't, for once, leave her much wiggle room. She is the archetype of the Woman Who Doesn't Care What the Snobs Think.

MAY 2010

SPEAKING IN TONGUES

It is a singular fate to be the last of one's kind. That is the fate of the men and women, nearly all of them elderly, who are—like Marie Wilcox of California; Gyani Maiya Sen of Nepal; Verdena Parker of Oregon; and Charlie Mungulda of Australia—the last known speakers of a language: Wukchumni, Kusunda, Hupa, and Amurdag, respectively. But a few years ago, in Chile, I met Joubert Yanten Gomez, who told me he was "the world's only speaker of Selk'nam." He was twenty-one.

Yanten Gomez, who uses the tribal name Keyuk, grew up modestly in Santiago. His father, Blas Yanten, is a woodworker, and his mother, Ivonne Gomez Castro, practices traditional medicine. As a young girl, she was mocked at school for her mestizo looks, so she hesitated to tell her children—Keyuk and an older sister—about their ancestry. They hadn't known that their maternal relatives descended from the Selk'nam, a nomadic tribe of unknown origin that settled in Tierra del Fuego. The first Europeans to encounter the Selk'nam, in the sixteenth century, were astonished by their height and their hardiness—they braved the frigid climate by coating their bodies with whale fat. The tribe lived mostly undisturbed until the late 1800s, when an influx of sheep ranchers and gold prospectors who coveted their land put bounties on their heads. (One hunter boasted that he had received a pound sterling per corpse, redeemable with a pair of ears.) The survivors of the Selk'nam Genocide, as it is called—a population of

about four thousand was reduced to some three hundred—were resettled on reservations run by missionaries. The last known fluent speaker
of the language, Angela Loij, a laundress and farmer, died forty
years ago.

Many children are natural mimics, but Keyuk could imitate speech
like a mynah. His father, who is white, had spent part of his childhood
in the Arauco region, which is home to the Mapuche, Chile's largest
native community, and he taught Keyuk their language, Mapudun-
gun. The boy, a bookworm and an A student, easily became fluent. A
third-grade research project impassioned him about indigenous
peoples, and Ivonne, who descends from a line of shamans, took this
as a sign that his ancestors were speaking through him. When she told
him of their heritage, Keyuk vowed that he would master Selk'nam
and also, eventually, Yagán—the nearly extinct language of a neighboring people in the far south—reckoning that he could pass them
down to his children and perhaps reseed the languages among the
tribes' descendants. At fourteen, he traveled with his father to Puerto
Williams, a town in Chile's Antarctic province that calls itself "the
world's southernmost city," to meet Cristina Calderón, the last native
Yagán speaker. She subsequently tutored him by phone.

If it is lonely to be the last of anything, the distinction has a mythic
romance: the last emperor, the last of the Just, the last of the Mohi-
cans. Keyuk's precocity enhanced his mystique. A Chilean television
station flew him to Tierra del Fuego as part of a series, *Sons of the
Earth*, that focused on the country's original inhabitants. He was interviewed, at sixteen, by the *Financial Times*. A filmmaker who knew
him put us in touch, and we met at a café in Santiago.

It was a mild autumn morning during Easter week. The city was
quiet after a series of student demonstrations protesting tuition costs.
Keyuk, who was studying linguistics on a scholarship at the University of Chile, supported their cause. ("The word 'Selk'nam' can mean
'we are equal,'" he noted, "though it can also mean 'we are separate.'")
Keyuk is tall, loose-limbed, and baby-faced, with a thatch of black
hair. His style is nonchalant—stovepipe jeans and a leather jacket.
Since his teens, Keyuk has composed songs in Selk'nam, and he

performs with an "ethno-electronic" band. But he carried himself with solemnity, as if conscious of the flame he tended—or, at least, said that he tended. How, I asked, could I be sure that he really spoke Selk'nam, if no one else did? He smiled slightly and said, "I guess I have the last word."

Keyuk's voice is a boyish tenor, but when he speaks Selk'nam it changes; the language is harsher and more percussive than Spanish. To master the grammar and the vocabulary, he had studied, among other texts, a lexicon published in 1915 by José María Beauvoir, a Salesian missionary. The sound of the language was preserved in recordings that the eminent anthropologist Anne Chapman made forty years ago. Chapman, a protégée of Claude Lévi-Strauss, was an early activist for endangered languages in Meso- and South America. Cristina Calderón, Keyuk's tutor, was one of her subjects, and, having heard of Keyuk's projects, Chapman sought him out in Santiago, about ten years ago. She was then in her mid-eighties; she died in 2010.

I joined Keyuk and his mother the next evening for dinner at a restaurant in the old fish market, where the local sea bass is a specialty. Ivonne is petite, blond, and animated, but, like Keyuk, she has a regal poise, and it is hard to imagine her as a bullied outcast. We shouted cheerfully above the din, though Keyuk seemed detached—as prodigies grow out of their teens, they sometimes mistrust the curiosity they have inspired. But when he spoke of the Selk'nam it was with intensity. "Our mythology is rich," he said. "Everything in our world—plants and animals, the sun and stars—has a voice. On our map of the universe, we called the east 'the space without time'"—the realm of the unknown. "We had a Paleolithic skill set yet a boundless imagination. They both existed with a high degree of social conformity. Long after we dispersed, we preserved our beliefs." He added, "One precious thing, to me, about the language is its vocabulary of words for love. They change according to the age, sex, and kinship of the speakers and the nature of the emotion. There are things you can't say in Spanish."

There are approximately seven billion inhabitants of earth. They conduct their lives in one or several of about seven thousand languages—multilingualism is a global norm. Linguists acknowledge that the data are inexact, but by the end of this century perhaps as many as fifty percent of the world's languages will, at best, exist only in archives and on recordings. According to the calculations of the Catalogue of Endangered Languages (ELCat)—a joint effort of linguists at the University of Hawaii, Manoa, and at the University of Eastern Michigan—nearly thirty language families have disappeared since 1960. If the historical rate of loss is averaged, a language dies about every four months.

The mother tongue of more than three billion people is one of twenty, which are, in order of their current predominance: Mandarin Chinese, Spanish, English, Hindi, Arabic, Portuguese, Bengali, Russian, Japanese, Javanese, German, Wu Chinese, Korean, French, Telugu, Marathi, Turkish, Tamil, Vietnamese, and Urdu. English is the lingua franca of the digital age, and those who use it as a second language may outnumber its native speakers by hundreds of millions. On every continent, people are forsaking their ancestral tongues for the dominant language of their region's majority. Assimilation confers inarguable benefits, especially as Internet use proliferates and rural youth gravitate to cities. But the loss of languages passed down for millennia, along with their unique arts and cosmologies, may have consequences that won't be understood until it is too late to reverse them.

Little is known about the origins of human speech. It seems unlikely, though, that there was ever a pre-Babel world. The geographic isolation of small groups breeds heterogeneity, both of dialects and of language isolates, as it probably did among Paleolithic hunters. Nowhere is there a richer or more concentrated cluster of languages, some eight hundred, than in Papua New Guinea, with its daunting topography of highlands and rain forests. In New Guinea, as in other hot spots of endangerment, indigenous languages are a user's guide to ecosystems that are increasingly fragile and—in the face of climate change—increasingly irreplaceable.

Richard Schultes, a professor of biology at Harvard, who died in 2001, is considered the father of modern ethnobotany. He was among the first to study the use of plants, including hallucinogens, by indigenous peoples in the rain forest and to publicize the alarming rate at which both were disappearing. (More than ninety tribes, he noted, vanished in Brazil between 1900 and 1975.) In the 1940s, doing fieldwork in the Amazon, Schultes identified the source of curare, a derivative of which, d-tubocurarine, is used to treat muscle disorders such as those associated with Parkinson's disease. His students Michael Balick, now the director of economic botany at the New York Botanical Garden, and Paul Alan Cox, executive director of the Institute for Ethnomedicine, in Jackson Hole, Wyoming, continued his explorations. They have written with authority on the "ethnobotanical approach to drug discovery," which is, in essence, fieldwork guided by shamans and healers.

In Samoa, Cox discovered that Polynesian herbal doctors had an extensive nomenclature for endemic diseases and a separate one for those introduced by Europeans. Their sophistication is not unique. The taxonomies of endangered languages often distinguish hundreds more types of flora and fauna than are known to Western science. The Haunóo, a tribe of swidden farmers on Mindoro, an island in the Philippines, have forty expressions for types of soil. In Southeast Asia, forest-dwelling healers have identified the medicinal properties of some 6,500 species. In the 1950s, drug researchers for Eli Lilly and Company, working on several continents, studied folk remedies for diabetes based on the rosy periwinkle, and isolated an active ingredient—vinblastine—that is used in chemotherapy for Hodgkin's disease. (The healers who led the researchers to their discoveries never saw any of the profits. Such "bio-prospecting" by pharmaceutical companies is a controversial practice that was largely unregulated until 1993.) Quinine, aspirin, codeine, ipecac, and pseudoephedrine are among the common remedies that, according to Cox and Balick, we owe to ethnobotanists guided and informed by indigenous peoples.

Daniel Kaufman, a linguist who directs the Endangered Language Alliance, a nonprofit institute on West Eighteenth Street, would be thrilled to hear that a cure for cancer had been discovered in a rainforest flower for which we have no name, other than one in a dying language, but saving the flower is not his concern. I was introduced to Kaufman last June at a screening of *Language Matters*, a documentary directed by David Grubin and hosted by the poet Bob Holman. Kaufman, who teaches at Columbia University, consulted on the film. He is a slight, studious-looking man in his late thirties, whose expertise is in the Austronesian languages of Madagascar and the Pacific. But the alliance, which he founded six years ago, grew out of his commitment to support the more than eight hundred endangered languages of the New York area, which has a higher concentration of them, Kaufman estimates, than any city in the world.

The alliance has recorded Shughni, from Tajikistan, which is spoken by a few families in Bay Ridge; Kabardian, from the northern Caucasus, which survives in a Circassian community in Wayne, New Jersey; and Amuzgo, from southwestern Mexico, still alive in Sunset Park, Corona, and Port Richmond—enclaves of immigrants from Oaxaca and Guerrero. Mandaic, an ancient Semitic language of Iraq and Iran, has only a few elderly speakers left, in Flushing and Nassau County. Garífuna, however, is firmly based in a mostly working-class community of some 200,000 people concentrated in eastern Brooklyn and the South Bronx. The Garífuna are descendants of West Africans who were shipwrecked in 1635 off the coast of Saint Vincent, where they intermarried with the indigenous Arawaks and Caribs. The language that evolved combines Arawak grammar with African, English, and Spanish loanwords. In the eighteenth century, the British deported the Garífuna to Central America; during the past fifty years, many have settled in New York.

"Let's be honest," Kaufman said. "The loss of these languages doesn't matter much to the bulk of humanity, but the standard for assessing the worth or benefit of a language shouldn't rest with outsiders, who are typically white and Western. It's an issue of the speakers' perceived self-worth." He suggested that I meet some of those speakers not far from home—members of the Mohawk nation. "The older people are the only ones who can tell you what their youth stands to lose," he said. "The young are the only ones who can articulate the loss of an identity rooted in a mother tongue that has become foreign to them." He told me about a two-week immersion program that takes place each summer at the Kanatsiohareke community center, in Fonda, New York, a village on the Mohawk River between Utica and Albany.

Until the eighteenth century, Fonda (which was named for the Dutch ancestors of Henry, Jane, and Peter), the neighboring town of Palatine (named for the Palatine Germans who took refuge there), and much of the land to the north and east, into Canada, was Mohawk territory. The Mohawk were feared for their ferocity, but it was chastened by a matriarchal system of consensus governance. One of the students in the intermediate class at Kanatsiohareke was a local IBM employee who told me that he was learning Mohawk because the tribe had saved the lives of his German ancestors.

During the American Revolution, the Mohawk supported the British, and after the defeat they were forced to cede their territory. Their chiefs led them to Canada, and most of their settlements are still on the border of New York and Ontario. In recent decades, two factions have divided Mohawk loyalties: a party of modernizers that has aggressively championed casino development, and an Old Guard that fears the corruption that casinos invite. The founder of the Kanatsiohareke center, Sakokweniónkwas, whose English name is Tom Porter, belongs to the latter.

Porter is a commanding figure in his early seventies, who speaks in a quietly hypnotic voice. He was born on a reservation, the son of an ironworker—one of the legendary Mohawk who built Manhattan's skyscrapers. Porter and his son both followed him into the trade. "It's a myth that Mohawk don't suffer from vertigo," he told me. "I was afraid of heights all my life." His grandmother encouraged him to marry a maiden of old-fashioned virtue, and while he was on a trip to Mississippi, a matchmaker introduced him to Alice Joe, a Choctaw. They settled on Mohawk land west of Albany, where he worked as an ambulance driver, a carpenter, and a teacher. Their six children were raised speaking both Choctaw and Mohawk. When Porter was twenty-one,

the clan mothers chose him as one of the nation's nine chiefs. He retired after twenty-five years, though he is still much in demand for his
eloquent funeral orations.

Porter bought the Fonda property at auction, twenty years ago,
with help from the local community. Kanatsiohareke was conceived as
a bulwark of "longhouse" values: reverence for nature, parents, ancestral spirits, and the language. "Mohawk isn't just a form of speech," he
said. "It's a holistic relationship to the cosmos." The Porters host concerts and lectures in addition to the language camp, and some of their
land is farmed organically. But Kanatsiohareke is a homespun operation: the compound includes an old red barn, a ramshackle farmhouse,
and a rustic B and B with a craft shop that sells T-shirts and baskets.

The Mohawk are one of 566 tribes recognized by the United States
whose presence on the continent predates "contact"—the advent of
Europeans. Only about 170 indigenous languages are still spoken, the
majority by a dwindling number of elders like Marie Wilcox, of the
Wukchumni, who is eighty-one and who spent her youth doing farm-
work south of Fresno. About fifteen years ago, she started recording
her tribe's creation myths and compiling a dictionary of its unwritten
language. Navajo, which helped to decide the outcome of the Second
World War (the Japanese were never able to decrypt messages relayed
among native speakers—the celebrated "code talkers"), is an exception.
It is used in daily life by two thirds of the nation's 250,000 citizens,
who refer to it as *"Diné bizaad,"* "the people's language." Fluency, however, is declining. The election of a new tribe president was suspended,
in October, by a dispute over the requirement that he or she speak
fluent Navajo. A leading candidate, Chris Deschene—a state repre-
sentative from Arizona and the grandson of a code talker—was dis-
qualified for that reason. "I'm the product of cultural destruction," he
told the *Navajo Times*, when he was asked why he couldn't speak Diné.
(He is a graduate of the U.S. Naval Academy, and, after retiring as a
major in the Marine Corps, he earned two graduate degrees, in engineering and law.) A new election will take place in April.

About 25,000 North Americans identify themselves as Mohawk,
but only about fifteen percent speak the language well enough to con-

duct their daily lives in it. Transcribing Mohawk is an arduous task. In
the 1870s, Alexander Graham Bell, a recent immigrant to Canada,
fell in love with its sound and created an orthography. (The Mohawk
made him an honorary chief.) The grammar is at least as challenging
as that of Latin. Noun roots are modified by a welter of adjectival
prefixes; the addition of the letter "h," for example, can alter a meaning dramatically. If you err in trying to describe a man as "tall," you
may have said that he has "long balls." Verbs are muscular and poetic.
"To bury" someone is "to wrap his body with the blanket of our
Mother Earth." A man who fathers a child "lends him his life." In the
ethos of Mohawk culture, as in its language, "I" cannot stand on its
own—the first-person singular is always part of a relationship. So you
don't say, "I am sick." "The sickness," in Mohawk, "has come to me."

In the advanced seminar at Kanatsiohareke, Mina Beauvais, whose
Mohawk name is Tewateronhiakhwa, was teaching students the opta-
tive, an arcane mood, akin to the subjunctive, that exists in Kurdish,
Albanian, Navajo, Sanskrit, and ancient Greek. The students also had
to contend with compound words, some longer than those of German,
which aren't pronounced as they are written. You need a bard's memory
and a singer's breath to speak Mohawk as Beauvais does: she makes it
sound incantatory. I took and failed a test that she gave her class: to
repeat *tahotenonhwarori'taksen'skwe'tsherakahrhatenia'tonháitie.* (It is a
single word that means "the fool comes tumbling down the hill.")

Beauvais, who grew up near Montreal, is a native speaker in her
late seventies. She is small and sturdy, with a wry patience bred of
hardship. When she was seven, the state compelled her parents to send
her to a school "for Indians," at which students were beaten for speaking their native tongue. Tom Porter's grandmother hid him, at the
same age, so that the authorities couldn't put him in a boarding school.
The forcible assimilation of First Nations children in punitively austere, mostly church-run institutions was made compulsory by Canadian law in the 1880s and continued until the 1970s. "That system
almost destroyed us," Porter said. "When you deprive a kid of his
language at the sponge time of life, the most precious learning years,
a bond is broken."

Attendance at the camp was lower than in the past; there were just four students in the advanced seminar, though all were parents who hoped to pass the language on to their young children. Gabrielle Doreen, a stately woman of thirty-seven, who wears her graying hair in a long braid, is the mother of four. While honing her grammar, she was teaching kindergarten at the Mohawk "nest" on the Tyendinaga Mohawk Territory in Ontario. The nest—*totahne*—is an immersion program for preschoolers. Doreen had enrolled in the camp with her fiancé, Lou Williams, an Oneida. He was moving from his native Wisconsin to Ontario, he told me, "because in Mohawk tradition men join their women's clan."

Iehnhotonkwas—Bonnie Jane Maracle—started as a student at the camp when it began, in 1998, and became its coordinator in 2005. "We originally had much better attendance," she said. "But eight Mohawk communities now have their own immersion classes, so people can study closer to home." Other First Nations—the Ojibwe in Minnesota; the Blackfoot in Montana; the Iñupiat of northern Alaska—also have nests, and the trend has been gaining momentum since the passage, in 2006, of the Esther Martínez Native American Language Preservation Act, which provided funding for language survival and restoration programs from pre-K through college. (Martínez, who lived in New Mexico, was a linguist, a storyteller, and a champion of her native Tewa. She died at ninety-four, the year that her namesake legislation was enacted.) There are now some thirty institutions of higher learning on or near reservations that offer instruction in indigenous languages.

K. David Harrison, an associate professor of linguistics at Swarthmore College, is the director of research at the Living Tongues Institute for Endangered Languages, based in Salem, Oregon, and heads *National Geographic*'s Enduring Voices Project. He is prominent in the field and writes prolifically about endangerment. Part of his mission, he told me, is to help communities "technologize their language." It heartens him, he said, to see "Mohawk kids texting in Mohawk." (The tribe also has its own television and radio stations.) The Yurok, of Northern California, are one of many tribes with a website. And smartphone users can download apps to study Nishnaabe (of Ontario), Salteaux (of Saskatchewan), Potawatomi (of the Great Lakes), Arikara (of North Dakota), or Mi'kmaq (of Canada's Atlantic Provinces and the Gaspé Peninsula). Harrison's institute also hosts a YouTube channel. "Living tongues have to evolve to deserve the term," he said. "I am working on a dictionary of Siletz"—a critically endangered language native to Oregon—"and the community is having an interesting dialogue about contemporary words like 'computer.' Should they import it from the English or coin a phrase that means 'brain in a box'?"

An app, however, can't replace the live transmission of a language to children at what Porter calls "the sponge time." The Maori of New Zealand were the first to develop the language-nest concept. (A nest is a sanctuary from predation as much as an incubator.) The nest movement in the United States, which began in Hawaii, where it is called Pūnana Leo, was inspired by the Maori movement, Kōhanga Reo. They both date to the early 1980s, although they have roots in years of community organizing to reverse colonial policies. The Hawaiian language was banned in public schools from 1896 until 1986—two years after activists, skirting the law, opened the first private nest. Today, some 2,400 students attend one of nineteen Hawaiian language-immersion sites around the state. Researchers have suggested that students taught in Hawaiian perform as well as, if not better than, their peers who, like most Americans, are educated monolingually. At the best immersion-program site, ninety percent of the class goes on to college. And graduate students at the University of Hawaii, Hilo, can now earn a doctorate in their native tongue.

Political activism has been a catalyst in nearly every narrative of a language rescued from the brink. The most famous example is that of Welsh. Resistance to English rule has an eight-hundred-year history in Wales that is intimately connected with the struggle to preserve its Celtic language, Cymraeg. In the documentary *Language Matters*, Bob Holman and David Grubin pick up the saga in the mid-1960s, when the British government flooded the ancient village of Capel Celyn, one of the few remaining Welsh-language communities, to create a reservoir that supplied water to Liverpool. This act fueled an independence movement and demands to give Cymraeg parity with English in the public sphere. The BBC launched a Welsh radio station in 1977. Since 1999, instruction in Welsh has been compulsory for students in state schools up to the age of sixteen. According to the most recent census, in 2011, nineteen percent of the population speak the language. That means, of course, that eighty-one percent do not.

The struggle to preserve a language often creates an atmosphere of siege. I felt that sense of embattlement at Kanatsiohareke and, again, last September, when I sat in on a radio show sponsored by Dan Kaufman and broadcast from the Endangered Language Alliance offices on Eighteenth Street. The show, *Voces sin Fronteras* (Voices Without Borders), was improvised—conversation punctuated by music. There were three hosts of indigenous descent—Leobardo Ambrocio Ajtzalam, José Juarez, and Segundo Angamarca—who alternated between Spanish and their respective native languages: K'iche' of Guatemala; Totonac of Mexico; and Kichwa of Colombia and Ecuador. Their listeners were a small online audience of fewer than two hundred people and a larger one of uncertain size in Guatemala. Radio, Kaufman noted, is an important tool for language activists. It reaches remote populations that might not have access to other media and boosts their morale.

The music was upbeat, but the faded maps on the office wall, the tangle of wires from a jury-rigged console, and the esprit de corps around a scuffed conference table might have been those of a guerrilla redoubt. A fourth endangered language crackled over the airwaves— that of left-wing revolution. "Fellow combatants!" the men exhorted. "A mother tongue is a human birthright. We must fight for our own!"

If peripheral languages are to survive, they will have to find a way to coexist with what Bob Holman calls the "bully" languages. David Harrison told me, "The ideal of stable bilingualism is a given. Nobody wants these communities to remain isolated." (China and Russia, however, consider ethnic languages a threat to their hegemony and have taken measures of varying severity to suppress them.) Even when there is persecution, the challenge, as Harrison sees it, is to "increase the prestige of a language so that the young embrace it." In that respect, the fate of endangered languages may ultimately rest, as Mohawk does, with couples like Gabrielle Doreen and Lou Williams. They are determined to set an example for their children—both of fluency and self-worth. Then it will be up to the kids. Mina Beauvais spoke Mohawk with her only son, but, she said, "he married a Canadian English lady and didn't pass it on." Tom Porter told me, "We will do what we can, and if the young don't cherish our way of life the Mother will take it back."

On rare occasions, an extinct language has been resurrected. Jessie Little Doe Baird, a member of the Mashpee Wampanoag tribe, in Massachusetts, received a MacArthur grant, in 2010, for her efforts to revive her people's extinct language, Wôpanâak. The tribe had been decimated by disease in the seventeenth century, and the last speakers died a hundred years ago. But written records of the language were relatively plentiful. A Wôpanâak Bible was published in 1663, the first translation of Scripture in Colonial America. John Eliot, a Puritan missionary who called himself "the Apostle to the Indians," created an orthography with the tribe's assistance, and taught its members to read. The Wampanoag welcomed literacy and left an archive of deeds and documents.

When Baird was pregnant with her fifth child, Mae Alice, she had a vision in which her ancestors called on her to fulfill an old prophecy that their language would come back to life. She was a social worker with no experience in linguistics, but she drafted a plan to revive Wôpanâak and was accepted into the Community Fellows Program at the Massachusetts Institute of Technology. A distinguished faculty of linguists, including Noam Chomsky, supported her project. Mae Alice is now the first native speaker of Wôpanâak in some seven generations.

Kaufman also cited the case of Daryl Baldwin—Kinwalaniihsia— a member of the Miami tribe of Oklahoma. The Miami (or Myaamia) originally lived in the Great Lakes area, where Baldwin was born. They spoke an Algonquian language that died out some fifty years

ago, but there were texts and recordings of it, and some elders—
"rememberers," as linguists call them—taught him a few words. Baldwin earned a linguistics degree, specializing in Native American
languages, from the University of Montana. He and his wife home-
schooled their children in the Miami language, and in 2013 he founded
the Myaamia Center, at Miami University in Ohio, to provide
the community with cultural resources. Miami is now a growing
language.

Kaufman was surprised when I told him about Keyuk—he hadn't
heard about his work with Selk'nam. I, in turn, was surprised to hear
from Keyuk that he had given up his formal studies of linguistics. "I
can reach more people through music than I could have as an academic," he told me in an e-mail. When I pressed him for details, he
was typically reticent, but he did mention that he had been working
on a new Selk'nam lexicon and that, last May, he and a friend had met
with a community in Tierra del Fuego. "We recorded some fragments
that the elders remembered," he said.

Keyuk's friend turned out to be a twenty-four-year-old linguist,
Luis Miguel Rojas-Berscia, who has corresponded at length on scholarly subjects with David Harrison. Rojas-Berscia himself is a prodigy.
I reached him by telephone in his native Lima, where he was visiting
his family. His childhood household was trilingual: his father is Peruvian, his mother is Italian, and his grandmother spoke Piedmontese.
English was his fourth language—he learned it as a toddler—and the
next seventeen tongues in which he is fluent, including Mandarin and
Quechua, were, he says, "relatively easy to master." (He has a working
knowledge of fifteen others.)

After graduating from the Pontifical Catholic University of Peru,
Rojas-Berscia moved to the Netherlands, where he does research on
language and cognition at the Max Planck Institute of Psycholinguistics. His doctoral thesis is on the Shawi, hunter-gatherers of the upper
Amazon. The Shawi, he told me, number "about twenty thousand, but
I give their language better odds than Quechua, which has ten million
speakers." That sounded counterintuitive but, he said, "Every language has its ecology. If it isn't useful, the community will be forced

to abandon it. Indigenous people in Latin America face all kinds of discrimination, and necessity dictates that, sooner or later, they adopt Spanish. Once that happens, the attrition is fast. Where a group is isolated from external pressures, they aren't forced to accept the dominant language. So you can't just go by the demographics."

Selk'nam was the subject of Rojas-Berscia's master's research. A colleague thought that a young Chilean might be of help. It was Keyuk. "When I heard about him, I had my doubts," Rojas-Berscia said. "I studied with some of the best linguists in the world, but how could a middle-school autodidact have mastered a language that died fifty years ago? I know that old Beauvoir lexicon he used—you can't learn much grammar from it. So I devised a test. I held up pictures and asked him to describe them. The man is a mystery, but his Selk'nam is good."

Rojas-Berscia had a travel stipend from the honors academy at Radboud University in the Netherlands, which paid for the trip to Tierra del Fuego. The Selk'nam survivors whom he and Keyuk interviewed had forgotten their language, though not their identity. One of the elders was a tiny woman named Herminia Vera. She hadn't spoken Selk'nam in eighty years, she told them, and initially she seemed suspicious of their interest. (Like Ivonne Gomez Castro, she had been mocked, as a girl, for her mestizo looks—though in her case it was because she looked "too European.") As she warmed to Rojas-Berscia, he gave her his picture test, and the language of her childhood began to thaw. She and Keyuk engaged in a halting conversation about food, farming, and family heritage. "I don't know who among us was the most surprised," Rojas-Berscia said. Perhaps it was the glaciers (*xɥṣ*), the rivers (*ṣịkịn*), the beaches *(kɥxhịjịk)*, and the sky (*sịɥn*) hearing their own voice. Herminia Vera died two months later.

MARCH 2015

Last May, Luis Miguel Rojas-Berscia, a doctoral candidate at the Max Planck Institute for Psycholinguistics, in the Dutch city of Nijmegen, flew to Malta for a week to learn Maltese. He had a hefty grammar book in his backpack, but he didn't plan to open it unless he had to. "We'll do this as I would in the Amazon," he told me, referring to his fieldwork as a linguist. Our plan was for me to observe how he went about learning a new language, starting with "hello" and "thank you."

Rojas-Berscia is a twenty-seven-year-old Peruvian with a baby face and spiky dark hair. A friend had given him a new pair of earrings, which he wore on Malta with funky tank tops and a chain necklace. He looked like any other laid-back young tourist, except for the intense focus—all senses cocked—with which he takes in a new environment. Linguistics is a formidably cerebral discipline. At a conference in Nijmegen that had preceded our trip to Malta, there were papers on "the anatomical similarities in the phonatory apparati of humans and harbor seals" and "hippocampal-dependent declarative memory," along with a neuropsychological analysis of speech and sound processing in the brains of beatboxers. Rojas-Berscia's PhD research, with the Shawi people of the Peruvian rain forest, doesn't involve fMRI data or computer modeling, but it is still arcane to a layperson. "I'm developing a theory of language change called the Flux Approach," he explained one evening, at a country inn outside the city, over the delicious *pannenkoeken* (pancakes) that are a local specialty. "A flux is a dynamism that involves a social fact and an impact, either functionally or formally, in linguistic competence."

Linguistic competence, as it happens, was the subject of my own interest in Rojas-Berscia. We first made contact three years ago, when I was writing about a Chilean youth who called himself the last surviving speaker of Selk'nam. How could such a claim be verified? Pretty much only, it turned out, by Rojas-Berscia. Luis Miguel is a hyper-polyglot, with a command of twenty-two living languages (Spanish, Italian, Piedmontese, English, Mandarin, French, Esperanto, Portuguese, Romanian, Quechua, Shawi, Aymara, German, Dutch, Catalan, Russian, Hakka Chinese, Japanese, Korean, Guarani, Farsi, and Serbian), thirteen of which he speaks fluently. He also knows five classical or endangered languages in addition to Selk'nam: Latin, Ancient Greek, Biblical Hebrew, Shiwilu, and Muniche.

Superlative feats have always thrilled average mortals, in part, perhaps, because they register as a victory for Team *Homo sapiens*: they redefine the humanly possible. If the ultra-marathoner Dean Karnazes can run 350 miles without sleep, he may inspire you to jog around the block. If Rojas-Berscia can speak twenty-two languages, perhaps you can crank up your high school Spanish or bat mitzvah Hebrew, or learn enough of your grandma's Korean to understand her stories. Such is the promise of online language-learning programs such as Pimsleur, Babbel, Rosetta Stone, and Duolingo: in the brain of every monolingual, there's a dormant polyglot—a genie—who, with some brisk mental friction, can be woken up. I tested that presumption at the start of my research, signing up on Duolingo to learn Vietnamese. (The app is free, and I was curious about the challenges of a tonal language.) It turns out that I'm good at hello—*chào*—but thank you, *cảm ơn*, is harder.

The word "hyperpolyglot" was coined two decades ago by a British linguist, Richard Hudson, who was launching an Internet search for the world's greatest language learner. But the phenomenon and its mystique are ancient. In Acts 2 of the New Testament, Christ's disciples receive the Holy Spirit and can suddenly "speak in tongues" (*glōssais lalein* in Greek), preaching in the languages of "every nation under heaven." According to Pliny the Elder, the Greco-Persian king Mithridates VI, who ruled twenty-two nations in the first century B.C., "administered their laws in as many languages, and could harangue in each of them." Plutarch claimed that Cleopatra "very seldom had need of an interpreter," and was the only monarch of her Greek dynasty fluent in Egyptian. Elizabeth I also allegedly mastered the tongues of her realm—Welsh, Cornish, Scots, and Irish, plus six others.

With a mere ten languages, Shakespeare's queen does not qualify as a hyperpolyglot; the accepted threshold is eleven. The prowess of Giuseppe Mezzofanti (1774–1849) is more astounding and better documented. Mezzofanti, an Italian cardinal, was fluent in at least thirty languages and studied another forty-two, including, he claimed, Algonquin. In the decades that he lived in Rome, as the chief custodian of the Vatican Library, notables from around the world dropped by to interrogate him in their mother tongues, and he flitted as nimbly among them as a bee in a rose garden. Lord Byron, who is said to have spoken Greek, French, Italian, German, Latin, and some Armenian, in addition to his immortal English, lost a cursing contest with the cardinal and afterward, with admiration, called him a "monster." Other witnesses were less enchanted, comparing him with a parrot. But his gifts were certified by an Irish scholar and a British philologist, Charles William Russell and Thomas Watts, who set a standard for fluency that is still useful in vetting the claims of modern Mezzofantis: Can they speak with an unstilted freedom that transcends rote mimicry?

Mezzofanti, the son of a carpenter, picked up Latin by standing outside a seminary, listening to the boys recite their conjugations. Rojas-Berscia, by contrast, grew up in an educated trilingual household. His father is a Peruvian businessman, and the family lives comfortably in Lima. His mother is a shop manager of Italian origin, and his maternal grandmother, who cared for him as a boy, taught him Piedmontese. He learned English in preschool and speaks it impeccably, with the same slight Latin inflection—a trill of otherness, rather than an accent—that he has in every language I can vouch for. Maltese had been on his wish list for a while, along with Uighur and Sanskrit. "What happens is this," he said, over dinner at a Chinese restaurant in Nijmegen, where he was chatting in Mandarin with the owner and in Dutch with a server, while alternating between French and Spanish with a fellow student at the institute. "I'm an *amoureux de langues*. And when I fall in love with a language, I have to learn it. There's no practical motive—it's a form of play." An *amoureux*, one might note, covets his beloved, body and soul.

My own modest competence in foreign languages (I speak four) is nothing to boast of in most parts of the world, where multilingualism is the norm. People who live at a crossroads of cultures—Melanesians, South Asians, Latin Americans, Central Europeans, sub-Saharan Africans, plus millions of others, including the Maltese and the Shawi—acquire languages without considering it a noteworthy achievement. Leaving New York, on the way to the Netherlands, I overheard a Ghanaian taxi driver chatting on his cell phone in a tonal language that I didn't recognize. "It's Hausa," he told me. "I speak it with my father, whose family comes from Nigeria. But I speak Twi with my mom, Ga with my friends, some Ewe, and English is our lingua franca. If people in Chelsea spoke one thing and people in SoHo another, New Yorkers would be multilingual, too."

Linguistically speaking, that taxi driver is a more typical citizen of the globe than the average American is. Consider Adul Sam-on, one of the teenage soccer players rescued last July from the cave in Mae Sai, Thailand. Adul grew up in dire poverty on the porous Thai border with Myanmar and Laos, where diverse populations intersect. His family belongs to an ethnic minority, the Wa, who speak an Austroasiatic language that is also widespread in parts of China. In addition to Wa, according to *The New York Times*, Adul is "proficient" in Thai, Burmese, Mandarin, and English—which enabled him to interpret for the two British divers who discovered the trapped team.

Nearly two billion people study English as a foreign language—about four times the number of native speakers. And apps such as

Google Translate make it possible to communicate, almost anywhere, by typing conversations into a smartphone (presuming your interlocutor can read). Ironically, however, as the hegemony of English decreases the need to speak other languages for work or for travel, the cachet attached to acquiring them seems to be growing. There is a thriving online community of ardent linguaphiles who are, or who aspire to become, polyglots; for inspiration, they look to Facebook groups, YouTube videos, chat rooms, and language gurus such as Richard Simcott, a charismatic British hyperpolyglot who orchestrates the annual Polyglot Conference. This gathering has been held, on various continents, since 2009, and it attracts hundreds of aficionados. The talks are mostly in English, though participants wear name tags listing the languages they're prepared to converse in. Simcott's winkingly says "Try Me."

No one becomes a hyperpolyglot by osmosis, or without sacrifice—it's a rare, herculean feat. Rojas-Berscia, who gave up a promising tennis career that interfered with his language studies, reckons that there are "about twenty of us in Europe, and we all know, or know of, one another." He put me in touch with a few of his peers, including Corentin Bourdeau, a young French linguist whose eleven languages include Wolof, Farsi, and Finnish; and Emanuele Marini, a shy Italian in his forties, who runs an export-import business and speaks almost every Slavic and Romance language, plus Arabic, Turkish, and Greek, for a total of nearly thirty. Neither willingly uses English, resenting its status as a global bully language—its *prepotenza*, as Marini put it to me in Italian. Ellen Jovin, a dynamic New Yorker who has been described as the "den mother" of the polyglot community, explained that her own avid study of languages—twenty-five, to date—"is almost an apology for the dominance of English. Polyglottery is an antithesis to linguistic chauvinism."

Much of the data on hyperpolyglots is still sketchy. But, from a small sample of prodigies who have been tested by neurolinguists, responded to online surveys, or shared their experience in forums, a partial profile has emerged. An extreme language learner has a more-than-random chance of being a gay, left-handed male on the autism spectrum, with an autoimmune disorder, such as asthma or allergies. (Endocrine research, still inconclusive, has investigated the hypothesis that these traits may be linked to a spike in testosterone during gestation.) "It's true that LGBT people are well represented in our community," Simcott told me, when we spoke in July. "And a lot identify as being on the spectrum, some mildly, others more so. It was a subject we explored at the conference last year."

Simcott himself is an ambidextrous, heterosexual, and notably outgoing forty-one-year-old. He lives in Macedonia with his wife and daughter, a budding polyglot of eleven, who was, he told me, trilingual at sixteen months. His own parents were monolingual, though he was fascinated, as a boy, "by the different ways people spoke English." (Like Henry Higgins, Simcott can nail an accent to a precise point on the map, not only in the British Isles but all over Europe.) "I'm mistaken for a native in about six languages," he told me, even though he started slow, learning French in grade school and Spanish as a teenager. At university, he added Italian, Portuguese, Swedish, and Old Icelandic. His flawless German, acquired post-college, as an au pair, made Dutch a cinch.

As Simcott entered late adolescence, he said, "the Internet was starting up," so he could practice his languages in chat rooms. He also found a sense of identity that had eluded him. There was, in particular, a mysterious polyglot who haunted the same rooms. "He was the first person who really encouraged me," Simcott said. "Everyone else either warned me that my brain would burst or saw me as a talking horse. Eventually, I made a video using bits and bobs of sixteen languages, so I wouldn't have to keep performing." But the stranger gave Simcott a validation that he still recalls with emotion. He founded the conference partly to pay that debt forward, by creating a clubhouse for the kind of geeky kid he had been, to whom no tongue was foreign but no place was home.

A number of hyperpolyglots are reclusive savants who bank their languages rather than using them to communicate. The more extroverted may work as translators or interpreters. Helen Abadzi, a Greek educator who speaks nineteen languages "at least at an intermediate level" spent decades at the World Bank. Kató Lomb, a Hungarian autodidact, learned seventeen tongues—the last, Hebrew, in her late eighties—and in middle age became one of the world's first simultaneous interpreters. Simcott joined the U.K. Diplomatic Service. On tours of duty in Yemen, Bosnia, and Moldova, he picked up some of the lingo. Every summer, he set himself the challenge of learning a new tongue more purposefully, either by taking a university course—as he did in Mandarin, Japanese, Czech, Arabic, Finnish, and Georgian— or with a grammar book and a tutor.

However they differ, the hyperpolyglots whom I met all winced at the question "How many languages do you speak?" As Rojas-Berscia explained it, the issue is partly semantic: What does the verb "to speak" mean? It is also political. Standard accents and grammar are usually those of a ruling class. And the question is further clouded by the "chauvinism" that Ellen Jovin feels obliged to resist. The test of a spy, in thrillers, is to "pass for a native," even though the English-speaking natives of Glasgow, Port of Spain, Delhi, Lagos, New Orleans, and Melbourne (not to mention Eliza Doolittle's East End) all sound foreign to one another. "No one masters all the nuances of a language," Simcott said. "It's a false standard, and one that gets raised, ironically, mostly by monoglots—Americans in particular. So let's just say that I have studied more than fifty, and I use about half of them."

Richard Hudson's casual search for the ultimate hyperpolyglot was inconclusive, but it led him to an American journalist, Michael Erard, who had embarked on the same quest more methodically. Erard, who has a doctorate in English, spent six years reading the scientific literature and debriefing its authors, visiting archives (including Mezzofanti's, in Bologna), and tracking down every living language prodigy he had heard from or about. It was his online survey, conducted in 2009, that generated the first systematic overview of linguistic virtuosity. Some four hundred respondents provided information about their sex and their orientation, among other personal details, including their IQs (which were above average). Nearly half spoke at least seven languages, and seventeen qualified as hyperpolyglots. The distillation of this research, *Babel No More*, published in 2012, is an essential reference book—in its way, an ethnography of what Erard calls a "neural tribe."

The awe that tribe members command has always attracted opportunists. There are, for example, "bizglots" and "broglots," as Erard calls them. The former hawk tutorials with the dubious promise that anyone can become a prodigy, while the latter engage in online bragfests, like "postmodern frat boys." And then there are the fauxglots. My favorite is "George Psalmanazar" (his real name is unknown), a vagabond of mysterious provenance and endearing chutzpah who wandered through Europe in the late seventeenth century, claiming, by turns, to be Irish, Japanese, and, ultimately, Formosan. Samuel Johnson befriended him in London, where Psalmanazar published a travelogue about his "native" island which included translations from its language—an ingenious pastiche of his invention. Erard pursued another much hyped character, Ziad Fazah, a Guinness record holder until 1997, who claimed to speak fifty-eight languages fluently. Fazah flamed out spectacularly on a Chilean television show, failing to answer even simple questions posed to him by native speakers.

Rojas-Berscia derides such theatrics as "monkey business," and dismisses prodigies who monetize their gifts. "Where do they get the time for it?" he wonders. Erard, in his survey for *Babel No More*, queried his subjects on their learning protocols, and, while some were vague ("I accept mistakes and uncertainty; I listen and read a lot"), others gave elaborate accounts of drawing "mind maps" and of building "memory anchors," or of creating an architectural model for each new language, to be furnished with vocabulary as they progressed. When I asked Simcott if he had any secrets, he paused to think about it. "Well, I don't have an amazing memory," he said. "At many tasks, I'm just average. A neurolinguist at the City University of New York, Loraine Obler, ran some tests on me, and I performed highly on recalling lists of nonsense words." (That ability, Obler's research suggests, strongly correlates with a gift for languages.) "I was also a standout at reproducing sounds," he continued. "But, the more languages you learn, in the more families, the easier it gets. Each one bangs more storage hooks into the wall."

Alexander Argüelles, a legendary figure in the community, warned Erard that immodesty is the hallmark of a charlatan. When Erard met him, ten years ago, Argüelles, an American who lives in Singapore, started his day at three in the morning with a "scriptorium" exercise: "writing two pages apiece in Arabic, Sanskrit, and Chinese, the languages he calls the 'etymological source rivers.'" He continued with other languages, from different families, until he had filled twenty-four notebook pages. As dawn broke, he went for a long run, listening to audiobooks and practicing what he calls "shadowing": as the foreign sounds flowed into his headphones, he shouted them out at the top of his lungs. Back at home, he turned to drills in grammar and phonetics, logging the time he had devoted to each language on an Excel spreadsheet. Erard studied logs going back sixteen months, and calculated that Argüelles had spent forty percent of his waking life studying fifty-two languages, in increments that varied from 456 hours (Arabic) to 4 hours (Vietnamese). "The way I see it, there are three types of polyglots," he told Erard. There were the "ultimate geniuses . . . who excel at anything they do"; the Mezzofantis, "who are only good at languages"; and the "people like me." He refused to consider himself a special case—he was simply a Stakhanovite.

Erard is a pensive man of fifty, still boyish-looking, with a gift for listening that he prizes in others. We met in Nijmegen, at the Max Planck Institute, where he was finishing a yearlong stint as the writer-in-residence, and looking forward to moving back to Maine with his family. "I saw only when the book was finished that many of the stories had a common thread," he told me. We had been walking through the woods that surround the institute, listening to the vibrant May birdsong, a Babel of voices. His subjects, he reflected, had been cut from the herd of average mortals by their wiring or by their obsession. They had embraced their otherness, and they had cultivated it. Yet, if speech defines us as human, a related faculty had eluded them: the ability to connect. Each new language was a potential conduit—an escape route from solitude. "I hadn't realized that was my story, too," he said.

Rojas-Berscia and I took a budget flight from Brussels to Malta, arriving at midnight. The air smelled like summer. Our taxi driver presumed we were mother and son. "How do you say 'mother' in Maltese?" Rojas-Berscia asked him in English. By the time we had reached the hotel, he knew the whole Maltese family. Two local newlyweds, still in their wedding clothes, were just checking in. "How do you say 'congratulations'?" Rojas-Berscia asked. The answer was "*nifraħ*."

We were both starving, so we dropped our bags and went to a local bar. It was Saturday night, and the narrow streets of the quarter were packed with revelers grooving to deafening music. I had pictured something a bit different—a quaint inn on a quiet square, perhaps, where a bronze Knight of Malta tilted at the bougainvillea. But Rojas-Berscia is not easily distracted. He took out his notebook and jotted down the kinship terms he had just learned. Then he checked his phone. "I texted the language guide I lined up for us," he explained. "He's a personal trainer I found online, and I'll start working out with him tomorrow morning. A gym is a good place to get the prepositions for direction." The trainer arrived and had a beer with us. He was overdressed, with a lacquered mullet, and there was something shifty about him. Indeed, Rojas-Berscia prepaid him for the session, but he never turned up the next day. He had, it transpired, a subsidiary line of work.

I didn't expect Rojas-Berscia to master Maltese in a week, but I was surprised at his impromptu approach. He spent several days raptly eavesdropping on native speakers in markets and cafés and on long bus rides, bathing in the warm sea of their voices. If we took a taxi to some church or ruin, he would ride shotgun and ask the driver to teach him a few common Maltese phrases, or to tell him a joke. He didn't record these encounters, but in the next taxi or shop he would use the new phrases to start a conversation. Hyperpolyglots, Erard writes, exhibit an imperative "will to plasticity," by which he means plasticity of the brain. But I was seeing plasticity of a different sort, which I myself had once possessed. In my early twenties, I had learned two languages simultaneously, the first by "sleeping with my dictionary," as the French put it, and the other by drinking a lot of wine and being willing to make a fool of myself jabbering at strangers. With age, I had lost my gift for abandon. That had been my problem with Vietnamese. You have to inhabit a language, not only speak it, and fluency requires some dramatic flair. I should have been hanging out in New York's Little Saigon, rather than staring at a screen.

The Maltese were flattered by Rojas-Berscia's interest in their language, but dumbfounded that he would bother to learn it—what use was it to him? Their own history suggests an answer. Malta, an archipelago, is an almost literal stepping stone from Africa to Europe. (While we were there, the government turned away a boatload of asylum seekers.) Its earliest known inhabitants were Neolithic farmers, who were succeeded by the builders of a temple complex on Gozo. (Their mysterious megaliths are still standing.) Around 750 B.C., Phoenician traders established a colony, which was conquered by the Romans, who were routed by the Byzantines, who were kicked out by the Aghlabids. A community of Arabs from the Muslim Emirate of Sicily landed in the eleventh century and dug in so deep that waves of Christian conquest—Norman, Swabian, Aragonese, Spanish, Sicilian, French, and British—couldn't efface them. Their language is the source of Maltese grammar and a third of the lexicon, making Malti the only Semitic language in the European Union. Rojas-Berscia's Hebrew helped him with plurals, conjugations, and some roots. As for the rest of the vocabulary, about half comes from Italian, with English and French loanwords. "We should have done Uighur," I teased him. "This is too easy for you."

Linguistics gave Rojas-Berscia tools that civilians lack. But he was drawn to linguistics in part because of his aptitude for systematizing. "I can't remember names," he told me, yet his recall for the spoken word is preternatural. "It will take me a day to learn the essentials," he had reckoned, as we planned the trip. The essentials included "predicate formation, how to quantify, negation, pronouns, numbers, qualification—'good,' 'bad,' and such. Some clausal operators—'but,' 'because,' 'therefore.' Copular verbs like 'to be' and 'to seem.' Basic survival verbs like 'need,' 'eat,' 'see,' 'drink,' 'want,' 'walk,' 'buy,' and 'get sick.' Plus a nice little shopping basket of nouns. Then I'll get our guide to give me a paradigm—'I eat an apple, you eat an apple'—and voilà." I had, I realized, covered the same ground in Vietnamese—*tôi ăn một quả táo*—but it had cost me six months.

It wasn't easy, though, to find the right guide. I suggested we try the university. "Only if we have to," Rojas-Berscia said. "I prefer to avoid intellectuals. You want the street talk, not book Maltese." How would he do this in the Amazon? "Monolingual fieldwork on indigenous tongues, without the reference point of a lingua franca, is harder, but it's beautiful," he said. "You start by making bonds with people, learning to greet them appropriately, and observing their gestures. The rules of behavior are at least as important in cultural linguistics as the rules of grammar. It's not just a matter of finding the algorithm. The goal is to become part of a society."

After the debacle with the "trainer," we went looking for volunteers willing to spend an hour or so over a drink or a coffee. We auditioned a tattoo artist with blond dreadlocks, a physiology student from Valletta, a waiter on Gozo, and a tiny old lady who sold tickets to the catacombs outside Mdina (a location for King's Landing in *Game of Thrones*). Like nearly all Maltese, they spoke good English, though Rojas-Berscia valued their mistakes. "When someone says, 'He is angry for me,' you learn something about his language—it represents a convention in Maltese. The richness of a language's conventions is the highest barrier to sounding like a native in it."

On our third day, Rojas-Berscia contacted a Maltese Facebook friend, who invited us to dinner in Birgu, a medieval city fortified by the Knights of Malta in the sixteenth century. The sheltered port is now a marina for superyachts, although a wizened ferryman shuttles humbler travelers from the Birgu quays to those of Senglea, directly across from them. The waterfront is lined with old palazzos of coralline limestone, whose façades were glowing in the dusk. We ordered some Maltese wine and took in the scene. But the minute Rojas-Berscia opened his notebook his attention lasered in on his task. "Please don't tell me if a verb is regular or not," he chided his friend, who was being too helpful. "I want my brain to do the work of classifying."

Rojas-Berscia's brain is of great interest to Simon Fisher, his senior colleague at the institute and a neurogeneticist of international renown. In 2001, Fisher, then at Oxford, was part of a team that discovered the FOXP2 gene and identified a single, heritable mutation of it that is responsible for verbal dyspraxia, a severe language disorder. In the popular press, FOXP2 has been mistakenly touted as "the language gene," and as the long-sought evidence for Noam Chomsky's famous theory, which posits that a spontaneous mutation gave *Homo sapiens* the ability to acquire speech and that syntax is hard-wired. Other animals, however, including songbirds, also bear a version of the gene, and most of the researchers I met believe that language is probably, as Fisher put it, a "bio-cultural hybrid"—one whose genesis is more complicated than Chomsky would allow. The question inspires bitter controversy.

Fisher's lab at Nijmegen focuses on pathologies that disrupt speech, but he has started to search for DNA variants that may correlate with linguistic virtuosity. One such quirk has already been discovered, by the neuroscientist Sophie Scott: an extra loop of gray matter, present from birth, in the auditory cortex of some phoneticians. "The genetics of talent is unexplored territory," Fisher said. "It's a hard concept to frame for an experiment. It's also a sensitive topic. But you can't deny the fact that your genome predisposes you in certain ways."

The genetics of talent may thwart average linguaphiles who aspire to become Mezzofantis. Transgenerational studies are the next stage of research, and they will seek to establish the degree to which a genius for language runs in the family. Argüelles is the child of a polyglot. Kató Lomb was, too. Simcott's daughter might contribute to a science still in its infancy. In the meantime, Fisher is recruiting outliers like Rojas-Berscia and collecting their saliva; when the sample is broad enough, he hopes, it will generate some conclusions. "We need to establish the right cutoff point," he said. "We tend to think it should be twenty languages, rather than the conventional eleven. But there's a trade-off: with a lower number, we have a bigger cohort."

I asked Fisher about another cutoff point: the critical period for acquiring a language without an accent. The common wisdom is that one loses the chance to become a spy after puberty. Fisher explained why that is true for most people. A brain, he said, sacrifices suppleness

MALTESE FOR BEGINNERS 305

to gain stability as it matures; once you master your mother tongue, you don't need the phonetic plasticity of childhood, and a typical brain puts that circuitry to another use. But Simcott learned three of the languages in which he is mistaken for a native when he was in his twenties. Corentin Bourdeau, who grew up in the South of France, passes for a local as seamlessly in Lima as he does in Tehran. Experiments in extending or restoring plasticity, in the hope of treating sensory disabilities, may also lead to opportunities for greater acuity. Takao Hensch, at Harvard, has discovered that valproate, a drug used to treat epilepsy, migraines, and bipolar disorder, can reopen the critical period for visual development in mice. "Might it work for speech?" Fisher said. "We don't know yet."

Rojas-Berscia and I parted on the train from Brussels to Nijmegen, where he got off and I continued to the Amsterdam airport. He had to finish his thesis on the Flux Approach before leaving for a research job in Australia, where he planned to study aboriginal languages. I asked him to assess our little experiment. "The grammar was easy," he said. "The orthography is a little difficult, and the verbs seemed chaotic." His prowess had dazzled our consultants, but he wasn't as impressed with himself. He could read bits of a newspaper; he could make small talk; he had learned probably a thousand words. When a taxi driver asked if he'd been living on Malta for a year, he'd laughed with embarrassment. "I was flattered, of course," he added. "And his excitement for my progress excited him to help us." "Excitement *about* your progress," I clucked. It was a rare lapse.

A week later, I was on a different train, from New York to Boston. Fisher had referred me to his collaborator Evelina Fedorenko. Fedorenko is a cognitive neuroscientist at Massachusetts General Hospital who also runs what her postdocs call the EvLab, at MIT. My first e-mail to her had bounced back—she was on maternity leave. But then she wrote to say that she would be delighted to meet me. "Are you claustrophobic?" she added. If not, she said, I could take a spin in her fMRI machine, to see what she does with her hyperpolyglots.

Fedorenko is small and fair, with delicate features. She was born in Volgograd in 1980. "When the Soviet Union fell apart, we were starving, and it wasn't fun," she said. Her father was an alcoholic, but her parents were determined to help her fulfill her exceptional promise in math and science, which meant escaping abroad. At fifteen, she won a place in an exchange program, sponsored by Senator Bill Bradley, and spent a year in Alabama. Harvard gave her a full scholarship in 1998, and she went on to graduate school at MIT, in linguistics and psychology. There she met the cognitive scientist Ted Gibson. They married, and now have a one-year-old daughter.

One afternoon, I visited Fedorenko at her home in Belmont. (She spends as much time as she can with her baby, who was babbling like a songbird.) "Here is my basic question," she said. "How do I get a thought from my mind into yours? We begin by asking how language fits into the broader architecture of the mind. It's a late invention, evolutionarily, and a lot of the brain's machinery was already in place."

She wondered: Does language share a mechanism with other cognitive functions? Or is it autonomous? To seek an answer, she developed a set of "localizer tasks," administered in an fMRI machine. Her first goal was to identify the "language-responsive cortex," and the tasks involved reading or listening to a sequence of sentences, some of them garbled or composed of nonsense words.

The responsive cortex proved to be separate from regions involved in other forms of complex thought. We don't, for example, use the same parts of our brains for music and for speech, which seems counterintuitive, especially in the case of a tonal language. But pitch, Fedorenko explained, has its own neural turf. And life experience alters the picture. "Literate people use one region of their cortex in recognizing letters," she said. "Illiterate people don't have that region, though it develops if they learn to read."

In order to draw general conclusions, Fedorenko needed to study the way that language skills vary among individuals. They turned out to vary greatly. The intensity of activity in response to the localizer tests was idiosyncratic; some brains worked harder than others. But that raised another question: Did heightened activity correspond to a greater aptitude for language? Or was the opposite true—that the cortex of a language prodigy would show less activity, because it was more efficient?

I asked Fedorenko if she had reason to believe that gay, left-handed males on the spectrum had some cerebral advantage in learning languages. "I'm not prepared to accept that reporting as anything more than anecdotal," she said. "Males, for one thing, get greater encouragement for intellectual achievement."

Fedorenko's initial subjects had been English-speaking monolinguals, or bilinguals who also spoke Spanish or Mandarin. But in 2013 she tested her first prodigy. "We heard about a local kid who spoke thirty languages, and we recruited him," she said. He introduced her to other whizzes, and as the study grew Fedorenko needed material in a range of tongues. Initially, she used Bible excerpts, but *Alice's Adventures in Wonderland* came to seem more congenial. The EvLab has acquired more than forty *Alice* translations, and Fedorenko plans to add tasks in sign language.

Twelve years on, Fedorenko is confident of certain findings. All her subjects show less brain activity when working in their mother tongue; they don't have to sweat it. As the language in the tests grows more challenging, it elicits more neural activity, until it becomes gibberish, at which point it elicits less—the brain seems to give up, quite sensibly, when a task is futile. Hyperpolyglots, too, work harder in an unfamiliar tongue. But their "harder" is relaxed compared with the efforts of average people. Their advantage seems to be not capacity but efficiency. No matter how difficult the task, they use a smaller area of their brain in processing language—less tissue, less energy.

All Fedorenko's guinea pigs, including me, also took a daunting nonverbal memory test: squares on a grid flash on and off as you frantically try to recall their location. This trial engages a neural network separate from the language cortex—the executive-function system. "Its role is to support general fluid intelligence," Fedorenko said. What kind of boost might it give to, say, a language prodigy? "People claim that language learning makes you smarter," she replied. "Sadly, we don't have evidence for it. But, if you play an unfamiliar language to 'normal' people, their executive-function systems don't show much response. Those of polyglots do. Perhaps they're striving to grasp a linguistic signal." Or perhaps that's where their genie resides.

Barring an infusion of valproate, most of us will never acquire Rojas-Berscia's twenty-eight languages. As for my own brain, I reckoned that the scan would detect a lumpen mass of mac and cheese embedded with low-wattage Christmas lights. After the memory test, I was sure that it had. "Don't worry," Matt Siegelman, Fedorenko's technician, reassured me. "Everyone fails it—well, almost."

Siegelman's tactful letdown woke me from my adventures in language land. But as I was leaving, I noticed a copy of *Alice* in Vietnamese. I report to you with pride that I could make out "white rabbit" (*thỏ trắng*), "tea party" (*tiệc trà*), and *ăn tôi*, which—you knew it!—means "eat me."

AUGUST 2018

TROUBLING LOVE

DARKNESS WEARABLE

———— ∞ ————

W hen Hubert de Givenchy, the aristocrat who had dressed Audrey Hepburn and Jacqueline Kennedy, retired, in 1995, he was replaced at the house he had founded in 1952 by John Galliano, a plumber's son from South London, who left after a year for an even more exalted job, at Christian Dior. (Galliano was fired this March, after a series of anti-Semitic rants.) Another working-class British upstart of prodigious talent and flamboyant showmanship then stepped up to the hallowed plate in his Doc Martens. The new chief designer at Givenchy was a chubby hellion of twenty-seven, with a buzz cut and a baby face, who once boasted, "When I'm dead and gone, people will know that the twenty-first century was started by Alexander McQueen."

McQueen committed suicide, at forty, in London, on February 11, 2010. The housekeeper found his body hanging in his Mayfair flat. He had been under treatment for depression, and a week earlier his mother, Joyce, had died of cancer. (Her funeral had been scheduled for February 12; the family went ahead with it.) In 2004, Joyce was invited to interview her famous son, by then at his own label, for the arts page of a British newspaper. In the course of an exchange that was fondly pugnacious on both sides (it was obvious where he'd got his scrappiness), she had asked him to name "his most terrifying fear." Without hesitation, he replied, "Dying before you." Normally, it is the parent who dreads losing the child, but the answer makes sense if you take it to mean "killing you with grief." You have to wonder if, for mercy's sake, McQueen hadn't been biding his time.

While McQueen had many anxieties, running dry wasn't among them. He was supremely confident of his instincts and his virtuosity. That ballast freed him to improvise, to take wild chances, and to jettison received ideas about what clothing should be made of (why not seashells or dead birds?), what it should look like (Renaissance court dress, galactic disco wear, the skins of a mutant species), and, above all, how much it could mean. The designer who creates a dress rarely invests it with as much feeling as the woman who wears it, and couture is not an obvious medium for self-revelation, but in McQueen's case it was. His work was a form of confessional poetry.

Last week, a retrospective of McQueen's two decades in fashion, *Savage Beauty*, opened at the Metropolitan Museum. Even if you never bother with fashion shows, go to this one. It has more in common with *Sleep No More*, the "immersive" performance of *Macbeth* currently playing in Chelsea, than it does with a conventional display of couture in a gallery, tent, or shop window. Andrew Bolton, the curator of the Met's Costume Institute, has assembled a hundred ensembles and seventy accessories, mostly from the runway, with a few pieces of couture that McQueen designed at Givenchy, and he gives their history and psychology an astute reading. McQueen was an omnivore (literally so; he always struggled with his weight), and the richness of his work reflects a voracious consumption of high and low culture. He felt an affinity with the Flemish masters, Gospel singing, Elizabethan theater and its cross-dressing heroines (a line from *A Midsummer Night's Dream* was tattooed on his right biceps), contemporary performance art, punk, Surrealism, Japan, the ancient Yoruba, and fin-de-siècle aestheticism. In most particulars, however—including his death—he was an archetypal Romantic.

Bolton has grouped the exhibits according to McQueen's "Romantic" fixations: historicism, primitivism, naturalism, exoticism, the gothic, and Darwinism. (In his last complete collection, *Plato's Atlantis*, McQueen envisaged the females of a devolved human species slithering chicly back into the sea in scaly iridescent minidresses.)

There is a section on "Romantic Nationalism," which in McQueen's case means Scottish tribalism. His paternal ancestors came from the Hebrides, and he never lost his abiding rage at England's treatment of his clansmen in centuries past. "Fucking haggis, fucking bagpipes," he said. "I hate it when people romanticize Scotland." The idea of its bleakness, though, seems to have warmed him—it resembled the climate of his mind.

McQueen's pride in his ancestry had been ingrained by his mother. (A collection on the theme of witchcraft was dedicated to one of her forebears, who was hanged in Salem.) His father, Ronald, drove a taxi, and Joyce stayed home until her son left school, at sixteen, when she took a teaching job. McQueen was the youngest of their six children—born in 1969—and they christened him Lee Alexander. (He started using his middle name at the outset of his career, because he was on welfare and he didn't want to lose his benefits.) When Lee was a year old, the family moved from South London to Stepney, in the East End. Trino Verkade, who was McQueen's first employee, and was part of the Met's installation team, told me that the area had been a skinhead bastion. "Lee was never a skinhead," she said, "but he loved their hard and angry look."

McQueen had realized very young that he was gay, but it took his family some time to accept him as what he called, with deceptive off-handedness, its "pink sheep." His puberty coincided with the explosion of AIDS, which is to say that he was forced to witness a primal scene that haunted the youth of his generation: sex and death in the same bed. Art, swimming, and ornithology were his primary interests at the tough local comprehensive school. He didn't have the credentials for university, but he always knew, he said, that he would "be someone" in fashion, and when Joyce heard that Savile Row was recruiting apprentices, he applied. At his first job, with Anderson & Shepherd, one of Britain's most venerable bespoke tailors, he learned, painstakingly, to cut jackets. (He later claimed that he had sewn an obscene message—"I am a cunt"—into the lining of one destined for Prince Charles. The firm is said to have recalled every garment for the prince that McQueen had worked on, but no message was found.) He moved to a competitor, Gieves & Hawkes, then to a theatrical costumer, and on to the atelier of an avant-garde designer, Koji Tatsuno. McQueen ended his adolescence in Milan, working for his idol, Romeo Gigli— the modern Poiret. Gigli, he said, taught him, by example, that a designer can't flourish without a talent for self-promotion.

When McQueen came home to London, about a year later, he thought that he might teach pattern-cutting at the art school that has educated the elite of British fashion, Central Saint Martins. There was no job for him, but the administration invited him to enroll as a postgraduate student, waiving the academic requirements. In 1992, McQueen presented a master's degree collection entitled *Jack the Ripper Stalks His Victims*. (At Givenchy, he based a collection on the character of a "mad scientist who cut all these women up and mixed them all back together.") There is a lot of sympathy for the devil in McQueen's work. Bolton suggests that you consider it as "a meditation on the dynamics of power, particularly the relation between predator and prey."

Isabella Blow, a freelance stylist who later became one of the great "noses" of the fashion world, saw the *Ripper* show, recognized McQueen's gifts, and bought the collection in its entirety. (A black tuxedo with a bustle and long dagger-shaped lapels lined in blood red is at the Met.) Blow and McQueen were inseparable for a while, then, as his fame increased, less so. She, too, suffered from depression, and killed herself in 2007. Her legendary collection of clothing was saved from dispersal on the auction block by her friend Daphne Guinness.

McQueen's five years in the Givenchy couture ateliers taught him, he said, to use softness, lightness, and draping as foils for the austerity of his tailoring—and of his temperament. Some of his best work is his most ethereal. But Paris didn't teach him docility, and he sometimes took impolitic swipes at his bosses. Givenchy is owned by the French luxury conglomerate LVMH. In 2001, when its chief rival, the Gucci Group, offered to back McQueen's own label, he and Givenchy parted company.

Alienation often accounts for a macabre sense of the marvelous. At the entrance to *Savage Beauty* there is an evening gown conjured entirely from razor-clam shells. Antelope horns sprout from the shoulders of a pony-skin jacket, and vulture skulls serve as epaulettes on a leather dress. There are angel wings made out of balsa wood, and worms encased in a bodice of molded plastic. "I'm inspired by a feather," McQueen said of all the duck, turkey, ostrich, and gull plumage in his clothing—"its graphics, its weightlessness, and its engineering." One of his most demented masterpieces is a glossy black-feathered body cast that transforms its wearer into a hybrid creature—part raptor, part waterfowl, and part woman.

Bolton had full access to the McQueen archives, in London, and the support of McQueen's associates (his house co-sponsored the show). Sarah Burton, who succeeded him, was busy in London with Kate Middleton's wedding dress, but she was interviewed for the catalogue. The Norwegian fashion photographer Sølve Sundsbø took the catalogue pictures. It looks as though he bought the mannequins from a junk dealer, and it is startling to learn that they are live models disguised as dummies. Their bodies were coated with white acrylic makeup, and articulated at the joints by black strings. In the retouching process, they lost their heads. But here and there—on a torso, a thigh, an arm—the makeup has worn away, and a bruise-like patch of pink skin shows through, as if the flesh of a corpse were coming to life. The freshness of the shock is pure McQueen.

Savage Beauty is a shamelessly theatrical experience that unfolds in a series of elaborate sets. In the first gallery, examples of McQueen's incomparable tailoring hug the walls of a raw loft. A silk frock coat from the *Ripper* collection, with a three-point "origami" tail, in a print of thorns (I mistook them for barbed wire), has human hair sewn into the lining. There are several versions of McQueen's signature "bumsters": drop-waisted trousers or skirts that flaunt the cleavage of the buttocks. But his outrages were generally redeemed by an ideal of beauty, and the point of the bumsters, he said, was not just to "show the bum"; they elongated the torso and drew the eye to what he considered the "most erotic" feature of anyone's body—the base of the spine.

The second gallery is an ornate, spooky hall of mirrors consecrated to McQueen's gothic reveries about bondage and fetishism. One of the loveliest dresses—with a lampshade skirt of swagged jet beading—has a necrotic-looking jabot of lace ivy that reminds you what a fetish mourning was to the Victorians. Leather abounds, masterfully tortured into submission, as in a zippered sheath with fox sleeves latticed by an elaborate harness. "It's like the *Story of O*," McQueen said. "I'm not big on women looking naïve. There is a hidden agenda in the fragility of romance."

Story of O proves that a work of art can be distilled from stock pornographic imagery, and McQueen—who has a lot to say, in the wall notes, about the sexual thrill factors of rot, fear, and blood—manages to find beauty, as he put it, "even in the most disgusting of places." Beyond the hall of mirrors is a "Cabinet of Curiosities," where inventive instruments of consensual torture in the form of jewelry, headgear, footwear, and corsets are displayed like talismans. Videos from selected runway shows flicker high on the black walls, and the animal sounds of a cheering crowd and a woman moaning issue from hidden speakers. In a clip from one of McQueen's most radical collections (Spring/Summer 1999), a homage to the German artist Rebecca Horn, the model Shalom Harlow revolves on a turntable, cringing in mock horror as two menacing robots spray her white parachute dress with paint guns. The most striking artifact from this collection is a pair of exquisitely hand-carved high-heeled wooden prostheses that McQueen designed for Aimee Mullins, a bilateral amputee and American Paralympic athlete. She modeled them on the runway with a bridal lace skirt and a centurion's breastplate of molded leather, sutured like Frankenstein's skull.

There were always critics who accused McQueen of misogyny, and he was chastised for "exploiting" Mullins's disability as a publicity stunt. He brazenly courted scandal, reveled in most of it, asserted that "hot sex sells clothes," and certainly subjected his models—like the mannequins in the catalogue—to extreme trials. They were caged in glass boxes or padded cells; half smothered or drowned; masked; tethered; tightly laced; straitjacketed; and forced to walk in perilous "armadillo" booties, with ten-inch heels. In *Highland Rape* (1995), the breakthrough collection that earned McQueen, at twenty-six, his notoriety as a bad-boy wonder, bare-breasted, disheveled girls staggered down the runway in gorgeously ravaged lace, sooty tartan, and distressed leather. According to feminist critics, the show eroticized violation. According to McQueen, it commemorated the "genocide" of his Scottish ancestors. "We're not talking about models' feelings here," he said. "We're talking about mine." In fact, he always was.

Therapists who treat children often use doll play as a tool for eliciting their stories and feelings, and one has the sense that the doll play of fashion was such a tool for McQueen. He was fascinated by the work of Hans Bellmer, the mid-century German artist who created a life-size, ball-jointed mannequin—the figure of a pubescent girl—and photographed it in disturbing tableaux. *La Poupée*, McQueen's Spring/Summer 1997 collection, paid tribute to an artist with whom he shared a kinship in perversity. Yet McQueen felt an even deeper sense of identity with the broken and martyred women who stirred his fantasies, and whom he transfigured. The real agenda of his romance with fragility may have been hiding in plain sight, tattooed on his arm, in the yearning line spoken by Shakespeare's Helena—a scrappy girl who feels that her true beauty is invisible: "Love looks not with the eyes but with the mind."

MAY 2011

1

Balthus, born Balthasar Klossowski in 1908, was sixty-two when we met, fifty years ago. I had never known a great artist, and he looked the part, especially in paint-splattered trousers and a rakish ascot. His manners were lordly, and his languid speech caressed the French language even when he was bemoaning something, especially his work, which was always going badly, or modernity, with which he was at odds. He affected an air of tragic weariness, yet he still had the agile grace of the ephebe he had been, as well as a bad boy's appetite for surprise.

I was in my early twenties, fresh out of college, living abroad, and unformed in every sense. Physically, I could have passed for one of the adolescents in Balthus's paintings. If they were not naturally ungainly, he posed them in awkward positions, kneeling on the floor over a book, or asleep on a divan with their heads thrown back and limbs splayed in such a way as to guarantee a stiff neck and numb extremities upon waking. They tend to have poignant bodies rather than model ones: dense and round, with legs that seem even shorter in childish white anklets. Their imperfection renders them vulnerable, the more so as they aren't conscious of it. In one of his most famous pictures, *Nude in Front of a Mantel* (1955), a plump girl, with flesh of white marble, like the fireplace she stands at, is rooted to the floor by her flat feet (my feet exactly). She is represented in profile, gazing at a pier glass, so that she is, in effect, faceless, as the young often are to themselves. She lifts her hair—a dark cascade—off her shoulders. It looks so heavy (my own hair weighed me down like a lead blanket) that her gesture seems to defy the gravity that her form conveys.

Balthus was, when we met, the director of the French Academy in Rome, which is housed in the sixteenth-century Villa Medici, on the Pincian Hill, above the Spanish Steps. He had overseen its restoration, and spent years trying to reproduce "Pieran blue," as he called it—the blue of Piero della Francesca's frescoes—for the walls. His chatelaine and second wife, Setsuko, née Ideta, was a woman of nubile charm, thirty-five years his junior, whom he had met on a cultural mission to Japan, where she had served as his group's interpreter. Setsuko exuded delicacy. She always dressed in a kimono (Balthus wore them himself from time to time), and she glided through the halls of the palazzo with birdlike steps.

I would never have been asked to the villa on my own account—I was of no account. But my boyfriend at the time was the son of distinguished figures in the French art world, and the four of us had been invited as a family. Our host spent most of the day in his atelier, and we met for meals. The spectral butler who served them wore white gloves, and called his master "Signor Conte." (Balthus styled himself "Le Comte de Rola," an invented title that he insisted upon even in the face of bohemian derision. He also claimed descent from Byron, the kings of Poland, and the Romanovs. But his father, Erich Klossowski, was a Polish émigré of genteel descent who lost what fortune he possessed in the Second World War, and Balthus's mother, Baladine, née Elisabeth Spiro, was the daughter of a cantor from Breslau, though her son always denied he had Jewish blood.) From the beginning, the great man addressed me familiarly, as one would a small child, and I took his *tu* as a mark of affectionate condescension. I always said *vous* to him—on the rare occasions when I dared to speak. "Your little Judith is quite pretty, but isn't she a bit stupid?" he asked my boyfriend's mother. She knew that I would treasure the remark.

Nude in Front of a Mantel was posed against a wall of Pieran blue. I also posed against such a wall—though not for Balthus. Setsuko had begun to paint (years would pass before she showed her work), and she asked me to sit for her. A baroque armchair covered in its original fraying damask was pulled up to a window that overlooked the villa's gardens, which had once belonged to Lucullus, and I stared at the venerable umbrella pines until lunchtime, when Balthus joined us at an antique table that gave off a scent of beeswax. I made an effort to eat as Setsuko did, taking dainty bites. I cannot remember the conversation, though I was struck by my hosts' demeanor as a couple. They performed their roles with a courtly, even ritualized, politesse beneath which hummed a sensual understanding. You would never have known they were mourning a child, their two-year-old son, Fumio, who had died that year of Tay-Sachs disease.

Balthus was avian in physique though feline in temperament, and his totem animal was the cat. He had made his artistic debut, at the age of thirteen, with a series of forty drawings, in pen and ink, that told the story of an Angora stray he had adopted. When the cat ran away, Balthus was heartbroken, and he turned to art for consolation. Rainer Maria Rilke, a family friend (he was having an affair with the tempestuous Baladine), was so impressed by the boy's gifts that he arranged for the drawings to be published as a little book, *Mitsou* (the defector's name, but also the title, not incidentally, of a novella by Colette, published that year), and supplied a preface.

Cats often figure in Balthus's dreamlike streetscapes, and as the house pets—or tutelary spirits—of the girls in his portraits. You cannot read the mind of a cat, and you have no idea what the girls are thinking, though their opaque reveries, you might suspect, resemble those of the eight-year-old provocateur whom Colette evokes in *My Apprenticeships*, a child who "already knew too much . . . of the various terrible ways of giving oneself pleasure." The beauty of Balthus's work is unsettling morally and visually, and the Italian title of Elena Ferrante's first novel, *L'amore molesto*, seems apt for it. Balthus himself described the style of these portraits with the untroubled phrase "timeless realism." Both timelessness and realism have long been out of fashion, and were still so when Balthus embarked on his adult career. His first show, in Paris in 1934, outraged critics both for its content—the precocious eroticism of pubescent subjects posed voyeuristically—and its technical "crudity." The artist of twenty-six became so depressed by this failure, which coincided with a lover's rejection, that he attempted suicide and stopped painting for a while. He also waited more than a decade to show his paintings in Paris again.

The charge of crudity is now hard to fathom. Few artists of the past century were more painterly than Balthus, whose masters were Courbet and della Francesca, and who worked so slowly, and with such tortured perfectionism, that he sometimes produced only two or three pictures a year. You can stare for a long time at the shadows on a wall in one of his interiors, rapt at their depth of nuance. Perhaps "crudity" was a Freudian slip on the part of a writer who meant to say "cruelty." There is a subtext of violation to the portraits (overt in a few of them), and the viewer is made complicit with it. Here one should note that none of the models or their chaperones ever accused Balthus of impropriety, and he indignantly defended his work against the charges that were leveled at it and at him. "Balthus has the immediacy of a naive painter," Guy Davenport writes, and one can best understand that naïveté not as a primitive state of mind but as an Edenic one—a trance of solitude insulated from any sense of wrongdoing. If one cannot quite understand it that way in 2020, we owe it to the art to examine the nuances of our discomfort. That is where Balthus's genius lies.

2

A Balthus Notebook was published thirty years ago, which is to say, an eon by the measure of social changes.* As the critic Michael Dirda put it, Guy Davenport possessed "a sensibility appealingly out of step with

* This essay introduced *A Balthus Notebook*, by Guy Davenport (David Zwirner Books, 2020).

our debased times." Few critics brought the depth of erudition to their work that Davenport did; fewer, if any, were his peers as a stylist. "Shoddiness demoralizes," he wrote succinctly. "Unless the work of art has wholly exhausted its maker's attention, it fails."

It is clear from the first lines of these lapidary aperçus that Davenport is addressing a reader undaunted by his references (the original edition had no footnotes). He free-associates symphonically in a scholarly language like Sanskrit or Mandarin. (The word "Mandarin," interestingly, may come from the Sanskrit *"mantri,"* referring to a councillor.) His own tastes, though, were refreshingly catholic. Davenport could write his name in Linear B, but he loved crime fiction and hillbilly slang. Tolkien was his tutor at Oxford, where he studied on a Rhodes scholarship, and he thought *The Hobbit* saga was a masterpiece. He translated Sappho, Heraclitus, Jesus, and Rilke, but he reveled in gossip. He rebelled against the prudery of his childhood, in a Southern Baptist family, in part by celebrating his bisexuality. (Some of his later stories and art are more explicitly homoerotic, courageously so for the time.)

Davenport's output was prodigious: nearly fifty books of criticism, poetry, drawings, cartoons, translations, collages, fiction, and correspondence; and the hunger that drove his reading, from the age of ten, when a neighbor in South Carolina gave him his first book (one of the Tarzan series), never flagged. If his works have a common thread, it may be ardor. He relates the art of Balthus to the philosophy of Charles Fourier, the French utopian socialist who argued that all expressions of desire and sexual identity, including (especially) those of children, should be respected. "The nakedness of human nature is clothed so soon by every culture," Davenport writes in these notes, "that we are at a wide variance . . . as to what human nature might be. It was one of the hopes of our century to find out, a hope wholly dashed."

A perfectionist is someone who despairs of perfection yet spares nothing in the vain attempt to achieve it. In that sense, Davenport and Balthus are kindred spirits. And also in that sense, every finished masterpiece is a work in progress that an exhausted maker had to abandon. It is useful to read these shimmering fragments with that warning in mind. They chart the struggle by which a true perception, feeling, or image comes into focus, even as they dramatize the truth that the wholeness of anything, or of anyone, is an illusion.

2020

DOLL'S PLAY

⸺&⸺

L ast Thursday, the clue for 1 Across in the *New York Times* crossword puzzle was: "1962 Kubrick film," six letters. Answer: "Lolita."

The next morning, I took the Eighty-sixth Street crosstown bus to the Jewish Museum, to see a new Laurie Simmons show, inspired by Doll Girls—young women who alter their appearance to look like Barbies or Japanese anime characters. The girl sitting next to me on the bus was reading *Lolita*. She looked about the age of Nabokov's heroine—the doll girl of another era. As we passed H&M, display workers were dressing the window mannequins. Spring is here, and it's time to bare some flesh. The plastic skin of a naked mannequin is, however, always unsettling. (I was already thinking about Laurie Simmons. Unsettling mannequins are her specialty.)

As a bus went the other way, the girl glanced up from her page, over her glasses, exactly as Sue Lyon did in the posters for *Lolita* that were plastered on New York buses fifty-three years ago. Lyon, the nubile blonde in the title role (she was fourteen when they cast her), was sucking on a lollipop that was, like her dark glasses, red and heart shaped. In the most shocking scene of the film—shocking for its time—Humbert Humbert (James Mason) gives Lolita a pedicure. He was grooming her in both senses.

When I got to the museum, it was filled with cheerful octogenarians in sensible shoes. (This is a crowd that shops at Harry's.) Most of them, apparently, had come to see *Helena Rubinstein: Beauty Is Power*, a large show of Rubinsteiniana—flattering portraits, important jewelry, opulent couture, and art from the collection of a formidable entrepreneur, not to mention a spendthrift. But Rubinstein's fortune was entirely self-made: she was born in a Polish shtetl, in 1872, and parlayed a recipe for homemade face cream into a global cosmetics empire. The show has been open since October (it closes this week), so it doesn't seem that there was any intent on the part of the curators to juxtapose it with the much smaller Simmons show of six photographs, upstairs. But the two exhibits do speak to each other.

The makeup business is a form of doll play, and Rubinstein loved dolls' houses. Some of the miniature interiors that she commissioned are on display. One has a Murano chandelier, Persian carpets, and French château furniture. Another is the atelier of a gentleman painter: slanted skylight, narrow mezzanine overlooking the vaulting studio space, easel by the window, and bohemian disarray. These dioramas are charming, but they are also claustrophobic, and they inspire creepy thoughts. The divan in the atelier, for example: Did its wolfish proprietor seduce his young models on it? Such notions may have been the influence of *Lolita*, but a doll's house invites voyeurism—the invasion of a private space.

A girl's body is also a private space, and child psychiatrists use doll play as a diagnostic tool, especially in cases of suspected abuse. Simmons's art uses dolls and mannequins in a related fashion—to explore the boundaries between innocence and perversion. She once bought a customized sex doll in Japan, then dressed it and undressed it for a series of photographs. They were published in a book, *The Love Doll*, which you can buy at the museum's gift shop. In the introduction, Jeanne Greenberg Rohatyn writes that "the surrogate sex partner arrived in a crate, clothed in a transparent slip and accompanied by a separate box containing an engagement ring and genitalia." Simmons starred as a dollhouse-obsessed artist much like herself in an indie film, *Tiny Furniture*, by her daughter Lena Dunham.

Mothers and daughters and feminine role-play: that is a theme here. Little girls love messing with their mothers' makeup. But when

Rubinstein was a little girl mothers didn't wear makeup; only actresses and prostitutes did. Rubinstein was determined to change that—she made painting your face respectable. "Nature always needs help," she says in an old film clip that runs on a loop in the exhibit. In another video, a group of docile, dewy-eyed young test subjects look as if they are being mummified in one of Rubinstein's salons. (They are actually just getting facials.) A lady next to me on the banquette laughed ruefully as she watched it. She quoted Yeats to her friend: "We who are born woman know that one must suffer to be beautiful." We also suffer being ridiculous.

The title of the Simmons show, *How We See*, is meant to be ironic or, more accurately, meta-ironic. First, there is not much to look at. Simmons photographed six plastic-looking professional models from the collarbone up against Life Savers–colored backgrounds. The models themselves are like Life Savers, too—they come in slight variations of the same sugary taste. The wall text notes that prominent in each portrait "are the girls' preternaturally large, sparkling eyes, which stare out at the visitor with an uncanny, alien gaze." (They are actually staring into space.) "Their arresting strangeness arises from the fact that they are painted on the models' closed lids, a well-known Doll Girls technique."

The girls and young women who identify as Doll Girls post images on social media in which they have transformed themselves with wigs and makeup—sometimes also with surgery and starvation—to look like a favorite doll or animated character. I am tempted to digress into the dialectical tension between the terms "anime" and "inanimate"— right next to the Simmons show is an installation based on the work of Gilles Deleuze, the French metaphysician, that plays with the same idea—but I fear that this is TMI. It's worth noting, though, that Simmons's doll girls have been rendered blind.

The title of the Rubinstein show is, I think, ironic unintentionally. Beauty is power? For the beautiful, certainly, and for beauty's eponymous purveyors, many of whom were, like Rubinstein, women of modest backgrounds. (Estée Lauder was a girl from Queens, and Elizabeth Arden—the former Florence Nightingale Graham—came from a small town in Canada.) Purveying beauty made Rubinstein so rich that when she was turned down for an apartment on Fifth Avenue, because she was Jewish, she bought the building. But power doesn't make you beautiful. Helena was a fireplug of four feet eleven. She had the looks of a priestess, not of a sacrificial virgin.

Mason Klein, the curator of the Rubinstein show, is aware that some museumgoers will not buy his premise, so he writes, "If latter-day feminist debates have focused on cosmetics as objectifying women, they were seen in the early twentieth century as a means of asserting female autonomy. By encouraging women to define themselves as self-expressive individuals"—painters, no less—"Rubinstein contributed to their empowerment." He concludes, "She offered women the ideal of self-invention."

If a female artist objectifies women ironically, is that empowerment? Perhaps it can be. As the Rubinstein show informs us, some suffragists wore rouge as a gesture of revolt. It aligned them with the "hussies" and "fallen women" who refused to let men's definitions of a "good" or a "bad" woman, or of lawful and shameful desire, cheat them of an erotic life. But Simmons's work also suggests how the "ideal of self-invention" can be self-subverted. When a young girl goes to extremes to embody the fantasies of a lecher, not to say of a pedophile—when Lolita and Humbert have the same taste for doll play—beauty is victimhood.

MARCH 2015

T he pseudonymous Italian novelist Elena Ferrante has written profoundly about two subjects for some thirty years: the fraught bond between mothers and daughters, and the brutality of life in proletarian Naples. Her latest work of fiction, *The Lying Life of Adults*, is a surprising deviation for her. Its narrator, Giovanna Trada, is a woman on the brink of middle age who is recounting the disaffections of her privileged adolescence, some thirty years ago. The teenager she conjures is obsessed with her looks, about which she despairs for three hundred pages. Just as doggedly, she moons after a local heartthrob who is dating a skinny friend. Familial rancors, long simmering, lead to the revelation that her parents are flawed human beings. Ferrante has a gift, perhaps even a genius, for making great literature out of melodrama. But the overwrought language of her new book doesn't illuminate the anguish that it seeks to plumb. Giovanna admits, in the first paragraph, that she is clueless about her own story: it may, she says, "merely be a snarled confusion of suffering." Had this been a young writer's coming-of-age story, one could praise its abundant flashes of brilliance and forgive its excesses. Coming from a master, its puerility is a mystery.

What does it mean to write like a woman? Ferrante posed that question, partly to herself, thirteen years ago, in an interview with the Italian magazine *Io Donna*. She had not yet published her Neapolitan quartet, an epic bildungsroman in four volumes, narrated by a writer named Elena, which has sold some sixteen million copies. But her earlier novels—*Troubling Love, Days of Abandonment,* and *The Lost Daughter,* a triptych of stories about women in extremis—were a preview of her power. This body of work defies the conventions of writing "like a woman" as radically as did Mary Shelley's *Frankenstein.*

In *Days of Abandonment* (2002), the narrator, Olga, who once had literary ambitions but shelved them when she married and had children, answers her author's question. "To write truly," she reflects, "is to speak from the depths of the maternal womb." Ferrante has an attunement to her characters that one might call maternal, yet she accepts no constraints on what a female can say, and, more fundamentally, on what she can feel. Her fiction rattles the cage of gender.

Interviews suggest that Ferrante found her vocation on the late side, around forty. Nothing verifiable is known about her youth, but, she told *Io Donna,* "I learned to write by reading mainly works by men." Their heroines (she specifies Emma Bovary, Anna Karenina, and Chekhov's lady with a little dog) engaged her more fully, she said, and seemed more like "real women" than did the female protagonists of women novelists.

There are writers of her sex whom Ferrante admires—Elsa Morante and Virginia Woolf among them. Those who disappoint her appear to have a common failing. "I always read stories by women with trepidation," she told another Italian magazine. "I expect something that seemed unsayable to appear miraculously on the page." The unsayable is either what you may not say, because of who you are, or what you cannot admit, because you have internalized a taboo.

Ferrante's style is blunt—at times even careless—as if she were deliberately rejecting centuries of preciosity in women's prose. "When I write, it's as if I were butchering eels," she told *Io Donna.* "I pay little attention to the unpleasantness of the operation." The word "revulsion" recurs so often in her pages that it is almost a tic. She revels in descriptions of incontinence: leaking tampons and spastic ejaculations. Women novelists before her have seethed at the benevolence expected of them—the Brontë sisters are a notable example. But Ferrante is a brawler, not a seether. She co-opts the pugnacity of a male voice to express the unsayable about female dilemmas, and this belligerence feels revolutionary.

A Ferrante novel typically begins with the violent rupture of a primal attachment, and a woman's discovery of how enslaved she has been to it. Delia, in *Troubling Love* (1992), is unhinged by her mother's apparent suicide. Olga becomes deranged when her husband deserts her for a younger woman. Elena learns, in the opening pages of *My Brilliant Friend* (2011), the quartet's first volume, that her best friend from childhood has abandoned her, after sixty years, by vanishing without a trace. Parents, children, and men back these women into corners, from which they lash out—sometimes viciously. But they are, above all, caged in their own bodies, taut to bursting with rage and shame. Ferrante perceives their claustrophobia as a conflict between their imperative desires and those of others, to whom their identity is beholden. In that respect, they are not unlike Shelley's monster.

There is a vast bibliography of analytic theory on this subject, much of it dating to the 1970s, when it electrified the young feminists of Ferrante's generation, and she has acknowledged its influence. The theory situated the roots of misogyny in an infant's conflicting impulses toward a mother's body: to devour, penetrate, and possess; to be cherished, mastered, and contained. Only later are these desires rigidly classified as male or female. Most cultures can't tolerate the ambiguity for long. A boy is socialized to suppress his "female" yearnings and is rewarded for it with the prestige of maleness; a girl's reward for surrendering to passivity is male approval. At their most unforgiving, these asymmetries help to sustain archaic patriarchies like that of Ferrante's Naples.

Male authors may have taught Ferrante to write, but none of them grew up as a girl. "A secret cord that can't be cut binds us to the bodies of our mothers," she wrote in a newspaper column. "There is no way to detach ourselves, or at least I've never managed to." But there is a way. Ferrante suggested it, cryptically, in response to a question about Olga's battles with her daughter: they lead her to accept her child's "hostile love as a vital feeling." Hostile love is also vital to literature.

The characters who seem most "real" to us were created by a writer unafraid of its contradictions.

Freud defines "the uncanny" as the terror of what is most familiar—what frightens us most about home, even as it compels us to return there. The Naples of Ferrante's work has precisely this gothic allure. The city is a mother's body, pungent and labyrinthine, loathsome and beloved, from which she cannot detach herself. It was there that I first read Ferrante in Italian.

Italians have been notably less smitten with Ferrante than her foreign fans have. They are famously pious about maternity, and Ferrante's narrators tend to be bad mothers who are emancipated by their neglect. Reading her in English isn't the same experience. Ann Goldstein has translated all of Ferrante's work, and many bilingual readers feel that she has improved the prose. It may not be a coincidence that Ferrante has called translators her "only heroes." Translation, she wrote recently, "draws us out of the well in which, entirely by chance, we are born." Goldstein has nearly perfect pitch for Ferrante's voice, yet it has an accent on the page that English cannot quite capture, which is itself the echo of another language—the harsh, often obscene dialect of Campania. Ferrante balks at using dialect explicitly, yet her prose bears its imprint like the welt marks of a slap.

Ferrante's early novels are rooted in the notion that primal attachments shape the way that human beings dominate and submit to one another. In the quartet, she gives that premise a vivid embodiment in the hostile love—empowering and subversive, jealous and reverent, steadfast and treacherous—between two friends whom we meet as girls of eight, in the slum where they were born, and follow for six decades, through the upheavals of postwar Italian society. Elena Greco and Raffaella Cerullo (Lenù and Lila) seem fated from the outset to become their mothers—weary drudges brutalized by their men, who wreak that violence on their daughters, if not by blows then by disparagement. In that respect, each of them has been invisible to herself until her friend gives her the gift of being seen.

Lila, a self-taught prodigy, will make her fortune as a pioneer of computer technology, but not before an abusive teenage marriage cuts short her education. She survives a hellish interlude in a sausage factory, which engages her in the violent class struggles that polarized Italy in the seventies. Her life is a series of insurrections against male despotism, beginning with her father's. Just as she threw rocks at the local boys who tried to bully her, she rebels against the institutions that do the same: daughterhood, wifehood, maternity, capitalism, the Camorra (Naples's Mafia). Not even love can hold Lila fast. She understands it as a form of martyrdom like all the others. When she disappears, leaving her best friend bereft, it isn't a surprise to Lenù: that is how Lila has always lived, beholden to no one.

Elena lacks Lila's courage for sacrilege; she is a female version of Balzac's provincial strivers, whose climb out of poverty is enabled by a vigilant false self and a talent for ingratiation. Decades pass, and she matures into a sexually liberated intellectual who juggles motherhood and a career. Her books on working-class Naples, appropriated from Lila's hardships, make her a famous writer. But whenever the story shifts away from Lila it loses a mythic dimension and becomes something more ordinary: a bourgeois novel.

Although Ferrante's audience isn't confined to women, she has inspired an ardent following among them, partly because few writers have evoked female friendship more truthfully, or have given it the place in an ambitious epic that male friendship has held in literature since the *Iliad*. (There is something of Achilles in Lila: a noble heart capable of feral cruelty.) And, if her readers tend to identify with one brilliant friend or the other, many feel a primal attachment to their creator.

In part for that reason, Ferrante's identity and gender—even her singularity (is she really one person?)—have been matters of fervid speculation. In 2016, Claudio Gatti, an investigative journalist for *Il Sole 24 Ore*, a business newspaper, claimed to have unmasked her. He had hacked into the royalty statements of Ferrante's Italian publisher, Edizioni E/O, a small house to which she has been loyal. Inexplicably vast sums, he discovered, had been paid to the account of Anita Raja, a translator from the German and an E/O stalwart. Raja, who is sixty-seven, was born in Naples, her father's native city, but grew up in Rome; her mother was a Polish Jew who had escaped the Holocaust. If she has published fiction, she has never signed any. But her husband, Domenico Starnone, is one of Italy's most prominent men of letters, whose best-known work is set in Naples, where he was born into the same generation and class as Lenù and Lila. He has vehemently denied having written or co-written Ferrante's novels. Yet if their author is a man he has pulled off one of the most improbable— not to mention galling—impersonations in the annals of fiction.

Whoever Ferrante may be, however, the author's relationship with the public resembles a game that mothers play with infants: peekaboo. Even as she dodges bounty hunters like Gatti, she seems to take unusual pleasure in explaining herself. In 2003, she published *Frantu-maglia*, a volume of letters and interviews with critics, reporters, filmmakers, fans, and her publishers, the earliest dating from 1991. Two subsequent editions enlarged the contents; an English translation appeared four years ago, with the subtitle "A Writer's Journey."

The reclusive cipher turns out to be a garrulous interview subject, so long as the conversations are conducted by e-mail. There is something poignant about her eagerness to hold forth, and it makes you wonder whether, over the years, anonymity hasn't become another experience of claustrophobia. Journalists ask versions of the same questions, and her replies run on for pages, sometimes donnishly. She corresponds with directors who have filmed her novels, and with fangirls who tell her that they were "blown away" by them. "Frantumaglia," Ferrante notes, is an expression in dialect that conjures "debris in a muddy water of the brain." She makes a creative-writing lesson of her own flotsam— reprinting manuscript pages from her early novels which didn't make the cut, often because they were, she felt, too explanatory. "It's my own fastidiousness that censors me," she tells a critic.

Last year, Ferrante published *Incidental Inventions*, a collection of weekly musings and personal sketches for *The Guardian*, which added to the inventory of what we know about her (or of what she wants us to think that we know). The prose is confiding and, in places, pontifi-cal. Those who are "given the job of telling stories," she notes, "should construct fictions that help seek the truth of the human condition." Ferrante the columnist claims to have more than one daughter and a granddaughter. Her daughters "let me know I should keep quiet" but help her with technology. She adores plants and cats. She hates exclamation points. Snakes are her worst fear, and failure used to be. Tobacco was once her drug of choice—she started smoking at twelve. At fifteen, she discovered sex, which she primly calls "love," in a deserted alley, with a skinny boy who was mainly interested in getting her to "caress" him. She still has a penchant for lean men, especially those with a receding hairline. Pregnancy was a "seesaw of joy and horror." She dislikes the way she looks in photographs and is the last guest to leave a party: "My problem is leave-taking itself. I don't like to separate from people."

What should readers make of these books—a slight, cozy memoir and a hefty intellectual autobiography that, together, run to nearly five hundred pages? At the very least, no one should entertain illusions about their veracity. "As I child, I was a big liar," Ferrante writes in a column. She put so much effort into her lies that she forgot they weren't true. *Frantumaglia* conveys a more explicit warning. A critic asks her for a "brief description" of herself, and she cites the response of Italo Calvino to a nosy scholar: "I don't give biographical facts, or I give false ones, or anyway I always try to change them from one time to the next. Ask me what you want to know, but I won't tell you the truth, of that you can be sure."

Mendacity is the theme of *The Lying Life of Adults*. Its title is the heading a teenager might give to a page in her diary, before filling it with evidence of her parents' hypocrisy. That, in essence, is the story that follows, which is set in Naples, in the 1990s. Its narrator is about forty. She has, she tells us portentously, "slipped away" from the places and the events that she is recounting, and is "still slipping away." The slippage, though, is never explained, except that the middle-aged Giovanna confounds herself uncritically with the teenager she was. That blurring of boundaries between an older and a younger woman, or an older and a younger self, is a Ferrante signature. Characters such as Delia, Elena, and Olga inhabit a troubled past, and relive its traumas with an immediacy that makes them visceral for the reader. But these women never relinquish their authority in the present to shape the story. In the course of events—a few days or weeks in the early novels, a lifetime in the quartet—a character separates from her avatars and comes to understand the nature of their attachment. One might call that achievement of consciousness hostile self-love. But its lucidity is missing from *The Lying Life*.

In the first chapter, Giovanna has just entered puberty. She is the cherished only child of an attractive couple, Nella and Andrea. Both parents teach high school, and her father is an intellectual of some note. They own an apartment in an upscale neighborhood, where they often entertain their best friends, whose two daughters are Giovanna's playmates. All three girls have been raised liberally—no nonsense about religion or abstinence. Illustrated primers taught them the facts of life, or at least its mechanics; they masturbate guiltlessly, sometimes together.

Giovanna is something new in Ferrante's fiction: a daddy's girl. She and Andrea share an enviable complicity. "I had much more fun with him than with my mother," she says. He lets her know that she is "indispensable." She ought to be on her way to becoming one of those lucky daughters who are at ease with their desires because an adoring father has sanctioned them. But puberty has made her moody, and, on the evening when the story begins, Andrea learns that Giovanna's latest report card is mediocre. She overhears him tell her mother that she is "getting the face of Vittoria." Vittoria is her father's younger sister, a plebeian virago who still lives in their parents' old tenement and works as a maid. She and Andrea hate each other incandescently.

"The face of Vittoria" is a coded expression that both parents use to describe a cultivated person who has revealed a hidden vulgarity. Muttered darkly, in the dialect of her father's childhood, the phrase shatters Giovanna like a curse. She takes it to mean that she has suddenly become "very ugly." Everyone assures her that she isn't ugly at all, but she ceases to believe any of the certainties she once accepted, starting with her sense of worth.

To assuage her angst, Giovanna seeks out the aunt whom she is said to resemble. Vittoria proves to be a beautiful, foulmouthed Fury out of Euripides by way of *The Sopranos*. She tells Giovanna an instructive story. Some twenty years earlier, she fell in love, for the first and only time, with a married policeman named Enzo, who fucked her like a god (she describes their coitus in detail to Giovanna), though only eleven times. Her happiness was destroyed when Giovanna's father revealed the affair to Enzo's wife and their three children. Soon afterward, the policeman "died of grief." Andrea, his sister explains, ruined her life on the pretense of saving it.

In the rendezvous that follows, Vittoria is alternately "threatening and enveloping." She introduces Giovanna to the working-class kin she has never met, and to Enzo's family, which embraces her. She also dares her niece to ferret out her parents' lies. When the girl discovers that they have been unfaithful, she loses respect for them—and any scruples about lying herself. As her breasts swell, and males take notice, Giovanna starts dressing like "a dissolute woman" in an effort to feel "heroically vile." She even gives a hand job to Enzo's hapless son. (Masochism has always been a quack remedy for a sense of unworthiness.)

Giovanna isn't blind to her aunt's coarseness, or insensible to her tyranny, yet she admires the code that Vittoria lives by, which consists of not taking shit from anyone and loving one man forever, even a dead one. Vittoria's fidelity extends to God. She drags her niece to church, where Giovanna has a *coup de foudre* for a charismatic lay preacher named Roberto, who was born in the slums but is now a theology student in Milan—and the fiancé of Enzo's daughter. Roberto is an evangelist for selfless love, rather than the hostile variety, and everyone reveres him. Giovanna's misery elicits his compassion, and he tells her the magic words: "You're very beautiful." This paragon of male virtue is such a rarity in Ferrante's fiction as to fairly guarantee a takedown in a sequel—one that the novel's loose ends seem to promise.

Three years pass as the men posture and the women weep over them. At nearly sixteen, Giovanna realizes belatedly, "I had been deceived in everything . . . But the mistake had been to make it a tragedy." Delivered of her virginity in a touchingly bathetic scene, she runs away to Venice with one of the sisters she used to play with, a budding novelist. "On the train," she concludes, "we promised each other to become adults as no one ever had before."

Great novelists conjure human beings under stress without making them case studies. "I think that authors are devoted, diligent scribes, who draw in black and white following a more or less rigorous order of their own," Ferrante told a journalist. But, she added, "the true writing, what counts, is the work of the readers." In *The Lying Life of Adults*, she seems to confuse her readers with the journalists to whom she has explained her work didactically. "Lies, lies, adults forbid them and yet they tell so many," Giovanna thinks.

The Lying Life has passages of electric dialogue and acute perception. But its crude hinting and telegraphing suggest an author who distrusts her reader's discernment, and they made me wonder if Ferrante hadn't drafted the story as a much younger writer, still honing her craft. Consider the artifice of the "cursed" bracelet that is coveted by every female character, and given to or stolen from each of them in turn. It winds up on the floor of the bachelor pad where Giovanna is deflowered. If you missed the symbolism, turn to page 135: Giovanna muses, "The bracelet, however you looked at it, in whatever type of story you inserted it . . . showed only that our body, agitated by the life that writhes within, consuming it, does stupid things that it shouldn't do." Who wrote this sentence? Not a master of the unsayable.

At a certain age, every artist contemplates her unfinished business. Having focused on mothers for three decades, perhaps Ferrante wanted to take on a father and a daughter. Since she has no comfort zone, it wasn't that she stepped out of it to imagine the bond between Andrea and Giovanna, and its disruption. In the absence of a mediating adult sensibility, however, the drama never transcends the emotional confines of the adolescence it depicts.

Ferrante's magisterial social history of class gave significance to events, in the quartet, that might otherwise have seemed like episodes in a telenovela. But *The Lying Life of Adults* affords no sense of Italy in the 1990s, except for the abstract Marxist chatter that excites Andrea and his friends, or the vague liberation theology that flavors Roberto's sermons. Giovanna's father and her aunt were born in a blighted neighborhood, but, thirty years after Lenù left one like it, its boundaries are porous: there is television reception and public transport; Vittoria tootles around Naples in her own car. Besides, Giovanna is only a tourist in the *città bassa*, beguiled by its exotic locals. She goes back to her studies, and makes up a lost year. With her father's encouragement, she starts reading the Gospels, in Greek. Yet she does so as a way into Roberto's heart. Like almost all the females in the novel, whatever their age or their class, Giovanna is abjectly dependent on the love of someone with a penis. In that respect, she represents a disheartening surrender of the ground that Olga, Lila, Elena, and Ferrante herself fought to liberate.

For all the signage in *The Lying Life of Adults*, it is hard to say what Ferrante's intentions were. She has chosen, for mysterious reasons, to abdicate the two greatest sources of her power: the hostile love of mothers and daughters, and the Vesuvian rumble beneath the surface of a squalid habitat where men and women are trapped in archetypal roles. Perhaps a sequel will give those intentions a more artful focus. Or perhaps something unsayable blocked her access to their truth.

AUGUST 2020

FAQs

Bergdorf Goodman has been dressing New York's one percent for more than a century—111 years, to be precise. The venerable retailer, on Fifth Avenue at Fifty-eighth Street, is celebrating that odd anniversary—chosen for its graphic symbolism: "one store" (Bergdorf has no branches), "one experience, one city"—with a season's worth of hoopla. It began in September, with the screening of a lavishly produced, ninety-minute documentary, *Scatter My Ashes at Bergdorf's*, directed by Matthew Miele. The title was taken from the caption of a cartoon by Victoria Roberts, which ran in *The New Yorker* in 1990. It pictures an old biddy cheerfully instructing a friend how to dispose of her remains. The conceit, Roberts told Miele, "wouldn't have worked with Macy's."

Betty Halbreich, one of Bergdorf's most senior employees—she joined the staff in 1976—appears only briefly in the film, though her peppery candor relieves its blandness. After the screening, she was mobbed by admirers, but she also wondered if she would have a job in the morning. Halbreich runs Betty Halbreich's Solutions, a personal-shopping service based in a suite—a corner office overlooking Central Park, and two private dressing rooms—on Bergdorf's third floor. She is a petite dynamo of eighty-five, with a svelte figure and a throaty laugh. Her grooming (artful makeup, short silver hair) and style of dress (sober tailoring, playful accessories) advertise the kind of secure identity that she helps her clients to project. "My work is like lay therapy," Halbreich told me. "You listen, you prescribe—clothes are a fix—and you hold up a mirror. Most people can't see themselves."

That evening, Halbreich was wearing a vintage tuxedo jacket by Issey Miyake, a Gucci blouse in animal-print chiffon, and, "for pizzazz," a bejeweled leopard brooch that had belonged to her mother. Sensible shoes and a good panty girdle are the only concessions that she makes to age. Her tolerance for constraint, however, seems limited to latex. Isaac Mizrahi was one of several fashion grandees who told Miele a typical "Betty story." He had heard her talking a client out of a dress, then abruptly changing her mind. "Buy it," she told the woman. "It's not as terrible as what you came in with."

Halbreich's bluntness is not universally applauded. An important buyer described her to me as "a curmudgeon." "Certain people are scared of me," Halbreich admitted, "and I probably can't help them." Psychoanalysis may be cheaper, though there is neither a charge for Halbreich's time nor a minimum-purchase requirement. Yet, for those who prefer tough love to servility, her office is ecumenical. Arrivistes alternate in the dressing room with the grandes dames they aspire to become, and athletes' wives follow oligarchs. Some of her regulars are women who, like Jo Carole Lauder, the art collector and philanthropist, "just don't like to shop," as Lauder told me. Others—media stars, corporate executives—don't have the time. Mothers send Halbreich their teenage daughters, often for the same reason that my mother enrolled me in driving school. Strivers upgrading their wardrobe for a promotion—in the boardroom or at the altar—invest in Halbreich's expertise, though on that score she has a "strict policy," she says. "I don't take the second wife if I've dressed the first one, and I don't take the mistress." Three of her best clients, however, are widows of the same man.

Even the buyer critical of Halbreich's manners lauded her "eye." (She possesses a matched pair, green and unclouded, which size you up, in all senses.) The costume designer Patricia Field, who shopped with her to dress Carrie Bradshaw and her friends on *Sex and the City*, considers Halbreich a fellow stylist. "Stylist is the new wannabe profession," Field said. "There are lots of studio services around"—shoppers who work in film and television—"but she's the go-to celebrity. She's also the most fun."

Halbreich estimates that about half her revenues are generated by fashion professionals. (Field sometimes "pulled" a hundred thousand dollars' worth of merchandise for a single episode of *Sex and the City*.) She has also collaborated on Woody Allen films, with the costume designers Santo Loquasto and Jeffrey Kurland, and on Broadway plays, with William Ivey Long, Ann Roth, and Jane Greenwood. Field's former protégé Eric Daman worked with Halbreich on the clothes for *Gossip Girl*. Candice Bergen, Meryl Streep, Stockard Channing, Joan Rivers, and Liza Minnelli are among her alumnae. Mia Farrow was the rare actress who balked at a dress—"a little hundred-dollar Adele Simpson number, so that dates the story," Halbreich recalled. "She said it would have fed a village in Biafra."

Soap operas cycle through more clothes than a laundromat, so they have always been lucrative for Solutions, especially *All My Children*, which ran for some forty years. (Susan Lucci, who played the glamorous villain, is also a private client.) In good times, Halbreich reckons, her office racks up annual sales of $2 million to $3 million, but, she added, "I ought to write a chapter for my memoirs called 'All My Recessions.'" The memoir, Halbreich's second book, is in the works. In 1997, she published *Secrets of a Fashion Therapist*, a volume of advice "for the ladies from Dubuque"—not flyover sophisticates—on "shopping for the truth."

Last June, at 8:30 on a sweltering morning, ninety minutes before Bergdorf opened its main doors to the public, Halbreich was waiting for me at the employees' entrance, next to the Paris Theatre, on West Fifty-eighth Street. When the security guard asked to see my ID, Halbreich gave her a cockeyed look. "I'm her ID," she said, and we waltzed through to the elevators. She had invited me to "walk the store" with her—all eight floors—a ritual that she performs at the beginning of every workday. "It's how I get a feel for what's new, because I don't read fashion magazines," she said. Tapping her head, she added, "And this is my computer."

Bergdorf's ground floor blazes with the opulence of its mirrors and chandeliers, but also with that of its merchandise, mostly jewelry and leather goods. A whimsical, beaded minaudière from Judith Leiber costs about as much (four thousand dollars) as a crocodile tote by Nancy Gonzalez. The upper stories have an amenity rare in New York: natural light on three sides. Five is a riot of noise and color, where the youthful wares of edgier designers compete for attention like the rugs in a souk. Halbreich hesitates to take clients there, she said, "unless they are twelve, but I'll bring Five to them." On the floors below, decorum is the rule (except during sales, when even Bergdorf turns into Fort Lauderdale). The aisles are flanked with richly appointed little chapels dedicated to a chosen saint (Chanel, Lanvin, Balenciaga). A hierarchy of prestige, like that among the dining rooms on a cruise ship, seems to govern the placement of Old Guard, newish-guard, and avant-garde designers.

Halbreich is "blind and deaf" to the siren call of a label. She sailed past a rack of Prada raincoats, in a drab palette. "Deluxe prison garb," she sniffed. A ruffled poet's blouse, by Alexander McQueen, was askew on its hanger. She jiggled it briefly, then put it back: "There's always a reason something is marked down." Alaïa's seams earned her approval: "I'm a nut for cut," she added, but "spare me the maid's-room pink." A "shepherdess" dress, in a floral print, by Jean Paul Gaultier, reminded her of Sarah Ferguson's daughter—"the blowsier one."

Whenever Halbreich paused to inspect a garment, she patted it down like a horse breeder at a yearling sale, checking for the flaws in an expensive animal. "How will it look when you walk or sit? How good is the fabric? What's the taste level?" After an instructive detour into the stockrooms (an alternative reality of concrete floors, fluorescent light, and rolling racks behind metal cages), we paused at the Row's fall pre-collection. The line is designed by the Olsen twins, and made in America. "If I have one prejudice," Halbreich said, "it's that I try to push brands manufactured here." A burgundy cashmere turtleneck "spoke" to her, though only after she had rubbed a sleeve on the underside of her chin. "Let's take it back with us," she said. "It looks like you, very Left Bank." The sweater wasn't something I would have leaped at. When I tried it on, though, I was smitten by its silhouette—

cropped and belled, with narrow armholes. "You're just necking with it," she warned me, as she checked the price tag and grimaced like a Kabuki actor at its four digits. "You're not going all the way on *my* watch."

Halbreich has lived in Manhattan long enough—for sixty-five years—to pass for a native. Patricia Field notes, "The wisecracks, the attitude, that El Morocco voice are all out of Damon Runyon." (Runyon's ashes were scattered on Broadway.) But Betty, née Stoll, was born in Chicago, in the heyday of Al Capone. Her father was a businessman who "ran department stores," Halbreich said. After his early death, her mother, Carol, had to reinvent herself, and she bought a bookshop on Oak Street, on the city's Gold Coast, "where she roped in interesting people, who stayed for hours. My mother's real vocation was running a salon."

Carol was famous for her hats, her jewelry, and her repartee. She may or may not have gone swimming in the Plaza fountain on a visit to Manhattan. She "smoked like a chimney," Halbreich said (and so did she, until a bout with cancer). In old age, Carol wore Pucci and Montana. She wasn't a beauty, yet men adored her. Viktor Skrebneski, the fashion photographer, was among her cavaliers. "He flew her around the world," Halbreich said. (They traveled with his longtime partner.)

Betty, too, adored her mother, but was somewhat overshadowed by her flamboyance. She wanted to become a painter or, better, a cartoonist, and she went to lectures at the Art Institute of Chicago. She married at twenty, however, before her ambitions had coalesced. (It was 1947, the year Dior launched his New Look; Halbreich had several original Diors in her trousseau.)

Sonny Halbreich was the real Runyon character, a dashing man who liked a good time. He owned a company in the garment district, called Uwana Wash Frocks, which manufactured drip-dry housecoats and bathrobes. (They weren't sold at Bergdorf.) Every season, he would ask his wife's opinion of the new designs, and, on the remote chance that she liked something, he knew that his customers wouldn't, so he pulled it from the line.

The Halbreichs had two children, Kathy and John, who are now in their early sixties. Kathy is the associate director of the Museum of Modern Art; John went into his father's business, and still works in the fashion industry, at a company that manufactures women's sleepwear. "We're a high-low family," he told me. "My sister runs the museum, and Mom was selling couture while Dad and I were servicing J. C. Penney." Kathy Halbreich said, "A clothes sense like my mother's is an artistic gift for experiment and composition, and I don't think it can be taught. She would have made a great curator—though, in a sense, she is one."

Halbreich's children both suggested that their mother's image of devil-may-care privilege and assurance is deceptive. "She's very good at the social part," John said, "and she's close friends with many of her clients. But she works in a corporate climate that didn't exist at Bergdorf when she started, and she has to make the sale." Kathy observed, "My mother likes to say, 'Everybody is the same without their clothes on,' by which she means, I think, that we're all vulnerable. Her buoyance of spirit is the product of a lifelong struggle because she really understands melancholy."

Halbreich went through a particularly melancholy period in the early 1970s, when her marriage was ending. "I forgave my husband many things," she said, "but I had a limit." She emerged, with the help of therapy, from "a doll-house existence," and found seasonal work in a series of designer showrooms on Seventh Avenue. Then Geoffrey Beene, whom she revered, and who wrote the foreword to her first book—"She enriches our lives"—hired her for a full-time sales job. But, once it was clear that the break with Sonny was irrevocable, she "couldn't get up in the morning," she told me. She eventually met a "good companion," who died four years ago, but a portrait of the Halbreichs as radiant newlyweds still hangs in her bedroom.

Chance meetings are a motif in Halbreich's biography. She had met Sonny in Miami Beach, while on vacation with her mother. She met Ira Neimark, Bergdorf's former CEO, while lunching with her mother at the Drake Hotel in Chicago. Neimark and Dawn Mello, the company's former fashion director, were at the next table. "When Ira saw me, he thought I was chic," Halbreich recalled. "'Get that girl,' he said."

The "girl," who was then forty-nine, was hired for a boutique that Beene had opened at Bergdorf. Halbreich had never worked a register, and she hated the sales floor. "I think you can do better with me," she told her bosses, after a year. "Let's set up a personal-shopping service." But the management wanted to see her in action, so they gave her a "test case": the immortally stylish Babe Paley. "It wasn't much of a test, since she was only looking at Givenchy," Halbreich said. "But I had the nerve to ask her what brand of hair rinse she used." (She allegedly used Tintex, a cheap fabric dye.)

Personal shoppers are now ubiquitous, and some are the algorithms that track your preferences on Net-a-Porter or Amazon. Lord & Taylor in New York, and Marshall Field's in Chicago, both claim to have been, in the early twentieth century, the first department store to offer one-on-one service. Halbreich created her own niche at Bergdorf, but when she started she had two rivals. (There are several more today.) One, she said, was a snob for French couture who spent her days on the phone, and the other catered exclusively to "the carriage trade" in an era when women of all classes were entering the workforce. "We had no office that really took care of people. There's a lot of pretension in this racket, but there's nothing glorified about what you do. It's a helping profession, with its menial aspects. You get nannies for your clients, even a date once in a while, and you listen to their woes. Oh, the stories these walls could tell."

Later on the morning of our walkabout, a young woman met us in the Solutions office. Olivia (not her real name) is a second-generation Halbreich client who had agreed to let me tag along on one of her shopping sessions. She is tall, poised, and voluptuous—a modern Gibson Girl.

HALBREICH: "You have a very expensive figure."
OLIVIA: "What is an expensive figure?"
HALBREICH: "Too womanly to go jeune fille."
OLIVIA: "That's fine with me, because I dress older than my age. My ideal is head-to-toe Saint Laurent from the seventies."

Olivia told us that she "didn't really need anything—my closets are full." But at our first stop, in the handbag department, she fell upon a Celine tote, reduced to fourteen hundred dollars, and would have bought it on the spot. "You're going to think about it," Halbreich said firmly. She also scotched Olivia's request to stop at the shoe salon. "You mean the candy store? I'll never get you out of there."

Some clients visit Halbreich every season when the collections arrive. Olivia and her mother come less often, and usually not together. "Our styles are too different for jubilant co-shopping," she said. "But I care about clothes less and less as I get older." To which Halbreich replied, "You could have fooled me."

We took the escalator to the fifth floor, and, as we worked our way down, I noticed a pattern. Olivia thought of her taste as "conservative." "You have your square days," Halbreich agreed. "I don't want my clothes to attract attention," Olivia said. (Her job involves diplomacy.) Yet she made a beeline for a racy sheath by Andrew Gn—black lace over nude chiffon, then an Alaïa ballerina dress, with tiers of crocheted ruffles ("Not with *your* behind, kid"), and a short Milly skirt, in a loud print, with flounces and a peplum. "It might look better than it ought to," Halbreich conceded, "at least to your boyfriend." Olivia parried the teasing, which she seemed to enjoy, but I thought she was going to cry when Halbreich asked the saleswoman for the Milly "in a size ten."

Halbreich sounds curmudgeonly only on the screen or the page, where you can't feel her visceral warmth. She isn't really a tyrant; she just doesn't pretend. And a client's fancy is the wind in her sails, so she tacks when she has to. As Olivia's choices piled up, Halbreich draped the garments over her arm. (Eric Daman told me that even with him, a buff male forty-two years her junior, "Betty insists on the heavy lifting.") But she added her own "pulls" to the mix, sometimes surreptitiously. There was a pattern there, too. She was dressing a statuesque figure with inspired severity; she was interpreting the adjective "conservative" as "patrician"; and she was reformatting Olivia's ideal of old Saint Laurent in the military swank of a jacket by Burberry, a Japanese print by Dries van Noten, and, in the day's pièce de résistance, the Row's "Left Bank" sweater. "I ask my clients to trust me," Halbreich said, on our way back to the dressing room, "but not to believe me. For that, we have a three-way mirror."

Halbreich suggested that our next meeting should take place at her apartment—she wanted to give me "the closet tour." (John Halbreich had described his mother's closets as "the Vatican library of vintage.") When she came to the door, on the appointed evening, I was somewhat surprised to find her in a black T-shirt and leggings, with a pair of moccasins. Below the neck, she looked about seventeen. "What's your poison?" she said, rattling the ice cubes in her glass like a maraca. She has lived in the same labyrinthine apartment on Park Avenue since her son was born. We threaded our way to an old-fashioned kitchen with poppy wallpaper and the original appliances. ("If it ain't broke, don't fix it. But it's a rental, so don't break it.") As she was pouring a vodka, I noticed some linens in the freezer. That might be a bad sign for an octogenarian who isn't Halbreich. "I freeze anything that I have to iron," she explained, "which is everything. It's a great trick, because the damp cold works better than starch." Halbreich's children once gave her what John calls the "Golden Sponge Award" for fanatical housekeeping.

You could not describe Halbreich's decor as soberly tailored. The den is paneled in knotty cypress ("big in the fifties"), with pink chintz upholstery ("It used to be tartan"). The master bedroom has gingham walls and needlepoint rugs. There is a laundry suite, and a walk-in closet dedicated to Christmas decorations. In the formal dining room (Wedgwood-blue walls, opaline-glass chandelier, antique breakfront groaning with heirloom china), Halbreich's banquet table was set for two. "I made us a little supper," she said. "You always look like you need a good meal."

After the cheese course, we started with the drawers in a massive bureau, where silk flowers and scarves, Bakelite "bug pins," wooden bangles and beads, evening bags in toile sleeves, gloves from Florence and Paris, monogrammed handkerchiefs, chunky stone necklaces, silver pens and pillboxes, clip-on earrings, and her mother's jewels all have separate compartments. Then came the clothes. Each of her closets (perhaps a dozen—I lost count) is a deep stall with high ceilings, sturdy poles along both sides, and, above them, shelving. The larger stalls might accommodate a Lipizzaner, with its tack. Their heavy doors are fitted with custom-made wooden shoe racks that open like a steamer trunk.

Halbreich organizes her wardrobe the way Bergdorf does its merchandise: by season, function, and style. Vintage evening wear has its own closet; sweaters are arranged by weight and color. Her summer day clothes were in the hall outside her bedroom, and every padded hanger had breathing room, "so the grabbing is easy." She explained, "I dress like a fireman, in about seven minutes." When the season changes, the woolens estivating in the apartment's hinterlands get pride of place. Twice a year, at the sartorial solstice, she empties every closet, triages its contents ("You wouldn't believe what I've given away—Jean Muirs!"), and cleans it with her golden sponge. It's an Augean labor.

My own closets are a study in senseless hoarding, and I told Halbreich that she had taught me the importance of knowing what you possess. "That's life," she said.

NOVEMBER 2012

Sexual intercourse," according to the British poet Philip Larkin, "began / In nineteen sixty-three / (Which was rather late for me)—/ Between the end of the *Chatterley* ban / And the Beatles' first LP." This, it turns out, is complete nonsense. Sexual intercourse began for Larkin, at the very latest, in the early 1940s, with his teen-aged girlfriend, and continued at an energetic pace with a variety of women, including his secretary and the wife of a colleague—at one point, he shared his favors among three lovers—until he died, in his early sixties. I mention Larkin's amorous history, and cite his succinct, famous poem "Annus Mirabilis" (the narrator goes on to describe the relations between men and women of his generation as "A sort of bargaining, / A wrangle for the ring, / A shame that started at sixteen / And spread to everything") because in 1963 Helen Gurley Brown, Larkin's elder by six months (they were both forty-one), had been fornicating shamelessly for half her life, and had proclaimed to the world, in *Sex and the Single Girl*, published a year earlier, that "nice girls" not only did it before and outside of wedlock but loved it, and were, just like men, entitled to obsess about it, to rack up conquests, and to trade in their partners, preferably for an upgrade.

Brown is now eighty-seven and, for the first time, the subject of a biography, *Bad Girls Go Everywhere*, by Jennifer Scanlon, a professor of gender and women's studies at Bowdoin College. Despite the title ("Good girls go to heaven, bad girls go everywhere" is one of Brown's favorite mottoes), this is a serious academic reconsideration of a figure who, Scanlon argues, has been slighted by feminist history, and deserves a place in its pantheon, particularly because she was speaking to and for the typists, the flight attendants, and the sales clerks who couldn't afford to burn a good bra, rather than the college-educated sisterhood that was "womanning" the barricades of the 1970s.

I'm happy to see Brown getting her due as a pioneer of libidinal equality, but I was also pleased to learn from the book that she has gained some weight. (She is now 125 pounds of fun, up from a hundred.) After a lifetime of ruthless dieting, daily weigh-ins, fasting to compensate for an extra bite, plus a ninety-minute exercise routine, with dumbbells, that she stuck to seven days a week (even on the day of her mother's funeral), she has finally decided that she deserves the odd chocolate-chip cookie. And she does deserve it. Her example of heroic discipline in the service of ageless sex appeal—at sixty-eight, she looked terrific frugging in a pink feather-and-sequin minidress—has been an inspiration to the millions of readers of her racy memoirs and self-improvement guides, and of *Cosmopolitan*, the magazine that she took over in 1965 and transformed from a venerable if moribund cultural monthly into a hot, upbeat sourcebook of advice for the working girl on beauty, money, makeup, dating, dieting, therapy, dressing for success, undressing for success, and driving men wild.

In everything that Brown has written or edited, she has promoted the message that sex is great, and that one should get as much of it as possible. (Ditto for money.) Just about everyone knows this, and has always known it, but in Brown's youth few women would admit it, even to themselves. So if, in 1963, sex did cease to be quite so clandestine a pleasure—especially for unmarried females—that was, in part, her doing.

Bad Girls Go Everywhere is the story of a woman who, mostly to her credit and greatly to her profit and glory, never knew how to blush, and who exhorted her readers to follow her example of self-invention in a buoyant, dishy, emphatic style that includes words like "pippypoo." Brown told her readers in 1962, "I think marriage is insurance for the *worst* years of your life. During your best years you don't need a husband. You do need a man of course every step of the way, and they are often cheaper emotionally and a lot more fun by the dozen."

Sex and the Single Girl, a primer for the would-be femme fatale, was addressed to the "mouseburgers" of America: average-looking, high-school-educated women with unrealized potential, like the hungry girl Brown had been. Helen Gurley was born in Green Forest, Arkansas, a hamlet in the Ozarks, into a family that she described as "hillbillies." She grew up comfortably in Little Rock until, when she was ten, her father died. During the Depression, her widowed mother had to take in sewing, and, as their poverty deepened, she moved with Helen and her older sister, Mary, to Los Angeles, where she eked out a living tagging merchandise at a Sears, Roebuck. Mary contracted polio and was crippled for life. Helen never went to college, despite having graduated from high school as her class valedictorian. (It's a shame that Scanlon didn't find that valedictory address in the Brown archives, which are at Smith College, but it's nice to think that they share space in a vault there with the papers of Sylvia Plath.) Yet, with "steely determination," Scanlon writes, and with steelier thighs, Brown cleared every hurdle on her path to the four-story penthouse on Central Park where she now resides.

There is nothing wrong, Brown has always said, with improving on nature where nature was stingy, as it was, she feels, in her own case. "What you have to do is work with the raw material you have, namely you, and never let up," she wrote. "Unlike Madame Bovary you don't chase the glittering life, you lay a trap for it. You tunnel up from the bottom." So, by all means, tunnel your way into the bank vault with a nose job, breast implants, and a face-lift when the time comes (it comes sooner than you think), starve yourself, and don't let your upper arms get stringy. Fake hair, too, is always an option. Long before Brown was earning a seven-figure salary—when she was, in fact, earning a four-figure salary—she scrimped and saved to dress like a million dollars. One suggestion for scrimping was to charm an out-of-town stranger you had picked up at a bar into giving you cab fare, let him hail you a cab, then jump out a block later and keep the change. Another hint: "Write fan letters to big companies. Sometimes they send samples."

Some of Brown's advice to the huntress was eccentric: "Driving in heavy traffic offers possibilities. Leave the window rolled down on your side and always look interestedly into the next car." Some, she admitted, was "almost ghoulish," as when she suggested trolling for a boyfriend at "a wealthy chapter of A.A. Might as well start with a *solvent* problem child, like say someone with liquid assets." And some, decades later, seems downright quaint, like her battle plan for furnishing an apartment to make it a mantrap: you should have a good TV (but not too big—you'd never pry him loose to start spending money on you), a brandy snifter filled with loose cigarettes, lots of sexy cushions, and a well-stocked liquor cabinet, with the proviso that your "beaux" should always replace at least as much of your booze as they drank. Also, a smart girl was tightfisted with her home cooking. Brown's formula was twenty restaurant dinners at his expense to one cozy supper whipped up by you as a little thank-you for his largesse, which, you hoped, included expensive "prezzies." Brown has always approved of making men pay for their pleasures—or, not to put too fine a point on it, of knowing how to "use" them. (Just remember to hang on their every word, and never say that you're too tired for sex.)

A sexy woman, according to Brown, is a woman who, at any age and under almost any circumstances, likes sex with men. (Gays and lesbians were always fine with her—they liked sex, too—but she couldn't relate.) In her most recent book of advice, *Late Show*, she urges her contemporaries to express their womanliness by "welcoming a penis," rather than, say, wasting their time "doling out money for a grandchild's college tuition." In *Sex and the Single Girl*, she affirmed that "liking men is . . . by and large just about the sexiest thing you can do. But I mean really liking, not just pretending. And there is quite a lot more to it than simply wagging your tail . . . His collie dog does *that* much." (It seems apropos to add here that if you have not yet figured out fellatio, or your technique needs remediation, see *Having It All*, page 225.)

Her own notable career as an anthrophile began, she recalled, at the age of nine, in Arkansas, when she fooled around with, or was fooled around with by, a thirteen-year-old uncle in the attic of a family house. She started dating at sixteen and lost her virginity at twenty, to a factory worker in Los Angeles, her boyfriend of two years. (If you are curious—and you are: "Deflowering didn't hurt, I didn't bleed, I had an orgasm.") Before that relationship was consummated, she had answered a help-wanted ad for an escort agency and, a bit naïve about the job description, spent an evening driving around the Hollywood Hills with a middle-aged client, who exacted five dollars' worth of kisses from her, and offered her another five to go all the way. She declined politely. She was, at the time, employed as a typist at a radio station whose male personnel enjoyed a game that they called Scuttle. They chased a female co-worker around the office until they cornered her, then pulled off her panties. Brown was hurt that, for some reason—maybe she was too flat-chested—she was never their scuttlebutt. It was eventually pointed out to her that scuttling constituted a rather egregious instance of sexual harassment. In her view, however, most advances, including unwanted ones, are a compliment, and a girl should have enough street smarts to deflect them without making it "a federal offense." She noted, "If you're not a sex object, you're in trouble."

Brown was always smarter, more ambitious, and better-looking than she let on—she didn't want to compromise her credibility as a mouseburger—even though she has never encouraged her followers to play dumb, just, perhaps, to look dumb. ("A man likes to sleep with a brainy girl. She's a challenge. If he makes good with her, he figures he must be good himself.") She spent her early twenties in a series of lowly clerical positions, rose to become an executive secretary, found a mentor in her boss at an ad agency, and by her early thirties was one of the most successful female copywriters on the West Coast. Advertising was, with publishing, a field in which a woman of her generation could, as she put it, be "paid handsomely not to think like a man."

It was always against her principles to quit her day job—"A job gives a single woman something to *be*"—but not against them to work the night shift as a kept woman. One of her bosses was a married studio executive who set her up in her own apartment, paid her an allowance, and promised her a stock portfolio. (I was touched to learn from Scanlon that Brown used some of the cash she pilfered from this man—she admitted to "stealing him blind"—to buy a *New Yorker* subscription for her sister, who was back in Arkansas, living miserably with their mother.) Married men made excellent "pets," she concluded, especially if you had more than one, although in *Sex and the Office*, a sequel to *Sex and the Single Girl*, which was published in 1964, she did not explicitly recommend sleeping with the boss—"I think it's better to keep this darling as a friend, someone who may from time to time advise you about *other* men."

Brown has always been a master of the mixed message, Scanlon observes, and the same woman who pitied housewives their drab domestic lives wrangled as expertly for a wedding ring as any of Larkin's teases. In 1959, at thirty-seven, she "hooked" the eminently eligible and attractive movie producer David Brown. She told her readers, "He was sought after by many a Hollywood starlet as well as some less flamboyant but more deadly types. And *I* got him!" She got him and kept him—"the world's best husband" is now ninety-two, and this year he and Helen will celebrate their golden anniversary. (David, according to his partner in the film business, Richard Zanuck, believed that if Helen had ever caught him having an affair she would literally have killed him.) Scanlon writes, "Consciously or not, the couple found a workable formula for their marriage: he would support her, unequivocally, in her professional life, and she would serve him, unequivocally, in their domestic world."

After reading a cache of her love letters to one of his predecessors, David decided that Helen had the material, and the talent, to write a bestseller, and *Sex and the Single Girl* was conceived. He has always acted as her mentor, agent, business manager, promoter, and confidant, and he helped with both moral support and editorial advice at *Cosmopolitan*, where he wrote the cover lines. (He had been the magazine's managing editor in the 1940s.) But the books and the magazine were *her* babies, and together the Browns had no others. "We're just too selfishly well-mated," David said. But pregnancy and motherhood repelled Brown for complex reasons: the privations they had imposed on her mother, Scanlon suggests, but also, perhaps, getting fat, and losing one's sex appeal—the illusion of nubility. The womb, Brown once wrote, was a "built-in mechanism" for turning women into drudges. She sympathized with the plight of single mothers, and sometimes featured stories about them, but *Cosmopolitan* was famously child-unfriendly. Gloria Steinem, among other critics, urged her to moderate her hostility, and even David told her to "shut up" about it— she was alienating her subscribers.

Had David Brown met Helen Gurley at twenty, she wrote, he wouldn't have looked at her, and she "wouldn't have known what to do with him." But he was, she believed, seduced by her independence and by her singularity, rather than by her feminine wiles. (She had just spent five thousand dollars of her savings on a new Mercedes sports car that symbolized to both of them how far she had come in the world on the strength of her own wits and determination.) To "package" her charms irresistibly for a good provider, she preached, a single girl should provide for herself. And that may be Brown's most enlightened lesson: that sexual autonomy and fulfillment are inseparable from the autonomy and fulfillment that a woman gets from her career.

At her most radical, Brown was a subversive rather than a revolutionary; a sexual libertarian rather than a liberator; and an unapologetic partisan of free enterprise. (She once called Margaret Thatcher a "Cosmo Girl.") "How could any woman not be a feminist?" she wondered, in 1985, in an interview on her twentieth anniversary at *Cosmopolitan*. "The girl I'm editing for wants to be known for herself. If that's not a feminist message, I don't know what is."

Feminists come in every bra size, and what feminist would deny or belittle Brown's achievements? But, whoever her reader was, the dewy model or celebrity who appeared on the cover of her magazine every month for thirty-two years never resembled Mrs. Thatcher, and, indeed, looked suspiciously like a bimbo to the older generation of militants for women's rights, who were less inclined than Scanlon is to acknowledge Brown's contributions to the history of the movement. Steinem suggested to Brown that she was a victim of the patriarchy. To Brown's chagrin, *Cosmo* was often described as *Playboy's* twin sister. A British journalist coined the indelible phrase "deep-cleavage feminism" to describe the magazine's philosophy. In 1970, Kate Millett led a group of protesters who occupied Brown's offices and demanded that she publish more articles with a feminist perspective. (She did publish an excerpt from Millett's manifesto *Sexual Politics*, and she agreed to participate in a consciousness-raising session, of which she later said, "I was only into my eighth hangup when I had to relinquish the floor to the next hangup-ee.")

One hesitates to seek a moral in the glittering life of a bad girl, and Helen Gurley Brown, thank goodness, is incorrigible. That is the dissonance in Scanlon's redemptive approach: the colorless prose that keeps its ankles decorously crossed on the dais; the savant discussions of second-wave and third-wave and "lipstick" feminism; and the vision of Brown as a transitional species of New Woman. No, she was a classic poor girl on the make, lusty and driven, who, with her husband's help, found a clever formula that wasn't unique, except perhaps in its crude honesty, for marketing her own worldly wisdom. And now she is a great old tough cookie, whose survival one applauds. Most of all, Scanlon's portrait reminds one that it has never been easy to be both a woman and a person—that femininity (like masculinity) is, to some extent, a performance. What has changed since Brown wrote *Sex and the Single Girl* is that women have more roles to play, on a greater stage. She helped—but only modestly—to expand the repertoire.

In one of her incarnations, Brown was the host of a radio talk show. A caller asked if she thought that diamonds really were a girl's best friend. That notion, Scanlon points out, was first proposed by another shameless, enterprising native daughter of and famous escapee from Little Rock: Lorelei Lee. She was the adorably mercenary heroine of Anita Loos's *Gentlemen Prefer Blondes*, and the first Material Girl in a lineage from which the Cosmo Girl, Madonna, and Carrie Bradshaw all descend. Brown began her answer by lamenting the demise of gold-digging: "I think all the sugar daddies dissolved in their own sugar or something, and chorus girls have to compete with all the other pretty girls there are nowadays." Then she added that one could marry a rich man for big diamonds, or a poorer man for smaller diamonds, but maybe the best idea was to buy one's own diamonds. Attention shoppers: a girl's best friend is herself.

MAY 2009

DEEP DIVES

D uring the Old Stone Age, between 37,000 and 11,000 years ago, some of the most remarkable art ever conceived was etched or painted on the walls of caves in southern France and northern Spain. After a visit to Lascaux, in the Dordogne, which was discovered in 1940, Picasso reportedly said to his guide, "They've invented everything." What those first artists invented was a language of signs for which there will never be a Rosetta stone; perspective, a technique that was not rediscovered until the Athenian Golden Age; and a bestiary of such vitality and finesse that, by the flicker of torchlight, the animals seem to surge from the walls, and move across them like figures in a magic lantern show (in that sense, the artists invented animation). They also thought up the grease lamp—a lump of fat, with a plant wick, placed in a hollow stone—to light their workplace; scaffolds to reach high places; the principles of stenciling and pointillism; powdered colors, brushes, and stumping cloths; and, more to the point of Picasso's insight, the very concept of an image. A true artist reimagines that concept with every blank canvas—but not from a void.

Some caves have rock porches that were used for shelter, but there is no evidence of domestic life in their depths. Sizable groups may have visited the chambers closest to the entrance—perhaps for communal rites—and we know from the ubiquitous handprints that were stamped or airbrushed (using the mouth to blow pigment) on the walls that people of both sexes and all ages, even babies, participated in whatever activities took place. Only a few individuals ventured or were permitted into the farthest reaches of a cave—in some cases, walking or crawling for miles. Those intrepid spelunkers explored every surface. If they bypassed certain walls that to us seem just as suitable for decoration as ones they chose, the placement of the art apparently wasn't capricious. In the course of some 25,000 years, the same animals— primarily bison, stags, aurochs, ibex, horses, and mammoths—recur in similar poses, illustrating an immortal story. For a nomadic people, living at nature's mercy, it must have been a powerful consolation to know that such a refuge from flux existed.

As the painters were learning to crush hematite, and to sharpen embers of Scotch pine for their charcoal (red and black were their primary colors), the last Neanderthals were still living on the vast steppe that was Europe in the Ice Age, which they'd had to themselves for two hundred millennia, while *Homo sapiens* were making their leisurely trek out of Africa. No one can say what the encounters between that low-browed, herculean species and their slighter but formidable successors were like. (Paleolithic artists, despite their penchant for naturalism, rarely chose to depict human beings, and then did so with a crudeness that smacks of mockery, leaving us a mirror but no self-reflection.) Recent genetic research proves that they mated, but there is no evidence that they cohabited. In any case, they wouldn't have needed to contest their boundless hunting grounds. They coexisted for some eight thousand years, until the Neanderthals withdrew or were forced, in dwindling numbers, toward the arid mountains of southern Spain, making Gibraltar a final redoubt. It isn't known from whom or from what they were retreating (if "retreat" describes their migration), though along the way the arts of the newcomers must have impressed them. Later Neanderthal campsites have yielded some rings and awls carved from ivory, and painted or grooved bones and teeth (nothing of the like predates the arrival of *Homo sapiens*). The pathos of their workmanship—the attempt to copy something novel and marvelous by the dimming light of their existence—nearly makes you weep. And here, perhaps, the cruel notion that we call fashion, a coded expression of rivalry and desire, was born.

The cave artists were as tall as the average southern European of today, and well nourished on the teeming game and fish they hunted with flint weapons. They are, genetically, our direct ancestors, although "direct" is a relative term. Since recorded history began, around 3200 B.C., with the invention of writing in the Middle East, there have been some 200 human generations (if one reckons a new one every twenty-five years). Future discoveries may alter the math, but, as it now stands, 4,500 generations separate the earliest *Homo sapiens* from the earliest cave artists, and between the artists and us another 1,500 generations have descended the birth canal, learned to walk upright, mastered speech and the use of tools, reached puberty, reproduced, and died.

Early last April, I set off for the Ardèche, a mountainous region in south-central France where cave networks are a common geological phenomenon (hundreds are known, dozens with ancient artifacts). It was here, a week before Christmas 1994, that three spelunkers exploring the limestone cliffs above the Pont d'Arc, a natural bridge of awesome beauty and scale which resembles a giant mammoth straddling the river gorge, unearthed a cave that made front-page news. It proved to contain the oldest paintings then known in the world—some 15,000 to 18,000 years older than the friezes at Lascaux and at Altamira, in northern Spain—and it was named for its chief discoverer, Jean-Marie Chauvet. Unlike the amateur adventurers or lucky bumblers (in the case of Lascaux, a posse of village urchins and their dog) who have fallen, sometimes literally, upon a cave where early Europeans left their cryptic signatures, Chauvet was a professional—a park ranger working for the Ministry of Culture, and the custodian of other prehistoric sites in the region. He and his partners, Christian Hillaire and Éliette Brunel, were aware of the irreparable damage that even a few indelicate footsteps can cause to an environment that has been sealed for eons—posterity has lost whatever precious relics and evidence that the carelessly trampled floors of Lascaux and Altamira, both now sealed to the public, might have yielded.

The cavers were natives of the Ardèche: three old friends with an interest in archaeology. Brunel was the smallest, so when they felt an updraft of cool air coming from a recess near the cliff's ledge—the potential sign of a cavity—they heaved some rocks out of the way, and she squeezed through a tight passage that led to the entrance of a deep shaft. The men followed, and, unfurling a chain ladder, the group descended thirty feet into a soaring grotto with a domed roof whose every surface was blistered or spiked with stalagmites. Where the uneven clay floor had receded, it was littered with calcite accretions—blocks and columns that had broken off—and, in photographs, the wrathful, baroque grandeur of the scene evokes some biblical act of destruction wreaked upon a temple. As the explorers advanced, moving gingerly, in single file, Brunel suddenly let out a cry: "They have been here!"

The question of who "they" were speaks to a mystery that thinking people of every epoch and place have tried to fathom: Who are we? In the century since the modern study of caves began, specialists from at least half a dozen disciplines—archaeology, ethnology, ethology, genetics, anthropology, and art history—have tried (and competed) to understand the culture that produced them. The experts tend to fall into two camps: those who can't resist advancing a theory about the art, and those who believe that there isn't, and never will be, enough evidence to support one. Jean Clottes, the celebrated prehistorian and prolific author who assembled the Chauvet research team in 1996, belongs to the first camp, and most of his colleagues to the second. Yet no one who studies the caves seems able to resist a yearning for communion with the artists. When you consider that their legacy may have been found by chance, but surely wasn't left by chance, it, too, suggests a yearning for communion—with us, their descendants.

Two books published in the past few years, *The Cave Painters*, by Gregory Curtis, and *The Nature of Paleolithic Art*, by R. Dale Guthrie, approach the controversy generated by their subject from different perspectives. Guthrie is an encyclopedic polymath who believes he can "decode" prehistory. Curtis, a former editor of *Texas Monthly*, is a literary detective (his previous book, on the Venus de Milo, also concerned the obscure provenance of an archaic masterpiece), and in quietly enthralling prose, without hurry or flamboyance, he spins two narratives. (The shorter one, as he notes, covers a few million years, and the longer one, the past century.)

I packed both volumes, along with some hiking boots, protein bars, and other survival gear, all of it unnecessary, for my sojourn in the Ardèche. My destination was a Spartan summer camp—a concrete barracks in a valley near the Pont d'Arc. It is owned by the regional government, and normally houses groups of schoolchildren on subsidized holidays. But twice a year, for a couple of weeks in the spring and the autumn, the camp is a base for the Chauvet team. They, and only they, are admitted to the cave (and sometimes not even they: last October, the research session was canceled because the climate hadn't restabilized). Access is so strictly limited not only because traffic causes contamination but also because the French government has been embroiled for thirteen years in multimillion-dollar litigation with Jean-Marie Chauvet and his partners, as well as with the owners of the land on which they found the cave. (The finders are entitled to royalties from reproductions of the art, while the owners are entitled to compensation for a treasure that, at least technically, is their property—the Napoleonic laws, modified in the 1950s, that give the Republic authority to dispose of any minerals or metals beneath the soil do not apply to cave paintings. Had Chauvet been a gold mine, the suit couldn't have been brought.)

By dusk on the first night, most of the researchers had assembled in the cafeteria for an excellent dinner of rabbit fricassée, served with a Côtes du Vivarais, and followed by a selection of local cheeses. (The Ardèche is a gourmet's paradise, and the camp chef was a tough former sailor from Marseille whose speech and cooking were equally pungent.) Among the senior team members, Evelyne Debard is a geologist, as is Norbert Aujoulat. He is a former director of research at Lascaux, and the author of a fine book on its art, who calls himself "an underground man." Marc Azéma is a documentary filmmaker who specializes in archaeology. Gilles Tosello and Carole Fritz, a husband and wife from Toulouse, are experts in parietal art, and Tosello is a graphic artist whose heroically patient, stroke-by-stroke tracings of the cave's signs and images are essential to their study. Jean-Marc Elalouf, a geneticist, and the author of a poetic essay on Chauvet, has, with a team of graduate students, sequenced the mitochondrial DNA of the cave's numerous bears. They pocked the floor with their hibernation burrows, and, in a space known as the Skull Chamber, a bear's cranium sits on a flat, altar-like pedestal—perhaps enshrined there by the artists. The grotto is littered with other ursine remains, and some of the bones seem to have been planted in the sediment or stuck with intent into the fissured walls. (No human DNA has yet surfaced, and Elalouf doesn't expect to find any.) Dominique Baffier, an official at the Ministry of Culture, is Chauvet's curator. She coordinates the research and conservation. Jean-Michel Geneste, an archaeologist, is the director of the project, a post he assumed in 2001, when Jean Clottes, at sixty-seven, took mandatory retirement.

Clottes is a hero of Gregory Curtis's *The Cave Painters*, one of the "giants" in a line of willful, brilliant, and often eccentric personalities who have shaped a discipline that prides itself on scientific detachment but has been a battleground for the kind of turf wars that were absent from the caves themselves. No human conflict is recorded in cave art, although at three separate sites there are four ambiguous drawings of a creature with a man's limbs and torso, pierced with spearlike lines. More pertinent, perhaps, is a famous vignette in the shaft at Lascaux. It depicts a rather comical stick figure with an avian beak or mask, a puny physique, and a long skinny penis. He and his erect member seem to have rigor mortis. He is flat on his back at the feet of an exquisitely realistic wounded bison, whose intestines are spilling out. The bison's glance is turned away, but it might have an ironic smile. Could the subject be hubris? Whatever it represents, some mythic contest—and the struggle of prehistorians to interpret their subject is such a contest—has ended in a draw.

Curtis profiles a dynasty of interpreters, beginning with the Spanish nobleman Marcelino Sanz de Sautuola, who discovered Altamira in 1879—it was on his property. (Parts of Niaux and Mas d'Azil, two gigantic painted caves in the Pyrenees, had been known for centuries, but their decorations were regarded as graffiti made in historic times, perhaps by Roman legionaries.) He was accused of art forgery, and his scholarly papers on the paintings' antiquity were ridiculed by two of the era's greatest archaeologists, Gabriel de Mortillet and Émile Cartailhac. Sautuola died before Cartailhac repented of his skepticism, in 1902. By then, the art at two important sites, Les Combarelles and Font-de-Gaume (which contains a ravishing portrait of two amorous reindeer), had come to light, and in 1906 Cartailhac published a lavish compendium of cave painting that was subsidized by the Prince of Monaco. The book's much admired illustrations of Altamira were the work of a young priest with a painterly eye, Henri Breuil, who in the course of half a century became known as the Pope of Prehistory. He divided the era into four periods and dated the art by its style and appearance. Aurignacian, the oldest, was followed by Perigordian (later known as Gravettian), Solutrean, and Magdalenian. They were named for type-sites in France: Aurignac, La Gravette, Solutré, and La Madeleine. But Breuil's theory about the art's meaning—that it related to rituals of "hunting magic"—was discredited by subsequent studies.

During the Second World War, Max Raphael, a German art historian who had studied the caves of the Dordogne before fleeing the Nazis to New York, was looking for clues to the art's meaning in its thematic unity. He concluded that the animals represented clan totems, and that the paintings depicted strife and alliances—an archaic saga. In 1951, the year before Raphael died, he sent an extract of his writings to Annette Laming-Emperaire, a young French archaeologist who shared his conviction that "prehistory cannot be reconstructed with the aid of ethnography." Beware, in other words, of analogue reasoning, because no one should presume to parse the icons and figures of a vanished society by comparing them with the art of hunter-gatherers from more recent eras. In 1962, she published a doctoral thesis that made her famous. "The Meaning of Paleolithic Rock Art" dismissed the various, too-creative theories of its predecessors, and, with them, any residual nineteenth-century prejudice or romance about the "primitive" mind. Laming-Emperaire's structuralist methodology is still in use, much facilitated by computer science. It involves compiling minutely detailed inventories and diagrams of the way that species are grouped on the cave walls; of their sex, frequency, and position; and of their relation to the signs and handprints that often appear close to them. In *Lascaux*, Norbert Aujoulat explains how he and his colleagues added time to the equation. Analyzing the order of superimposed images, they determined that wherever horses, aurochs, and stags appear on the same panel, the horse is beneath, the aurochs in the middle, and the stag on top, and that the variations in their coats correspond to their respective mating seasons. The triad of "horse-aurochs-stag" links the fertility cycles of important, and perhaps sacred or symbolic, animals to the cosmic cycles, suggesting a great metaphor about creation.

Laming-Emperaire had an eminent thesis adviser, André Leroi-Gourhan, who revolutionized the practice of excavation by recognizing that a vertical dig destroys the context of a site. In twenty years (1964–84) of insanely painstaking labor—scraping the soil in small horizontal squares at Pincevent, a 12,000-year-old campsite on the Seine—he and his disciples gave us one of the richest pictures to date of Paleolithic life as the Old Stone Age was ending.

A new age in the science of prehistory had begun in 1949, when radiocarbon dating was invented by Willard Libby, a chemist from Chicago. One of Libby's first experiments was on a piece of charcoal from Lascaux. Breuil had, incorrectly, it turns out, classified the cave as Perigordian. (It is Magdalenian.) He had also made the Darwinian assumption that the most ancient art was the most primitive, and Leroi-Gourhan worked on the same premise. In that respect, Chauvet was a bombshell. It is Aurignacian, and its earliest paintings are at least 32,000 years old, yet they are just as sophisticated as much later compositions. What emerged with that revelation was an image of Paleolithic artists transmitting their techniques from generation to generation for twenty-five millennia with almost no innovation or revolt. A profound conservatism in art, Curtis notes, is one of the hallmarks of a "classical civilization." For the conventions of cave painting to have endured four times as long as recorded history, the culture it served, he concludes, must have been "deeply satisfying"—and stable to a degree it is hard for modern humans to imagine.

Jean Clottes is a tall, cordial man of seventy-four, who still attends the biannual sessions at Chauvet, conducting his own research (this April, he and Marc Azéma found a new panel of signs), while continuing to travel and lecture widely. The latest addition to his bibliography, *Cave Art*, a luxuriously illustrated "imaginary museum" of the Old Stone Age, is due out this summer.

Clottes's eminence in his field was never preordained. He once taught high school English in Foix, a city in the Pyrenees, near the Andorran border, which is an epicenter for decorated caves. He studied archaeology in his spare time, and earned a doctorate at forty-one, when he quit teaching. He had been moonlighting in a job that gave him privileged access to new caves, and an impressive calling card—as the director of prehistory for the Midi-Pyrenees—but a nominal salary. The appointment was made official in 1971, and for the next two decades Clottes was usually the first responder at the scene of a new discovery. The most sensational find, before Chauvet, was Cosquer—a painted cave near Marseille that could be reached only through a treacherous underwater tunnel, in which three divers had drowned. Like Altamira, Cosquer was, at first, attacked as a hoax, and some of the press coverage impeached Clottes's integrity as its authenticator. He could judge its art only from photographs, but in 1992, a year after Cosquer was revealed, carbon dating proved that the earliest paintings are at least 27,000 years old. That year, the Ministry of Culture elevated him to the rank of inspector general.

At the base camp, Clottes bunked down, as did everyone, in a dorm room, and braved the morning hoarfrost for a dash to the communal showers. There is a boyish quality to his energy and conviction. (At sixty-nine, he learned to scuba dive so that he could finally explore Cosquer himself.) One evening, he showed us a film about his "baptism," in 2007, as an honorary Tuareg; the North African nomads crowned him with a turban steeped in indigo that stained his forehead, and he danced to their drums by a Saharan campfire. Among his own sometimes fractious tribesmen, Clottes also commands the respect due an unusually vigorous elder, and it was hard to keep pace with him as he scampered on his long legs up the steep cliff to Chauvet, talking with verve the entire way.

The path skirts a vineyard, then veers up into the woods, emerging onto a corniche—a natural terrace with a rocky overhang on one side, and a precipitous drop on the other. "En route to Chauvet, the painters might have sheltered here or prepared their pigments. Looking at the valley and the river gorge, they saw what we do," Clottes said, indicating a magnificent view. "The topography hasn't changed much, except that the Ice Age vegetation was much sparser: mostly evergreens, like fir and pine. Without all the greenery, the resemblance of the Pont d'Arc to a giant mammoth would have been even more dramatic. But nothing of the landscape—clouds, earth, sun, moon, rivers, or plant life, and, only rarely, a horizon—figures in cave art. It's one among many striking omissions."

Where the terrace ended, we plunged back into the underbrush, following a track obstructed by rocks and brambles, and, after about half an hour of climbing, we arrived at the entrance that Jean-Marie Chauvet and his partners discovered. (The prehistoric entrance has been plugged, for millennia, by a landslide.) A shallow cave at the trailhead has been fitted out as a storeroom for gear and supplies. From here, a wooden ramp guides one along a narrow ledge, shaped like a horseshoe, that was formed when the cliffs receded, to a massive metal door that's as well defended—with voice alarms, video surveillance, and a double key system—as a bank vault. Some members of the team relaxed with a cigarette or a cold drink and a little academic gossip, but Clottes immediately changed into his spelunking overalls, donned a hard hat with a miner's lamp, and disappeared into the underworld.

On a map, Chauvet resembles Great Britain, and, like an island with coves and promontories, its outline is irregular. The distance from the entrance to the deepest gallery is about eight hundred feet, and, at the northern end, the cave forks into two horn-shaped branches. In some places, such as the grotto that Éliette Brunel first plumbed in 1994 (it is named for her), the terrain is rocky and chaotic, while in others, like the Chamber of the Bear Hollows, the walls and floor are relatively smooth. (In the 1990s, a metal catwalk was installed to protect the cave bed.) The ceilings of the principal galleries vary in height from about five to forty feet, but there are passages and alcoves where an adult has to kneel or crawl. Twenty-six thousand years ago (six millennia after the first paintings were created), a lone adolescent left his footprints and torch swipes in the farthest reaches of the western horn, the Gallery of the Crosshatching.

The Megaloceros Gallery—a funnel in the eastern horn named for the huge, elklike herbivores that mingle on the walls with rhinos, horses, bison, a glorious ibex, three abstract vulvas, and assorted geometric signs—is the narrowest part of the cave, and it seems to have been a gathering point or a staging area where the artists built hearths to produce their charcoal. Dominique Baffier, the curator, and Valérie Feruglio, a young archaeologist who arrived at the base camp with her new baby during my visit, were moved to write in *Chauvet Cave*, a book of essays and photography on the team's research, "The freshness of these remains gives the impression that . . . we interrupted the Aurignacians in their task and caused them to flee abruptly." They dropped an ivory projectile, which was found in the sediment.

From here, one emerges into the deepest recess of Chauvet, the End Chamber, a spectacular vaulted space that contains more than a third of the cave's etchings and paintings—a few in ocher, most in charcoal, and all meticulously composed. A great frieze covers the back left wall: a pride of lions with pointillist whiskers seems to be hunting a herd of bison, which appear to have stampeded a troop of rhinos, one of which looks as if it had fallen into, or is climbing out of, a cavity in the rock. As at many sites, the scratches made by a standing bear have been overlaid with a palimpsest of signs or drawings, and one has to wonder if cave art didn't begin with a recognition that bear claws were an expressive tool for engraving a record—poignant and indelible—of a stressed creature's passage through the dark.

To the far right of the frieze, on a separate wall, a huge, finely modeled bison stands alone, gazing stage left toward a pair of figures painted on a conical outcropping of rock that descends from the ceiling and comes to a point about four feet above the floor. The fleshy shape of this pendant is unmistakably phallic, and all of its sides are decorated, though only the front is clearly visible. The floor of the End Chamber is littered with relics. In order to preserve them, the catwalk stops close to the entrance, and the innermost alcove, known as the Sacristy, remains to be explored. But one of the team's archaeologists, Yanik Le Guillou, rigged a digital camera to a pole, and was able to photograph the pendant's far side. Wrapped around, or, as it appears, straddling the phallus is the bottom half of a woman's body, with heavy thighs and bent knees that taper at the ankle. Her vulva is darkly shaded, and she has no feet. Hovering above her is a creature with a bison's head and hump, and an aroused white eye. But a line branching from its neck looks like a human arm with fingers. The relationship of these figures to each other, and to the frieze on the adjacent wall, is among the great enigmas in cave art. The woman's posture suggests that she may be squatting in childbirth, and the animals, on a level with her loins, seem to be streaming away from her. Gregory Curtis, who fights and loses a valiant battle with his urge to speculate, admits in *The Cave Painters* that he can't help reading a mythical narrative into the scene, one that relates to the Minotaur—the hybrid offspring of a mortal woman and a sacred bull "who lived in the Labyrinth, which is a kind of cave." Art on the walls of Cretan palaces depicts the spectacle of youths leapfrogging a charging bull, and that public spectacle—in the guise of the bullfight—has, he points out, endured into modern times precisely in the regions where decorated caves are most concentrated. "European culture began somewhere," he concludes. "Why not right here?"

In the course of a friendly correspondence, Yanik Le Guillou gave Curtis a warning about indulging his imagination. Perhaps that sin might be forgiven in an American journalist, but not in Jean Clottes. The book that sets forth his controversial theory about the art, *The Shamans of Prehistory*, co-written with the South African archaeologist David Lewis-Williams, and published in 1996—the year Clottes took over at Chauvet—detonated a polemical firestorm that hasn't entirely subsided. Defying the prohibitions against importing evidence to the caves from external sources, the authors grounded their interpretation in Lewis-Williams's studies of shamanism among hunter-gatherers, historical and contemporary, and of African rock art, specifically the paintings of a nomadic people, the San, whose shamans still serve as spiritual mediators with the powers of nature and with the dead. In an earlier article, "The Signs of All Times," written with the anthropologist T. A. Dowson, Lewis-Williams had explored what he called "a neurological bridge" to the Old Stone Age. The authors cited laboratory experiments with subjects in an induced-trance state which suggested that the human optic system generates the same types of visual illusions, in the same three stages, differing only slightly by culture, whatever the stimulus: drugs, music, pain, fasting, repetitive movements, solitude, or high carbon-dioxide levels (a phenomenon that is common in close underground chambers). In the first stage, a subject sees a pattern of points, grids, zigzags, and other abstract forms (familiar from the caves); in the second stage, these forms morph into objects—the zigzags, for example, might become a serpent. In the third and deepest stage, a subject feels sucked into a dark vortex that generates intense hallucinations, often of monsters or animals, and feels his body and spirit merging with theirs.

Peoples who practice shamanism believe in a tiered cosmos: an upper world (the heavens); an underworld; and the mortal world. When Clottes joined forces with Lewis-Williams, he had come to believe that cave painting largely represents the experiences of shamans or initiates on a vision quest to the underworld, where spirits gathered. The caves served as a gateway, and their walls were considered porous. Where the artists or their entourage left handprints, they were palping a living rock in the hope of reaching or summoning a force beyond it. They typically incorporated the rock's contours and fissures into the outlines of their drawings—as a horn, a hump, or a haunch—so that a frieze becomes a bas-relief. But, in doing so, they were also locating the dwelling place of an animal from their visions, and bodying it forth.

This scenario has its loose ends, particularly in the art's untrance-like fidelity to nature, but it fits the dreamlike suspension of the animals

in a vacuum, and it helps to explain three of the most sensational figures in cave art. One is the bison-man at Chauvet; another is the bird-
man at Lascaux; and the third, known as the Sorcerer, looks down
from a perch close to the high ceiling at Les Trois Frères, a Magdalenian cave in the Pyrenees. He has the ears and antlers of a stag; hand-
like paws; athletic human legs and haunches; a horse's tail; and a long,
rather elegantly groomed wizard's beard.

Clottes was hurt and outraged by the rancor of the attacks that
greeted *The Shamans of Prehistory* ("psychedelic ravings," one critic
wrote), and the authors defended themselves in a subsequent edition.
"You can advance a scientific hypothesis without claiming certainty,"
Clottes told me one evening. "Everyone agrees that the paintings are,
in some way, religious. I'm not a believer myself, and I'm certainly not
a mystic. But *Homo sapiens* is *Homo spiritualis*. The ability to make
tools defines us less than the need to create belief systems that influence nature. And shamanism is the most prevalent belief system of
hunter-gatherers."

Yet even members of the Chauvet team feel that Clottes's theories
on shamanism go too far. The divide seems, in part, to be generational. The strict purists tend to be younger, perhaps because they
came of age with deconstruction, in a climate of political correctness,
and are warier of their own baggage. "I don't mind stating uncategor-
ically that it's impossible to know what the art means," Carole Fritz
said. Norbert Aujoulat tactfully told me, "We're more reserved than
Jean is. He may be right about the practice of shamanism in the caves,
but many of us simply don't want to interpret them." He added with a
laugh, "If I knew what the art meant, I'd be out of business. But in my
own experience—I've inventoried five hundred caves—the more you
look, the less you understand."

For an older generation, on more intimate terms with mortality, it
may be harder to accept the lack of resolution to a life's work. Jean-
Michel Geneste, a leonine man of fifty-nine with a silver mane, told me
about an experiment that he had conducted at Lascaux in 1994. (In
addition to directing the work at Chauvet, he is the curator of Lascaux, and last winter he had to deal with an invasion of fungus that

was threatening the paintings there.) Geneste decided to invite four elders of an Aboriginal tribe, the Ngarinyins—hunter-gatherers from northwestern Australia—to visit the cave, and put them up at his house in the Dordogne. "I explained that I would be taking them to a place where ancients had, like their own ancestors, left marks and paintings on the walls, so that perhaps they could explain them," he said. "'They're your ancestors?' they asked. I said no, and that stupid reply made them afraid. If we weren't visiting my ancestors, they wouldn't enter their sanctuary, and risk the consequences. I was terribly disappointed, and finally, as good guests, they agreed to take a look. But first they had to purify themselves, so they built a fire, and pulled some of their underarm hair out and burned it. Their own rituals involve traversing a screen of smoke—passing into another zone. When they entered the cave, they took a while to get their bearings. Yes, they said, it was an initiation site. The geometric signs, in red and black, reminded them of their own clan insignia, the animals and engravings of figures from their creation myths."

Geneste agrees with their reading, but he also believes that a cave like Lascaux or Chauvet served many purposes—"the way a twelfth-century church did. Everyone must have heard that these sanctuaries existed, and felt drawn to them. Look at the Pont d'Arc: it's a great beacon in the landscape. And, like the art in a church, the richness of graphic expression in the caves was satisfying to lots of different people in different ways—familial, communal, and individual, across the millennia—so there is probably no one adequate explanation, no unified theory, for it."

For the next week, I climbed the hill to Chauvet once a day. A guardian, Charles Chauveau, who, by law, has to be present when the scientists are underground, took me hiking, and we scaled the cliffs to sun our faces on a boulder, watching the first rafters of the season negotiate the river and pass under the Pont d'Arc. Only a few members of the team enter the cave at a time, each to pursue his or her research, though because of potential hazards, especially carbon-dioxide intoxication, no fewer than three can ever be alone there. "In the old days, when you sometimes had Chauvet to yourself, it was awesome and a little frightening," the geologist Evelyne Debard said. But Aujoulat felt more intimidated at Lascaux. "I used to spend a solitary hour there once a week," he said. "I rehearsed all my gestures, so I wouldn't lose time. But after a while it became oppressive: those huge animals staring you down in a small space—trying, or so it feels, to dominate you."

Those who have elected to stay behind spend the day in a prosaic annex next to the camp parking lot which was built to provide the team with office space and computer outlets. Marc Azéma, who has collaborated with Clottes on books about Chauvet's lions (he also filmed the Tuareg baptism), gave me a virtual cave tour on a big monitor. Of necessity, Fritz and Tosello spend more time photoshopping their research than conducting fieldwork. (Henri Breuil made tracings directly from cave walls—an unthinkable sacrilege to modern archaeologists.) They digitally photograph an image section by section, print the picture to scale, and take it back underground, where Tosello sets up a drawing board as close as possible to the area of study. The digital image is overlaid with a sheet of clear plastic, and he traces the image onto the sheet, referring constantly to the original painting as he does so. This dynamic act of translation gives him a deeper insight into the artists' gestures and techniques than a mere reading would. He repeats the process on successive plastic sheets, each one focused on a separate aspect of the composition, including the rock's contours. Then he transfers the tracings (as many as a dozen layers) onto the computer, where they can be magnified and manipulated. Describing the detail in a monumental frieze of horses between the Megaloceros Chamber and the Skull Chamber, Fritz and Tosello wrote in *Chauvet Cave*:

> Once again, the surface was carefully scraped beneath the throat, which suggests to us a moment of reflection, or perhaps doubt . . . The last horse is unquestionably the most successful of the group, perhaps because the artist is by now certain of his or her inspiration. This fourth horse was produced using a complex technique: the main lines were drawn with charcoal; the infill, colored sepia and brown,

is a mixture of charcoal and clay spread with the finger. A series of fine engravings perfectly follow the profile. With energetic and precise movements, the significant details are indicated (nostril, open mouth). A final charcoal line, dark black, was placed just at the corner of the lips and gives this head an expression of astonishment or surprise.

While the team was at work, I often stayed on the cliff with Chauveau, reading Dale Guthrie's book at a picnic table. Guthrie, a professor emeritus of zoology at the University of Alaska, specializes in the paleobiology of the Pleistocene era. Not only is he an expert on the large mammals that cavort on cave walls; he has spent forty years in the Arctic wilds hunting their descendants with a bow and arrow. In that respect, perhaps, he brings more empiricism to his research than other scholars, though he also brings less humility. *The Nature of Paleolithic Art*, as its title suggests, aspires to be definitive.

It is a handsome, five-hundred-page volume composed, like a mosaic, of boxed highlights, arresting graphics, and short sections of text that distill a wealth of multidisciplinary research. The prose, like the layout, is designed to engage a layman without vulgarizing the science, or, at least, not too much. Guthrie, who sounds and looks, in his author's photograph, like an earthy guy, has fun with occasional rib-nudging subtitles ("Lesbian Loving or Male Fantasy?," "Graffiti and Testosterone"), but they promote a premise at least as audacious as that of Clottes and Lewis-Williams: that our biology, expressed in our carnal appetites and attractions, including an attraction to the supernatural, is a "baseline of truth" for the cave artists' symbolic language.

Nearly all the illustrations are Guthrie's own renderings or interpretations of Paleolithic imagery (there are no photographs). A number of prehistorians are and have been, as he is, gifted draftsmen and copyists. But unlike the devout Breuil, or the cautious Tosello, Guthrie is a desacralizer. He admires the creative "freedom" of cave art—an acuity of observation coupled with, in his view, a nonchalance of composition. He stresses its erotic playfulness, even straining to discern evidence of dildos and bondage, despite the rarity of sexual

acts depicted on walls or artifacts. ("No Sex, Please—We're Aurignacian" was the title of a scholarly paper on the period.) The reverence
with which certain researchers—including, one infers, the Chauvet
team—treat even the smallest nick in a cave strikes him as a bit too
nice, and where they perceive an elaborate, if obscure, metaphysics, he
sees high-spirited improvisation. "Some Paleolithic images identified
as part man and part beast may simply be artistic bloopers," he writes.
(But the artists sometimes did correct their work, Azéma told me, by
scraping the rock's surface.)

Paleobiology is, in part, a science of statistical modeling, and, analyzing the handprints in the caves, Guthrie argues that many, perhaps a majority, of the artists were not the "Michelangelos" of Lascaux
or Chauvet but teenage boys, who, being boys, loved rutting and rum-
bling and, in essence, went on tagging sprees. It is true that among the
masterpieces there are many line drawings, including pubic triangles,
that seem hasty, impish, or doodle-like. In Guthrie's view, prehistorians have imported their mandarin pieties, and the bias of a society
where children are a minority, to the study of what, demographically,
was a freewheeling youth culture.

Guthrie is both provocative and respected—Clottes wrote one of
the cover blurbs on his book—but some of his methods make you
wonder how much of the light that he throws onto the nature of the
art owes to false clarity. By culling examples of erotica from a huge
catchment area without noting their size, date, or position, he distorts
their prevalence. His cleaned-up drawings minimize the art's bewildering ambiguity and the contouring or the cave architecture organic
to many compositions. As for the bands of brothers spelunking on a
dare, and leaving what Guthrie calls their "children's art" to bemuse
posterity, the life expectancy for the era was, as he notes, about eighteen, since infant mortality was exorbitant. But those who lived on
could, thanks to the rarity of infectious diseases and the abundance
of protein, expect to survive for thirty years more—considerably
longer than the Greeks, the Romans, or the medieval peasants who
built Chartres. Can puerility as we know it—horny, reckless, and

transgressive—be attributed to a people for whom early parenthood and virtuosity in survival skills were, as Guthrie acknowledges, imperative? Rash spelunkers die every year, yet no human remains have been discovered in the caves (with the exception of a single skeleton, that of a young man, at Vilhonneur near Angoulême, and those of five adults who were buried at Cussac in the Dordogne). That is a staggering testament to the artists' sureness of foot and purpose, if not to their solemnity.

A few days before Easter, I left the camp and drove southwest, over the mountains, stopping at the town of Albi, where the Toulouse-Lautrec Museum, in a thirteenth-century palace off the cathedral square, has a small gallery of Stone and Bronze Age artifacts. I wanted to see the museum's tiny Solutrean carving, in red sandstone, of an obese woman with impressive buttocks. She seemed well housed among Toulouse-Lautrec's louche Venuses. By the next evening, in a thunderstorm, I had reached Jean Clottes's hometown of Foix, and found an old-fashioned hotel that he had recommended. From a corner table in the dining room, I could watch the swollen Ariège River flowing toward a distant wall of snow-covered peaks—the Pyrenees—that were black against a livid sunset. The Neanderthals had come this way.

Pascal Alard, an archaeologist, met me the next morning at Niaux, where he has conducted research for twenty years. It is one of three caves (with Chauvet and Lascaux) that Clottes, who had arranged the rendezvous, considers paradigmatic. I had driven south for about forty minutes, the last few miles on a road with hairpin turns that wound up into flinty, striated hills. The site was nothing like Chauvet. There was, for one thing, a parking lot at the entrance, deserted at that hour, a bookshop, and an imposing architectural sculpture, in Corten steel, cantilevered into the cliff. (It is supposed to represent an imaginary prehistoric animal.)

Niaux is Magdalenian—its walls were decorated about 14,000 years ago—and it was one of the first caves to be explored. Visitors from the seventeenth century left graffiti, as did pranksters for the next three hundred years. In 1866, an archaeologist named Félix

Garrigou, who was looking for prehistoric relics, confessed to his journal that he couldn't figure out the "funny-looking" paintings. "Amateur artists drew animals here," he noted, "but why?"

Niaux's enormity—a network of passages that are nearly a mile deep from the entrance gallery, which was used as a shelter during the Bronze Age, to the Great Dome, at the far end, branching like a cactus into narrow alcoves and low-ceilinged funnels, but also into chambers the size of an amphitheater—helps to give it a stable climate, and small groups can make guided visits at appointed times. But when Alard had unlocked the door, and it closed behind us, we were alone. He had two flashlights, and he gave me one. "Don't lose it," he joked. He told me that he and some colleagues, all of whom know the cave intimately, decided, one day, to see if they could find their way out without a light source. None of them could.

The floor near the mouth was fairly flat, but as we went deeper it listed and swelled unpredictably. Water was dripping, and sometimes it sounded like a sinister whispered conversation. The caves are full of eerie noises that gurgle up from the bowels of the earth, yet I had a feeling of traversing a space that wasn't terrestrial. We were, in fact, walking on the bed of a primordial river. Where the passage narrowed, we squeezed between two rocks, like a turnstile, marked with four lines. They were swipes of a finger dipped in red pigment that resembled a bar code, or symbolic flames. Farther along, there was a large panel of dots, lines, and arrows, some red, some black. I felt their power without understanding it until I recalled what Norbert Aujoulat had told me about the signs at Cussac. He was the second modern human to explore the cave, in 2000, the year it was unearthed, some 22,000 years after the painters had departed. (The first was Cussac's discoverer, Marc Delluc.) "As we trailed the artists deeper and deeper, noting where they'd broken off stalagmites to mark their path, we found signs that seemed to say, 'We're sanctifying a finite space in an infinite universe.'"

Beyond the turnstile, the passage widens for about six hundred feet, veering to the right, where it leads to one of the grandest bestiaries in Paleolithic art: the Black Salon, a rotunda 130 feet in diameter. Scores of animals were painted in sheltered spots on the floor, or etched in charcoal on the soaring walls: bison, stags, ibex, aurochs, and, what is rarer, fish (salmon), and Niaux's famous "bearded horses"—a shaggy, short-legged species that, Clottes writes in his new book, has been re-introduced from its native habitat, in Central Asia, to French wildlife parks. All these creatures are drawn in profile with a fine point, and some of their silhouettes have been filled in with a brush or a stumping cloth. I looked for a little ibex, twenty-one inches long, that Clottes had described to me as the work of a perfectionist, and one of the most beautiful animals in a cave. When I found him, he looked so perky that I couldn't help laughing. Alard was patient, and, since time loses its contours underground, I didn't know how long we had spent there. "I imagine that you want to see more," he said after a while, so we moved along.

Every encounter with a cave animal takes it and you by surprise. Your light has to rouse it, and your eye has to recognize it, because you tend to see creatures that aren't there, while missing ones that are. Halfway home to the mortal world, I asked Alard if we could pause and turn off our torches. The acoustics magnify every sound, and it takes the brain a few minutes to accept the totality of the darkness— your sight keeps grasping for a hold. Whatever the art means, you understand, at that moment, that its vessel is both a womb and a sepulcher.

JUNE 2008

W hen I am falling asleep, I sometimes hear voices. They are not hallucinations—I am perfectly aware that they are inside my own head. It feels as if my brain had pulled them down from the airwaves, or up from storage in my synapses. Their speech has meaning, though it comes in snatches. The closer I get to going under, the more indistinct the buzz becomes, until I am hearing not language but an oceanic murmur.

Alice Oswald eerily evokes that state in her eighth and most enigmatic volume of poetry, *Nobody: A Hymn to the Sea*. The book has had several incarnations. It began as a collaboration with the British artist William Tillyer, to accompany a 2018 show of his lyrical, semiabstract watercolors. Her wall text and his images were later published as an art book; Oswald then rewrote the text to stand on its own—or perhaps, like the sea, to keep moving. In a note to the American edition, she writes, "The poem is designed to be mobile."

I am, by chance, reading *Nobody* by the sea. This morning, the tide is coming in aslant, while a black cormorant skims the waves in a straight line, from left to right, as if it were writing a sentence. I keep looking out the window, partly to rest from an exertion that feels like swimming in open water, but partly to ask the waves for help in deciphering Oswald's dreamlike dissolves:

the same iridescent swiftness and the same
uncertain certainty either brimming or rippled
or swelling over of hollowing water
as one thought leads to another if you stand
here on these boulders with your back to the earth
you can see the whole story of the weather
the way the wind brings one shadow after another
but another one always sweeps up behind
and no-one can decipher this lucid short-lived
chorus of waves it is too odd and even
as if trying to remember some perfect prehistoric
pattern of spirals it is too factual too counter-factual
too copper-blue too irregular-metrical
listen

Oswald studied classics at Oxford, and *Nobody* is the second of
her book-length homages to Homer. The first, *Memorial: A Version of
Homer's Iliad*, published in 2011, was short-listed for the T. S. Eliot
Prize, which Oswald had won nine years earlier, for her second book,
Dart. But the prize now had a new sponsor—a hedge fund—and
Oswald withdrew the poem from consideration. Explaining her decision in *The Guardian*, she defined her art as a form of dissidence. "I
think it's often assumed that the role of poetry is to comfort," she
wrote, "but for me, poetry is the great unsettler. It questions the established order of the mind. It is radical, by which I don't mean that
it is either leftwing or rightwing, but that it works at the roots of
thinking."

Memorial* thinks radically about violence, and it has earned a place
in the canon of great antiwar poems. Simone Weil believed that the
Iliad itself was a great antiwar poem, perhaps the greatest treatise ever
written on the nature of force, but also on the nature of compassion,
and she argued that conviction in a celebrated essay, published in 1940,
during the Nazi occupation of Paris. There are echoes of Weil's mystical activism in Oswald's "version" of the *Iliad* (the British edition was
subtitled "An Excavation of the Iliad"), although in paying homage to

Homer's masterpiece with one of her own, she tacitly reproaches his hero worship, a foundation of patriarchies.

Oswald's work is not widely known in the United States, but in her native Britain she is justly considered a major poet. Last year, she became the first woman to serve as the Oxford Professor of Poetry, a chair established in 1708 which has, since then, been held by forty-five white men, including Matthew Arnold, W. H. Auden, and Seamus Heaney. Edmund Blunden, who assumed the professorship in 1966, the year Oswald was born, was the last incumbent obliged to give a biennial oration in Latin. Oswald could certainly manage a speech in the language of Cicero. She commands a stage to mesmerizing effect, according to those who have heard her perform her longer works, including *Memorial* and *Nobody*, by heart. In oral cultures, bards have been revered for their power to enrapture. Oswald, who acted in her youth (she met her husband, the playwright Peter Oswald, when he cast her in a student production of Shakespeare), has noted that the fear of forgetting one's lines, or of losing one's place, was an occupational hazard of the Homeric tradition. In her view, that anxiety helped to keep the poetry alive.

Too many artists to name have appropriated Homer. A notable recent one—Oswald's compatriot Christopher Logue, who died at eighty-five, the year that *Memorial* was published—spent four decades writing *War Music*, a multivolume modernist adaptation of the *Iliad* that he never finished, but that runs to more than three hundred pages. Logue, who cheerfully admitted he knew no Greek, offended purists with what one critic called his "flagrantly anachronistic" imagery. (Logue's epithet for Aphrodite was "Miss Tops and Thongs.")

Oswald, at the other extreme, dispenses with narrative. She distills the carnage of the *Iliad* into an elixir of grief: 214 capsule obituaries of the fallen on both sides—young foot soldiers throwing themselves at death, or helplessly being thrown at it. It would be a searing lament for any murderous conflict since the Bronze Age (when the Trojan War may or may not have been fought), but what feels most radical about *Memorial*, in 2020, is Oswald's determined focus on the lives that didn't matter, except to the families gutted by their loss. The briefest of her cameos are often the most devastating:

> POLYDORUS is dead who loved running
> Now somebody has to tell his father
> That exhausted man leaning on the wall
> Looking for his favourite son

The original Greek served Oswald "as openings through which to see what Homer was looking at," she explains in a preface. The obituaries are her "paraphrases" of the original, and the pastoral similes planted between them—as if to give them breathing space, like the melancholy willows in a graveyard—are "irreverent" translations:

> Like leaves who could write a history of leaves
> The wind blows their ghosts to the ground
> And the spring breathes new leaf into the woods
> Thousands of names thousands of leaves
> When you remember them remember this
> Dead bodies are their lineage
> Which matter no more than the leaves

But what Oswald sees, more clearly than Homer could—not least, perhaps, because she is a woman and a mother—is the obscenity of the human sacrifice. The last of her obituaries leaves nothing to be said: "And Hector died like everyone else." The chasteness of her style recalls that of a different memorial, one that is also a roll call: Maya Lin's monument to the American dead of the Vietnam War. In both cases, you find yourself mourning other people's children as if they were your own.

Memorial waylaid Oswald from her poetry's Ithaca: the English countryside. Her mother, Lady Mary Keen, is a well-known garden designer, whose job often came with housing, and the four Keen children grew up on the estates where Lady Mary was employed. After

Oxford, Oswald studied horticulture and became a gardener herself. Until recently, she lived with her husband and children in Devon, at a bend of the Dart River, where she worked in an unheated writing hut. (The family now lives in Bristol.) She relishes research in the field, and spent three years following the river's course and interviewing people whose livelihoods depend on it: a salmon poacher, a tin extractor, a worker in a woolen mill. In *Dart* (2002), their voices—which have the twang of folk song, along with its stoic nonchalance toward hardship—flow together with mythical and imagined ones. *A Sleepwalk on the Severn* (2009) was another river project that got Oswald out in her Wellingtons, with a notebook, at ungodly hours. She aimed to chart the phases of the moon as it rose, in the course of a month, over the flooded fields and chalky cliffs along the Severn's banks, recording the effect of the moonlight on water and voices. "This is not a play," she advises the reader—paradoxically, since she presents it as one, with stage directions and dialogue, some of it slapstick, for a cast of locals. Her disclaimers are worth attention. They speak to the mistrust that she wants you to feel toward the way that language betrays reality by stabilizing it.

Light, time, water, weather, growth, and decay: transience is Oswald's muse, and it inspires startling, almost fugitive leaps of syntax and perception. She often asks one of her senses to do the work of another: her eyes to feel, her touch to hear, almost as if she were retraining them, like participants in an acting workshop instructed to change places with someone or something alien—a stranger, a foe, a bird, a plant, even a corpse—and to inhabit that otherness. In a poem from her collection *Falling Awake* (2016), she seems to envy the clouds reflected in a puddle, which are "without obligations of shape or stillness." "I'm going to flicker for a moment," she announces in another poem, "and tell you the tale of a shadow . . . not yet continuous / no more than a shiver of something." In "A Rushed Account of the Dew," she writes:

> I want to work out what it's like to descend
> out of the dawn's mind
> and find a leaf and fasten the known to the unknown

with a liquid cufflink
    and then unfasten
to be brief
to be almost actual

Anyone who has tried to write an artful sentence knows that it involves fastening the known to the unknown by some mysterious process that takes place "at the roots of thinking," where the brain wrests an idea from an inchoate mass of sensory data and encodes it in parts of speech that another mind can decrypt. Pedestrian language bears few traces of the staggering richness and particularity that are lost in the transaction. The work of visionary poets such as Rimbaud or Gérard de Nerval, or of modernists, like Pound in the late *Cantos*, who write at the edge of intelligibility, gives you a glimpse of what it signifies "to be almost actual" while refusing to simulate reality. Oswald belongs to their lineage, and she writes at that edge, too. But in *Nobody* she goes over it.

Oswald's intention in *Memorial*, she tells us in the preface, was to translate the "atmosphere" of the *Iliad*, seeking "translucence" rather than fidelity. That is what she aims to accomplish in *Nobody*. In another of her brief prefaces (many of her books require a word of explanation), she writes that "this poem lives in the murkiness" between two stories from the *Odyssey*. One is of King Agamemnon's murder by his wife, Clytemnestra, and her lover, Aegistheus. The other is of Odysseus's ten-year voyage home from Troy. But a minor figure in the tale seems to have hijacked the telling: a court poet whom Agamemnon hired to guard his wife when he sailed off to war. Aegistheus, the evil usurper, maroons the poet on a stony island so that he and the queen can commit adultery undisturbed. Presumably, the castaway goes mad with thirst and solitude, since Oswald seems to be channeling his delirium:

These voices flit about quick-winged
with women's faces or land on a clifftop singing
so that here and there you find fading contrails of song

and a swimmer slooshing along breathing in and out
with the purple sea circling his throat always
thinks he can hear something which nevertheless escapes him

The title *Nobody* is a gender-neutral translation of Outis, the alias
that Odysseus uses to deceive the Cyclops. (For centuries, it was rendered in English as "Noman.") But it also alludes to the bodiless anonymity of the sea, and to the unmoored voices that the castaway
hallucinates. They ostensibly belong to the main characters of the *Odyssey*, though a few, like Icarus, seem to have flown into the poem from
elsewhere in Greek mythology—or from the future. Oswald's sea
proves no less vulnerable to pollution by the debris of modernity than
oceans everywhere. The poet pacing his rocky outcrop is "dry as an
ashtray"; a drowning man's will to live—his "upwardness"—keeps
him afloat "like a wedge of polystyrene."

Memorial, for all its translucence, feels carved in stone; its combatants are conjured so precisely that their sufferings become indelible.
Nobody is written in disappearing ink. None of its phantoms have a
stable contour, and if you are not a student of the classics you can chafe
at Oswald's donnish presumption that you should recognize their
fleeting apparitions. (Their names do appear, teasingly, in an unpunc-
tuated frieze that runs across the bottom half of six pages, in Attic-
style font, bleached out in places, bold in others, as if randomly
timeworn.)

An "old sea-god sometimes surfaces"—Proteus, perhaps—shifting
shape to avoid capture:

and became a jellyfish a mere weakness of water
a morsel of ice a glamour of oil
and became a fish-smell and then a rotting seal
and then an old mottled man full of mood-swings

Odysseus materializes from the murk more distinctly, telling a lis-
tener how he took leave of "our hostess who is a goddess long-haired
inhuman / but her language is human except when she sings."

A woman who may be that hostess wryly addresses a messenger: "You've come to remove my lover / who is tired of this hotel life." We last glimpse her as she "shrieks and flies up laughing and loudspeakering / and turns and dives unable to be anything for long / and the black wave covers her."

The *Odyssey* plays loose with chronology, almost like a modern novel, though without sacrificing suspense. The tension in *Nobody* is generated by bewilderment, as one shimmering mirage supplants another. It unsettles your senses the way some avant-garde music does, and its vexing beauty invites surrender to incomprehension. But rarely does it unsettle your heart. Oswald's perceptions are variously too personal, unique to her; or too impersonal, too purely literary; or, in the case of her phantoms, too disassociated to forge a sustained connection between sensation and insight. The intimacy of her best work is absent. I even felt, at times, that she had devised the poem as a cognitive experiment to test a reader's tolerance for disorientation.

As an experiment, however, *Nobody* dramatizes Oswald's audacity with language. The extremes she goes to may have been emboldened by Tillyer. He turned eighty in 2018, and their show was one of five mounted by his London gallerist to celebrate a career of mercurial engagement, formal and spiritual, with the flux of nature. In that respect, his work and Oswald's have an obvious affinity. Yet Oswald says she hates being told that she is a "nature poet." Perhaps she's mindful that the pastoral idyll, since Theocritus, has been a luxury for poets and readers with clean fingernails. More to the point, Oswald has spent her writing life refusing to be told who she is. Like Proteus, she keeps wriggling out of confinement to one body, and its finality.

AUGUST 2020

I n 1946, Simone de Beauvoir began to outline what she thought
would be an autobiographical essay explaining why, when she had
tried to define herself, the first sentence that came to mind was "I
am a woman." That October, my maiden aunt, Beauvoir's contemporary, came to visit me in the hospital nursery. I was a day old, and
she found a little tag on my bassinet that announced, "It's a Girl!" In
the next bassinet was another newborn ("a lot punier," she recalled),
whose little tag announced, "I'm a Boy!" There we lay, innocent of a
distinction—between a female object and a male subject—that would
shape our destinies. It would also shape Beauvoir's great treatise on
the subject.

Beauvoir was then a thirty-eight-year-old public intellectual who
had been enfranchised for only a year. Legal birth control would be
denied to French women until 1967, and legal abortion until 1975.
Not until the late 1960s was there an elected female head of state anywhere in the world. Girls of my generation searching for examples of
exceptional women outside the ranks of queens and courtesans, and
of a few artists and saints, found precious few. (The queens, as Beauvoir remarks, "were neither male nor female: they were sovereigns.")
Opportunities for women have proliferated so broadly in the past six
decades, at least in the Western world, that the distance between 2010
and 1949, when *The Second Sex* was published in France, seems like an
eternity (until, that is, one opens a newspaper—the victims of misogyny

and sexual abuse are still with us, everywhere). While no one individual or her work is responsible for that seismic shift in laws and attitudes, the millions of young women who now confidently assume that their entitlement to work, pleasure, and autonomy is equal to that of their brothers owe a measure of their freedom to Beauvoir. *The Second Sex* was an act of Promethean audacity—a theft of Olympian fire— from which there was no turning back. It is not the last word on "the problem of woman," which, Beauvoir wrote, "has always been a problem of men," but it marks the place in history where an enlightenment begins.

⎯⎯⎯ ⊗⊗⊗⊙ ⎯⎯⎯

Simone-Ernestine-Lucie-Marie Bertrand de Beauvoir was born in 1908 into a reactionary Catholic family with pretensions to nobility. She had a Proustian childhood on the Boulevard Saint-Germain in Paris. But after the First World War, her father, Georges, lost most of his fortune, and without dowries, Simone and her sister, Hélène, had dim prospects for a marriage within their class. Their mother, Françoise, a banker's daughter who had never lived without servants, did all the housework and sewing for the family. Her pious martyrdom indelibly impressed Simone, who would improve upon Virginia Woolf's famous advice and move to a room of her own—in a hotel, with maid service. Like Woolf, and a striking number of other great women writers,* Beauvoir was childless. And like Colette, who wasn't (she relegated her late-born, only daughter to the care of surrogates), she regarded motherhood as a threat to her integrity. Colette is a ubiquitous presence in *The Second Sex*, which gives a new perspective to her boast, in a memoir of 1946, that "my strain of virility saved me from

---

* Jane Austen, George Eliot, Emily Brontë, Charlotte Brontë, Emily Dickinson, Louisa May Alcott, Christina Rossetti, Lou Andreas-Salomé, Gertrude Stein, Christina Stead, Isak Dinesen, Katherine Mansfield, Edith Wharton, Simone Weil, Willa Cather, Carson McCullers, Anna de Noailles, Djuna Barnes, Marianne Moore, Hilda Doolittle, Marguerite Yourcenar, Sigrid Undset, Else Lasker-Schüler, Eudora Welty, Lillian Hellman, Monique Wittig, to name a few.

the danger which threatens the writer, elevated to a happy and tender parent, of becoming a mediocre author . . . Beneath the still young woman that I was, an old boy of forty saw to the well-being of a possibly precious part of myself."

Mme. de Beauvoir, intent on keeping up a façade of gentility, however shabby, sent her daughters to an elite convent school where Simone, for a while, ardently desired to become a nun, one of the few respectable vocations open to an ambitious girl. When she lost her faith as a teenager, her dreams of a transcendent union (dreams that proved remarkably tenacious) shifted from Christ to an enchanting classmate named ZaZa and to a rich, indolent first cousin and childhood playmate, Jacques, who took her slumming and gave her a taste for alcohol and for louche nightlife that she never outgrew. (Not many bookish virgins with a particle in their surname got drunk with the hookers and drug addicts at Le Styx.) Her mother hoped vainly that the worthless Jacques would propose. Her father, a ladies' man, knew better: he told his temperamental, ill-dressed, pimply genius of a daughter that she would never marry. But by then Simone de Beauvoir had seen what a woman of almost any quality—highborn or low, pure or impure, contented with her lot or alienated—could expect from a man's world.

Beauvoir's singular brilliance was apparent from a young age to her teachers, and to herself. An insatiable curiosity and a prodigious capacity for synthetic reading and analysis (a more inspired grind may never have existed) nourished her drive. One of her boyfriends dubbed her Castor (the Beaver), a nickname that stuck. She had a sense of inferiority, it would appear, only in relation to Jean-Paul Sartre. They met in 1929, as university students (she a star at the Sorbonne, he at the Ecole Normale Supérieure), cramming, as a team, for France's most brutal and competitive postgraduate examination, the *agrégation* in philosophy. (On their first study date, she explained Leibniz to him.) Success would qualify her for a lifetime sinecure teaching at a lycée, and liberate her from her family. When the results were posted, Sartre was first and Beauvoir second (she was the ninth woman who had ever passed), and that, forever, was the order of precedence—Adam before Eve—in their creation myth as a couple.

Even though their ideal was of a love without domination, it was part of the myth that Sartre was Beauvoir's first man. After Georges de Beauvoir confronted them (they had been living together more or less openly), Sartre, the more bourgeois, proposed marriage, and Beauvoir told him "not to be silly." She had emerged from her age of awkwardness as a severe beauty with high cheekbones and a regal forehead who wore her dark hair plaited and rolled—an old-fashioned duenna's coif rather piquantly at odds with her appetites and behavior. Both sexes attracted her, and Sartre was never the most compelling of her lovers, but they recognized that each possessed something uniquely necessary to the other. As he put it one afternoon, walking in the Tuileries, "You and I together are as one" (*on ne fait qu'un*). He categorized their union as an "essential" love that only death could sunder, although in time, he said, they would naturally both have "contingent" loves—freely enjoyed and fraternally confessed in a spirit of "authenticity." (She often recruited, and shared, his girls, some of whom were her students, and her first novel, *She Came to Stay*, in 1943, was based on one of their ménages à trois.) "At every level," Beauvoir reflected, years later, of the pain she had suffered and inflicted, "we failed to face the weight of reality, priding ourselves on what we called our 'radical freedom.'" But they also failed to fault themselves for the contingent casualties—the inessential others—who were sacrificed to their experiment. And the burden of free love, Beauvoir would discover, was grossly unequal for a woman and for a man.

If Beauvoir has proved to be an irresistible subject for biographers, it is, in part, because she and Sartre, as a pharaonic couple of incestuous deities, reigned over twentieth-century French intellectual life in the decades of its greatest ferment. But the most fascinating subjects tend to be those richest in contradictions, and *The Second Sex*, no less than

Beauvoir's prolific and important fiction, memoirs, and correspondence, seethes with them. Deirdre Bair, Beauvoir's biographer, touches
upon a fundamental paradox in the introduction to her admirable life.
She and Sartre's biographer Annie Cohen-Solal had been lecturing
together at Harvard. At the conclusion of their talk, she writes, "I
could not help but comment to my distinguished audience that every
question asked about Sartre concerned his work, while all those asked
about Beauvoir concerned her personal life." Yet Sartre's work, and
specifically the existentialist notion of an opposition between a sovereign self—a subject—and an objectified other, gave Beauvoir the
conceptual scaffold for *The Second Sex*,* while her life as a woman (indeed, as Sartre's woman) impelled her to write it. He had once told her
that she had "a man's intelligence," and there is no evidence that he
changed his mind about a patronizing slight that she, too, accepted as
a compliment until she began to consider what it implied. It implied,
she would write, that "humanity is male, and man defines woman, not
in herself, but in relation to himself," and by all the qualities (Colette's
strain of "virility") she is presumed to lack. Her "twinship" with Sartre
was an illusion.

The Second Sex has been called a "feminist bible," an epithet bound
to discourage impious readers wary of a sacred text and a personality
cult. Beauvoir herself was as devout an atheist as she had once been
a Catholic, and she dismisses religions—even when they worship a
goddess—as the inventions of men to perpetuate their dominion. The
analogy is fitting, though, and not only to the grandeur of a book that
was the first of its kind but also to its structure. Beauvoir begins her
narrative, like the author of Genesis, with a fall into knowledge. The
two volumes that elaborate on the consequences of that fall are the

* It has been credited by Beauvoir and others for having given her the scaffold,
although a journal from her university years, which was discovered after her death
by her companion and adopted daughter, Sylvie Le Bon de Beauvoir, suggests
that Beauvoir had arrived at the notion of a fundamental conflict between self and
other before she met Sartre, partly through her reading of Henri Bergson, but
partly through her own struggle—an explicit and implicit subtext of *The Second
Sex*—with an imperious need for love that she experienced as a temptation to
self-abnegation.

Old and New Testaments of an unchosen people with a history of enslavement. ("Facts and Myths" is a chronicle of womankind from prehistory to the 1940s; "Lived Experience" is a minutely detailed case study of contemporary womanhood and its stations of the cross from girlhood through puberty and sexual initiation to maturity and old age, with detours from the well-trodden road to Calvary taken by mystics and lesbians.) The epic concludes, like Revelation, with an eloquent, if utopian, vision of redemption:

> The same drama of flesh and spirit, and of finitude and transcendence, plays itself out in both sexes; both are eaten away by time, stalked by death, they have the same essential need of the other; and they can take the same glory from their freedom; if they knew how to savor it, they would no longer be tempted to contend for false privileges; and fraternity could then be born between them.

The first English-language edition of *The Second Sex* was published in 1953.* Blanche Knopf, the wife of Alfred Knopf, Beauvoir's American publisher, had heard of the book on a scouting trip to Paris. Thinking that this sensational literary property was a highbrow sex manual, she had asked an academic who knew about the birds and the bees, H. M. Parshley, a retired professor of zoology at Smith College, for a reader's report. His enthusiasm for the work ("intelligent, learned, and well-balanced . . . not feminist in any doctrinaire sense") won him the commission to translate it. But Alfred Knopf asked Parshley to condense the text, noting, without undue masculine gallantry, that Beauvoir "certainly suffers from verbal diarrhea." Parshley appealed to the author for advice on the "minor cuts and abridgments" that Knopf felt were essential for the American market. She was either too busy or unwilling to reply, because he heard nothing until he received an indignant letter protesting that "so much of what seems important to

* This essay introduced the most recent and only complete English-language translation of *The Second Sex*, by Constance Borde and Sheila Malovany-Chevallier (Alfred A. Knopf, 2010).

me will have been omitted." But she signed off graciously on the edition.

While the translation was a labor of love from which Parshley nearly expired, he lacked a background in philosophy, or in French literature. He also lacked a credential more pertinent, perhaps, to the audience for a foundational work of modern feminism, a second X chromosome. This eagerly awaited new translation, by Constance Borde and Sheila Malovany-Chevallier—the first since Parshley's—is a magisterial exercise in fidelity. The cuts have been restored, and the English is as lucid and elegant as Beauvoir's ambition to be exhaustive permits it to be. She is a bold, sagacious, often dazzling writer and a master aphorist,* but no one would accuse her of being a lapidary stylist. It is hard to find a description for the prose that does justice both to its incisive power and to its manic garrulity. Elizabeth Hardwick came closest, perhaps, when she called *The Second Sex* "madly sensible and brilliantly confused."

The stamina that it takes to read *The Second Sex* in its entirety pales before the feat of writing it. (Sartre was happy when his beaver was busy, Beauvoir told Bair, because "I was no bother to him.") One is humbled to learn that this eight-hundred-page encyclopedia of the folklore, customs, laws, history, religion, philosophy, anthropology, literature, economic systems, and received ideas that have, since time began, objectified women was researched and composed in about fourteen months,† between 1946 and 1949, while Beauvoir was also engaged with other literary projects, traveling widely, editing and contributing to *Les Temps Modernes*, Sartre's leftist political review, and juggling her commitments to him and "the Family" (their entourage of friends, groupies, disciples, and lovers) with a wild transatlantic love

---

* The cult of the Virgin is "the rehabilitation of woman by the achievement of her defeat"; "The average Western male's ideal is a woman who . . . intelligently resists but yields in the end"; "The traditional woman . . . tries to conceal her dependence from herself, which is a way of consenting to it." Examples are numerous.

† In reference libraries and in lecture halls—Beauvoir audited classes by Lacan and Lévi-Strauss, among others—and in interviews with women of all backgrounds on two continents.

affair. On a trip to America in 1947, she had met the novelist Nelson Algren, the most significant of her male others, and it was he who advised her to expand the essay on women into a book. He had shown her the "underside" of his native Chicago, and that year and the next they explored the United States and Mexico together. Her encounter with a racism that she had never witnessed firsthand, and her friendship with Richard Wright, the author of *Native Son*, helped to clarify her understanding of sexism, and its relation to the anti-Semitism that she certainly *had* witnessed firsthand before and during the war, but, with Sartre, had never openly challenged. The Black, the Jew, and the woman, she concluded, were objectified as the Other in ways that were both overtly despotic and insidious, but with the same result: their particularity as human beings was reduced to a lazy, abstract cliché ("the eternal feminine"; "the black soul"; "the Jewish character") that served as a rationale for their subjugation.

Not all of Beauvoir's staggering erudition and mandarin authority in *The Second Sex* is reliable (she would repudiate a number of her more contentious or blinkered generalities, though not all of them). Her single most famous assertion—"One is not born, but rather becomes, woman"—has been disputed by more recent feminist scholars, and a substantial body of research in biology and the social sciences supports their argument that some sexual differences (besides the obvious ones) are innate rather than "situational." Instead of rejecting "otherness" as an imposed cultural construct, women, in their opinion, should cultivate it as a source of self-knowledge and expression, and use it as the basis to critique patriarchal institutions. Many readers have also been alienated by Beauvoir's visceral horror of fertility—the "curse" of reproduction—and her desire, as they see it, to homogenize the human race.

Yet a revolution cannot begin until the diffuse, private indignation of individuals coalesces into a common cause. Beauvoir not only marshaled a vast arsenal of fact and theory; she galvanized a critical mass of consciousness—a collective identity—that was indispensable to the women's movement. Her insights have breached the solitude of countless readers around the world who thought that the fears, transgressions, fantasies, and desires that fed their ambivalence about being female were aberrant or unique. No woman before her had written publicly, with greater candor and less euphemism, about the most intimate secrets of her sex.

One of those secrets—the hardest, perhaps, for Beauvoir to avow—is that a free woman may refuse to be owned without wanting to renounce, or being able to transcend, her yearning to be possessed.* "As long as the temptations of facility remain," she wrote, by which she meant the temptations of romantic love, financial security, and a sense of purpose or status derived from a man, all of which Sartre had, at one time or another, provided for her, a woman "needs to expend a greater moral effort than the male to choose the path of independence." Colette, who would have smiled, and not kindly, at the phrase "moral effort," states the problem less cerebrally: "How to liberate my true hope? Everything is against me. The first obstacle to my escape is this woman's body barring my way, a voluptuous body with closed eyes, voluntarily blind, stretched out full, ready to perish."

To a reader of this new translation—a young feminist perhaps, for whom the very title may seem as quaint as a pair of bloomers—I would suggest that the best way to appreciate *The Second Sex* is to explore it as a deep and urgent personal meditation on a true hope that, as she will probably discover, is still elusive for many of us: to become, in every sense, one's own woman.

2010

---

* It was a source of her bad faith in fictionalizing the affair with Algren in her finest novel, *The Mandarins*.

Fifty years ago, I was a guest at the baptism of a friend's son in the ancient church of a Tuscan hamlet. It was Easter, and lambing season. A Sardinian shepherd who tended the flocks of a local landowner came to pay his respects to the new parents. He was a wild-looking man with matted hair whose harsh dialect was hard to understand. Among our party was a beauty of fifteen, an artist's daughter, and the shepherd took such a fancy to her that he asked for her hand. The girl's father politely declined, and the shepherd, to show that he had no hard feelings, offered us a lamb for our Paschal dinner. My friends were penniless bohemians, so the gift was welcome. It came, however, with a condition: we had to watch the lamb being slaughtered.

The blood sacrifice took place after the baptism. That morning, the baby's godfather, an expatriate writer, had caused a stir in the church, since none of the villagers, most of them farmers, had ever seen a Black man in person. Some tried to touch his hands, to see if the color would rub off; there was a sense of awe among them, as if one of the Magi had come to visit. Toward the end of the ceremony, the moment came for the sponsors to "renounce Satan and . . . all his seductions of sin and evil." The godfather had been raised in a pious community, and he entered into the spirit of this one. His own experience of malevolence had taught him, as he wrote, that life "is not moral." Yet he stood gravely at the font and vowed, "*Rinuncio.*"

I thought of those scenes last spring when I began reading three new translations of Purgatory, being published to coincide with the seven hundredth anniversary of Dante's death, at fifty-six, in September 1321. The speech of the hamlet had primed my ear for the poet's tongue. "*Di che potenza vieni?*" an old farmer had asked the godfather: "From what power dost thou come?" Purgatory, like the other two canticles of what Dante called his "sacred" epic, Inferno and Paradise, takes place during Easter week in 1300. In Canto I, the pilgrim and his cicerone, Virgil, emerge from Hell and arrive at the mountain "of that second kingdom where the human spirit purges itself to become worthy of Heaven." Dante's body, still clad in its flesh, inspires marvel among the shades because it casts a shadow. They mob him with questions: From where has he come?

Dante was a good companion for the pandemic, a dark wood from which the escape route remains uncertain. The plagues he describes are still with us: of sectarian violence, and of the greed for power that corrupts a regime. His medieval theology isn't much consolation to a modern nonbeliever, yet his art and its truths feel more necessary than ever: that greater love for others is an antidote to the world's barbarities, that evil may be understood as a sin against love, and that a soul can't hope to dispel its anguish without first plumbing it.

An underworld where spirits migrate after death has always been part of humankind's imagination. Nearly every culture, including the most ancient, has a name for it: Diyu, Naraka, Sheol, Tartarus, Hades. But there is no Purgatory in the Bible, or in Protestantism, or in Eastern Orthodoxy. In current Catholic dogma, it is a state of being rather than an actual realm between Hell and Heaven: an inner fire in the conscience of sinners that refines their impurities.

The concept of Purgatory was relatively new when Dante was born; it came into currency in the twelfth century, perhaps among French theologians. This invention of a liminal space for sinners who had repented but still had work to do on their souls was a great consolation to the faithful. It was also a boon for the Church. By the late Middle Ages, you could shorten your detention by years, centuries, or even millennia by paying a hefty sum to a "pardoner," like Chaucer's pilgrim. A popular ditty captured the cynicism this practice inspired: "As soon as a coin in the coffer rings / The soul from Purgatory springs." Before Dante, though, the notion of Purgatory was an empty lot waiting for a visionary developer. His blueprint is an invention of exquisite specificity. A ziggurat-like mountain ringed with seven terraces, one for each of the cardinal sins, rises from the sea in the Southern Hemisphere, opposite the globe from Jerusalem, with the Earthly Paradise at its summit. According to Dante, this mountain was formed by the impact of Satan's fall to Earth. His descent brought grief to the children of Eve—those "seductions of sin and evil" that every godparent must renounce. But it also created a stairway to Heaven.

Dante's conception of Purgatory is remarkably like a wilderness boot camp. Its terrain is forbidding—more like an alp than like a Tuscan hillside. Each of the rugged terraces is a setting for group therapy, where supernatural counselors dispense tough love. Their charges are sinners, yet not incorrigibles: they all embraced Jesus as their savior. But, before dying, they harmed others and themselves, so their spirits need reeducation. They will graduate to the Earthly Paradise, and eventually to Heaven, after however much time it takes them to transcend their mortal failings by owning them.

For many students of Dante, Purgatory is the *Divine Comedy*'s central canticle poetically, philosophically, and psychologically. It is, as one of its best translators, the poet W. S. Merwin, noted, the only one that "happens *on* the earth, as our lives do. . . . Here the times of day recur with all the sensations and associations that the hours bring with them, the hours of the world we are living as we read." And here, too, he reflects, there is "hope, as it is experienced nowhere else in the poem, for there is none in Hell, and Paradise is fulfillment itself."

The Dante we meet in the first lines of Inferno is a middle-aged man who wakes after a night of terrors to find himself in the wilderness. How did he get there? The Republic of Florence was his crucible. He was born in 1265, under the sign of Gemini. According to a recent biographer, the Italian scholar Marco Santagata, he believed that his natal horoscope had destined him for glory as both a poet and a messiah who would save the world. There was little in his background to justify such grandiosity. Santagata calls Dante's father, Alighiero, "a small-time moneylender." His mother, Bella, came from a wealthier family. Both parents were respectable citizens, though not members of the elite. Their son's pretensions to nobility weren't warranted by his birth.

Dante was the youngest of his parents' children, and he was possibly just a toddler when his mother died. His father died when Dante was about ten. The boy suffered from poor health and bad eyesight. The fits and visions that his works allude to may have been caused by epilepsy. Yet his intellect seems always to have been exceptional. However Dante was educated (likely in a plebeian public school, according to Santagata), he mastered Latin and became "a great epistolographer"—a composer of artful letters, official and private. When he waded into his city's roiling politics, that talent anchored his career.

Florence was a hub of banking and the wool trade. By the late 1200s, two rival parties, the Guelfs and the Ghibellines, had been fighting for nearly a century to dominate its government. The Guelfs were allied with the Pope, the Ghibellines with the Holy Roman Emperor. In 1289, the Ghibellines were defeated in a decisive battle at Campaldino. But the victors then splintered into two factions—the White Guelfs, with whom Dante sided, and the Black Guelfs, his sworn enemies.

Dante fought in the cavalry at Campaldino, and war must have given him a foretaste of Hell. But then he went back to civilian life, becoming a nova in Florence's literary firmament. He made princely friends who admired his poetry. Among them was another of Italy's greatest poets, Guido Cavalcanti, although Dante wouldn't spare his father from damnation for heresy.

By 1295, Dante had finished *Vita Nuova*, a stylized autobiography. Its author is a self-absorbed youth with the leisure to moon after an aloof woman. He knows he's a genius and can't help showing off. Passages of prose alternate with sonnets and canzoni on the theme of love, but the author doesn't trust us to understand them. His didactic self-commentary has been hailed as the birth of metatextuality, though it also seems to mark the advent of mansplaining. The *Vita*, Dante tells us in the penultimate chapter, is addressed to a female readership (one presumably unversed in poetics). "It is to the ladies that I speak," he writes.

Several ladies elicit Dante's gallantry in the *Vita*, but only one, Beatrice, inspires his adoration. Her probable model was Beatrice di Folco Portinari. Her father and husband were rich Florentine bankers; she died in her early twenties. Details of her life are scarce, and Dante doesn't supply many. Their families may have been neighbors. Her father's testament left her fifty florins. Dante claims that he was first smitten with Beatrice as a nine-year-old; she was a few months younger and dressed fetchingly in crimson. At that moment, he "began to tremble so violently that even the least pulses of my body were strangely affected." He next catches sight of her at eighteen, now "dressed in pure white," and when she greets him he feels he is experiencing "the very summit of bliss." That night, he dreams of her asleep, "naked except for a crimson cloth," in the arms of a "lordly man." The man wakes her, holding a blazing heart—Dante's—and compels her to eat it, which she does "unsurely."

There are, regrettably, no more naked bodies or scenes of erotic cannibalism in the *Vita*—it's all courtly love from here on. Dante chronicles his brief encounters with Beatrice on the street or in church (today, one might say that he stalked her), fainting with joy if she acknowledges him and plunging into depression after a snub. He mourns her untimely death abjectly. But not long afterward his head is turned by another lady, "gracious, beautiful, young, and wise." Why not console himself, he reasons, "after so much tribulation"?

This "other woman" of the *Vita* was not the girl to whom Dante had been betrothed when he was not quite twelve, and whom he had married as a young man. His lawful wife was Gemma Donati. Her family was nobler and richer than the Alighieris, and they led the Black Guelfs. He mentions several of his wife's relatives in the *Comedy*. (One, the virtuous Piccarda, whose odious brother tore her from a convent and forced her to marry, greets him in Paradise; another, Forese, a friend of his youth, is a glutton in Purgatory.) But he never acknowledged Gemma's existence in any of his works. One would like to think that Dante ghosted her out of discretion—she was beholden to his persecutors. Perhaps, though, the rueful shade of Ulysses hits upon the real reason in Inferno:

> Neither tenderness for my son,
> Nor duty to my old father,
> Nor the debt of love I owed Penelope,
> To make her happy, could compete
> With my ardor to know the world,
> And all things human, base and noble.

If Gemma was Dante's Penelope, Beatrice was his Athena—the divine protectress of his odyssey. And the final chapter of the *Vita* announces a future joint enterprise. The guilty swain vows to atone for his betrayal by writing of Beatrice "what has never been said of another woman."

In 1301, the White Guelfs sent Dante to Rome on a mission to secure the Pope's support for their cause. But while he was away from Florence the Black Guelfs seized power. They banished Dante in absentia and confiscated his property; he would burn at the stake should he ever return. He never did, even in 1315, when the city offered to commute his sentence if he repented publicly. Exile was preferable to abasement for a man of his temperament, which was reported to be vain and contentious. After leaving Purgatory's terrace of pride, he worries that he'll be remanded there after death.

Dante spent the last nineteen years of his working life as an itinerant diplomat and secretary for the lords of northern Italy. The poem that he called, simply, the *Comedy* (a Venetian edition of 1555 added the adjective "Divine," and it stuck) is the work of an embittered asylum seeker. Its profoundest lesson may be that love's wellspring is forgiveness. Yet Dante never forgave Florence. Even in Paradise, he can't resist a swipe at his fellow citizens. They are "little brats who swat away their nurse's breast though they're dying of hunger."

The *Comedy* is both an epic road trip indebted to Homer and a medieval pilgrimage, though it is also a landmark in Western literature: one of its first masterpieces in a Romance vernacular. Dante's art heralds the beginning of the Renaissance for the same reason that Giotto's does. The two great Florentines were contemporaries, and they may have been friends, despite a disparity of class. According to legend, the painter spent his boyhood as a shepherd. (He would have known how to butcher a lamb.) They both inherited an allegorical tradition, and their themes are faithful to its doctrine, yet their protagonists are radically human. A fresco on the walls of Florence's Podestà Chapel, attributed to Giotto, represents the saved in Paradise. Among them is a young man presumed to be Dante, holding a book. He is dressed sumptuously in red, with an aquiline profile and a steely gaze. Dante celebrates Giotto's fame, somewhat sarcastically, in the eleventh canto of Purgatory. A lust for fame was one of his own failings.

As the narrator of the *Comedy* and its central persona, Dante wrestles with his fellow-feeling for sinners condemned to torments that he has invented. Nowhere is the tension between his orthodoxy and his nascent humanism more acute than in Canto XV of Inferno, when a shade with features scorched by the flames clutches at the poet's hem. "Brunetto, master, you are here?" Dante cries out, palpably shocked.

Brunetto Latini, a Florentine poet and statesman, had been Dante's mentor after his parents' deaths. He has been condemned to the Seventh Circle for practicing the vice of sodomy, about which, apparently, he was unrepentant. But the tenderness both men express, and their mourning for what they have lost in each other—a father and a son—is in its way a heretical rebuke to the implacable order that forbids their reunion in Heaven. "If all that I ask were fulfilled," Dante says, "you wouldn't be an outcast from human nature."

Virgil, who died two decades before Christ's coming, is also excluded from Heaven, yet he bears that sorrow stoically. He tells Dante that it's a presumption to question divine justice, even when it seems unfair, and to confuse "piety" with "pity" (the same word in Italian, "*pietà*"). Salvation, Dante will discover, requires the surrender of precisely that attribute to which he is most attached as an artist, a lover, and a man: his ego.

As Dante and Virgil make their arduous circuit of Purgatory's terraces, they ask directions from the shades, who share their stories and explain their penances. Like birds of prey being tamed by a falconer, the envious have their eyes sewn shut. The gluttons are mortified by starvation amid tormenting aromas. The lustful must pass through a wall of flames. The proud stagger beneath a sack of boulders, and the slothful atone with manic activity. But Dante is an embed, rather than a mere tourist. A sword-wielding angel scarifies his brow with seven letters—"P"s, for *peccato*, or sin. Once he understands a sin humbly and viscerally, he ascends to the next terrace, and a "P" is erased. Fear and exhaustion sometimes tempt him with dejection, but, Virgil tells him,

> This mountain's nature
> Is to seem steepest from below;
> The climb is less painful the higher you go.

Finally, in the Earthly Paradise situated at Purgatory's summit, Dante reunites with Beatrice. She has descended from her place in Heaven, near the Virgin Mary's, not to welcome but to confront him:

> . . . In your desires for me,
> Which led you to love the good
> Beyond which one can't aspire,
> What ruts or chains in the road
> Forced you to ditch any hope
> Of advancement?
> And what bribes or lures
> In others' eyes enticed you
> To dally so idly there?

"Answer me!" she commands, as Dante cowers mutely. He compares himself with a naughty little boy being scolded.

No one has told Beatrice that, according to St. Paul, women are forbidden to teach men. She chastises Dante with a pontifical authority that few members of her sex would have then dared to vaunt. In her perfect beauty and wisdom, she explains, she embodies God's love, so Dante's fickleness toward her is ingratitude to the Creator. His repentance ultimately wins her absolution and consummates their love story.

But, for all her endearing feistiness, Beatrice is uniquely implausible among Dante's major characters. She's an abstract mouthpiece for her creator's philosophy who lacks her own vital substance. (The Virgin Mary, by comparison, is a relatable woman who has labored and suffered.) In that respect, the poet's otherwise incomparable powers of imagination slight Beatrice and us.

Even as a figment, however, Dante's Beatrice has an enduring prestige as the object of a man's ardent longing. Did her halo of romance tantalize the poet's daughter? Dante and Gemma had at least three children. Two of their sons were among the *Comedy*'s first commentators. The boys' younger sister, Antonia, became a nun in Ravenna, where Dante died and is buried in a splendid tomb. She is said to have taken the name Suor Beatrice. The poignancy of that detail haunts me. Antonia was a baby when her father was exiled, so she grew up without knowing him—yearning, it would seem, to be worthy of the love that he had vowed so publicly to an ideal woman.

Since Dante's death, more than a hundred writers in English have produced a version of the *Comedy* in part or whole or have channeled it into their own work. It's a roll call of the big guns: Chaucer, Milton, Shelley, Keats, Byron, Tennyson, Longfellow, Swinburne, and the Brownings, to name a few. Dante inspired Pound and Eliot to write some of the twentieth century's finest poetry. He was also a Virgil to Beckett, Joyce, Yeats, Auden, Robert Lowell, and the Nobelists Derek Walcott and Seamus Heaney. Robin Kirkpatrick, a Cambridge don, did a masterly translation for Penguin Classics. But two of my favorites are Dorothy L. Sayers, the crime novelist, and C. H. Sisson, a civil servant, like Dante, whose modernist tercets capture the *Comedy*'s austere intensity. ("I think Sisson / Got it, don't you?" his friend Donald Davie wrote. "Plain Dante, plain as a board / And if flat, flat. The abhorrent, the abhorred / Ask to be uttered plainly.")

That saga of translation resembles the slopes not so much of Mount Purgatory as of Mount Everest, littered with the debris of the climbers who have attempted to summit, some coming closer than others. But reaching Dante's Heaven by following faithfully in his footsteps isn't possible in English, which lacks the luxuriance of rhyme native to Italian. The epic's terza rima is a propulsive schema of three-line stanzas in a chain-linked pattern (aba, bcb, cdc) that Dante invented. It acts as a vessel—in the sense not only of a container but of a conveyance for the narrator's passage toward sublimity. (James Merrill compared the schema's momentum to the motion of oars.) His words and music are inextricable.

Many readers don't get further with Dante than Inferno, for obvious reasons: depravity is a more compelling subject than virtue, as you discover when you reach Paradise. Inferno's denizens are our familiars—we meet their avatars every day. It's a place, as Merwin put it, where "the self and its despair [are] forever inseparable," a predicament we think of as modern, perhaps because it suggests the claustrophobia of narcissism.

Translators have also preferred Inferno: its tableaux of carnage are so thrillingly obscene. In a famous passage, Dante meets Muhammad in the "bedlam" of the Eighth Circle, where the sowers of discord get their comeuppance. (Muhammad's "sin" was to have lured his followers away from the true church. Dante was a fierce critic of the papacy but a militant defender of Catholic theology.)

I never saw a barrel burst apart,
Having sprung a hoop or slipped a stave,
Like that man split down to where we fart,
His guts between his legs, his body splayed,
Its organs hanging out, among them that foul sac
Which turns to shit all that we eat.
As I beheld this gore he looked at me
And even wider tore his breast apart
"See how I spread myself," said he.

Evil is never banal in Dante's depiction. Nor are the traitors, coun-
terfeiters, rabble-rousers, thieves, hypocrites, corrupt pols, charlatans,
flatterers, pimps, blasphemers, usurers, sodomites, suicides, plunder-
ers, murderers, heretics, spendthrifts, melancholics, gluttons, sex
addicts, or, at the threshold of Hell, those apathetic souls whose sin
was ingratitude for the life force they were born with. Each one is indelibly individual. Yet, if Dante can show a bodhisattva's compassion
for the sufferings he has devised, he is also susceptible to that most
human of guilty pleasures: schadenfreude. At every opportunity on
his journey to beatitude, he settles a score.

For Dante's septicentennial, however, the latest crew of translators
has chosen to assault Mount Purgatory. They include the American
poet and professor Mary Jo Bang; the Scottish poet and psychoanalyst
D. M. Black; and the sixteen contributors to a new anthology, *After
Dante: Poets in Purgatory*, edited by Nick Havely, a prolific Dante
scholar, with Bernard O'Donoghue, an eminent authority on medieval literature. Perhaps it's Purgatory's moment because, in an era of
cataclysmic strife, weather, and unreason, hope is as precious as it is
scarce. But, before one asks how they measure up, one has to wonder
why they would try to.

In my own pilgrimage through Dante, it was revealing to see
how many of the passages I underlined evoked the angst of a first
draft—

I am conquered here by my defeat
In satisfying what my theme demands
More so than all before me in whatever genre.

—or the ephemeral elation of achieving what Dante calls
"*significando*":

I am one who pays close heed
When love inspires me, then as bidden
I proceed inwardly making meaning.

It was a solace to me that the greatest of poets was often stymied, overwhelmed, or speechless. Even with the muses' help, he writes, in Paradise, "I'd still not reach one thousandth of the truth." It isn't surprising, then, that the *Comedy* has been translated for seven hundred years. It's a writer's bible.

It's also an old mansion that invites renovation. Mary Jo Bang was discouraged, she tells us in an introduction, by the "elevated register" of previous versions, because it was "a continually distracting reminder of the fact that the poem was written in a long-ago era." Her *Purgatory* is a retranslation—she doesn't speak Italian. In places, though, her terse syntax generates lines that glide with the grace of a scull:

> The curtain over the real is so thin
> The light makes certain you can see within.

But I'm leaving out the first sentence of that tercet:

> Here, Reader, keep your eye on the prize.

Bang's remedy for elevation is philistinism. She almost jealously disrupts our immersion in Dante, and the poem's unity, by bombing the text with jokey anachronisms. These "contemporizing moments," as she calls them, include allusions to baseball, Candy Land, Wall Street, hustlers, Houdini, animation, *West Side Story*, and the Little Red Hen. Where Dante's poetry doesn't suffice, Bang throws in some of Shakespeare's. She also samples, among others, Amy Winehouse, Allen Ginsberg, and Elton John.

Although Bang's license is extreme, every translator of Dante makes some compromise with the original. (Any passages from the *Comedy* otherwise uncredited here are mine.) You haggle with the Italian in every line. How much of the poetry will you concede for semantic fidelity? How much fidelity for the music or the form? How far can you go in modernizing the tropes? As the editors of *After Dante* suggest in their introduction, answering such questions may require the collective bargaining of a "community." In fact, the *Comedy* itself is

one. As Dante and Virgil make their way toward Paradise, they speak
with or evoke the spirit of poets whose craft they revere—their
"singing-masters," in Yeats's phrase.

The *Comedy*'s community of translators isn't unlike a monastery,
where the spiritual ambitions of the ordained vie (even as Dante's did)
with their profession of humility. The title *After Dante* alerts us to
those conflicts, and the polyphony of its voices may be more instructive than their harmonies.

There are too many fine translations here to cite. But in braving
Canto XVIII, in which Virgil enlightens Dante on the nature of love,
Jonathan Galassi smoothly turns a lock that others have forced. Lorna
Goodison, a former poet laureate of Jamaica, summons the landscape
and speech of her island to powerful effect. At the end of Canto XII,
where a chastened Dante leaves the terrace of pride, she imagines the
loads of rocks that bow the backs of its penitents as the burdens of her
own people,

> who do not notice that they
> still bear the weight of slavery days on their heads

A. E. Stallings finesses Canto III in terza rima. Her diction cap-
tures a quality of Dante's sentences that Erich Auerbach marveled at
in 1929, when he called them as "simple as the lines of a primer . . .
which pierce the heart":

> And just as, from the fold, come sheep—
> first one, then two, then three; the flock
> stand meek, and faces earthward keep,
> and if one walks, the rest will walk;
> and when he stops, huddle in place,
> meek, mild, not knowing why they balk

That passage reminded me of the Sardinian shepherd, coaxing a
ewe and her suckling from the flock. He chose a lamb with a fleece of
pure white and was careful not to bloody it. (He could sell the fleece

later, he explained, to line a cradle.) The mother followed mutely and trustingly until he slit the lamb's throat. Then, with heart-piercing bleats, she charged us.

D. M. Black's Purgatory is the most satisfying complete translation since Merwin's. Black is a South African–born Scot who has studied Eastern religions, taught philosophy and literature, and published seven collections of his own poetry. He has practiced psychoanalysis in London, and he was drawn to the *Comedy*, he writes in an illuminating introduction, partly because he reads it as "a sort of gigantic encyclopedia of human motives" which examines the nature of psychic conflict. Black admits that Dante wouldn't have read his poem that way, since his "ultimate concern is with Christian 'salvation,'" and not "with understanding what impedes someone from living a fulfilling life." Yet that, I suspect, is exactly why Dante still speaks to us. The afflictions that Freud baptized "the psychopathology of everyday life," and that Dante calls "the senseless cares of mortals," are sins against love; like Satan, they dupe an individual into rejecting, perverting, violating, or despairing of it.

The *Comedy* is a morality tale designed, in part, to scare its readers straight, not to free them from their hangups. But in Purgatory Dante describes a process—slow and arduous, like analysis—of unriddling the mysteries of self-sabotage. As Beatrice puts it to him:

> From dread and shame I want you
> To evolve, so you no longer speak
> As in a dream.

In his commentary on the poem, Black likens the terraces where the penitents "go round and round" to the "circling thoughts of those who can't let go of the past." That describes most of history. There seems to be no escape from our worst natures; it would take a miracle no deity has ever wrought.

"People who shut their eyes to reality simply invite their own destruction," James Baldwin wrote, "and anyone who insists on remaining in a state of innocence long after that innocence is dead turns

himself into a monster." But Dante (here in Black's thoughtful rendering) invites us to believe that we can banish our demons, alone and
together, if we resist unconsciousness:

> As a man dismayed who turns to face the facts
> changes his fear to trust in his own strength
> when to his eyes the truth has been uncovered
> So I changed; and when my leader saw me freed
> from those anxieties, up by the rampart
> he moved, and I behind him, toward the height.

SEPTEMBER 2021

ACKNOWLEDGMENTS

There is always someone crucial whom one forgets to thank, especially for a book some fifteen years in the making. So, please forgive me if these notes are more categorical than specific.

I am boundlessly grateful to David Remnick and my colleagues at *The New Yorker* who suggested, assigned, copyedited, titled, illustrated, promoted, signed off on and/or nurtured this work, but particularly to my fact-checkers, who interrogated every line without compromise, and to my editors, who did the same, not only for truth but for beauty—Virginia Cannon, Nick Trautwein, and Henry Finder.

I am humbly indebted to the readers who astutely critiqued and ultimately rescued an Introduction that gave me exorbitant trouble, but particularly to Carl Bernstein, Phillip Blumberg, Suzanne Brøgger, Mary Karr, David Rieff, Phyllis Rose, Kitty Ross, Martha Saxton, and my son, Will Thurman.

I am grateful to my peerless agents Jin Auh and Andrew Wylie, to Katie Liptak for her generous editorial help at FSG, and to the skillful assistants who provided technical and practical support: Debbie Kapsch and Chase Berggrun.

I give thanks every day for my extended family of beloved friends (of whom I will single out my stepchildren Liese Mayer and Stefan Block), without whom I couldn't have weathered the trials of the last fifteen years.

My deepest debts are to my publisher, Jonathan Galassi, who met me as a young poet, half a century ago, and whose faith in my writing has been greater than my own; and—incalculably—to my subject-collaborators, who entrusted me with their stories and, in doing so, illuminated mine.

JUDITH THURMAN
NEW YORK
JANUARY 7, 2022